v9

TWENTIETH-CENTURY WOMEN OF COURAGE

SQUADRON LEADER BERYL E. ESCOTT

SUTTON PUBLISHING

First published in 1999 by
Sutton Publishing Limited · Phoenix Mill
Thrupp · Stroud · Gloucestershire · GL5 2BU

British Library Cataloguing in Publication Data
A catalogue record for this book is available from the British Library

ISBN 0-7509-1892-6

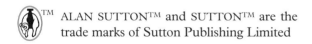

Typeset in 10/12pt Plantin Light.
Typesetting and origination by
Sutton Publishing Limited.
Printed in Great Britain by
WBC Ltd, Bridgend.

Contents

Introduction

Collectors of medals are often intrigued less by the beauties of the award or its ribbon than by the stories of its winning. Parents or grandparents can frequently be persuaded to tell tales of gallantry but when it comes to their own acts of courage, they sometimes brush them off, or say modestly that others did as much without reward. Or falling silent, touching their own precious medals, their eyes glaze over as they look back into the past. They hear sirens wail amid heavy explosions, and recall the difficulties, the friendships, the sadness and the laughter of living in dangerous days. But peace has its memories, too!

The stories behind the medals are many and various, and of particular interest are those given for bravery. When we speak of courage, we first think of war and men. But over half the population is female and women, too, have played their part. Nevertheless bravery awards for women are much rarer and often more difficult to find, scattered through nondescript indices, or even lost without trace.

To those people who have assisted me in finding out some of the information, please accept my thanks. They are too many to name here. This frustrated researcher has had to hunt in a hundred places and use oceans of ink, often to find just one small nugget of information. So here, before they slip away and are lost, is my attempt to collect together in one book the stories of some of the awards for courage given by governments and leading societies to women during the twentieth century.

A book twice this size could scarcely do justice to so vast a subject, and I was forced to limit its scope to only the four Old Commonwealth Countries, as defined by the 1931 Statute of Westminster, besides that of the UK and the USA. I have therefore, regretfully, had to leave out the European countries and those of the later Commonwealth, including the vast continent of Asia, with India. But they doubtless know their own worth.

Towards the end of this book is an abnormally long Appendix giving the many names the text cannot cover. The work of nurses calls for many degrees of courage and I have therefore included the award of the Florence Nightingale Medal. Despite my best efforts, I am still very conscious that there are gaps in all the lists throughout the book, and for these I apologise. I have tried! In the arrangement of awards in the text and Appendix, I have often ignored the correct orders of precedence so that periods and types could be grouped together. I have also included illustrations of the medals and some of the people about whom you read. A picture can often tell a thousand words.

I regret that I have been limited to those women who have received medals or awards for their actions but, in the nature of things, these are usually the only ones that have been recorded. I know there must be many more whose equally brave deeds have gone unrecognised. Courage comes in many forms, but usually involves some sort of sacrifice. Women are very familiar with this, whether it be the silent unwitnessed kind, or the more public deeds that win rewards. Sometimes it lasts a lifetime, and often it takes a life. Bravery is not the preserve of any one nation or age group, nor is it limited only to the Armed Forces, but rather it is widespread among the general population. It is not the privilege of the chosen few. It can descend on any man, woman or child in the blinking of an eye, and the next moment they will have joined the company of the great.

In this book I have tried to chart a few of the peaks of human courage shown by some of the bravest women of the twentieth century, from all walks of life. Here the reader may linger for a while, warmed by their devotion, inspired by their sacrifice and proud that such women should exist among us. Their deeds must not be forgotten, and perhaps they may inspire others to follow in their footsteps!

CHAPTER ONE

The Military Medal

War has always been terrible! Before the twentieth century most conflicts had been relatively limited. Weapons, armies, the scale of pitched battles and even the casualty lists seem small to our eyes. Sightseers often watched battles from nearby hills, safe from involvement. The First World War changed everything. Despite the saturation by film and the media, it is still hard for us to comprehend the full horror and misery of that war, and the conditions endured by those involved. New and ever more fearsome weapons appeared – tanks, planes, mechanised transport, submarines and radio – it was the first truly 'modern' war, yet it was waged with out-of-date methods and manpower. Blind patriotism and reckless ideals persisted, cavalry charged on horseback, light guns and supplies were transported by mules and horse-drawn wagons, soldiers became cannon-fodder and generals wasted their resources with obsolete tactics. The result was too frequently static battles and pointless slaughter. But in a curious way it brought women their hour of glory. Long accepted as 'hangers-on' wherever there were soldiers and camps, they had been regarded as little more than necessary baggage, servicing the men's needs in sex, comfort and everyday life, occasionally tending wounded or sick individuals. In civilian life, except among the poor, it was felt that women's only career was home and family.

Several factors now appeared to change this long entrenched attitude. Firstly, Florence Nightingale, in her long battles with authority, stemming from the mid-nineteenth-century Crimean War, almost single-handedly established nursing as an honourable profession, and the need of nursing for the wounded became accepted in any future wars. Secondly, developments in education and technological inventions had led to the tentative emergence of a further small band of professional women, who sought a new freedom outside the home to exercise their skills.

The First World War (and to some extent the earlier Boer Wars) provided the catalyst, presenting many other women with their long-desired opportunities. Moreover, these came with the blessing of both home and government. The war's extreme manpower shortages were suddenly to catapult women into many hitherto restricted fields, and ultimately into those bastions of tradition, the Armed Forces.

It is probably no exaggeration to say that many diehard leaders were staggered by the range of ordinary women's extraordinary abilities and enthusiasm. The government became more willing to recognise their dedication and courage, especially in close proximity to fighting or other dangers, and of course there was the propaganda value in encouraging others to follow.

During the First World War nurses outside Britain could be found in Western and Eastern Europe and the Middle East, for wherever the troops went, there the nurses went too, tending friend or foe alike. They worked in great hospitals, in requisitioned buildings, or in huts, tents, ambulance trains and ships. Nor was their work limited strictly to nursing. Women drove cars and makeshift ambulances into the thick of battle, or across no-man's-land, to pick up casualties. Dazzled by the sun or blinded by blizzards, they lurched through shell craters, sometimes getting stuck in the ever-present mud or sand, hopelessly vulnerable to air or land attacks. Under fire many were wounded or died, but still the dedicated work carried on.

During both world wars nurses served in the Army, the Territorials, the First Aid Nursing Yeomanry (FANY), the combined Red Cross and St John Ambulance Brigade Volunteers, or Voluntary Aid Detachments (VADs). Some were professional civilian nurses, others were women with a rudimentary knowledge of first aid – but all were caught up in the effort to help the wounded at home or overseas.

In the well-regulated, tightly controlled hospitals where they trained and worked, very few nurses could ever have imagined the awfulness of nursing abroad in the First World War. Many of them were young and had never before seen such carnage, nor lived and worked in such conditions. Yet they endured – and some died – uncomplaining, giving their best care and comfort to the wounded and showing unforgettable shining courage. Unlike the men, they had not been trained for this kind of work, but they did it just the same.

War was blazing heat and pestilential swarms of flies, or slimy slit trenches, with ceaseless deafening gunfire, flying shrapnel, and planes dropping indiscriminate bombs that blew away or mutilated people and buildings. Nurses had to work with insufficient beds, few bedclothes, inadequate medicines and equipment, unclean water and poor sanitation, amid dying men with torn bodies and gangrenous wounds. There was the constant danger of explosions, fire and gas attacks and the unpredictable behaviour of men half-crazed with fear or pain. But always, in the eye of the storm, was a little haven of calm and sanity – the hospital, no matter how makeshift, with its nurses. In their starched white aprons and headdresses, nurses worked calmly, exuding confidence, whatever their true feelings, impressing on the wounded the belief that they would soon be safe and well.

Military Medal (obverse). (*R.J. Scarlett*)

For soldiers who were not officers and showed exceptional courage on the field of battle, King George V in 1916 created the Military Medal (MM); within months this was extended to

Sister Norah Easby MM. (*QARANC Museum*)

include women of any nationality and, later, civilians. The silver medal was round, like a coin, with the monarch's head and titles on one side, and, on the reverse, a crowned royal cipher above the words 'For Bravery in the Field', the whole surrounded by a laurel wreath. Its ribbon was dark blue with white and red stripes. Holders are entitled to put the letters MM after their names.

One of the earliest women nominated for this award was Sister Norah Easby. She was called up from the reserve of the Queen Alexandra's Imperial Military Nursing Service (QAIMNS) and sent to serve in a hospital that had been set up and run by English nurses in the Balkan War of 1913. She and her colleagues did their best despite tough conditions: the weather swinging between extremes of temperature; insufficient and slow delivery of supplies due to the difficult terrain; and the hospital overwhelmed with wounded soldiers. Norah did such sterling work there that it was recognised by a Montenegrin decoration. For this she travelled for two bumpy, dusty days to the capital in an evil-smelling ox cart – the only transport available – to receive it from the hands of King Nicholas himself. Later, this dumpy, sometimes fierce, little sister, in ankle-length skirt and flyaway cap, was sent to France, where she worked at various tented casualty clearing stations just behind the front line.

Eventually Sister Easby found herself at a makeshift hospital near Béthune. It was in an exposed position and occasionally in the line of fire. One particular night it was very heavily shelled by the enemy and she and several of the staff were blown off their feet and wounded by flying glass and shrapnel. Although her white uniform was torn and blood-stained, and she had cuts and bruises to her face and arms, Norah refused to abandon her post, knowing this would alarm her patients and leave them unattended. Ignoring her wounds, and despite the tumult of shells exploding outside, she continued her work calmly thereby giving the impression that there was nothing to fear.

Her cool courage so impressed the authorities that she was given her Military Medal in September 1916. Subsequently, she received the Royal Red Cross (RRC) and became an Officer of the Order of the British Empire (OBE), the first being most precious to her, as it concerned her skills as a nurse.

For similar actions on that same night four others were awarded the Military Medal: Matron Mabel Tunley, Sister Beatrice Allsop and Staff Nurse Ethel Hutchinson – all from the QAIMNS – and Staff Nurse Jean Wyte of the Territorial Force Nursing Service (TFNS).

A sixth name was added to this first list of women's military honours, that of Lady Dorothea Feilding, not a nurse but a driver. A Dr Hector Munro had provided several motor ambulances for use in France and to drive them he chose women with special qualities of character. They had to have a spirit of adventure, together with adaptability, and bravery enough to continue through any hazard, even if under fire. Dorothea was one of these special women. In France she frequently drove her ambulance into the teeth of battle, picking up wounded; she was noted for driving with complete disregard for her own safety and in what might be described as a reckless manner. Among those doing similar work, Dorothea's actions were pre-eminent and her courage not only impressed the authorities but also exceeded Dr Munro's criteria.

Sister Dorothy Foster was already a member of the TFNS when called up in August 1914. She travelled to France alongside the British Expeditionary Force, where she was made Sister-in-Charge of a front-line casualty clearing station, a location in great danger of being overrun by the Germans when the enemy launched a big offensive. She, like the others with her, were half deafened by the great guns growing ever louder and nearer and accompanied by a steady stream of shells. Many landed close by, bringing the hazard of flying shrapnel. Although the shells seemed to her to be directed at the hospital, she ignored them, and with a stern look or word – almost more intimidating than the advancing enemy – she quelled any appearance of panic in her staff. Coolly Sister Foster supervised the slow-moving stream of men from the hospital tents to a patiently waiting ambulance train. Those who could walk, shuffled or hobbled there, assisted by male orderlies, nurses or even their own numbers; others were carried on stretchers. Nowhere did there seem to be any rush, despite the impending disaster. Sister Foster's composure reassured everyone and the evacuation was completed successfully. It was only just in time, as the post was shortly afterwards overrun by the enemy. She was cited as showing conspicuous courage and organisation in the midst of what could have turned into a shambles. Her Military Medal is now to be seen in Liskeard Town Museum, together with her RRC.

Nurse Annie Weir of the Red Cross Society enrolled as a VAD and at the age of twenty-four volunteered to work with the QAIMNS in France. There she served in one of the front-line casualty clearing stations, her wellington boots wallowing deep in mud before being discarded to enter any tented wards. Patients who were able to walk were usually asked to help the orderlies, not only because of insufficient staff to tend the more needy patients, but also because it was considered therapeutic for them to be so employed. One in particular, however, was slow and clumsy, so that at times even Nurse Weir's patience ran out and she had to tell him off. Interestingly, after the war she eventually married him.

In October 1917, her hospital fell victim to a severe bombing with much damage and loss of life. Undismayed by the danger, Nurse Weir felt it her duty to remain in the tented ward with her soldiers, rather than run and take shelter as they had been instructed. Throughout the raid she stayed, comforting and tending the men, though the ground shook under her feet and, hearing the bombs landing all around, she expected every moment to be her last. Her most terrible experience was when she saw a fellow nurse – a friend with whom she had trained – blown to bits before her eyes; it was something that haunted her for the rest of her life. Later she added to her Military Medal, the RRC and the Special Service Cross of the Red Cross.

Ethel Watkins was another Red Cross nurse who in 1915 joined the QAIMNS reserve and served at various casualty clearing stations and base hospitals in France. Her medal was for gallantry and devotion to duty at Aubigny in July 1918, during an enemy air raid which lasted four hours. Throughout she behaved with the utmost coolness, and when wounded by a jagged piece of shrapnel, made light of her injury, setting a magnificent example to those around her.

Anna Violet Thurstan, known better as Violetta Thurstan, was an amazingly diverse and gifted woman. At the ripe age of thirty-five, she joined the FANY before the First World War. She was sent by the Red Cross to a variety of postings, often with a field ambulance and sometimes as matron or administrator. She served in Belgium (where she was briefly a prisoner of war), Russia, Poland and France, interspersed by recovery periods for wounds and shell-shock. In July 1917, she was sent to the main dressing station of Y Corps in France. A month later it came under heavy shelling from the Germans. The hut where she was working was struck by a shell, and, hit by a falling timber, she was concussed and injured. In the hut there was carnage, but regardless of her own suffering, she turned her attention to her patients and helped in the evacuation of the building, where most of the men were wounded and helpless. Her actions provided a stimulating example to all, and for her bravery she added the Military Medal to her Russian Red Cross.

Muriel Thompson was a noted racing driver and the first woman to win Brooklands in 1907. She joined the FANY in 1915 and served in France, always showing conspicuous devotion to the soldiers in her care during enemy

Violetta Thurstan MM. (*Royal Artillery Institute*)   Driver Muriel Thompson MM. (*WTS (FANY)*)

air raids. During one particular raid on an ammunition dump, six other FANY drivers were out with her in their cars, picking up and assisting the wounded and injured. They showed the greatest of bravery in working calmly through the raid, ignoring their own danger, and concentrating on the task in hand. Miss Thompson received not only the Military Medal but also French and Belgian honours. In 1918 she joined the WRAF.

Among the great efforts and courage displayed by women on the battlefields, two in particular stand out. They were known simply as the 'Women of Pervyse'. Neither were in any military or other nursing service, and it was not until a year later, in 1915, that the Army authorities, deigning to recognise their presence and value, grudgingly allowed them to remain. One was an older woman, Elsie Knocker (on her marriage to a Belgian pilot, known as Baroness de T'Serclaes), and the other, eighteen-year-old Mairi Chisholm. In 1914 they had set up a dressing station in the bombed-out Belgian village of Pervyse, where Elsie, being a former trained nurse, dealt with the serious casualties and Mairi, only superficially trained in first aid, handled the lesser injuries. In reality they should not have been in such a dangerous place five yards from the trenches; their searches for wounded men in the marshes and mud-churned former farmland sometimes brought them within reach of the bayonets of advancing soldiers. Frequently, too, they had to stagger back alone with heavy stretchers loaded with badly injured men and their gear. Then after emergency treatment and sufficient time allowed for their patients to recover from the shock of their wounds, Mairi, using a Munro ambulance, would ferry them through the shelling to the nearest hospital, perhaps fifteen miles back. The two women tended not only the living of all nationalities, but also the dead, collecting the mangled bodies to nail into coffins.

This incredible bravery eventually caught up with them in 1918, when they both succumbed to a mustard gas attack launched by the enemy, which invalided them back to Britain; Mairi, returning alone later, suffered a second dose. Although their valuable work was now finished, it was recognised by the Military Medal and Belgian and St John awards.

An unusual group of four Military Medals went to women in the Queen Mary's Army Auxiliary Corps (QMAAC). On a May night in 1918, enemy planes attacked Abbeville, where there was also a WAAC camp. A trench sheltering a number of members suffered a direct hit, killing eight and wounding seven, one fatally. Forewoman

Elsie Knocker, Baroness de T'Serclaes MM. (*Royal Artillery Institute*)

Ethel Cartledge limped from one injured woman to another, until it was found she had a nail embedded in her foot. She and Miss Cross, the administrator, helped Dr Chappel bandage and tend those wounded, while Mrs Margaret Gibson, another administrator, calmed and organised everyone, keeping up their spirits and preparing alternative accommodation for those shocked but unhurt.

Many brave nurses and drivers won the First World War Military Medal (listed in the Appendix) and although there has been room for only a few of their stories to be recounted here, two women in a slightly different situation should be mentioned. In 1916, during the Easter Rising in Ireland, nineteen-year-old Louisa Nolan and Florence Williams, a civilian housewife living in Dublin, used their homes, and later just one, to shelter and nurse those wounded in the conflict. As this act of mercy placed them in grave danger from both sides of the fighting, it called for great courage to take such a risk. But they both felt that saving life was better than standing by and doing nothing; their unusual action was recognised by this award.

It is strange to record that no Military Medals were given to nurses after the First World War. It is as if the surprise at their exceptional courage, in later years gave way to acceptance that this was their normal function. Political considerations also shifted the emphasis, as theatres of war widened to include the whole of the civilian population, and new awards were appearing which were deemed more suitable. Whatever the reason, over 100 Military Medals went to women of Britain in the First World War, but fewer than 10 have been given since, and those were to women of the Armed Forces.

The Medal of the Order of the British Empire 1917–22

Medal of the Order of the British Empire 1917–22 (obverse). (*R.J. Scarlett*)

A similar situation seems to have arisen with the Most Excellent Order of the British Empire. Created in 1917 by King George V among the orders of chivalry, it could be given to men or women equally, including other nationalities. Special service to the empire was its criterion. It was divided into five classes, and subdivided in the following year into military and civil lists. In the last two divisions of Officer (OBE) and Member (MBE), a few gallantry actions were sometimes recognised.

In 1917, a special award was also added to the five classes, known as the Medal of the Order of the British Empire. It was a silver disc on a purple ribbon with the royal cipher on one side, and Britannia encircled by the words 'For God and the Empire' on the other. When a military division was added at the end of 1918, this was indicated by a red stripe on the purple ribbon. In its early days the medal was aimed chiefly at the civilian population, in recognition of 'acts of great bravery, self-sacrifice or high example, of initiative or perseverance, of skill, resource or invention'.

The hazards of the First World War had reached beyond mainland Europe to the British Isles, where those doing dangerous work in munitions factories or employed in proximity to air raids and bombing displayed as much courage or devotion to duty as those in the Armed Services. As a result, the recipients of the medal included a large proportion of women working in such situations, replacing men who were in the Forces. As such, it proved a popular and human feature of the honours list.

The Industrial Revolution had created new heavy industries based on coal, and workers' houses were built around the places of employment. They were crowded together, frequently back to back, dark and insanitary, with outside pumps or cold-water taps, open drains and communal privies. In these conditions large families were brought up, sometimes more than one sharing the same tiny terrace house. As time passed wages and conditions of work improved, and slum clearance programmes demolished many of the infamous, disease-ridden courtyard houses, but still much housing was too near the workplace with its attendant dangers, particularly in inner cities like London, with its pressure of a rapidly growing population.

Thus many factories, ordnance depots, iron and steel works and similar installations remained in the midst of their workers' homes, leaving little space between them should there be any accidents. Fires, explosions and enemy air raids targeting these very workshops would therefore inevitably and easily destroy with them large areas of housing and the people who lived there.

War brought increased activity, and the demand for munitions and equipment necessitated more workers and local factories. The military reverses of 1915 were blamed on a lack of shells, so a Ministry of Munitions was set up to increase output, and new factories were hastily erected under an amended Explosives Act licence. They were often little more than wooden sheds and highly inflammable, being filled with components of armaments and equipment. Their tall chimneys belched continuous clouds of smoke and poisonous chemicals into the surrounding atmosphere. Large, dangerous machinery had to be fenced off, but there were still smaller machines, in which a careless operator could lose a limb, or in an extreme case be killed.

Women and men were urged to take jobs in munitions factories by compelling posters appealing to their patriotism; work was described in glowing colours, highlighting the advantages, the wages, the opportunity for doing their bit to help Tommy in the trenches. Danger was never mentioned. Army volunteers and then conscription had milked the male workforce, so that factory employees came to consist mainly of young girls, housewives and older men – themselves often Army rejects or invalids.

The workplaces, too, were pretty dismal, often dark, cold and damp, with tasks frequently repetitive, as this was considered all that most girls could manage. It was little wonder that the young – in high spirits, away from home constraints – were sometimes real daredevils, who larked about and ignored the consequences. Inside, the factories would be enlivened by the voices of the girls calling to one another or singing snatches of the latest songs. Despite warnings, what young girl would worry that her job was highly risky, with the guncotton, detonators and shells she processed, and other substances used, often being volatile and highly combustible? Girls handling TNT were nicknamed 'Canaries', since exposure to it turned the skin yellow. Munitions work was a hazardous occupation – well paid, but beset with accidents large and small.

However, many of these same girls could meet emergencies with cool heads and great courage. They helped in accidents and risked their own lives in rescuing others, and they were not too frightened afterwards to return to the same work, even if they or others had been injured.

The first roll of medallists, published on 24 August 1917, included the names of eleven women. Violet Golding was one, and at sixteen was among the youngest. She worked at the George Kent Munitions Factory at Chaul End, Luton, for which she had volunteered. Her task was putting caps on detonators. On a busy day in July 1916, when she was leaning over to take a

Violet Golding, munitions worker.
(*Mrs B. Abbitt*)

detonator out of the press, it suddenly exploded in her hand. The tips of one finger and thumb of her left hand were so badly injured that when she was sent to hospital they had to be amputated. Her left arm also had extensive burns, so that she spent some time in hospital. Undeterred by her accident, she returned to the same work three months later, setting an excellent example to her fellow workers. Impressed by her courage, the directors of her firm recommended her for the new medal. In addition she received £50 compensation for her accident, part of which she used to buy a bike because, until that time, she had had to walk to the factory from her home in Dunstable.

Inspecting the same workshops shortly after the award was announced, King George V asked one young girl, 'How many of these can you do in a day?' The girl replied shyly, 'I don't know, sir. We don't count. We just carry on.' 'Capital,' said the King. He also had a few words with Violet who was standing nearby, and congratulated her on a well-earned medal. 'Is your hand better?' he asked.

In April 1918 she was formally handed her new medal at Dunstable town hall by the Lord Lieutenant of Bedfordshire, having earlier had her photograph taken for the records kept at the Imperial War Museum, cleverly hiding her damaged left hand. Fifty years later, she attended a service at St Paul's Cathedral to commemorate the inauguration of the Order of the British Empire.

Emily (Dolly) Vickers was another sixteen-year-old who appeared in the same list of medal workers. She worked at a factory in the vicinity of Warwick. As sometimes happened, a fuse on which she was working exploded and burned her hand badly. But this young girl, realising the danger to others, had the presence of mind in the midst of her pain to pick the fuse up while it was still burning and take it several yards to the nearest window, hurling it as far as she could outside the building, where it exploded harmlessly. Her action saved the detonation of the other explosives around – there were many piled up in the section waiting for collection – and thus saved the building and the lives of those within it.

It was noted that, in among the older men receiving the medal with her in the formal presentation, she looked ridiculously young, in shorter skirts than more mature ladies would wear and with a big satin bow at the back of her head.

The number of recipients of the medal in the New Year's Honours List of January 1918 was topped only by those in January and July 1920 (which were mainly of firemen and soldiers). Among the names was included the youngest girl to date, Violet Davies, who was only fifteen when involved in a munitions works explosion.

Faversham in Kent had several factories making high explosives and inevitably there were a number of serious explosions with considerable loss of life, such as the one in the Explosives Loading Company and the nearby Cotton Powder Company in April 1916 and another in 1917. In the first, 106 died and 97 were injured. For showing courage in rescuing workers at great personal risk from the burning explosives shops of the Cotton Power Company in 1917, ten people were recommended for the award – seven men and three women. They were of all ages, and photographs taken at the time show some women in their best factory uniform, award winners in front. Their belted and buttoned overalls are short for the period – just below the knee – with an armband and a triangular badge which reads 'On War Service'. They are wearing specially tailored hats, resembling mob caps with elasticated sides, necessary in an age when women had long hair, which could be dangerous in proximity to machines or chemicals unless closely confined.

The three young women in their smartest civilian dresses received their awards from the uniformed Marquess of Camden, in an open-air ceremony in the town square at Maidstone – quite an ordeal as there were speeches and individual citations read out before each person stepped up to the platform for the marquess to pin on the medal – the whole event being watched by the Mayor, his mace bearer, the civic clerk, all the town dignitaries and a vast crowd of people, many in uniform. The town had also been decorated with bunting and flags for the occasion. The women honoured were Mary Croucher, Mabel Edwards and Daisy Marsh.

Munitions workers, award winners in front. (*Fleur de Lis Heritage Centre, Faversham*)

Mary Croucher receives her medal. (*Fleur de Lis Heritage Centre, Faversham*)

However, they were only three in a list of more than a hundred medal winners from all over the country, most of whom were involved in fires or explosions in different types of munitions factories. As a result, some were badly injured: Margaret Burdett-Coutts lost a finger on a circular saw, but did not tell her fellow workers, worried that it might frighten them; Louisa Busby lost her hand and had other injuries; Gertrude Coles's hand was badly mutilated; and Rosa Finbow had injuries to her face (a serious matter, as a facial disfigurement could ruin a woman's chances of marriage at a time when this was considered a necessity for every woman). Edna Goodenough lost her right eye; Mary Harley was badly injured; Annie Holly had severe injuries to both eyes; Mrs Holttum saved many lives but was seriously injured; and Rosa Kipling was so badly injured that she had to endure 7½ months of operations. Mabel Lethbridge lost one leg and the other was damaged; Nora Morphet spent so long in a poisonous atmosphere that her health was permanently affected; Violet Newton was severely injured in an accident that killed two others; Agnes Peters was blinded and injured; and Hannah Spash was injured three times, the last time seriously. Most of these women eventually returned to work, but there were other injuries of varying severity and in many sad cases the women suffered for the rest of their lives, while others not mentioned here died.

It is heartening, nevertheless, to see recorded individual acts of bravery in trying to preserve the lives of others. Edith Butler saved two fellow workers; Ethel Head went back to pull out a colleague after an explosion; Agnes McCann rescued a workmate entangled in machinery and saved his life at great risk to her own; Mollie Mason helped to avert panic in Chatham Dockyard when a railway carriage overturned in which she was a passenger; Georgina Peeters stopped a machine at considerable personal risk and extricated a fellow worker; Lily Stanyon saved a crane driver, while putting herself in great danger; and Frances Watson rescued a fellow worker after an explosion, taking a big chance on her own survival in doing so. In different circumstances, while out fishing and accompanied by a boy of ten, Ella Trout saw an old steamer, that had been torpedoed, sinking rapidly. Though well aware of the danger from enemy submarines, she quickly manoeuvred her boat to the wreck and rescued a drowning sailor.

This New Year 1918 list also contained a number of telephonists or telegraphists. Such work needed intelligent women, with clear voices, accuracy, tact and nimble fingers, skills which were increasingly required, even in peacetime. Many had a very steadying influence on those working alongside them, particularly in the increasing day and night air raids by planes and Zeppelins, and they showed great enthusiasm for and devotion to their work. A few stories will give an idea of their courage.

Myra Bessent was a sorting clerk, working on telegraph duties in Chatham, handling high security Navy and Army messages, when the location was attacked by enemy aircraft in September 1917; the din of earth-shaking anti-aircraft guns was continuous. Being on duty that night, she twice attempted to walk to her office from her home a mile away, and was twice driven back by the bombs and falling shrapnel. Finally during a lull, she succeeded in cycling there, remaining on duty all night in the instrument room as the only telegraphist in the post, with messages passing constantly. Later she was very complimentary about the telephone girls; they carried on through every raid: 'When a warning is notified we say, "the Bang Boys are coming". We treat the matter with humour, though it is no joke to be turned out of bed in the middle of the night to lend a hand in the busy time that follows a raid.'

Mabel Clarke, telephonist. (*Mrs B. Richards*)

Louise Carlton was a telephone supervisor at Margate. She often came in while off duty, and continued without sleep, working for long periods. During the bombardment of Margate by German destroyers in February 1917, at great risk to herself she came through the shattered streets to her post and worked there calmly as if nothing was wrong. She also remained at work and in danger during a particularly bad air raid in August of that year, giving a fine example of courage.

Mabel Clarke was a 23-year-old telephonist working in London. Gunfire and air raids never stopped her reporting for duty. In January 1917 there was a huge explosion and fire at Silvertown Gas Works, not far from Woolwich Arsenal, where there were about 14,000 women packing shells. The fire soon spread to the explosives, and the blast sent flames up two miles into the air, high over East London, showering metal over the surrounding area. Buildings rocked as if shaken by an earthquake, and after a lull, an ear-splitting roar was followed by buildings, chimneys and tanks being blown into the air, and rows of houses near the factory collapsing like a pack of cards. On duty when this happened, Mabel took the alarm call for the fire brigades and ambulances, and directed and coordinated the emergency services. For thirty-six hours she remained at her post relaying messages, and this was despite the danger of the glass roof above her head disintegrating in the minor explosions that continued. Finally leaving work, she found that all the trams had been commandeered by the Army, so she had to walk all the way home. Her medal was given to her in April 1918 by the Marquess of Crewe.

Annie Merralls was a telephone supervisor at Dover, in control of a very important exchange. She was off duty during the first daylight air raid there, but she decided to go and help just the same and walked to the exchange. On her way she was stopped and detained by the police for her own safety, despite her protestations, as shells and shrapnel were falling all over the town. Subsequently, anticipating moonlight raids, she remained at her post, whether on or off duty, until she was satisfied that the danger had passed. She never showed concern, even when bombs fell near the exchange, and continued her work, setting an excellent example to her girls.

Agnes Pearson was a telephonist at Bradford when there was a very serious explosion in August 1916 at the Low Moor Munitions Works nearby. She remained at her post despite continuous explosions, which threw her to the ground three times from their force, and although the police advised everyone to leave, she stayed and continued working until finally relieved. Eventually she was forced to retire on sickness grounds.

Florence Steggel was often called to her post in London for emergencies during air raids. In September 1917 she narrowly escaped death on her journey to the exchange, when the woman with her was killed.

Fanny Steward was assistant telephone supervisor at Folkestone, a town often attacked because of its harbour and several Army camps nearby. This increased the workload of the exchange, and in a particularly violent air raid in May 1917 she continued work in terrifying conditions, calming and encouraging her frightened staff.

Amelia Ward was telephonist in charge of the exchange at Great Yarmouth. She was responsible for the anti-aircraft arrangements and telephone training, as well as being in charge of the military operators there. She tried to get to work during the town's first bombardment from the sea, and eventually arrived in the middle of the second, setting a fine example to her staff.

So the tales of courage continue. Many ports suffered enemy bombardment from the sea, and many telephone exchanges were sited near or actually inside factories. There the telephone women were often the last people to leave, being too busy in summoning help to care for themselves when explosions broke out or air raids put the place in danger, and as one graphic account describes, 'when the whole exchange rocked'.

The long medal winners' list of 11 June 1918 again concentrated on telephone operators and munitions workers, but three teachers were also included, who showed great courage during air raids. Two of them rescued their pupils when a bomb actually exploded in the classroom where they were teaching – a terrifying experience. Misses Cunnington, Middleton and Watkins certainly deserved their awards.

Nurses, too, appeared on this and the next two lists for January 1919 and July 1920. Nurses Cope and Shepherd were both on the staff of munitions factories, engaged to deal with the frequent accidents; they not only treated their patients but also rescued them in the resultant fires. Nurses Waddell and Westrope worked in a local hospital and helped to rescue people from a fire there, and in a home-based hospital for the wounded, Superintendent Thompson assisted when an air raid set the wards on fire. Matron Spink handled the situation well when bombed in an air raid, and Nurse Jacobs, working in a field hospital, rescued patients during heavy bombing. Three nurses in 1920 were VADs from the British Red Cross Society: Alice Fenwick was involved in a hospital fire caused by an air raid; Agnes Kent rescued patients from a burning marquee; while Lily Rushton's efforts were centred on her hospital, struck by a shell.

In a more unusual case, Margaret Waller of Long Eaton won her medal in January 1919 for her deeds after a great explosion at Chilwell in July 1918.

Seriously wounded in the back by falling glass, she remained behind to give the first aid she had learned in the Girl Guides to over fifty people, undoubtedly saving several lives. She then helped to extinguish the fire in her wrecked canteen in the works. Afterwards, with the doctor, Margaret helped to search in the dangerous buildings for further casualties since only she knew the way around, proceeding through escaping gas and choking smoke. Finally she was overcome by the fumes and fell unconscious.

To a large extent, the remainder of the 1920–3 lists were dominated by awards to firemen, policemen and the Services, with a few women mentioned in May and June 1919, and a variety of awards for Commonwealth ladies who, often in committees, gave time and money to help in the war effort.

CHAPTER THREE

The Albert, Edward and Empire Gallantry Medals

In 1856 Queen Victoria instituted the Victoria Cross for supreme acts of valour and self-sacrifice on the field of battle, and it has remained to this day at the pinnacle of all gallantry awards.

The decoration, hanging from a dull red ribbon, was forged from the guns captured from the Russians during the Crimean War. Because it is only for fighting personnel, it has never officially been given to a woman. There is, however, an apocryphal tale that the old Queen, long shut away mourning her dead consort Albert, had later come to take an active interest in foreign affairs, especially those affecting her empire. She had been most impressed by the dedication of the nurses in the Boer War, and the courageous actions of one in particular. Nursing Sister Frances Bell had rescued some patients ambushed in an ambulance convoy and brought them safely back, at the cost of serious injuries to herself. The Queen, ignoring the advice of her ministers, sent for the lady and handed her the Victoria Cross, saying she could think of none more worthy. Unfortunately the award was unofficial and never gazetted.

Prince Albert in his lifetime shared the Victorian sentiment of admiration for the doer of brave deeds. It was therefore fitting that, five years after his death, the Queen should name the new medal of 1866 as a memorial to her beloved husband – the Albert Medal (AM). It is the highest and the earliest of the awards for courage for which women could qualify alongside men. At first it was only intended for saving life at sea, but in 1877 this was extended to saving life on land, the risk of the saver dying in the attempt being greater than the likelihood of survival. A beautiful unusual medal, it

Victoria Cross (obverse). (*Spink*)

Albert Medal, land type (obverse). (*Savannah Publications*)

was oval in shape, headed with a crown. Around the edge was a garter, and in the centre the letters V and A were entwined. The land medal had a red enamelled centre, with the words 'For Gallantry in Saving Life on Land' within the garter. It hung upon a crimson ribbon with white stripes. The name, date and deed were engraved on the reverse. Eventually the gold medal, representing the greatest risk, carried four white stripes on the ribbon, while the bronze, for slightly less risk, had two. As this award was really the civilian equivalent of the Victoria Cross it is not surprising to see a number of women included among the recipients, some of these being nurses.

The first woman to receive the medal would have been Nurse Edith Reynolds, at the Bristol General Hospital in February 1911. A mentally unstable patient smashed a window of the ward where Nurse Reynolds was on night duty, and climbed onto the roof. Catching hold of his nightshirt, she followed him, risking a fall of thirty-five feet. Had he gone higher, they would both have been killed, but in the darkness he misjudged the tiling and fell through a skylight, thus saving both their lives. Nurse Reynolds modestly declined the offer of the medal, saying that the account of her bravery had been greatly exaggerated. An unusual woman and a humble heroine.

Hilda Wolsey lived to exchange her Albert Medal for the George Cross. In June 1910 she was a 23-year-old nurse at Hanwell Mental Asylum in Southall. In the women's wing, the patients were taking supervised exercise in a courtyard. Suddenly one woman broke away and began climbing the wire netting which covered an outside staircase, used as a fire escape. On reaching the top, she clambered onto the roof of the laundry building, and balancing herself upright, ran along the metal gutter fastened to the edge of the roof. Nurse Wolsey followed her, realising the woman could be killed. Fortunately the nurse was young and agile, but even so she was fully aware of the danger, with the ground twenty-five feet below her and only a fragile gutter to hold their combined weight. Resting one hand against the sloping roof, Hilda reached the now frightened inmate and held her, praying that she would do nothing more unpredictable to send them hurtling to their deaths in the courtyard below. Ropes and ladders were fetched and eventually the patient was lowered to the ground, followed by a shaken Nurse Wolsey, whose concern for the inmate had overcome any fear for herself.

Equally lucky was Nurse Elizabeth Holley, who worked in another mental institution, Kingsdown House in Box, Wiltshire. In November 1912, she was escorting a woman elsewhere and waiting quietly on the railway station platform for the train to arrive. The signals changed and the train appeared in the distance. Then without any warning, the patient tore herself from her nurse's hands and ran across the platform, intending to leap onto the rails right into the path of the approaching train. Nurse Holley grabbed at the woman's coat and at great risk to herself tried to pull her back to safety, but the train was unable to stop in time and to her horror and that of the waiting passengers, the patient was mowed down in front of them. However, Nurse Holley was fortunate to escape with only cuts and bruises from her struggle with the disturbed woman, who had deliberately taken her own life.

An unusual award went to four nurses, who acted together during a frightening incident at a casualty clearing station at Rousbrigge, Belgium, during the First World War. Sister Gertrude Carlin and Staff Nurse Harriet Fraser were from the TFNS, Sister Gladys White was from the British Red Cross Society (BRCS) and Nurse Alice Batt was a VAD. Casualty clearing centres were usually tented, but in this one the operating theatres were in wooden huts. Early in the morning of October 1918, a fire broke out in part of the camp and it rapidly spread along the tented wards until it reached the theatres. Serious abdominal cases were already on the operating tables. The first intimation of danger was when the electric lights failed, and while jury rigging gave enough light to continue, the air began to fill with smoke and the wooden walls burst into flames. Coolly, surgeons and nurses finished the operations, though the heat was intense. Then the nurses rushed the unconscious patients to safety, while around them ether bottles and nitrous oxide cylinders were constantly exploding, filling the air with fumes and flying fragments of steel. Through this inferno the nurses continued, afterwards returning to the burning wards to evacuate the other patients, helpless in the advancing path of the fire. Coughing and grimy from smoke, they worked together, regardless of their own safety, until all the patients were out of danger.

In 1934, another nurse, Ethel Hopkins, gained the same medal for bravery, closely followed by Florence Allen in 1935, who was invested with the medal by King Edward VIII, in the few months before he became the Duke of Windsor. Florence was a children's nurse in Quetta, which today is in Pakistan and in those days contained a military garrison to guard the North-West Frontier of India. She was looking after Christopher, the infant son of Flt Lt Turner. At the end of May 1935, the child was sleeping quietly in his cot when suddenly the floors and walls began to shake and buckle. Knowing that the area was subject to earthquakes, but not realising its severity, instead of finding safety outside, Florence dragged herself to the baby's cot – both legs having been injured by falling debris – and threw herself across it, making her body a living shield to protect the child underneath. The building collapsed on top of them. Two days later, and with Florence in great pain, they were both growing weaker. Then came the noise of pickaxes and voices, and at length they were hauled out, the baby uninjured. Florence, however, required six months in hospital and never fully recovered; later her medal was changed to the George Cross.

Quite ordinary people, too, were unexpectedly faced with potential tragedy, and found the courage to combat it. In 1919, Florence Emmett was in India. She was middle-aged, the wife of the station master of Peshawar, a North-West Frontier province now in Pakistan. With many fighting men, both British and Indian, away in the First World War, frustrated Indian political aspirations and expectations resulted in occasional riots and attacks by terrorist groups, within a population inclined to be excitable and easily inflamed. Religion, poverty, racism, local affairs and other factors all had a hand in the unrest.

On this December day, Mrs Emmett and her children were sitting at the bedside of her husband, who was sick with fever, when she heard her seventeen-year-old son screaming for help. Mrs Emmett immediately left her husband and ran into the sitting room, where she saw the boy being attacked by a madman. The assailant had been forced to drop his axe, which had broken the boy's arm, and was now stabbing at him with a dagger. To save her son she seized the man's arm, calling for help all the while. In the struggle, he stabbed her in the side, but it only made her hang on more tightly. Hearing the commotion, her husband staggered into the room to rescue his wife. The Indian, seeing him, wrenched himself free and succeeded in stabbing the sick man in the thigh, before Mrs Emmett again caught at the attacker's wrist. To shake her off, the man stabbed at her arm and hand, but this time she managed to wrestle the handle of the dagger, now slippery with blood, into her own hands.

By now their cries had brought her servants onto the scene and with their aid the man was overcome. Even then, Mrs Emmett ignored her own wounds until both her husband and son had been attended to and sent to hospital. All three recovered, but it was the sheer courage of Mrs Emmett that saved them – a woman without weapons, tackling an armed man so much stronger than herself, in such frightening circumstances.

Elizabeth Everitt was a heroine of the Second World War. She was a widow, living alone in 1944, when an American bomber crashed in a field near Street Farm, her home, not far from Saffron Walden. This intrepid woman ran to rescue any of the crew who might have survived the crash. She knew the danger, but her desire to save others overrode her fears. Ammunition was exploding as she ran in to search the wreckage and two of the bombs subsequently exploded, killing her instantly. She was posthumously awarded the Albert Medal.

In 1949, a party of Boy Scouts on their bicycles had been visiting Sully Island off the coast of South Wales under the leadership of their Scoutmaster. They had, however, left it late to return across the causeway to the mainland. The tide had risen quickly, cutting the island off, so that though most of the boys had managed to cross safely, two were being swept off the causeway by the force of the waters. Their Scoutmaster, realising their plight, turned back and managed to grasp the elder boy, but in the struggle they both grew weaker and could make no headway.

Margaret Vaughan, a small but sturdy fourteen-year-old schoolgirl, was on the beach with friends, having a picnic. As it was a bright day in May, she had cycled the ten miles from her home and was wearing her swimsuit under her clothes, although she had been forbidden to swim (or cycle) by her parents, since she had undergone an appendix operation only two weeks before. She saw a lot of people in the water and some, holding their bicycles above their heads, were shouting and gesticulating.

Although she had been a keen long-distance swimmer, she had no life-saving training, but this did not stop her. Throwing off her clothes she swam out to help the Scoutmaster and the boy. The sea was cold and rough, with a very strong current now running, which could sweep weaker swimmers out to sea. Despite this, she managed to reach them and, partly aided by the man, began to tow the boy, who was holding on to her costume straps, towards the

Margaret Vaughan (age 14)
AM/GC. (*Mrs M. Purves*)

beach. Others threw a lifebelt to them when they neared the shore, and with its help they were pulled the last few feet to safety. Another boy had tried to save the second Scout but they were both swept away and drowned.

On her return home Margaret was severely scolded by her parents for swimming so soon after her operation and was packed off to the doctor. Both children received the Albert Medal, the boy who had attempted a rescue, posthumously. Margaret was its last living recipient. This was because in 1949 it had been decided that the Albert Medal should no longer be given, except posthumously in bronze, since it overlapped two more recently established awards. Then in 1971, to prevent any further misunderstandings, the Albert Medal finally ceased to exist, and any holders still living were considered to have won the George Cross, and could, if they wished, change their medal for this one.

Between these two dates came a last award to a woman. It was a dull November day in 1968. At St John's Roman Catholic Secondary School in Dundee, a class of fifteen-year-old girls were having a needlework lesson. Their teacher was Nanette Hanson, a pretty 26-year-old woman, who had been married for only six months. The lesson was continuing as normal when, looking up, the teacher saw in the doorway a nineteen-year-old soldier, an ex-pupil of the school, holding a loaded shotgun. At first he sent her and the girls to the opposite end of the room, and barricaded the two classroom doors. Then he drove them into a small adjoining fitting room. There Mrs Hanson tried to quieten the hysterical girls. Meanwhile, the disturbance had brought the headmaster and some school staff to the classroom door, and when they could not open it they shouted to Mrs Hanson, asking what was wrong. In answer the young gunman fired at the door. Alerted to the danger within, they immediately sent for the police, had the school evacuated and tried to talk to the man. In answer, he brought Mrs Hanson out of the fitting room. Fearing for her girls, she realised they needed quiet to calm the highly excitable man and told those on the other side of the door that she must be left to handle the situation herself. Then she began to talk to him. He was, however, very unpredictable, still threatening the girls and assaulting two of them until Mrs Hanson intervened. Later, feeling that Mrs Hanson had somehow tricked him, he sprang up and fired at her at point-blank range. Mercifully the gun misfired, but the teacher knew it could happen again, and that only her life stood between him and the children. In conversation he had mentioned a certain Marion Young, for whom he appeared to have some regard. She could make him feel better. 'What if we could bring her here?' suggested Mrs Hanson gently. The idea appealed to him, and he agreed to release the girls in the fitting room if he could see Marion. With his permission, Mrs Hanson conveyed this to those outside.

When Marion Young arrived at last, fully aware of the situation, the barricade was removed and she and Mrs Hanson eventually secured the release of the girls unharmed, but not of themselves. The barricade was replaced and the talking resumed, but in his deranged state the man needed a scapegoat. During this time he had been firing occasionally at the door and now he noticed that the window behind Mrs Hanson was open. Motioning with his gun, he told her to shut it. As she turned to close it, he shot her in the back, killing her almost instantly. After well over an hour, he at last gave himself up, but it was too late to help the teacher who had sacrificed her life to save her pupils. What happened to Marion Young appears in Chapter Eight.

At the beginning of the twentieth century, Edward VII, son of Queen Victoria and Prince Albert, came to the throne. He was a sociable, rather corpulent man, whose talents had been squandered by waiting too long for his kingly inheritance from his long-lived mother. He was probably still influenced by many of the ideas of his revered father, who had a great interest in the burgeoning science and technology of his day and the conditions of the industrial classes. Also, Edward, much closer to his people that either of his parents, had always been genuinely distressed by the frequent disasters in mining and its allied industries with their terrible loss of life. The result was the introduction of a new medal in 1907 – the Edward Medal (EM) – to recognise the great heroism shown by individuals in endangering their own lives to save others in mines and quarries. In 1909, these areas were extended to industry in general.

The medal was round and minted in silver or bronze according to the degree of bravery. The 1907 medal intended for the mines showed a miner in rolled-up sleeves rescuing another, and above them the word 'Courage'. Until 1911, the medal for industry featured a workman supporting a fallen man, his upheld arm holding a broken beam against a huge approaching wheel, with the words 'For Courage' written on the wood; to their left was a factory with tall chimneys. After that year, the medal for industry showed a Grecian lady holding a laurel branch above her shoulders, the words 'For Courage' alongside her, and at her feet an industrial landscape with chimneys. On the obverse (front) of the medal was the King's head, with his titles around the edge. The whole was suspended from a dark blue ribbon with yellow borders, shaped into a bow for women. It ranked slightly below the Albert Medal.

Edward Medal, early type for Industry (reverse). (*R.J. Scarlett*)

Few women gained the Edward Medal. The first went to Hannah Hugill, four years before the First World War. She was a young woman in Great Busby, Stokeley, near Middlesbrough in Yorkshire, labouring at Court House Farm, which belonged to her parents. One day in September 1909, while working, she heard loud screams and roars coming from a nearby field. Running there she saw that her mother was being gored by an enraged bull, and could not get away. Without thought for herself, she immediately attacked the bull to draw him off, and so enabled her mother to crawl out of danger. Eventually Hannah, too, was able to escape, although not before she was herself injured; but there was no doubt that her mother would have been killed had she not intervened at the risk of her own life, and in such frightening circumstances.

The Holdsworth Brothers' Factory in Plumstead, south-east London, used great machines to grind up used rags into flock, which fell to the floor in a snow of tiny particles. Some, in the air, settled on the clothing of the women who were piling it into large bags. On a warm June day in 1925, fire suddenly broke out in a machine tended by a young girl. Unfortunately, she was in a corner of the room, trapped between the wall behind her and the machine in front of her. The flock falling out of the machine caught fire, which swiftly spread to that around her feet, the bag she was filling and the particles covering her clothes, so that she became a ball of fire, and the whole corner with her.

Lilian Peyto, working on the opposite side of the same machine, saw this happen and immediately ran to help her workmate, but although the girl tried to escape from behind the machine, she stumbled and fell. Mrs Peyto tried to lift her and drag her clear, despite the flames all round, but just then – by ill luck – a heavy sack of blazing waste material, hanging on the end of the machine,

Lilian Peyto EM shows her medal to her mother, outside Buckingham Palace. (*Mr D. Peyto*)

collapsed over the girl. Blinded for a moment Mrs Peyto let her go, but, realising her friend's life was in her hands, she did not give up and fought her way into the flames for a second time. Grasping the girl hard, she at last managed to drag her away, though her friend's clothing was still on fire. A foreman ran up and threw some empty sacks over the girl to put out the flames.

Everything happened so quickly that the other women working in the room were frightened and ran away. It was only Mrs Peyto's presence of mind and speed of reaction that rescued the girl unaided. She was also aware of the danger to her own clothing and it required a special kind of courage to tackle the flames a second time. Sadly the girl died from her burns.

After 1949, only a bronze version of the Edward Medal remained and this was for posthumous awards, but by 1971 so few had been given that it was decided to discontinue it, and that any holders still living could, if they wished, exchange it for the George Cross. No women were then alive to do so.

The Empire Gallantry Medal (EGM) took over from the earlier medal of the Most Excellent Order of the British Empire. Introduced by King George V at the end of December 1922, this type was to reward acts of gallantry in two categories: military and civil. It was short-lived, being replaced in 1940 by the George Cross, at which time all living holders had to exchange it for the new medal, recipients being deemed to have been awarded the George Cross.

The medal itself was a larger silver coin shape than the earlier medal, and so also was the seated figure of Britannia. The words, making a quarter circle on either side of her, were 'For God and The Empire'. To the right of her head was a large sun and below the line under her feet was a sprig of laurel with the words 'For Gallantry'. The reverse side carried the royal cipher below the crown, except that those medals given in the next king's reign also carried the words 'Instituted by King George V'. Lions couchant formed a circle around the whole. The ribbon was purple for civilians, the military having a red stripe in the middle, but in 1937 at Queen Mary's request, the colour was changed to a rose-pink edged with pearl-grey, the military having a pearl-grey stripe in the centre. At this

Empire Gallantry Medal after 1937 (obverse). (*V. Scott*)

time too, a laurel branch was fixed diagonally to the ribbon when the medal was given for gallantry.

As this was a British Empire Medal, it was only right that one of the recipients should be a woman of the British Empire. She was Begum Ashraf-un-Nisa of Hyderabad, the elderly wife of a retired Indian Army officer. In 1936 when she gained this award, the custom of purdah meant that Indian women of high rank, whether Hindu or Muslim, should not be seen by men or strangers. Therefore on this June day, the Begum and many other ladies were sitting in a screened balcony enjoying a film at the Moti Mahal cinema in Hyderabad City. Their pleasurable outing was tragically cut short when a fire broke out in the cinema, and the two exits from the balcony to the ground floor became a mass of flames. To break purdah was a serious matter, but since there was no alternative, the Begum's practical sense overrode custom. She stripped off her long sari, making it into a rope with which she lowered five women down to the ground floor. Other women copied her example. But the balcony was now on fire and some women were too afraid or half stupified by the smoke to escape. Trying to help them, the Begum nearly left it too late to help herself, and finally had to jump down from the balcony, hurting herself badly as a result. She was then taken outside, where a huge crowd had gathered to watch the building burn, almost to the ground. No one else escaped the blazing inferno. Of the forty-four women on the balcony fourteen died, but had it not been for the Begum the death toll would have been higher.

In May 1932, during a quiet, ordinary visiting hour for patients at the South Hams small cottage hospital at Kingsbridge, Devon, Emma

Townsend, a grey-haired lady of fifty-four, was sitting by the bedside of her sister. Suddenly she heard cries for help; suspecting a patient in pain, she went to investigate. In a nearby ward a little boy was being attacked by a man with a gun. There was no time to go for assistance, so Miss Townsend ran to grapple with the man, who had fired two shots, wounding the boy, and was now attempting to beat him to death with the butt. The nine-year-old boy was weeping pitifully and begging his father to stop. Angered by Miss Townsend's interference the man tried to turn the gun on her and as they struggled she was hit over the head with the gun barrel, cutting her head open and showering her with blood. The noise brought others onto the scene, and eventually the man was overpowered. Miss Townsend, with stitches in her head, became an in-patient herself, and others hearing of her brave actions flooded her room with flowers. The man turned out to be a local farmer who that day, having murdered his wife and two of his children, had come to the hospital to kill the third. Sadly, after lingering for two days, the young boy whom Miss Townsend had fought so hard to save – nearly losing her own life in the process – finally died.

From these illustrations, it can be seen that none of the women were prepared for the circumstances in which they found themselves, but they had all deliberately risked their lives to save another, at whatever cost. They set an example few could equal.

CHAPTER FOUR

The George Cross and George Medal

Towards the end of the First World War, the civilian population of Britain was beginning to realise that conflict was not only confined to far-off lands, but could be brought to their very doors by the implementation of a terrible new weapon – first the Zeppelin and then the aeroplane with its lethal cargoes. Attacks were intended to damage installations connected with war, but targeting was often inaccurate, and indeed sometimes deliberately aimed at damaging civilian morale – something common on all sides in war.

At home enemy air raids took their toll and in their turn proved that men and women could be called to deeds of daring and courage in saving life, the equal of those displayed on the field of battle. Indeed, the Second World War made the small island of Britain itself not only the arsenal and powerhouse of war, but almost another battleground. This was true of the large cities that nightly endured pulverising raids, and in the camps, airfields and factories that had sprouted everywhere.

George Cross (obverse). (*R.J. Scarlett*)

Two new medals were created especially to meet the wartime emergency, and to mark and encourage the bravery of civilian men and women not eligible for military awards. Consequently in 1940, the awarding of the Albert, Edward and Empire Gallantry Medals almost disappeared, the latter completely, and the first two being only given posthumously after 1949, so that by 1971 all three awards were deemed to have become the George Cross (GC).

The highest of the two new awards, ranking only just below the soldier's Victoria Cross, and the highest that could be bestowed on any civilian, was named the George Cross after King George VI who had instituted it. This was earned by displaying the most conspicuous courage in circumstances of extreme danger. Like the Victoria Cross, it is a simple medal, in the shape of a plain Greek Cross and fashioned in silver. Its centre is a roundel showing in high relief St George killing the dragon, within a surround carrying the words 'For Gallantry'. On its reverse is the name of the recipient and the details. It hangs from a plain dark blue ribbon; for women, the ribbon is in the shape of a bow.

So rare is it that very few have been awarded and only four to women: three for actions overseas during the Second World War, of which more later, the fourth to Barbara Harrison, the only postwar woman to receive it. She was twenty-three, a beautiful, lively, conscientious young woman, and a stewardess in the British Overseas Airways Corporation (BOAC). On an April day in 1968, she was on a Boeing 707 jet aircraft, G-ARWE, which was taking off from Heathrow Airport for Singapore. Soon after they were in the air, one of the four jet engines on the wing nearest the fuselage of the aircraft caught fire and after burning fiercely fell off, leaving flames flaring from where it had been. The plane could still fly on three engines but because the fire seemed to be worsening, the pilot requested permission from Heathrow to return, and made an emergency landing there about two and a half minutes later. The fire on the wing, meanwhile, was spreading out of control. Miss Harrison, together with the steward, had been assigned to the tail end of the aircraft. As soon as the plane landed, they followed the normal emergency procedure, opening the plane's rear door to let down and inflate the escape chute, from which the hundred or so passengers could slide to the ground. Unfortunately the chute twisted as it fell, closing its exit. Realising what had happened, the steward climbed down and straightened it out, but once outside he could not climb back. It was therefore left to Miss Harrison on her own to guide the rear passengers out of the aircraft, and quell the rising panic. It was a frightening experience amid explosions, flames and smoke spreading inside the cabin, with the long black tunnel of the chute the only way of escape. Many passengers were afraid to enter the chute but, by dint of encouraging some and firmly pushing others, Barbara managed to get a number of passengers out, until it was no longer possible to exit the aircraft from the rear. Calmly she directed her remaining passengers to another chute. An elderly, crippled passenger was having difficulty leaving his seat so she turned back to help. By then the smoke from the burning upholstery was thick and suffocating, so that they could neither see nor breathe. Eventually Miss Harrison's body was found beside that of the crippled passenger, whom she had given her life to try to save. In addition to the George Cross, she was posthumously given the Flight Safety Foundation's Heroism Award.

The second award, sanctioned by the King in September 1940, was the George Medal (GM). It ranked second to the George Cross. It was a silver coin shape, bearing the monarch's crowned head and titles on one side, and on the other, inspired by a bookplate in Windsor Castle Library, the outline of St George with a halo slaying the dragon, with the words 'The George Medal' in bold letters around the rearing horse. The ribbon is in red with five narrow blue stripes and for women worn as a bow. Mainly intended for civilians, especially those who distinguished themselves in the 1940 bombing of cities, it could also be given for actions by any member of the Armed Services not covered by military honours, and was for 'acts of great bravery'.

The First World War had for the first time begun to draw in the ordinary civilian women of Britain, who carried out the jobs that men vacated when they joined the Forces, and they had many brave actions to their credit as a result of enemy shellings or air raids on their homes and workplaces. The onset of the Second World War changed the picture still more because the population of the British Isles was small. In order to free the numbers of men needed for the Armed Forces or essential war work, women had to be much more active and organised. In 1941 came Registration for Employment for women of certain

George Medal (obverse). (*R.J. Scarlett*)

ages, rapidly followed by National Service Regulations, which were eventually to call up mostly childless or single women for the Services or other war work. By 1944, the registration of all women between the ages of eighteen and fifty with no valid exemption had been completed. As a result many women joined the women's Services or nursing, but housewives, mothers, single women and the small number of unemployed, who were not already working in munitions or war industries, were urged to join one of the many organisations for Civil Defence, of which the Women's Voluntary Service (WVS) was the most prominent.

Apart from their many-faceted kinds of work, the WVS also acted as a clearing house, directing the most suitable women into other organisations, since many who volunteered wanted a change of work from what they already knew. They joined Air Raid Precautions (ARP) – later renamed the Civil Defence Corps – Fire Watching, the Auxiliary Fire Service (AFS), the Civil Nursing Reserve (NA), the Auxiliary Ambulance Service, and even the Home Guard Auxiliary. There were other official and unofficial bodies, too. Statistics of the time indicate that older women preferred canteen work, arranging evacuations and supplying hospitals. The average single 35-year-old – many of whom worked in offices and shops during the day – gravitated into ARP. Those who chose transport work were often around twenty-nine, married, and relatively well off. Ambulance drivers were a bit younger, on average about twenty-seven, and married without children. Those under twenty-five and coming from shops or offices and occasionally factories often preferred to be nursing auxiliaries, and the under eighteens chose play or recreation centres. As can be seen, many of these occupations were part-time, as these women were also running a home and holding down a job; they were giving up their spare time to training or turning out in an emergency, and there were many emergencies in those wartime days.

One such occurred in the quiet Suffolk village of Aldeburgh, today famous for its music festival. Divided from inland by barbed wire, the marshes and beaches along the coast had been heavily seeded with mines against an expected German invasion: already Hitler's Operation Sealion was in preparation, with the collection of barges and craft for the expedition.

In July 1940, two middle-aged married women were sent by the ARP with their ambulance to give help to two injured soldiers who had wandered into the coastal minefield. Dorothy Clarke was the driver and Bessie Knight-Hepburn her attendant. The men had stepped on a mine, causing an explosion that was heard for miles around. A crowd had gathered nearby and when the women arrived, they were warned to go no further for fear of detonating further mines. 'It's our job to look after the wounded wherever they may be,' responded Mrs Knight-Hepburn. Shrugging off efforts to stop them, the two women took a stretcher and, treading as lightly as they could, made their way to where the two men lay. One was already dead, the other had terrible injuries. Applying first aid, they then placed him on their stretcher and struggled back to the ambulance. By a miracle they returned without setting off any more mines, though they knew the risk, and drove the soldier straight to hospital, waiting anxiously for the outcome. However, despite endangering their own lives, they were not able to save him.

These were the first two women invested by the King with the George Medal, and on that day they were joined by a third. She was Sonia Straw, a part-time warden with the ARP. The Battle of Britain was at its height. The Luftwaffe had switched their raids from coastal targets to front-line airfields and then inland bases, mainly in daylight. So it was a sunny September day in 1940 when the German bombers came swooping down on Caterham and its nearby Kenley Fighter Station. Many people were watching a cricket match between the Army and the Air Force and there was no time for warning before the bombs came raining down. Sonia, a very frightened nineteen-year-old, arrived during the air raid and was appalled at the carnage. Dead and dying were strewn everywhere. She set herself to treat those suffering from shock. For others who were injured and bleeding, and having no equipment, she had to improvise tourniquets, pads and slings. So intent was she on her task that she did not realise that she was the only person present able to give assistance, and that she was working completely on her own. It was some time before the ambulances got through the cratered roads, and many that day owed their lives to her presence of mind, prompt attention and courage.

Only six days later, Hitler, in a rage at two RAF raids on Berlin, which he had sworn would always be inviolate, switched the German Air Force attacks to London. Throughout that afternoon and night, the sprawling mass of docks along the Thames – their warehouses and yards filled with essential foods and supplies, cranes, bridges and the crowded housing of the dockers' families – fell victim to the fires and explosions of the heaviest bombing they had ever known.

Grace Rattenbury was a member of the Bermondsey WVS centre, a little south of the river. Although it was her Saturday off, hearing the sirens

The ruins of bombed London.
(*Imperial War Museum*)

wailing, the roar of the planes and the crash of the bombs, she volunteered to help. An urgent request for blankets from Bermondsey arrived. When she managed to reach her destination in her WVS van, she found the docks ablaze and she was immediately enrolled to do whatever was needed. First she went to a block of flats, almost completely cut off by flames, and assisted with its hurried evacuation. After that she drove all night over burning bridges and along burning streets, with bombs constantly falling, ferrying to safety not only families of fleeing people, but also firemen injured in their dangerous work. When she finally finished, her battered van was full of the signs of a heavy night's work, such as steel helmets, blood-soaked bandages, and a fireman's axe. Neither strong, nor young at forty, this indomitable woman had kept going on her rescue missions throughout that terrible night.

Attacks in September were not just confined to London. An unexpected raid took place in a quiet village near Horsham. Here Dorothy White was a member of the BRCS and, as an original member of the Horsham WVS, had been assigned with two other VADs to a first aid post in the village hall. She was on duty with them when they heard a bomb explode nearby. Running out they found it had demolished the district's nurse's house next door. The nurse herself was in the crater made by the bomb, badly injured. Slipping and sliding, they managed to lift her out from the rubble and onto a stretcher which they carried to their post, but another bomb fell directly on the end of the hall where they were, killing the nurse and severely injuring the two VAD rescuers. Miss White, who had been boiling a kettle further away, and although hurt, with no thought for herself scrambled back over the rubble and dug them out. She applied first aid and used her belt as a makeshift tourniquet. Making them comfortable, she then set off to visit the other cottages in the village to offer her assistance. All this time enemy planes were overhead dropping bombs, some of which exploded later, but through this mayhem forty-year-old Miss White carried on her self-appointed task doggedly, bringing comfort, confidence and help to the shaken villagers.

Bombers and bombs often went wide of their targets, as happened at Horsham, and this also occurred in one of the last day raids at the end of September at Sherborne, near the aircraft factory at Yeovil. The hub of organising the relief and rescue services for Civil Defence was the telephone exchange. The fine traditions established by women telephone operators during the First World War continued into the Second World War, as shown by one supervisor's report: 'I said, "All right, girls. Time to get out!" but none of them moved, although . . . [they were] coughing and spluttering from the effects of smoke. . . . "But we've still got calls coming in," one said, and I had to pull the plugs out before they would leave their seats.' Something similar happened in the case of Maude Steele, working with an assistant in the Post Office Telephone Exchange at Sherborne. One bomb landed within the building, and most of the telephone lines were put out of action. She then organised runners to go out of the town to make calls from outside telephone boxes, while she remained bravely at her post until the position became absolutely impossible. She was forced to leave only after being of maximum assistance to the emergency services and the populace of the badly hit town.

Bombs also came that night to the rural quiet of Uckfield, Sussex. One fell on a family farmhouse, which was reduced to rubble. Neighbours quickly appeared to help, among them eighteen-year-old Rose Ede, a member of the Housewives Service of the WVS. Though the adults had been killed, the family's three children could be heard crying in the debris. With bare hands and the nearest implements, everyone began digging, the light of torches slanting through the driving rain. Overhead there was the drone of planes and the danger of more bombs falling.

At length the two older children were extricated, but the rescuers could not reach the baby, who was in a hole protected by some timbers likely to fall if disturbed. There was just enough room for a small person to creep underneath to reach the child. Miss Ede, the smallest person there, volunteered, knowing full well the risk of being crushed to death. Tunnelling her way into the debris, she managed to loosen the baby from the surrounding rubble, and then remained to comfort him, while those outside struggled to raise the entrapping beams, every movement sending rivulets of mud and stones onto the crouching girl and baby. Half an hour later there was enough room for Rose to pull the child free and crawl with him through the hole to freedom, having saved his life at the greatest risk of her own.

By now Hitler's invasion plans had been shelved indefinitely, and Operation Sealion was beached. Instead, the Germans turned to a war of attrition to starve or incapacitate Britain. The big cities with large engineering works attracted their quota of air attacks, but, as has been seen, lesser towns and rural communities were sometimes mistaken for them. There was no mistake on 10 October 1940, however, when Coventry suffered its first bombing of the war. Incendiary and high-explosive bombs peppered the city and it became an inferno.

Betty Quinn was a seventeen-year-old clerk working there. She was also a St John Ambulance Brigade member and a volunteer ARP warden in the Foleshill division. On the night of the raid, she was busy dowsing incendiary bombs in her area when a message came through about a family trapped in a bombed Anderson shelter in their garden. Because of the danger she was ordered to stay at her post but she insisted on going, knowing that her first-aid training would help.

Being the first to arrive, and hearing the cries of those still alive inside, she started digging at the mass of rubble covering them. She was joined after a while by others who had striven to get through the hazardous streets, and eventually seven survivors were painstakingly extracted. These she treated successfully and stayed with them, until the much-delayed ambulances managed to reach them. Afterwards she returned to her post to continue her warden duties.

One of the early consequences of an air raid (and bad weather) was the destruction of telephone wires, still vulnerable because they were not yet buried underground. Coordination of rescue and emergency services depended on them. Anticipating the need, a Civil Defence controller at West Ham created a band of young sixteen- to eighteen-year-old cyclists, known as 'Gilman's Daredevils', to carry messages between control and vital ARP and other posts when the telephones failed. The idea quickly spread.

Charity Bick was one such cyclist at West Bromwich outside Birmingham, though underage at fourteen. She came on duty with her father when her town was bombed on a night in November 1940. Incendiary bombs with their resultant fires – intended to guide the bombers to their targets – could cause as much damage as high-explosive bombs, but could be extinguished by relatively untrained civilians. Charity and her father saw incendiaries land on the roofs of the surrounding houses and, with the hose of a stirrup hand pump, they put them out. One incendiary went through the roof of the pawnbroker's next door, so they had to climb into the false roof space above the bedroom to get at it. When the neighbour's stirrup pump refused to work, Charity's father passed her a bucket of water that she splashed over the bomb, extinguishing it. As she returned, the ceiling gave way, and she fell into the bedroom below, hitting her back on the bedrail as she landed and lying half across the thick eiderdown on the bed. For the rest of the night she was in considerable pain, moving with an increasing limp, but she tried not to show it lest she be sent home.

By now most telephone wires were down, so borrowing a bike Charity was sent numerous times to the control room, a round journey of over a

Charity Bick (age 14) GM, Despatch Rider. (*Miss A. Bick*)

mile each time, through the roaring of fires and the explosions of nearby bombs, often falling flat on her face in the gutter when one fell too near. With incredible courage, this child carried out her duties, despite her injury, throughout the raid.

The control centre of Croydon was in its town hall. On an evening in November 1940, a bomb crashed through the building into the basement, used as the control message room, killing three of the five telephonists on duty and injuring the other two, one badly. Pauline Hollyer was one. When the dust and debris had settled, rescuers tried to evacuate the seriously injured woman, but Miss Hollyer refused to go. She had been in an adjoining room, also wrecked, and a large window frame had severely wounded her in the neck; woodwork blasted across the message room had pinned her underneath. Despite this, hearing a telephone ringing, she managed to reach and answer it. She then tested the other telephones and, finding some in working order, cleared enough space and then calmly continued her vital work of receiving and transmitting messages for the emergency services. She continued maintaining this essential link until finally relieved next morning, when she at last allowed herself to be treated for her injuries.

Coventry was the target for two other great raids in November 1940 and April 1941, but there were smaller raids at other times. During this baptism of fire, many ordinary women showed great courage and selflessness, among them Margaret Brown, who was a 22-year-old St John Ambulance Brigade member, acting as a nurse at Herbert's Works. During an air raid on an April night in 1941, she was hurrying to her parent's home along a street where a house had received a direct hit, when she fancied she heard a cry for help. The roof beams were swaying, leaning over the rubble from where the sounds were coming. Without waiting for assistance to arrive, Margaret started to tunnel very carefully beneath the roof, and eventually located a youth, fearfully injured but still alive. Unable to free him, she stayed with him in the tunnel, talking to keep him conscious and promising help would soon come. It was about an hour before the rescue teams arrived and dug them out, relieving Margaret of her dangerous and lonely vigil. That same night, her Brigade Hall was also bombed, causing many casualties. She attended efficiently to the wounded and although by then she was exhausted and in pain, many of them undoubtedly owed their lives to her prompt attention.

Another brave Coventry woman was Mary Beardshall. She was a nursing orderly and helper at the Coventry and Warwickshire Hospital and on night duty in April 1941 when a raid started. Her head was cut when a bomb exploded outside the room where she was operating the telephone switchboard. Later, alone on the top floor, finding fires caused by incendiaries, she extinguished them with sand and beat out smouldering mattresses with her bare hands, knowing that any fire there might bring the ceiling down on the patients in the ward below. She helped an injured nurse to safety, and then supported a beam while patients were being extricated from the debris caused by other bombs. At another time, the Alexandra Ward where she was working received a direct hit, and she had to climb along a ledge to reach patients trapped beneath blocks of concrete. These and other patients she helped to remove by stretcher to the basement. Then a delayed-action bomb went off and she was badly injured, remaining unconscious for some weeks, during which she had several stitches in her scalp and treatment for a long facial scar. She did not leave hospital until ten weeks later.

Mary Fitzgerald was a full-time ambulance driver in Plymouth, one of the Channel ports frequently attacked by the Luftwaffe. She was on duty on a night in August 1941 when a huge landmine exploded, causing many casualties and much damage. As she raced to pick up the injured, another bomb landed so close that the ambulance was blown into the air, landing with its upper framework flattened over her and her attendant. Extricating them both with difficulty, she then took the shocked woman back to the ambulance centre and asked for another ambulance to pick up her original casualties. She then set up a shuttle service, ferrying the many injured back and forth to the hospital, and continuing throughout the whole, long, frightening raid. When it finished, she retrieved her first ambulance – valuable if only for reuse of its parts – and managed to make it crawl back to the centre. Afterwards she volunteered to try to bring in another ambulance, damaged and abandoned on a hill, and again succeeded – completing all this in virtual darkness, her blacked-out headlights showing only a narrow slit of light, and with the greatest of driving skills.

Though all these endeavours would be considered brave in normal times, they were rendered much more so because most took place in fearful circumstances – falling buildings, fractured gas mains, flooding sewers, fires, craters, explosions and continuing air raids – when the women involved knew they could be blown to bits at any moment. The George Medal was thus only a small mark of the appreciation of the country for the courage and sacrifice of these wartime women.

Outside Britain, three intrepid civilian women with English connections who gained the George Medal should also be mentioned. Sylvia Apostolides, who lived in Greece, was the daughter of a Greek doctor and an Englishwoman. After the German conquest of Greece, her work in her father's surgery gave her considerable scope for activities in intelligence, supply gathering and assisting with escape lines. Caught in 1944 with her parents, she was brutally interrogated, imprisoned, condemned to death and finally freed.

Helen Rodrigues was the daughter of a Scottish mother and a Portuguese doctor who took his final qualifications in Britain. As a nurse, she became matron of a hospital in Burma some time before the 1942 Japanese invasion. She refused evacuation, remaining to continue tending her patients. Later transferring her patients to a safer location, she was wounded while a battle raged around her area. The George Medal for her bravery being announced that year caused the Japanese to imprison and torture her, before interning her in a prison camp where she continued her selfless nursing work before her release in 1945.

Berthe Fraser was married to a First World War British Sergeant Major. After her husband's arrest following the German occupation of France, she became intensely active and innovative in organising a French resistance group, gathering supplies and intelligence, and assisting with escape lines. Twice arrested, she was mercilessly tortured and imprisoned, only just escaping death by the unexpected arrival of the Allies.

There were a number of other women – mostly civilians, of French, Belgian and Dutch nationalities, as well as an extraordinary Eurasian nurse in Malaya – whose great bravery was acknowledged with an honorary George Medal for their activities on behalf of their country and the Allied cause in enemy-occupied territories during the war.

Peace, however, brought its own dangers. In a semi-detached farm cottage at Worlington, Devon, Marjorie Vearncombe lived with her elderly uncle and aunt. One evening in June 1951, she heard screams coming from her neighbour's home. Calling to her relatives, she ran into the adjoining cottage through the back door, and saw the farmer's wife, with a bleeding cut on her forehead, wrestling with her crazed husband for possession of a double-barrelled shotgun. Realising that in this state he would hurt someone, Marjorie tried to intervene, but her strength proved not enough, and the farmer turned the gun on her, her fingers over the muzzle receiving the bullet. The farmer regained possession of the gun and ran after his wife, who had fled to Marjorie's uncle and aunt. He fired at her and she fell to the floor with a head wound. When help eventually arrived, it was to find that the man had shot himself in the kitchen and his wife's life was hanging in the balance. By her intervention, Marjorie had succeeded in saving her friend's life, but lost the top of her finger in the process.

In July 1996, at St Luke's Primary School, Wolverhampton, Lisa Potts, a 21-year-old nursery nurse and teacher of the infants' class, was beginning to tidy up after a teddy bear's picnic outside with her four-year-olds. Suddenly she saw a man waving a machete; he hit one of the mothers on the head and then, jumping a low fence, struck at two more. Fearing for the children, Lisa grabbed a few of them and took them inside, returning to fetch more. The attacker was now among the children, who were screaming and running, some wrapping themselves around their teacher's long skirts so that she could hardly move. As she put out her hand to protect a little girl beside her,

Lisa Potts GM. (*Mr D. Tamea*)

the man slashed at the child's face, cutting both her and Lisa. Tucking the girl under her arm, Lisa Potts ran indoors with her, where most of the children now were, while the man turned to attack a small boy still outside, cutting him across the head.

Three times she had run out to rescue the children, and finally with them all safely inside, she was shutting the door when the man forced it open behind her and started to slash at her back as she stood shielding the children. Meanwhile, the commotion had brought parents and staff to the scene, and the attacker ran off, to be later captured. In four terrifying minutes, three parents and four children were injured and Lisa Potts more seriously; her hand will never fully recover and she suffers blackouts. Fortunately in such a vicious attack, there were no fatalities. She was the last woman to win this award in the twentieth century.

The George Medal has certainly marked out and upheld the high standards of courage displayed by women, whether in times of war or peace.

CHAPTER FIVE

Women in the Armed Services

In two world wars, women have served officially in all three of the Armed Services. They were always kept as separate organisations, non-combatant and usually in the support role, so that they might release men for more active duties. Nevertheless, the women's Services have often created a mixed response in the public at large, the misconception being that women had been transformed into fighting machines, with either too much or too little sex. This was wrong on all counts – the few bad cases called forth investigations that always proved that servicewomen were not only very human but that, spending their days in an ordered, regulated working and living environment, they were better in percentage terms than their civilian counterparts.

With so many women in uniform it is not surprising that, particularly in time of war, their actions have won them medals or awards – despite their work in the past having been auxiliary rather than active; from the former must be excluded those women who served abroad in the Second World War with the Special Operations Executive (SOE), who were certainly not passive, and where there was the daily necessity of showing great courage.

The changing names of the women's Services in past years have often caused confusion, so a brief summary is given here. The Women's Army Auxiliary Corps (WAAC) came into existence in March 1917, and shortly after changed its name to the Queen Mary's Army Auxiliary Corps, (QMAAC). The Women's Royal Naval Service (WRNS) emerged in February 1918. It was closely followed by the Women's Royal Air Force (WRAF), created on the same day as the Royal Air Force (RAF) on 1 April 1918 – by far the youngest of all Britain's three Services. The interwar years saw all three male Services affected by economies, resulting in the disbanding of their women's arms, until late in 1939, just before the Second World War. Then the Auxiliary Territorial Service (ATS) was formed for the Army, the Women's Royal Naval Service (WRNS, sometimes called the Wrens) for the Navy, and the Women's Auxiliary Air Force (WAAF) for the Royal Air Force. After the Second World War, it became accepted that a nucleus of women must be kept to start a new Service in case of future emergencies. Two of them were renamed the Women's Royal Army Corps (WRAC) and the Women's Royal Air Force (WRAF), and those names have remained until approaching the 1990s, when their roles became more active, and they were absorbed into their parent services.

Corporal Daphne Pearson EGM/GC.
(*This England*)

The following are the actions of a few of the women in the Services, who can lay claim to some of the most revered medals of the Second World War – those given for gallantry.

Outstanding among these was the Empire Gallantry Medal given to Corporal (Cpl) Daphne Pearson of the WAAF in the early part of 1940 (it was shortly turned into the George Cross). She was at RAF Detling, working as an attendant in its sick quarters. No. 500 Squadron of Coastal Command was based there, flying Avro Ansons. On the last night of May, and off duty, she had just dozed off into a fitful sleep – it was difficult to sleep long and soundly with the noise of planes revving up or patrols going out. Her medical work, too, always kept her on the alert for accidents to aircraft, and that night she became aware that an incoming plane was in trouble; one engine was cutting out. It landed heavily and slid across a field, flames spreading from the engine and along the fuselage, towards the full load of bombs it had not been able to drop.

Hastily donning slacks, wellington boots, a thick fisherman's jersey and tin hat, Daphne ran out across the wet grass to the guard room. There was a dull glow where the plane had come to rest. A twinkling light had been switched on at the station headquarters. As she rushed headlong past the guard, she shouted to him to undo the gates as the ambulance would be on its way. She scrambled over a fence – an RAF policeman tried to stop her – fell down an incline, was stung by nettles in the ditch, and finally reached the field with the blazing plane. Men were shouting for a doctor, an ambulance. She yelled 'Coming'. One or two others appeared, silhouetted against the flames. Running towards them, Daphne helped someone dragging a harnessed figure out of the wreckage. 'Leave him to me,' she cried. 'Race and get the fence down for the ambulance.' On her own she tried to drag the pilot further away from the blaze but he was groaning with pain, so she decided to render first aid immediately. Unclipping his parachute harness, she found his neck was injured, and feared a broken back. The pilot mumbled he had a full load of bombs on board and to keep clear. Realising this, she managed to drag him over the ridge just before the petrol tanks blew out. She threw herself over him, placing her own helmet over his head to protect him, and to shield him from the light as he was in shock. A huge bomb exploded and Daphne held his head to prevent any further dislocation; as she did so he mumbled something about his face. There was a lot of blood around his mouth and a tooth was protruding from his upper jaw. A soldier crawled up and lent her a handkerchief so that she could clean him up. She was just going to examine the pilot's ankle when the plane went up in a tremendous explosion. They were only thirty yards from it, and there was only the ridge and Cpl Pearson's body to protect the pilot. All the breath was sucked out of them, the air around seeming to collapse, and they were showered with splinters and debris. Other helpers were blown flat as before a gale-force wind.

Knowing that more bombs would go off, Daphne ran to the fence to help the medical officer over with the stretcher. Shortly after the pilot had been removed by ambulance, there was another explosion, worse than the first, but Cpl Pearson then went back to the wreckage to see if the fourth member of the crew had survived, but he was already dead. Afterwards she returned to help the doctor, and was on duty as usual at 8 a.m. the next day. The courage of this woman was remarkable, since she knew full well the dangers from a crashed aircraft, yet she was willing to risk her own life in order to save others.

A George Medal went to a member of the ATS in early 1948, in the most frightening of circumstances. Several soldiers of the Royal Ordnance Corps and Royal Pioneer Corps, in the remote area of Saxelby, not far from Melton Mowbray, were in an iron-roofed hut defusing anti-tank mines – delicate and highly dangerous work. Suddenly one of the mines blew up; two men were killed outright and others severely injured, one of whom died later. Lance Corporal (L/Cpl) Margaret Richards was a medical orderly at the ordnance depot, Old Dalby, and was with her medical officer visiting an outpost not far away. Both were immediately summoned to the scene. When they arrived, what met their eyes was heart-rending and fearful: the hut was wrecked, with jagged pieces of roof, glass, wood and shell splinters strewn around, together with many other mines, unbalanced and ready to go off at any minute. Personnel, stunned and horrified, advised them not to enter the hut, but neither the medical officer nor his orderly baulked at the danger if there were lives to save. As they entered, L/Cpl Richards could see bits of two badly mangled dead bodies on the floor. There was a third person lying there, still alive, surrounded by other mines, and Margaret was aware that any movement could set off another deadly detonation. But he needed their help and although shouted warnings reached them as they worked, L/Cpl Richards displayed cool, clinical care, as she and the medical officer attended his grave injuries. Afterwards they were shown into another hut nearby, where other soldiers were lying. They were also badly injured and complaining that they could neither breathe nor see properly. They were sad cases, but hiding her feelings Margaret talked cheerfully to them, calming and encouraging them. At the same time she applied first aid and helped the medical officer as they tried to stop haemorrhages, splint broken bones and, cutting away the men's uniforms, dress the most serious of their wounds. The cheerfulness and courage of this gallant 24-year-old were outstanding in such acutely dangerous conditions, and her skill and efficiency enabled the medical officer to get the men ready quickly for their removal to hospital, and in all probability contributed to saving any further loss of life.

After the large numbers of Military Medals given to military nurses and ambulance drivers in the First World War, only a few were awarded to women later, the majority of these in the Second World War to women of the Armed Services, and not for bravery overseas but in Great Britain. Here they acted as the front line of defence. They flew protective balloon barrages. They worked on searchlights and guns targeting enemy raiders. They manned telephones and teleprinters. In lonely cabins around the coast they strained to hear enemy messages or worked at decoding them. They watched radar screens on stations festooned with give-away masts and aerials – the eyes of the RAF. They assisted the search and rescue service around the coast and worked on aircraft on exposed airfields. They also performed many other vital functions, all three women's Services taking their share.

It was to members of the WAAF, however, that the Military Medals of the Second World War were given, and it is noticeable that all the recipients worked on airfields.

August and early September 1940 saw the German Air Force fighting for command of the air in the Battle of Britain.

Sergeant (Sgt) Joan Mortimer was at RAF Biggin Hill, a key Fighter Command station, situated on a plateau of the North Downs. Today a chapel commemorates the 450 fighter pilots who died there. Sgt Mortimer's office was in the station armoury. Nearby was stored a vast amount of live ammunition, making it a dangerous place to be in when enemy heavy bombers attacked in late August 1940. Ignoring the danger, she remained at her telephone in her office, passing instructions to the various defence posts and shouting encouragement to the airmen in the armoury. Fortunately her building suffered no direct hits. Afterwards, picking up a bundle of red flags, she proceeded to mark out the craters of unexploded bombs – a fearful hazard to any landing aircraft, and dangerous work for her. One bomb did explode nearby as she worked, damaging her hearing, so that she was later discharged with a disability pension. But her brave actions ensured that no one else would be harmed.

Two other airwomen received the Military Medal at the same time as Joan Mortimer and they, too, were at Biggin Hill, but in the communications centre. It was the beginning of September, and they were working in different buildings. Cpl Elspeth Henderson, aged twenty-two, was in charge of a special telephone line in one building, and Sgt Helen Turner, a former First World War WRAF known as Jimmy to her friends, had the switchboard next door, outside the operations room. Had the women been able to look outside, they would have seen many dogfights between planes in the sky above them, but on this day some bombers managed to raid the station, dropping their loads to explode near the communications centre, and cutting all the lines except those to 11 Group headquarters. In this disruption, the women's work was more essential than ever and they stuck grimly to it, carrying on as calmly as they could. Sgt Turner was in a small room of a long hut above ground, with only a slight roof over her head. When it became too dangerous they were both advised to leave, but they refused. They were unlucky, when eventually a 500-lb bomb fell through Sgt Turner's roof and, bouncing off a steel safe, exploded in the next building, where Cpl Henderson was working, throwing them both to the ground and damaging their telephone instruments. Not even that deterred them. With some equipment still operative, they resumed their work. Conditions, however, were against them. The bomb had started a fire and soon they were given no option but to leave the blazing buildings, which burned to the ground. After the raid, they were left to contemplate a smouldering ruin, but they had kept open essential communications, at great risk to themselves, until the very last moment.

Awarded later, but from earlier August events, was the Military Medal of Cpl Josephine Robins. Like Cpl Pearson she was also at RAF Detling. During one of the intense air raids the operations room suffered a direct hit, killing the station commander and many plotters. The aircraft hangars were also set on fire. Nevertheless, within hours, owing to the incredible efforts of everyone, it was back in operation. In another raid, a bomb fell through the earth, metal and concrete casing of a shelter, where a number of airmen and airwomen were taking cover, killing several outright and injuring others, two seriously. Cpl Robins was inside and, though shaken and bruised, she made her way through the dust and fumes to where the wounded lay. With no thought of herself or the danger of further explosions, she gave them first aid and, as they were trapped, tried to calm those around by sheer force of her personality. When rescue parties finally reached them, she encouraged an orderly removal of those injured and stayed with the wounded until they were all taken to hospital. Her efficiency and unruffled good sense probably saved lives and certainly quelled any incipient panic.

Also in August, at another RAF station, Sgt Joan Youle was on duty in the station telephone exchange when they were bombed by five enemy aircraft. The exchange was in a long hut, at the opposite end of which a bomb landed, destroying part of it. Other bombs fell close around. Sgt Youle steadied her staff and persuaded them, by pressing their earpieces against their ears, to ignore the heavy rain of splinters scattering about and the terrible roaring of exploding bombs. It was solely due to her bravery and example that she was able to rally the operators to continue with their essential work, since none knew whether the next bomb might completely wipe them out.

Radar was one of the chief early warning systems which gave the RAF their superiority. It allowed fighter control to place fighters in the right place at the right time, but it did have its limitations, and mainly scanned the sea approaches. Consequently most radar stations were located near the coast. Its pioneer, Robert Watson-Watt, was very proud of the personnel who made it so effective and said, 'Anti-hamfistedness is women's greatest attribute in war work, whether it is in radio-location or potato-peeling.'

RAF Poling operated the chain home system. German aerial photographs prove that they knew the station's location and something of its importance. It was thus an obvious target. Acting Cpl Avis Hearn, a vivacious 24-year-old, was a newly trained radar operator posted there. In mid-August 1940,

A/Corporal Avis Hearn MM. (*Mrs A. Parsons*)

she was alone on the afternoon shift in a brick-built block, her officer and sergeant in a wooden hut some distance away. She was the link between Truleigh Hill and the Fighter Command headquarters at Stanmore Park.

From the plotting on the map in front of her, Cpl Hearn knew that a raid was developing. It was, in fact, intended for RAF Thorney Island, Ford and Poling itself, to which thirty-one Stuka aircraft had been detailed. Her sergeant had just managed to get through to warn her of the raid and was saying, 'Duck', when she heard the scream of the diving Stukas and the whistle of the falling bombs. All the doors and windows were blown in, heavy walls cracked and the noise was deafening. Amid this crescendo, the corporal never moved from her instruments. Steadily she plotted the course of the enemy bombers, knowing how much the RAF fighters and anti-aircraft gunners were depending on her calculations. She passed these on with coolness and accuracy, feeling herself unable to leave her place of duty because of the importance of her work. Enquiries came through her headphones on the raid at Poling and, in a most dramatic message, she said, 'The course of the enemy bombers is only too apparent to me, because the bombs are almost dropping on my head.' At about 2 a.m. the raid ceased, but it was found that eighty-seven bombs had fallen on Poling, several huge ones around the block where she operated.

Because of the nature of their peacetime work, there was little chance later for women to win these high awards, but one more Military Medal has been given. It went to a member of the WRAC, L/Cpl Sarah Warke, who in 1973 was posted to the troubled area of Northern Ireland. Together with an Army man, they dressed in civilian clothes and posed as laundry workers in Belfast. In a white van they collected laundry, to check for bloodstains or explosives, before it was cleaned and returned. The purpose of the undercover operation was to locate stores of ammunition or hidden gunmen, and it was therefore a very dangerous mission calling for considerable bravery. Some months later, L/Cpl Warke was outside her van talking to a woman when it was ambushed by gunmen in another van, who shot both her and her companion. Fortunately she survived.

Among the earlier awards in the First World War, the first servicewomen to receive the Medal of the Order of the British Empire in its Military Division came from the WRNS in May 1919 and there were twenty-two of them. They were, however, 'for service in connection with the war', and probably not for bravery. Among the number, from the lower ranks, were stewards, some shorthand typists, clerks, drivers, an electrician, a mechanic, a draughtswoman and a telephone operator.

They were followed in June by Member Marjorie Brisley of the WRAF. In December of the previous year, single-handed she had extricated an airman from his crashed plane and assisted a second to move away from the wreckage before it burst into flames.

The MBE denoted a Member of the last of the five classes of the Most Excellent Order of the British Empire, founded in 1917. The holder became a member of a British Order of Knighthood.

During the Second World War, 3rd Officer (3/Off) Pamela Grace received the MBE in 1942 for bravery in an air raid, as did 2nd Officer (2/Off) Alexandra Whittacker for courage and presence of mind in helping to remove four American Army vehicles from burning garages during an air raid in 1944. Both women came from the WRNS. Additionally, several junior officers of the ATS Anti-Aircraft Command received this honour.

The Air Transport Auxiliary (ATA) must not be forgotten. It was neither part of the Armed Services nor exactly of civil status. Formed in 1939 by men who were experienced pre-war pilots but ineligible for the RAF, the ATA ferried newly built aircraft from factories to airfields, and undertook minor transport tasks. In the following year, because of the shortage of men, women were introduced and by the end of the war there were nearly 1,000 women ground crew and over 100 pilots. The ATAs valuable contribution to the war effort, with its strain and danger, should not be dismissed. One of those who died carrying out its work was aviator Amy Johnson. Pauline Gower started the UK women's organisation, headed it and flew for it. For her enormous efforts she received the MBE.

There are many more gallantry British Empire Medals (BEMs) but only a few can be mentioned. One of the earliest in 1940 went to Leading Wren Nina Marsh. She was an eighteen-year-old steward at a naval shore establishment. During an air raid the shelter trench used by those in the sickbay suffered a direct hit. Although wounded in her back and elbow, Wren Marsh made light of her injuries and started helping others in the shelter, until the casualties had been evacuated to hospital. Only then did she allow herself to be sent for medical care.

In May 1943, on a fine cloudless night, the important supply harbour of Cardiff in South Wales was attacked, together with the surrounding area. Houses in the town were flattened, damage was widespread and some industrial premises were hit, with a number of civilian casualties.

There were about eight balloon sites around the city; one was at Colchester Avenue, four miles from Llandaff. There the balloons, which had been flying at 500 feet, were raised finally to their full operational height, but despite this the bombs still rained down, one scoring a direct hit on the site. It killed three WAAF operators and badly injured four others, one very seriously. Although Cpl Lilian Ellis was one of the injured, she took charge of the situation and maintained the balloon in its operational position until help arrived. She also organised relief for the casualties, and by doing so undoubtedly saved the life of at least one airwoman, who might have died without immediate treatment, with an arm and shoulder blown off and a dreadful wound to one side of her face. Throughout the raid, Cpl Ellis displayed leadership, calmness and courage, only afterwards allowing her injuries to be treated.

A further two WAAFs received a gallantry BEM during the war. Leading Aircraftwoman (LACW) Kathleen McKinlay was duty ambulance driver to a balloon squadron in Dover, when in 1944 the Allied troops were taking the French Channel ports and Dover was being shelled continually by the Germans. In September she and her medical officer

> had been out all morning and went back to headquarters to get something to eat. Just as we parked the ambulance, there was a thud. We shot behind the blast wall and there was an almighty bang. Glass, dust and rubble flew everywhere. The medical officer put his arm around me and said, 'Hold tight'. We both ended up on the floor, and when things cleared I got up

LACW Kathleen McKinlay BEM and her ambulance. (*Mrs K. Harding*)

and said, 'Are you all right?' I got no reply. He was dead! After covering him up, I didn't have a great deal of time to think, as there was a yell for an ambulance, which fortunately was in one piece. The medical orderlies were busy, so one of the RAF sergeants dealt with my wounds (in the thigh and hand) and as I could still drive we started getting the injured to hospital (one and a half miles away). I don't really remember much about the journeys, as I think I was just acting like a robot, but the sergeant told me later that I scared the hell out of him. I remember creating a fuss at the hospital, because all the stretchers had been taken into casualty and I couldn't get them back. I was worried that if they got lost I would have to pay for them (as they were my responsibility). The next thing I remember was waking up next morning in hospital myself and demanding to know what they had done with my uniform.

Another to win this special BEM was Alice Holden, a 22-year-old corporal, who was on radio-telephone duty in October 1943 when a Wellington bomber crashed and caught fire. Hearing cries for help, she ran towards the wreckage, through the flying debris from exploding petrol tanks and ammunition. Despite the searing heat she managed to wrench open the escape door to the burning turret of the rear gunner, freed him from his harness and dragged him out. The others were beyond help.

The final two years of the war brought a number of gallantry BEMs. Wren Elizabeth Booth was a mechanised transport (MT) driver at Machrihanish

Corporal Alice Holden BEM.
(*Mrs A. Horton*)

Wren Elizabeth Booth BEM, after her investiture. (*Mrs B. Hutchinson*)

on Kintyre. When a blazing plane crashed nearby on one of her journeys, she and her officer passenger drove quickly to it and, running to the wreckage, dragged the observer from the aircraft, though explosives were scattering burning debris and petrol all round. With her bare hands, Wren Booth beat out the flames enveloping the man and tore off his smouldering clothing. Then, unable to do anything for the other crew of the plane, she hurriedly carried the observer into her vehicle and drove him nine miles along a dangerous and tortuous route to a doctor. Despite her efforts, the man was too seriously burned and later died.

After the Allied invasion, feeling that Europe might slip from his grasp, Hitler unleashed his secret revenge weapons, first the V1 – a jet-powered robot aircraft, dubbed by Britain a buzz-bomb – and then the V2 rocket bomb, a far more sinister device. Fortunately the production of the V3 was prevented when its gun sites were overrun by the Allies.

At the time of the V1 flying bomb, L/Cpl Harradine of the ATS was one day on duty on the tracker tower of an anti-aircraft battery, following their course to enable the guns to pinpoint and then shoot them down. One V1, hit by the guns, exploded in the air close overhead, followed almost immediately by another, which fell only 100 feet away from the tower where she was standing. Although shaken by the blast and knocked hard against the tower rail, she still had the presence of mind and courage to drag herself back and continue directing the tracker onto yet another flying bomb with scarcely an interval in between. Her coolness in such essential work was outstanding.

Leading Aircraftwoman Ivy Cross BEM.
(*Mrs W. Newton*)

In March 1945, at RAF Langham, Norfolk, a heavily loaded Wellington bomber crashed in flames near the airfield just after take-off. LACW Ivy Cross, an MT driver employed at flying control, drove her van across several fields to arrive first at the stricken aircraft. She helped to drag clear several of the crew thrown out of the plane, though ammunition and explosives were going off very close to her. She gave first aid to these airmen but was unable to rescue the remainder because of the intense heat. Shortly afterwards she was again called out to another crashed Wellington, and again was the first to arrive. Most of the crew had already escaped but she helped to smash the rear turret so that the rear gunner could be rescued and treated. During the year she attended fourteen crashes and on twelve occasions aided in rescuing aircrew, with complete disregard for her own safety.

By 1945, the Allied armies were in Europe, with the women's Services not far behind. One contingent of the ATS was in Belgium at Bruges, a fine city sometimes called the Venice of the North because of its many canals. In May that year, a child fell into one of the canals, at a place where it was hemmed in by unscalable vertical walls, with water like a boiling cauldron below. He was being carried by the strong current beyond the reach of help, since this spot was fraught with danger for even the strongest swimmer. Pte O'Brien, who was passing at the time, shook off her shoes and coat and plunged into the canal without hesitation. By swimming hard she overtook the child, caught him and supported him in the swirling water. The current took them both downstream until they reached a point where the wall disappeared and she was able to make for the bank, where people were waiting to pluck them both out. There is no doubt that but for her brave action and disregard for her own safety, the child would have drowned.

These are only a brief selection of gallantry awards to servicewomen in war, but they serve to show that from highest to lowest, women could exhibit outstanding courage in the face of great personal danger, particularly in saving life, and that this bravery was not limited to a very rare few.

CHAPTER SIX

Service Nurses

The first women's military Services to be formed involved nursing, a vital function, particularly in wartime. The pioneer Army nurse was Florence Nightingale in 1854 in the Crimea. The Army Nursing Service was founded in 1881, but the official Queen Alexandra's Imperial Military Nursing Service (QAIMNS) really began in 1902, and served under that name in both world wars. There was also a territorial Service, known as the Territorial Force Nursing Service (TFNS) or the Territorial Army Nursing Service (TANS) in the First World War and the latter in the Second World War. Afterwards they became the Queen Alexandra's Royal Army Nursing Corps (QARANC).

The Navy had ten nursing sisters in 1884, but in 1902 its nurses became part of the Queen Alexandra's Royal Naval Nursing Service (QARNNS), a name they have kept through the years.

The new Royal Air Force in 1918 produced the Princess Mary's Royal Air Force Nursing Service (PMRAFNS) and it also has continued to retain this name.

Thus each of the Armed Services had its own body of nurses, whose dedication and care has always met with approval. The main difference today, in all three nursing Services, is that men can now be enrolled in their numbers.

Throughout the century the Army, being the largest of the Services, has needed the greatest body of nurses. By the end of the First World War there were nearly 10,500 nurses and to this total must be added the VADs supplied by the Order of St John and the BRCS. There were many more than that in the Second World War. The Navy and RAF being smaller had correspondingly fewer nurses.

Nursing calls for courage above the ordinary in everyday tasks but even more in the dangers of war and in dealing with hideously wounded servicemen. Thus many gallantry medals have been given to nurses of all the Services, but most to Army nurses, particularly in France during the First World War, as mentioned previously. In Italy, towards the end of the Second World War, one of its nursing sisters won the George Medal.

On a cold early morning of March 1944, Lieutenant (Lt) Sheila Greaves was attending to patients in No. 15 casualty clearing station – dug in near the Anzio beachhead – when suddenly its flimsy tents were attacked by enemy aircraft. Although her unit was not hit, she could tell that the reception camp, not far away, was in trouble. She could have stayed in the

Lieutenant Sheila Greaves GM.
(*QARANC Museum*)

comparative safety of her own post-operative ward but, being more concerned for the well-being of those attacked, she instead ran the 200-odd yards in the open towards the reception camp, shells and bombs falling around her as she went. On reaching it, she immediately began to dress the wounds of those injured and apply first aid, undoubtedly saving some lives by the speed of her treatment. Unfortunately, as soon as one attack finished another began, and Lt Greaves found the tents again mercilessly machine-gunned. Through all the carnage that followed, the nursing sister demonstrated great fortitude in carrying out her duties and directed the removal of the casualties to her own part of the hospital with the same calm and care that she had formerly shown.

Some honours went to the Navy and RAF nurses, and extended to those working on home bases as well as overseas. In August 1942, at the Royal Naval Hospital of Cullercoates, near Newcastle, Acting Superintendent Sister Muriel Cawston of the QARNNS became an Officer of the Order of the British Empire (OBE) for her coolness and devotion to duty during a severe air raid on her hospital. Her badge of silver gilt was worn on her left shoulder in a bow of rose-pink ribbon with its edges and centre stripe of pearl-grey. Also at the presentation were three VADs – Nursing Members Fay Caplan,

Officer of the Order for the British
Empire OBE (obverse). (*V. Scott*)

Sister Muriel Cawston OBE.
(*Mrs H. Cawston*)

Susan Tait and Joan Wylie – who all received the BEM for their courageous
actions in the same air raid. Their actions can be conjectured as those of all
good nurses in any emergency. Sister Letitia Jones of the PMRAFNS also
gained an MBE for courage and devotion to duty in June 1942.

Security in this war was tight and very often did not allow much
information to be made public, as in these last cases, but happily there is
more on the next ones.

On a night in April 1943, Sister Stone of the PMRAFNS was in her
quarters when a Halifax aircraft crashed into three huts where the WAAF
were sleeping. Although Sister Stone had completed twelve hours of
continuous duty already, she was soon on the scene of the accident where
she immediately took control, quelling what could have been a serious panic
among the victims and rescuers alike. Small fires had ignited inside the
crushed huts from the lighted stoves and these threatened to spread. Despite
this, the falling debris and the fact that the crashed aircraft was lying beside
one of the huts with its attendant danger of an explosion, Sister Stone
organised those who had emerged unharmed and helped to extricate many
of the injured, administering aid to those hurt and in distress.

After the arrival of the medical officer, Sister Stone went to the operating
theatre, where she spent the rest of the night helping the doctor deal with
the most serious cases. At 8 a.m. the next day she was on duty as usual. For
her exemplary conduct and efficiency during that terrible night, she also
was made an Officer of the Order of the British Empire.

In July 1943, Sister Innes of the QAIMNS was in a hospital ship taking wounded soldiers from landing crafts attempting landfall on the beaches of Sicily as a preliminary to their September invasion of Italy. The huge flotilla of Allied troop-carrying ships assembled for this undertaking was fiercely attacked by enemy aircraft. They made no distinction between the ships, in spite of the fact that the *Talamba*, Sister Innes' ship, displayed its huge white crosses prominently. A bomb landed, sinking the vessel.

At the time the bomb struck, Sister Innes was on a lower deck, used as a hospital ward, tending her patients. Warned that the ship was sinking, she tried to help as many of them as she could to the lifeboats. Badly holed, the ship went down quickly, with much loss of life, and Sister Innes found herself adrift in a lifeboat with some patients, two doctors and the hospital padre. They drifted at sea for days, but finally were picked up by another hospital ship, the *Alba*, before being landed in Tripoli. For her devotion and courage during the long voyage she received an OBE.

Matron Spedding of the QAIMNS also received an OBE much later, for her bravery and tireless care of the sick during her internment by the Japanese with many hundreds of other women, at the Bankinang Prison Camp in Sumatra.

Overseas, nurses worked not only in hospital ships at sea but on land in purpose-built hospitals, in casualty clearing stations – mobile units set up in areas of heavy casualties, often in tents – and in ambulance trains – well-planned small hospitals which shuttled between casualty clearing stations and base hospitals. The trains were usually staffed with three nurses and forty orderlies, all under the direction of three medical officers.

The first MBE awarded to a woman in the Second World War was to Sister Kathleen Davies of the QAIMNS for gallantry. She was in charge of the nurses on an ambulance train in the days just before the British Forces left France in the great evacuation of Dunkirk in 1940. The train was to make a three-day journey from Dieppe to Armentières to take on British and Allied wounded servicemen and a few injured civilians. Among the servicemen was a young RAF officer who had been terribly burned and blinded in the fire of his crashed aircraft. Sick and half-delirious as he lay in his bunk, he begged the sister not to lose his wings, of which he was so proud, as they cut his uniform from his scorched body. 'We'll keep them safe,' she assured him and carefully pinned the precious symbol onto his pyjama jacket.

Blocked by slow-moving trains and damaged rails, as sappers struggled to repair the track ahead of the train, it made an easy target for enemy planes to machine-gun and bomb, despite the cross clearly painted on its roof. Once, when the train came under fire from five German aircraft, the German prisoner/patients and orderlies tried to jump from the train to take cover in the fields. The young pilot became delirious on hearing the planes and in his fear tried to roll off his bunk to take shelter on the floor. Sister Davies stooped over him and then lying beside him, protected him with her own body. 'It's all right! It's all right!' she comforted him. 'Keep still. It won't last long.' When the raid had finished and they were unharmed, he became quieter, and the sister succeeded in keeping the spark of life, already flickering, alight, but unfortunately he died on the ship taking him home. Another of her patients, an older RAF officer who survived, made a point of delivering the young pilot's wings to the Air Ministry, for passing on to his parents, and wrote of Sister Davies, 'It was an act of extreme bravery the way she knelt by his bunk and comforted him with words and tender care, and it will always be one of my treasured memories of what military nurses really mean to the wounded.'

At the end of August 1944 came the first proof of the hardly believed rumour of Hitler's systematic extermination of individuals who opposed his regime, or who were considered by the Nazis to be of the wrong race or nationality. As the Allied armies moved across Europe, they started coming across concentration camps with their gas chambers and crematoria. They saw the pathetic walking skeletons and began to hear terrible stories of what had happened there. The first Russian nursing and medical staffs who entered the Polish concentration camps were horrified at what they saw but, as the Allies advanced into Germany, they discovered even worse places, like Auschwitz, Belsen and Buchenwald.

Doctors and nurses alike, often wearing masks against the stench of rotting corpses and the fearful diseases of the pitiful survivors, did what they could to save the inmates. It was often to no avail; those remaining died in their hundreds, rescued too late. Army and Air Force nurses made heroic efforts with these patients and their makeshift accommodation, while Europe was being liberated.

In recognition of their brave conduct in carrying out their hazardous work so courageously, three nurses of the QAIMNS were awarded gallantry MBEs – Sisters McNickolas, Hourigan (both from the reserve) and Roberts. Other gallantry MBEs for north-west Europe went to Sisters Stainton, Stringfellow, Thompson and Thorpe (all from the reserve). These awards were announced at the end of 1944.

The war in the Far East and the release of Japanese prison camp victims took longer, since so many had to be found before they could be rescued. The Indian Command covered a vast area and Sister Huskin received a gallantry MBE in 1945, while Temporary Matron Walden in the Far East was not given her gallantry OBE until 1947.

One other gallantry MBE stands out among those awarded to nurses of the three Services. It was for the incredible experiences of Sister Margot Turner of the QAIMNS, before she returned to Britain in 1946. In December 1941, at the age of twenty-nine, she was at a hospital at Kuala Lumpur, Malaysia, at the time when the Japanese Air Force attacked and almost destroyed the Hawaiian base of the American fleet in Pearl Harbor. As a result, the USA and her European, British and Commonwealth Allies declared war on Japan. Shortly afterwards, Sister Turner's hospital was bombed by the Japanese and it was decided to transfer the medical services to Singapore. On the ominous date of Friday 13 February, the nurses and VADs were ordered to leave. During their embarkation on SS *Kuala*, they were dive-bombed and machine-gunned, causing many fatalities and casualties among the women and children, and a few military personnel, crammed on board. The nurses were asked to change from their tropical white dresses into something darker, in order to make them less conspicuous in the night.

The voyage was a nightmare. Japanese planes soon discovered them and their accompanying ship and eventually sank both vessels, even machine-gunning the survivors as they swam from the sinking ships. A few managed to reach the beach of the nearby island of Pompong, among whom was Sister Turner. After crossing the island and nursing those who survived, they were picked up by another ship, the *Tanjong Penang*, already full of survivors from other wrecks, and Nurse Turner did the best she could to help those who needed it. Shortly afterwards, while she was sleeping on deck in the great heat, that ship too was bombed and sunk, with only time to release some of the liferafts. With another nurse, Sister Turner fastened two of the rafts together and, next day, swam out to bring back more people, collecting sixteen men, women and children. Room was scarce, so some swam along hanging onto ropes, and the women took the children on their knees. The nurse with her, obviously in pain and sorely wounded, refused a place on the raft and, at the end of the day, died. During the long days they were adrift on the ocean, the survivors gradually died – first the babies and the children, then the adults, until only two were left, lashed by the tropical storms and seared by the heat. One tried to save a piece of driftwood they were using as an oar, and then there was only Sister Turner left.

At the end of the fourth day, burned black by the sun and dying of thirst, she was picked up by a Japanese ship, where an American-trained doctor helped her recover enough to be landed at Muntok, an island in Sumatra, where she was carried on a stretcher to a hospital run by Dutch nurses. After recovering she was sent to a women's prison camp, with its brutal treatment and starvation rations. Here she found 30 Australian Army sisters, 8 British civilian nurses, 2 Dutch ones and 2 more members of her own Service. She and three other nurses were sent to help in a Malay hospital, but after a while all four of them were thrown into a tiny, fetid, vermin-infested cell for three months, with no explanation, and then released just as suddenly into a different prison camp, where one of the four shortly died.

The management of the camps changed from civil to military Japanese control quite frequently, usually resulting in worse treatment and rations, and prisoners were often moved on from one camp to another, each more terrible than the last. Increasingly more women in the camps fell ill and died, and Sister Turner did her best to nurse them, with no facilities or medicines to save them or ease their suffering.

An unexpected concert in May 1945, given by their captors, made some of the prisoners suspect that the war was drawing to a close. In August 1945, they were told that the war was over (shortly after the atom bombs had fallen on Japan) and the Japanese personnel left the camp. Men from a nearby camp told them to stay where they were for their own safety, as they were so far from civilisation. At this time Sister Turner was laid up with a high temperature. It took the British Army three weeks to locate and reach the women in the thick jungle, but US planes dropped supplies in between times.

Finally, in mid-September, the airlift began to empty the camps. Sister Turner was eventually shipped back to Britain and reported for duty again two months later. Incredibly she had survived all the privations and traumatic experiences that would have killed a less determined woman. Her proudest moment, apart from the award of her MBE, was in 1946 when she led the contingent of the QAIMNS in the Victory Parade in London.

In this context Superintending Sister Olga Franklin should also be mentioned. She was a member of the QARNNS, serving in the Royal Naval Hospital in Hong Kong. Her MBE was announced after the Japanese invaded in December 1941. She was moved to Stanley Internment Camp in Hong Kong, along with thousands of other prisoners. Here she continued her nursing in a makeshift camp hospital, though short of all medical equipment and supplies, which the Japanese denied them. Despite her efforts, disease, cruelty and malnutrition carried off many inmates, forced to do hard physical labour under the hot sun in indescribable conditions. After the camp was liberated, she was given the much coveted Royal Red Cross for her work.

When the frenzy of war had passed, the RAF continued its Aero-Medical Evacuation services to all Service personnel abroad. In 1950, during one of the many three-hour flights between Germany and Britain, the Anson aircraft carrying an Air Force nurse, Sgt Ethel Ferris, crashed into the English Channel off Felixstowe. Using great presence of mind, and with the aid of both navigator and pilot, she calmly assisted her two tuberculosis patients, an army Sergeant and a woman, from their stretchers into a dinghy. There she attended to the Sergeant's head injury and comforted both until they were all picked up, although the Sergeant had great difficulty

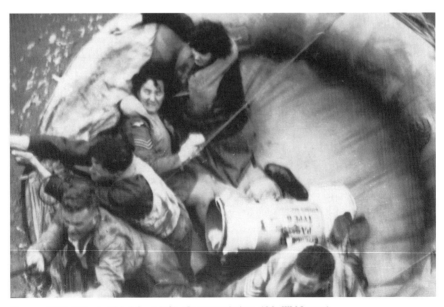

Sergeant Ethel Ferris (third from left), Commendation. (*Mr W. Newton*)

in climbing the rope ladder of the rescue vessel owing to a further muscular disease. When they arrived in Britain, the patients were quickly removed to hospital, and Sgt Ferris was reprimanded for showing her knees in the rescue picture. Nevertheless she was given a Commendation for Bravery.

Another award given to nurses, both Service and civil, is the Royal Red Cross. It is to recognise cases of special devotion by nurses towards the sick and wounded, or to those especially exerting themselves in providing care. Created in 1883, it was originally meant for women, but in 1976 male nurses were included. In 1915, the award was divided into two classes, the first becoming known as the Royal Red Cross (RRC), the second as an Associate member of the Royal Red Cross (ARRC) and being of a slightly lower standard. In 1920, an extra clause was added to the RRC award, to cover 'a very exceptional act of bravery and devotion (of a nurse) at her post of duty', and this, of course, meant gallantry, though it is rarely indicated when the award is published.

The medal itself in its earliest days was made of gold, but soon it became silver gilt. It is in the shape of a cross, the middle of each arm being enamelled, edged with gold and carrying the single words, 'Faith, Hope, Charity' and '1883', on each arm. The centre of the cross carries a side view of the monarch's head in relief, and on the opposite side the crowned royal cipher. The latest ones also have the year of the award. The ARRC is identical but is made of silver. Both have a dark blue ribbon with red edging, the women's version being shaped into a bow.

Royal Red Cross, King George VI type (obverse). (*R.J. Scarlett*)

Many nurses have received these awards through the years. Nurse Florence Harley, a young VAD of the QAIMNS in France during the First World War, gained her RRC in rather peculiar circumstances. She saw a pile of bodies in a grave having quicklime scattered over them, prior to being covered with earth. Suddenly one of the bodies moved and she realised that the man was alive. Shocked, she had him pulled out just in time. He had terrible injuries to his arm and needed urgent surgical treatment, but there were no doctors available. In the chaotic conditions of the first year of the war, with disorganised medical facilities frequently unable to cope with the unexpected, enormous death toll, these conditions sometimes existed. Nurse Harley, therefore, took it on herself to amputate the arm at the shoulder, and, against the odds, her patient recovered. This was certainly saving life to the ultimate degree.

Staff Nurse Minnie Byrne of the TFNS also received a gallantry RRC in 1920 for saving a patient from a fire in his bed at the Northern Hospital, Leeds. She suffered extreme burns herself in doing so.

The Second World War brought a number of special mentions, but strangely they only seem to appear for the ARRC. Nursing Sister Phyllis Shipton gained hers with a special commendation on the SS *Britannia*, sunk by an enemy raider in the Atlantic in 1941. Senior Nursing Sister Norah Brown achieved her mention on the SS *Alpacca* in 1942. Several received theirs in 1942 for their work in the siege of Malta, and Nursing Sister Georgina Moore had her mention when serving during the Salerno landings. All were from the QARNNS. Lt Audrey Jones of the QARANC was awarded the ARRC for brave conduct in the fire that sank the ship *Empire Windrush* off Algiers in March 1954. It was carrying 250 women and children and 1,000 troops, many wounded from the Korean War Service. Nurses were, of course, present in the many trouble spots where British troops were involved after the war, in such places as Korea, Malaya, East Africa and the Middle East.

The very rare award of the Florence Nightingale Medal in 1920 included nurses from both Army and Navy, but none in the Services seem to figure later. A list of names of those awarded the Florence Nightingale Medal is given in the Appendix.

CHAPTER SEVEN

The Women of SOE in France

During the black days of 1940, when the enemy armies had overrun a large part of Europe, France had signed a humiliating armistice with Germany. Among its terms, the French not only had to pay a huge indemnity to the Germans for every day their country was occupied but they also had to send a large part of their industrial and farming produce to Germany, together with forced labour drafts of their young men and women. Worse followed. Certain groups of their population, hated by the Nazis – Jews, Communists, gypsies, homosexuals, Freemasons and others – were imprisoned or deported and when 'incidents' occurred, as they inevitably did, hostages were taken and shot in increasing numbers. Little wonder that French opposition started to grow and underground resistance to the German occupation began, although weak and disorganised at first.

Across the Channel, Britain remained the only free country still at war with Germany. It was at this juncture, when all seemed doomed, that Winston Churchill and his War Cabinet decided to create a small secret organisation dedicated to encouraging resistance against the Germans, wherever it might exist in occupied Europe, or even in Germany itself. No less a person than the former prime minister Neville Chamberlain – whom many blamed for encouraging Hitler by his policy of appeasement – gave this body its terms of reference and even its name: the Special Operations Executive (SOE). It was, in Winston Churchill's phrase, 'to set Europe ablaze', by working through its 'agents' and what sabotage and guerrilla supplies Britain could provide.

The SOE agents were not spies – that role was reserved for the Special Intelligence Service (SIS) – but rather would act as enabling services for the resistance. They were trained in Britain and then sent 'into the field' in groups of normally three, though later more were added. The first agent acted as an organiser to the varied and often conflicting resistance groups within large geographical areas of land known as circuits; the second was a courier, a wide-ranging role that included linking them all together; and the third was a wireless operator, a key person of the enterprise, who kept in contact with Britain to arrange supplies. Unfortunately the operator was also the most vulnerable agent, since the Germans had an organisation listening for the messages and were able to track down the wirelesses and the operators using them. In mid-1943, SOE estimated a wireless operator's chances of survival to be about six weeks before capture.

Anyone working for SOE in the field – and there were many more working for them at home in Britain – had to be very brave to undertake such dangerous work against a cruel enemy, but most agents volunteered from altruistic motives – to free a country from the domination and oppression of a conqueror, and to save the lives and souls of its people. Thus it was in the spirit of self-sacrifice that most agents undertook their work. When deaths occurred, it was only for the aim of the greater good. On the way, of course, there was excitement, friendship and a gruelling test of the human spirit, but there was also fear, loneliness, hard work and sometimes torture and death.

SOE sent around 500 agents to France, and of those over 50 were women (most of British nationality; the 3 Americans and 1 Australian are mentioned later) but owing to the dangers, many never came back. Women came to the SOE by various routes, often by accident, and mainly through fluency in a language. They ranged across the spectrum from princess to shopgirl. Some were civilians – working women or housewives – and some came from the Armed Services, primarily the WAAF. At this point there is a strange, probably intentional imprecision about SOE women in the field, due to the secret nature of their work.

Firstly, as Service women were supposed to be non-combatant and could not use weapons, SOE aspirants had to be trained outside this umbrella, and the only uniformed body that had no pre-commitments was the civilian Women's Transport Service (WTS), the FANY. Besides giving cover to SOE women's warlike activities, the FANY also supplied signallers, coders, conducting officers, forgers and trainers to the SOE at home and abroad. They staffed SOE's wireless stations, rest homes and depots, keeping them and their work shrouded in a secrecy never broken.

Founded in 1907 as an all-woman medical unit on horseback, the FANY had rapidly mastered mechanised transport. In the First World War they had driven ambulances in Flanders for the British, French and Belgian armies. The only women's service to continue training after the armistice, in 1938 the FANY provided 1,500 trained driver-mechanics to form the nucleus of the new ATS motor companies. (The WTS (East Africa) was an overseas branch.) Other FANYs were attached to the Polish Army. Today the FANY – still civilian – is known simply as the WTS, and supports civilian and military authorities in emergency communications.

Secondly, at the start of the Second World War, apart from nurses, the women's element of the Armed Services did not go overseas. The FANY, however, could do so as, despite being in uniform, FANY personnel were deemed to be civilians and their recruits could thus break the rules.

Thirdly, in contradiction of these features, when SOE women did go into the field, though technically civilians, they were granted (honorary) officer ranks. This was in the hope that, if captured, they would be treated as prisoners of war and officers. Both proved to be wrong.

Fourthly, controversy still rankles in the area of bravery decorations. Many could not be given because the would-be recipient was dead. A number were citizens of another country, who worked for the SOE with no training or other links. No one knows how many died, unrecognised and silent, but displaying the ultimate in bravery. Allied women or foreign nationals helping the SOE, or linked organisations no matter how deserving, were not eligible for the Victoria or George Crosses and, until later and except in certain circumstances, the George Medal.

British women could not qualify for the Distinguished Service Order, the Military Cross or the Distinguished Conduct Medal. These were reserved for men. They could qualify for the Victoria Cross (never officially given to a woman), the George Cross and the George and Military Medals. They could be included in the various classes of the Order of the British Empire, the British Empire Medal and Mentions in Despatches. If dead, they were not allowed the George Medal (until 1977) or the much lower Member of the Order of the British Empire, the award given to the majority.

SOE was not the only secret organisation working against Germany. Among others, General (Gen) de Gaulle set up his own Bureau Central de Renseignements et d'Action (BCRA), which operated in France, and the Americans had their Office of Strategic Services (OSS), which functioned there and in the Pacific area. In all directions there were also escape lines for all kinds of people, and there were additionally other resistance and intelligence groups and individuals working against the enemy.

Only four women have ever won the George Cross outright; three of them came to the women of SOE, two posthumously.

One of the best known of these is Frenchwoman Lt Odette Sansom. Married to an Englishman, with whom she had three daughters, Odette was living in England. In 1942, aged thirty, she joined SOE almost accidentally by responding to a request for translators. When her husband was killed, the FANY claimed her and she undertook intensive training, which showed her to be friendly, patriotic, determined, but rash. She failed her parachute instruction, so that she had to be landed by boat in the south of France on Hallowe'en night in October 1942, although her circuit was to be in the north.

Fate intervened, and in her first 'safe' house (a hairdresser's) in Cannes, she met Peter Churchill, an extrovert, rather credulous organiser, and agreed to remain there as his courier. She liked his wireless operator, code-named Arnaud, but was horrified at the French resisters' lack of security – men talking loudly in public on the most secret matters, with the town being full of rich and dangerous people.

Then her life as a courier began, in taking messages, codes and even radios on trains and buses along the Riviera coast. Sometimes caught by the nightly curfew, she had to take shelter in unusual hiding places, including brothels, as most prostitutes were anti-Nazi. She had a number of narrow escapes. In February 1943, the Gestapo started arresting members of Churchill's group at Cannes, but the three agents found shelter at St Jorioz in the Haute Savoie. The next month Churchill flew back to Britain for briefing. A friendly Colonel (Col) Henri – supposedly a German officer opposed to Hitler and trusted by Peter Churchill – turned out to be a

Lieutenant Odette Sansom GC.
(*Mr G. Hallowes*)

German agent who, awaiting Churchill's return, arrested both him and Odette in the middle of a night in April 1943.

Over the following months they were moved and questioned separately in several prisons in Italy and France. Soon Odette realised that the Germans wanted to know the whereabouts of Arnaud, who had evidently escaped. To protect herself and Churchill, she claimed to be his wife and that he was closely related to Winston Churchill, the Prime Minister. She also tried to turn the attention from Churchill to herself by saying he only acted on her suggestions. Finally they arrived at Fresnes Prison, where she was taken and interrogated under torture at the notorious Gestapo headquarters in Avenue Foch, Paris, but she gave nothing away. At last, infuriated by her intransigence, her captors told her she would be shot. Instead, she found herself on a train with six other British women agents, being sent first to the women's prison at Karlsruhe, and then in July 1944 to the terrible women's concentration camp at Ravensbrück. Here, she was subjected at various times to starvation, solitary confinement, extremes of heat or cold and prolonged darkness, and she became so weak and ill that she was moved to a better cell.

At the beginning of May 1945, the camp commandant drove her to the nearest American unit and handed her over, before making his own escape, afraid to harm her because he still believed her story. There followed a long period of hospitalisation in Britain, the awarding of the George Cross and MBE, and in 1947 her marriage to Peter Churchill.

Ensign Violette Szabo joined the ATS while her husband was abroad with the Army. In 1942, when she became pregnant, she left the ATS but lost her husband in the same year that her daughter was born. Her English father and French mother gave her a burning love for both countries and, as a beautiful widow of twenty-two, she was accepted by SOE and sent for training with the FANY. She sailed through her course and was reputed to be one of SOE's finest shots.

In April 1944 she was dropped by parachute to act as courier to a Frenchman who had survived the

Ensign Violette Reine Elizabeth Szabo GC. (*Special Forces Club*)

break up of his Rouen-based circuit and was trying to rebuild it. Her task was to investigate any survivors, but it soon became clear that the circuit could not be restored. The two returned by Lysander to Britain, six weeks later. She was again parachuted into France on the day after D-Day in June 1944 to join a large Maquis group near Chateauroux as courier, with instructions for them to interfere with the German troop reinforcements being sent to Normandy. A young Maquis leader, code-named Anastasie, was to show her the routes for the first few days. On 10 June, driving along in an old car, they saw a German patrol round the next bend. The Germans saw them taking to a cornfield to evade them and started firing, wounding Violette in the arm. When the two managed to reach a woodland they could have escaped had Violette not fallen and twisted her ankle. Anastasie wanted to carry her, but she knew that way they would both be caught so she urged him to flee while, cradling her gun on her hip, she started firing on her pursuers to cover his flight. The Germans encircled her, but she continued firing until her ammunition ran out and she threw the gun away, physically fighting her captors, showing she would not be an easy prisoner.

Violette retained her defiance and her fiery spirit throughout her painful interrogations and imprisonment, divulging nothing. At Limoges prison, where she was first taken, the resistance planned to rescue her, but their attempt was foiled as on the very day she was unexpectedly transferred to Fresnes Prison and the expert Gestapo questioners at Avenue Foch. After several weeks of treating her brutally, the Germans, realising that by now any information she might have had was out of date, put her on a train to the Ravensbrück women's concentration camp. During an air raid on one of the several days the journey took, and despite being chained by the ankle,

Noor-un-Nisa Inayat-Khan GC. (*This England*)

she managed to pass a bottle of water to some British prisoners in a stifling cattle truck next door.

Hard physical labour on a starvation diet awaited her but, amid the cruelty, disease and filth of the camp, she found two other SOE women whom she knew. With them she was sent to a labour camp at Torgau, where food and conditions were slightly better, and they began planning an escape, defeated by their early return to Ravensbrück. Hoping for easier treatment, they again volunteered for another labour camp, but this time it involved building an airfield at Konigsberg and conditions were so bad that they nearly died. In January 1945 they were recalled and placed in the death cells. About 5 February, with the Allies advancing on all sides, they were taken across to the wall outside the cremation block. Their sentence was read out to them, then they were brought forward one by one and shot through the back of the neck, their bodies immediately being removed and cremated.

The last of the three wartime George Cross awards to a woman was to one who was probably the most unusual, and certainly the most exotic, of agents. She was Assistant Section Officer (ASO) Noor-un-Nisa Inayat-Khan, the first female wireless operator to be sent to France. Born in the Kremlin, Moscow, the eldest child of the Indian leader of the Sufi sect – a mystical branch of Islam – and his American wife, Noor came from a royal line. Brought up in the suburbs of Paris, she escaped to Britain after the German invasion of France and in 1940 joined the WAAF as a wireless operator. In February 1943, she was transferred to SOE and began her training. She was a shy, softly spoken, unworldly woman with a noticeably foreign accent and appearance. Opinions on her suitability as an agent were divided in SOE, but they were so desperately short of wireless operators that it outweighed other considerations.

Noor arrived in France with three others on a double Lysander landing in June 1943, to work in Paris, where she was to be known by the code name of Madelaine. Hardly had she settled in than the Germans began arresting the chief men in her circuit, and Noor narrowly avoided this fate several times. When she managed to find a safe place, she informed London of the disaster but, realising that she was the only operator at large in Paris, she refused to return to Britain, saying she did not want to leave her French resisters without communications and hoped herself to rebuild the circuit.

In a twilight world, she flitted from one house to another, often only a few hours ahead of the searching Gestapo, who did not then know she was a woman. With her bulky suitcase containing her incriminating wireless, she tried various ways to disguise it – once in a violin case. For her own safety, friends put her on a train out of Paris but, by some misunderstanding, she returned.

It was inevitable that she would soon be caught, and it came about not by her own fault but as a tip-off from an informer, for the reward offered. In October 1943, she was arrested in a shared flat, with her wireless set and, worse still, her messages and codes neatly filed in an exercise book near her bed; another misunderstanding had caused her to keep them. Noor fought violently with the man arresting her and, when captured, nearly managed to escape through the bathroom window after asking if she could take a bath. Kept in the Avenue Foch, the Germans used her radio and her innocent answers to trick a suspicious London into believing that she and her wireless were still free. Her captors never used torture, finding that kindness drew more out of her, of which she was unaware since directly questioned she would give no information. Her main interrogator considered her utterly unworldly and truly good. She nearly escaped again, through the grating above her cell and across the flat roof of the adjacent properties, but unfortunately an air raid alerted the guards to her disappearance and she was recaptured, still defiant.

As Noor would not give her word not to try to escape again, she was transferred in November 1943 to a women's prison at Pforzheim, where she was chained and kept in solitary confinement as a particularly dangerous and uncooperative prisoner, but her sweet nature persuaded the prison governor to relax her conditions. In September 1944, she was sent to Dachau concentration camp. Here on 12 September, her death sentence and that of three others – Madeleine Damerment, Elaine Plewman and Yolande Beekman – was read out. They were brought forward in pairs, holding hands, and were shot through the back of their heads before being cremated. Her last word was 'Liberté'.

The lesser award of the George Medal went to several civilian women who worked mainly for the escape lines or in other secret operations against the enemy. One, however, was given to a member of SOE. She was a Polish countess by birth and marriage called Krystina Gizycka, but she became known by her Anglicised name of Christine Granville.

Christine Granville GM (Krystyna Skarbeck). (*Special Forces Club*)

She was extremely beautiful, dangerously attractive, highly intelligent, and excelled at all sports including skiing, which enabled her to take escapees from Poland over the mountains in winter. She also had a gift for picking up languages, a sometimes ripe sense of humour, and lived an unconventional wealthy lifestyle. Moreover she thrived on action. From her base in London – to which she had escaped in 1939 after the Germans had overrun her beloved Poland – she darted all over Europe and the Middle East on her self-appointed mission to work against the hated Germans. It is ironic that most sides, at some time or other, suspected her of being a spy.

Eventually in July 1944, as a Flight Officer (Flt Off), Christine parachuted into France from Algiers in a gale as seemingly tempestuous as her life. Based on the plateau of Vercors, she became an SOE courier to a very successful organiser. She was soon constantly on the move, arranging and taking part in drops of arms for the active Maquis, accompanying them on their sabotage raids – impressing everyone by her reckless courage – and taking messages up and down the precipitous mountain slopes to the villages below.

In mid-July, the Germans began an all-out onslaught on their troublesome region of Vercors. Despite heroic efforts by the Maquis, they were forced back and had to disperse, leaving the plateau undefended. There the Germans took a barbaric revenge on those captured, whether resistance or civilians. Christine, her organiser and a few companions escaped to a second base at Seynes-les-Alpes.

Now Christine's mission changed. She was to contact Italian partisans on the border and win their active cooperation with the Allies. This mission successfully completed, not without danger, she was next sent off to win over the Russians serving with the Oriental Legion of the German 19th Army. Her gift for languages and ability to inspire affection made her welcome and she again succeeded in her object. Once on the journey, while hiding from a German patrol, she was scented by one of the Alsatian tracker dogs which, coming under her strange charm, lay down beside her, instantly changing its loyalties and never afterwards leaving her side. At another time she was sent to subvert soldiers in a mountain fort. On her arrival she found many were Poles, and their conversion was easier than her ascent or descent of the mountain.

Near the end of the occupation, Christine's organiser and a newly arrived agent were stopped by the enemy, questioned and sent to the death cell. While they were there the Allied landings on the Riviera took place and, with scarcely any opposition, they quickly advanced inland. In the nick of time, by a mixture of disguises, threats and bribery, she got them released. Shortly afterwards, hearing that the Americans had arrived, she and her organiser went to offer help, the Maquis protecting the American Army flanks as it advanced.

When this task was finished, SOE planned to use this remarkable woman in Italy but, the end of the war being in sight, Christine was sent instead to Cairo to await demobilisation, in 1945.

Although other women working in the field for SOE F (French) Service were equally as brave and useful, most received the MBE – far inferior to their merits – and they had to be alive when the award was announced. The MBE for Section Officer (SO) Diana Rowden was withdrawn when it was discovered after the war that her death by lethal injection at Natzweiler concentration camp in July 1944 had pre-dated her award. France, however, with no such inhibitions, awarded her a Croix de Guerre. SOE women given the George Cross and George Medal were also awarded an MBE.

Space forbids more than a very short summary of the activities of the other female SOE F Service holders of the MBE, who worked in the field. Fuller accounts of those from the WAAF can be found in my earlier book, *Mission Improbable*.

Captain (Capt) Lise de Baissac was born in the British Crown Colony of Mauritius, but brought up in Paris. She escaped to England after the German occupation and at the age of thirty-seven trained for SOE. In September 1942, she parachuted into France to build up a successful circuit in Poitiers, though she ranged more widely, acting as liaison to others. Recalled to London in August 1943, she again landed in France in April 1944 to work as a courier, first at Lyon and then with her brother in the area around Chartres. She was brave, intelligent and steady. After D-Day they moved to Orne and in July 1944, dressed in her FANY uniform, she met the Americans.

Flt Off Yvonne Baseden, brought up in Paris, moved from the WAAF to SOE, where she trained as a wireless operator code-named Odette. In March 1944, at twenty-two years of age, she parachuted into France to work in the Jura mountain area. In June 1944, she was captured by the Germans, who, not entirely certain that she was an agent, kept her in an underground cell, beaten, starved and tortured. Eventually she was sent to the concentration camp of Saarbruken and then Ravensbrück. Sick with tuberculosis, she was saved from being sent to Belsen, and in April 1945 was released.

ASO Sonya Butt, deceptively innocent looking, joined the WAAF in 1943 and, at nineteen, SOE. She arrived in France in May 1944 to act as courier and weapons training officer to the Maquis in a circuit around Le Mans. Once, she was imprisoned by the Germans, who, not realising who she was, let her go. After the area was liberated by the Americans, she agreed to several more dangerous missions into German-occupied territory, on one of which she was assaulted. She returned home in October 1944, her cool head having won the respect of all with whom she worked.

Flt Off Yvonne Cormeau's education had been in France. When her French husband was killed, leaving her with a young daughter, she joined the WAAF and later passed into SOE. At the age of thirty-three, in August 1943, she parachuted into France to join a circuit based at Castelnau, acting as wireless operator and sometimes courier. Her circuit developed into one of the most active in France. During her thirteen months there she never had a day's rest, sending about 400 messages without a single miscode. She was at the liberation of Toulouse before returning home.

Ensign Marguerite Knight, who was educated in Paris, joined the WAAF, and by accident gained her entry to SOE. Rushed through training, she was parachuted into France as a courier in the Yonne in May 1944. It was a disruptive and confused time in her group; her resistance specialised in sabotaging trains – helped by Marguerite – but, nearly captured by the Germans, they had to disperse, only slowly re-forming. When the Americans occupied the area, she often had to cross German lines to both groups. Her courier work by bicycle was gruelling, but finally she returned home to recover.

SO Phyllis Latour's parents were French, but her mother lived in South Africa. In England she joined the WAAF at twenty and then was trained by SOE as a wireless operator. She parachuted into France in May 1944 to work in the Orne region, where Lise de Baissac was courier and her brother organiser. She was continually on the move and narrowly escaped capture several times, but she sent over 135 messages before the Americans occupied her village, when she was able to return home safely.

Lt Eileen Nearne was already working in the FANY at an SOE listening station in Britain. Her elder sister opposed her being sent to France, considering her too young and vulnerable at twenty. Finally, though, she was able to go, and landed in France in March 1944 as the wireless operator of a circuit around Paris. Always on the move, she sent a record 105 messages in less than three months. Tracked down by the Gestapo, she was tortured and, when moved, tried to escape. In August of that year, she was sent to Ravensbrück and, while being moved again in April 1945, she escaped with two others, wandering through Germany for some days before being rescued by the advancing Americans.

Lt Jacqueline Nearne of the FANY was Eileen's elder sister. Educated in France, the family escaped to Britain and in January 1943 SOE sent her into France to be courier to a circuit stretching from Chateauroux to Tarbes and Pau. Based at Clermont-Ferrand, as a chemist's sales representative, her life was one of constant train travel. A gruelling fifteen months later, London became concerned about her health and recalled her in April 1944.

SO Patricia O'Sullivan, born in Dublin and educated at a French convent, joined the WAAF and thereafter SOE to train as a wireless operator. Partly trained, she was hurriedly parachuted into the Limoges area in March 1944 in answer to an urgent request. The squalid conditions of

Lieutenant Jacqueline Nearne MBE. (*Special Forces Club*)

her lodgings were outweighed by its safety. Heavily overworked, she transmitted over 300 messages and still managed to train two local operators, as well as act as courier, with several narrow escapes. Her health was not good, so she was glad to return home in August 1944.

ASO Lilian Rolfe, educated in France, joined the WAAF and later SOE. She landed in France in May 1944 to act as wireless operator to a circuit based on Orleans. After a month of frantic activity, her organiser was captured by the Gestapo and she had to carry on alone. In July, on a snap raid on Nangis, the Germans accidentally captured her but, despite intensive interrogation in Paris, she divulged nothing. She was sent to Ravensbrück with two SOE companions, where in February 1945 they were shot and their bodies cremated.

Ensign Yvonne Rudellat, educated in France and a grandmother in her forties, was an unexpected SOE agent. Code-named Jacqueline, she landed in France in July 1942 as a courier to a sub-circuit in Paris. During a car chase in June 1943, she was shot in the head. An operation saved her life and, after hospitalisation, when taken to Fresnes Prison and questioned by the Gestapo she was able to claim that she had lost her memory. With other SOE prisoners in August 1944 she was sent to Ravensbrück and afterwards Belsen, where she died unrecognised after its liberation. Her success led to other women agents being employed by SOE.

ASO Anne-Marie Walters had a French education and joined the WAAF and subsequently SOE. She was parachuted into France in January 1944 to act as courier in the area of Landes and Gascony. At twenty-one she was bubbling with life, charm and reckless courage. To help her in her work, she learned to drive in the hair-raising French style, and also used bikes, trains and buses as well as travelling on foot. She escorted escapees to the Pyrenees, helped the local Maquis when they were cornered and had many narrow escapes. She returned over the Pyrenees just ahead of the Germans.

Flt Off Pearl Witherington was a member of the WAAF and one of the most successful SOE women in France. She took over the circuit after her organiser was caught, although she came by parachute in September 1943 to be his courier in the Auvergne and to act as liaison officer to the local Maquis. In May 1944, she halved the circuit and concentrated on arming and training her Maquis group, which grew to 3,500 men, whom she used to constantly harass the German troop reinforcements intended for the north. They fought many pitched battles and caused one German Army unit to surrender at Issoudun. She returned home, her mission successfully accomplished.

Others just as courageous took part in the fight for freedom in Europe, but had no British award – some because they died in the field. Thirteen Frenchwomen, working for SOE in liaison with Gen de Gaulle's Free French Forces (a few being members of the French Women's Army) came through the war unharmed. Those working for SOE under British control in the French section were all equally as brave and their fates were various: Marie-Thérèse Le Chene (aged about fifty-five), Julienne Aisner and Francine

Sibyl Sturrock MBE. (*Lady S. Stewart*)

Agazarian returned safely during the war by plane; Odette Wilen escaped capture by crossing the Pyrenees on foot, as Blanche Charlet only just failed to do, but achieved almost the impossible by escaping from her French prison first; Mary Herbert remained in hiding until the end of the war, after a spell in prison where her quick wits talked her out of Gestapo suspicions; Yvonne Fontaine, Ginette Jullian and Madeleine Lavigne were still at their posts when the Allied Forces freed their areas, though Ginette risked her life a second time in another area, till that too was liberated, and Madeleine died shortly afterwards; Muriel Byck died in harness of meningitis, only five weeks after arriving.

Denise Bloch was shot at Ravensbrück concentration camp, her death shortly followed by that of Cécile Lefort, who, by a cruel irony of fate, died unrecognised after the camp was liberated. In the previous year of 1944, two groups of four women were executed at concentration camps. Diana Rowden, Andrée Borrel, Vera Leigh and Sonia Olschanesky (the latter, a French-born daughter of Russian parents, only loosely connected with SOE but part of the French Resistance) were given lethal injections at Natzweiler. Two months later, the group with Noor Inayat Khan were shot at Dachau. And there were others. They were all young, full of patriotism and brave, willing to sacrifice their lives in the liberation of France. Unsung heroines all.

In 1997, Squadron Leader (Sqn Ldr) Vera Atkins was made a Companion of the Order of the British Empire (CBE) as a recognition of a woman who had been so much involved in organising, preparing, accompanying and advising those who went to France for SOE. For a year after the war and SOE's hasty winding-up in 1946, she had made it her task, single-handed, to investigate the fates of 118 missing men and women agents, and it is to her that we owe the knowledge of how 117 of them died.

Not to be left out, too, are the agents of the SIS, most of whom remain in the shadows. They also worked behind enemy lines gathering information useful to the Allies. One such was Sibyl Sturrock, who received an MBE for the difficult and dangerous work of acting as courier to one of the teams helping the partisan Tito in Yugoslavia against the German occupiers. She returned safely.

In this listing of heroic women, it must not be forgotten that many people, both civilian and Service, on both sides of the Channel, contributed to the work of SOE, and many abroad paid with their own and their families' lives. Few gained official recognition, despite the dangers they ran, sometimes on a day-to-day basis. Bravery, it seems, is more widespread than may be realised.

CHAPTER EIGHT

Civilian Nurses

In civil life bravery can be found in any emergency situation, and this can quite regularly occur in hospitals and with the nursing profession. During the First World War, in munitions factories up and down the land, the skills of civilian nurses on their staffs were often necessary for the horrific injuries that arose from the frequent explosions and fires. At home and abroad, many civilian nurses were volunteers from the British Red Cross and St John Ambulance Brigade, and women like the FANY drove ambulances. A number gained the medal of the Order of the British Empire, and several were awarded the Albert Medal, both then and later.

Dorothy Thomas was a 29-year-old staff nurse in the operating theatre of the Middlesex hospital, which was a large and busy place. The main operating theatre was on the ground floor, with the anaesthetic room, filled with equipment, next door. In an early January morning in 1934, Sister Thomas was on duty as theatre sister. Suddenly there was a flash, and flames and sparks shot out from the open door of the anaesthetic room, across the theatre to the opposite wall. One of the large oxygen cylinders had caught fire. Sister Thomas remained calm in this dangerous situation and coolly organised everyone to evacuate the theatre. She was the last to leave but not before bravely removing the ether from the room and firmly closing the theatre doors behind her, to minimise any explosion. Outside, realising that a blast would not only wreck the theatre but also damage other wards, she decided to enter the anaesthetic room. Shutting the door she hurried over to the cylinder, which was now almost red hot and burning fiercely, and struggled with the tap to switch off the oxygen supply. If it had then exploded, she would have been killed instantly. Fortunately, just in time, the tap turned. Her selfless action and courage were rewarded by the Empire Gallantry Medal, in 1942 replaced by the George Cross.

In war, nursing courage shows, not only in the front line of battle but also in civilian towns and cities subjected to air raids. The George Medal was created in 1940 to reward such civilian heroism during the Second World War, as some of the following stories show.

After the evacuation of Dunkirk and the Battle of Britain, the German Luftwaffe turned its attention to the day and night bombing of London. In the stricken city, reports poured in of people hurt or killed, homes demolished, factories going up in flames and hospitals almost overwhelmed with sick and injured, if not themselves badly damaged.

Staff Nurse Patricia Marmion was in charge of the men's ward in the

Royal Chest Hospital. When it was bombed in September 1940, the windows of her ward were blown out, glass wounding her in several places. The patients had to be evacuated as quickly as possible through the debris, but first she had to deal with a crazed man, who would have thrown himself from the empty window shouting, 'This isn't going to happen to me again', had she not caught and pacified him in time. Then she had to free a man from a heavy window frame that had fallen across his broken legs. She somehow lifted him onto her back and carried him downstairs to the basement. Afterwards she helped stretcher parties rescue other patients, and secured any dangerous drugs. Only then did she allow herself to be hospitalised further away, where later, barefoot, she once again helped to evacuate patients when that hospital, too, was bombed.

At the same time, 52-year-old Acting Matron Catherine McGovern, hardly able to walk from glass embedded in her thigh and bleeding badly, assisted in the evacuation of patients. One of the relief party acted as her crutch, when, feeling faint, she nevertheless considered it her duty to make the rounds of the hospital to check for any stray patients, before accepting medical treatment.

At the Grove Park Hospital in November 1940, a bomb fell through from top to bottom, causing the floors to tilt downwards at a dangerous angle, the beds gradually sliding downwards and in danger of falling off with their occupants. Assistant Nurse Aileen Turner released several patients trapped on the first floor by crawling to them, after climbing through a first floor window, and encouraged them to follow her out. Staff Nurse Mary Fleming helped to rescue other bedridden patients by herself crossing the tilting floor to them. Staff Nurse Ruby Rosser had meantime hurried to a ground floor ward, where there was only one patient. Flinging herself on top of the woman, she protected her body and injured head from the debris and equipment falling on them from the ward above. There was also a danger of the roof collapsing on top of the two of them.

Marion Boulton was Matron of the Sir Robert Geffrey's Homes for the Sick and Elderly at Mottingham. In September, a bomb landed on part of the building setting it alight. All the patients save two had been evacuated to the shelter. Fighting her way through the flames, Matron Boulton dragged the infirm old women forcibly from the burning building. Afterwards she directed the removal of other patients from another wing.

Nor must female doctors be forgotten in London's baptism of fire. Dr Laura Bateman was working at Brook Hospital on a night in January 1941, when a bomb trapped two maids in the ruins. Dr Bateman ran to the scene and the first girl was extracted from the wreckage. The second was trapped under girders and masonry. Being small, Dr Bateman volunteered to hang down, head first under the ruins, her feet held by a porter, to give morphia to the suffering maid, risking the danger of being fatally trapped and crushed as she did so.

Dr Hannah Billig, as a member of the local Emergency Medical Service, in March 1941 was in the shelters tending casualties. When a bomb landed on the street nearby, she left the shelter to tend the dying and wounded there. Bombs dropped within 20 yards of her and she was badly injured. However, she insisted on treating others for up to four hours, before dealing with her own injuries.

Airfields, of course, were important targets. Thus, the little town of Montrose in Scotland was attacked in October 1940, since it was close to an RAF airfield. Bombs fell onto part of the Montrose Royal Asylum. Of the two nurses in the kitchen at the time, one was severely injured. The other, Nurse Violet Reid, although herself wounded, ran to the female patients in the block, who were confused and frightened in the dark, and quelled their rising hysteria. Then she carried her colleague to a bed and tended her until the arrival of the doctor. Returning to her shivering patients, she quietened them again and put them into warm clothing. Only when their needs were attended to, did she allow herself to be helped.

The city of Coventry was the target of two of the biggest provincial raids. In the November 1940 pre-flight briefing to the German aircrew, they were told: 'We shall not repay [the attack on Munich] by smashing up harmless dwelling houses, but we shall do it in such a way that those over there will be completely stunned. . . . We have therefore received orders to destroy the industries of Coventry tonight. This place is one of the chief armament centres of the enemy air force, and has also factories which are important for the production of motor vehicles and armoured cars. . . . Amongst other aircraft factories, the Rolls-Royce aero-engine works are worthy of note.'

It was a bright, moonlit night when the bombers first attacked. The bombs came raining down for hours on end, until the whole city was alight with explosions and fires. Among the buildings hit was the weaving factory of Pattison and Hobourne, where its works nurse, 25-year-old Marjorie Perkins, was on duty. Many people on the late shift were injured, Miss Perkins herself being injured twice, the second time blown across her surgery and knocked unconscious. Recovering and ignoring her wounds, she tended first to those hurt in the factory then, realising there were others injured in the streets outside and regardless of the still-falling bombs, she left for a public shelter where many had been taken, and continued her ministrations there. She did not stop until the following morning. Her own injuries prevented her from returning to work for some weeks.

Surveys later showed that the Luftwaffe did indeed attack industrial targets, but in a city crowded with dwelling houses and shelters, cheek by jowl with their workplaces, it was inevitable these also would be caught. There was another sharp attack on Coventry in April 1941. All the civilian and nursing staff of the Coventry and Warwickshire Hospital had been told to come to the hospital if there was another big raid, and they did so, but the hospital itself was hit. Its heroine was Matron Joyce Burton, a 38-year-old with nerves of steel. As her actions and those of her devoted nursing staff are typical of what happened elsewhere, it is interesting to examine them in more detail.

At the beginning of the raid, after visiting the wards, Matron Burton went to the enquiry office to collect information on casualties. On her way there a bomb landed, the lights failed and a patient was blown off the table of an emergency operating theatre. The sister of the X-ray department and her assistant were killed instantly, together with two stretcher-bearers. Another bomb fell directly in front of the enquiry office, blasting the matron and those with her through a doorway but, unfazed, she got up and helped with the stretcher-bearers. After getting water for one of the injured, she hurried to a severely injured sister in the resuscitation ward, where she stayed until morphia was found for her pain. Her nurses were inspired by her encouragement, falling flat when the bombs fell near and talking to the patients in calm voices, and even laughing when one man accidentally squirted soda water over the Matron.

As the basement was warm and dry and its lights still worked, some patients were taken there while others were driven by ambulance and car to Warwick Emergency Hospital, supervised by the indefatigable Matron, who seemed to be everywhere at once. Other patients had been placed under their beds for safety and were now moved to the basement. Those in plaster, and covered in debris of the same colour, were sometimes hard to identify, so the matron and a sister shone their torches under the beds to ensure that none had been left behind, and indeed found two still there, side by side and quite calm, waiting to be moved. A nurse from the children's ward was hidden with the babies under the nurses' dining table. Another, with older children, felt that they were quite safe as there was now nothing overhead to come down on them. Going to investigate, Matron Burton found that an ambulance, lifted by a bomb blast, was perched on top of their balcony.

During a lull, the Matron crossed the bomb crater outside the enquiry office on some planks and went to survey the devastation, then answered queries from relatives before checking on her casualties and arranging some drinks and food. In one wing of the quadrangle a nurse waved from her smashed window. Suddenly the huge delayed-action bomb in the crater – which the Matron had so casually crossed on planks shortly before – blew up, and the whole wing and basement caved in. Scraps of nurses' uniform stuck out from under the debris, and then hands and tops of heads could be seen. A casualty sister took hold of a hand, and found it belonged to the sister who had just waved at them, fortunately still alive. Matron Burton told her they would get her out very soon, after the enormous piece of wall which covered her was removed. As she ran up the side of the crater to get more help, the Matron saw patients climbing out of a basement window at the back.

The rescue squads were soon there at work, passing patients out through the window and stairway. Nurses and Matron Burton acted as stretcher-bearers until relieved by others. Those removed were put on seats until cars could be brought for them, but some walked home, which later made it difficult to check up on numbers. Rescue work went on all day; the most gruesome and heartbreaking task for the Matron was trying to identify her own staff. By late afternoon everything was finished; a roll-call was completed and weary, dazed staff could finally rest. But the high morale of

Nurses examine damage in a
bombed Liverpool hospital.
(*Imperial War Museum*)

patients and nursing staff of the hospital throughout the long ordeal was
largely attributable to the cheerfulness, courage and example of Matron
Burton.

Another sister, forty-year-old Emma Horne, whose ward was partly
demolished by one of the bombs in the same incident, also won the George
Medal.

A few nights later it was the turn of Birmingham, another big industrial
centre in the Midlands. Here, Matron Evelyn Thomas was in charge of the
West Bromwich and District Hospital. It was surrounded by incendiary
bomb fires, with several parts of the hospital either on fire or devastated.
She managed to douse one incendiary, which could have destroyed a block,
but another landed nearby and knocked her to the ground. Picking herself
up and retrieving her cap, she continued organising the evacuation of the
hospital throughout the raid in a calm and unhurried manner, requisitioning
the necessary vehicles. Never once did she show any fear, and she inspired
her staff to act in the same way.

The raids continued. Southampton, one of the south coast ports, was
regularly bombed and shelled. On a November night in 1940, eighteen-
year-old Nurse Mary Newman was on her way to visit her parents when a

bomb struck some houses nearby, killing several people. Nurse Newman tended a man who had been blown into the roadway and then, hearing of his son who was trapped upside down in the building, she climbed into a hole made by the rescuers to comfort the frightened boy. Gas was escaping and the atmosphere very poisonous. Several times she almost collapsed, but she held on until the boy was released and the ambulance had arrived.

The dockyards, warehouses and port installations of Bristol also came in for numerous raids. On a night in March 1941, a woman trapped in the wreckage of her home in the city was about to give birth. Staff Nurse Violet Frampton and Assistant Matron Elsie Stevens from the Bristol Maternity Hospital volunteered to run the gauntlet of the bombing to help her. The woman lay with several others in a rubble-covered cellar. Lowered feet first through a narrow grating, the nurses managed to extract two children and a woman. Matron Stevens had by now located the pregnant woman and both midwives managed to clear her head from the debris entirely covering her, but they could not release her. So they stayed as the rescuers fought to clear a way to them in a building liable to collapse and in an atmosphere noxious with escaping gas. Nevertheless it was not until the next afternoon that they were freed. The trapped woman, taken straight to hospital, gave birth shortly after to a healthy infant.

Yet another south coast town under frequent attack was Hastings. Here on a night in April 1941, Dorothy Gardner, a probationer nurse, was on duty at the Royal East Sussex Hospital when the air raid sirens sounded. She was about to remove patients to safety when she heard the whistle of a falling bomb. Careless of her own safety, she threw herself over the bed of the nearest patient. The bomb hit the balcony outside causing the roof to fall in, covering Nurse Gardner with thick debris. When she was dug out some time afterwards she was severely injured, but the patient was only bruised.

In the darkness of an early morning in May 1941, Nurse Vera Anderson was finishing her night duty when the busy manufacturing town of Nottingham experienced one of its heaviest raids. She was clearing up her surgery in Boots the Chemist's building when it was hit by a bomb. Moving a seriously injured casualty to the basement, she risked running up to the top of the building to find hot water. Another explosion threw her hard against the stair wall, but indomitably she returned to her patient. When the basement started to flood, she helped carry him to a safer place, and finally they were driven from that to shelter under the arch of a railway bridge. She tried to get hold of an ambulance without success, but stayed with her patient, comforting him until he died. Being unable now to return to her surgery, Nurse Anderson trudged through the shattered streets to the town's central control post to help there, and she was once more busy with numerous casualties. Again threatened by the advancing fires, she had to move on to another shelter, where she continued calmly with her ministrations. Later, almost dead with fatigue, she was relieved by another nurse.

Dr Alison McNairn was Assistant Medical Officer in the City General Hospital of Plymouth, another coastal town that was a frequent enemy target because of its shipping. On a night in March 1941 the hospital was bombed and Dr McNairn was buried in rubble up to her head. When freed, although injured and in pain, she dragged herself along to help another nurse dig out and remove children who were still alive. In between, she treated other casualties as they were brought in. She did not allow her own extensive injuries to be tended until things started to return to normal.

These are only a few examples of the bravery shown by nurses during the Second World War. However, even when bombs and casualties had become just a bad memory, there were still some George Medals to be awarded to nurses.

Night Nurse Freda Holland was doing her rounds with another sister during an early morning in April 1954 at Dellwood Maternity Home, Reading. When she opened the door of the nursery, where fifteen babies were sleeping, she was met by a thick cloud of smoke and flames. With complete disregard for her own safety she ran into the room and started picking up the babies, one by one, finding them more by feel than sight. The floor was also on fire, so that her whole body and face were scorched as she entered the room time and again, until she had succeeded in bringing out all fifteen. Downstairs she insisted on tending them, before collapsing from the smoke and her very serious burns, from which she never properly recovered.

It was a dark, wet Christmas Eve in 1965 and the Middlesex Hospital in London was busy with last-minute preparations for Christmas. Word came to Ward Sister Fiona Chard that one of the patients had climbed out of a fifth-floor window onto the ledge, saying he was going to jump from it. Going upstairs, she immediately climbed out of another window and worked her way along the slippery, narrow ledge to reach him. She tried reasoning but he would have none of it. Nevertheless, she stayed with him, finding out as she talked that he was also carrying a knife. Meanwhile, a surgeon had climbed onto the ledge from the other side and joined her, sometimes holding onto the patient when he seemed to be ready to carry out his threat. At last the man was persuaded to go back inside, followed by the brave sister and surgeon.

A third medal was awarded in 1968 to Pupil Nurse Marion Young, mentioned in Chapter Three. It was for her bravery in assisting the teacher, Mrs Hanson, in a secondary school in Dundee. Off duty, she was brought to the school by the police, after their needlework teacher had appealed for her to come and try to pacify an armed soldier she knew, who was threatening to shoot her class of girls. He had said he would let them go if she came. With so many lives at stake, she volunteered to enter the barricaded classroom. The man opened the door and after some persuasion let one of the girls go. Nurse Young then tried to convince him to release the rest of the girls. During this time he occasionally fired at the door to prevent anyone from entering, but at last agreed to let the terrified girls leave unharmed. Marion and Mrs Hanson remained and they continued their joint efforts to persuade the gunman to give himself up. At one point he told

Mrs Hanson to close a window behind her. As she did so, he shot her in the back, killing her. Nurse Young saw death staring her in the face, but she continued calmly talking to the unstable soldier, who a short time later gave himself up. In addition to the Albert Medal given posthumously to Mrs Hanson and the George Medal to Nurse Young, they were awarded the first two Sir James Duncan Medals for bravery in helping the police.

Several civil nurses were made Members of the British Empire (MBE) for what amounted to bravery during the Second World War in unusual circumstances.

In 1939, Matron Alexandrina Marsden, who had settled in Brittany, volunteered for nursing at Dinard Hospital in France at the age of sixty-two, and became its Matron. When the Germans occupied her hospital she refused to work for them. Later she was arrested and put in charge of British prisoners in a prison camp and then a concentration camp hospital, where she fell ill; her life was saved by the devoted nursing of some nuns. By 1941, considering her more as a nuisance, the Germans sent her back to Brittany under open arrest, where she soon became involved with a resistance group. In Rennes she set up a clinic for treating wounded resistance workers. She also helped in the escape lines, vetting escapees in her hospital and collecting useful intelligence information, which she managed to pass on to Britain. She was arrested and freed twice more, with many narrow escapes. Undeterred, she continued her work until her town was bombed on D-Day, when she was badly injured, her life again being saved by the nuns. In August 1944, she acted as interpreter to the driver of a French ambulance and was treated as a conquering heroine. Later she helped the Allies with lists of collaborators and examples of German brutality. She was irrepressible, and as well as the MBE was also given the French Croix de Resistance.

Two further unusual MBEs should be recorded. The dividing line between those willing to risk their lives in dangerous situations to help others is a very narrow one. This very much applies to nurses in the Queen Elizabeth Overseas Nursing Service, who served loyally the coloured or white populations in Britain's former colonies. The following examples stand for many.

Ida Race was Matron of the Provincial Hospital in the central province of Kenya during the Mau Mau emergency, in 1952. Here nurses in the outlying area continued to run their hospitals, antenatal and outpatients clinics for Africans, with no regard for their own safety and unsure if any of their own staff might be ordered to kill them by the ritual Mau Mau oaths. The nurses also travelled through hazardous areas to reach their patients and some died trying to help. Matron Race faced similar dangers in her own hospital.

In 1970, Marjorie Spencer was sister in charge of a group of nurses during the reopening of the University Hospital of Enugu in Nigeria during the Biafran civil war. She was the first of the medical team to go to Lagos. Two weeks later, with a doctor, they organised the equipment needed for the

Nurse Daisy Jerome BEM.
(*Miss D. Jerome*)

hospital and travelled from Lagos to Enugu by Land Rover. Their risky journey took three days; several times they had guns pointed at their windscreens. Fortunately Sister Spencer had picked up the Hausa language and she was able to convince the men of their peaceful mission. Even so, on arriving and setting up the hospital, they were often in fear of their lives.

Sister Spencer had also been in Sarawak, Malaysia, in 1965–8 and later Sumatra in Indonesia, where during a terrorist attack on an oil installation she was called to tend a man suffering from a massive heart attack and bullet wounds, and another with a bullet in his back. The latter she escorted to Singapore, on a journey of terror.

In Britain many wartime awards of the British Empire Medal (BEM) were given for bravery. One example was Nurse Daisy Jerome, who was tucking up her patients on a night in March 1941 in the London Chest Hospital when it was hit by bombs. In a ward of sixteen patients, there was an enormous bang when a landmine exploded in the nearby courtyard, almost blowing Daisy onto one of the patient's beds. When she surfaced, the bedscreen was around her neck like a collar, and some of the flying glass had lodged above her eye. Extricating herself she managed to carry one patient into the corridor and then returned to convey four more to safety. When another bomb fell, it knocked her unconscious and debris hitting her hand broke four fingers. Recovering sufficiently, she managed to evacuate the rest of her patients before collapsing. She remained dangerously ill for several months.

In Manchester, Evelyn Leaver, retired from midwifery since her marriage twenty years before, volunteered to help a woman in labour at her home. In frightful conditions, with care and patience, Mrs Leaver managed to get her patient down to the cellar and tended her until the doctor arrived. She remained with her until after the child was born.

In Portsmouth, Mary Farr was also attending a woman in labour, making her own body a shield to protect the expectant mother from the blast of the bombs. The labour continued as normal and at the end of the raid the baby was born.

Another gallantry BEM went to Nurse Elizabeth Baker in Kent. During a bombing raid a woman was trapped in debris in her ruined house, although she was not seriously injured. Rescuing her was a long and difficult process but eventually the team made a small opening in the collapsing wall of an adjoining house and Nurse Baker volunteered to crawl through the hole, in order to comfort the woman. She remained there for the dangerous hours it took to free the woman, in the choking gas and dust, with the wall ready to fall at any time.

On a night in March 1941, the staff of the Knightswood Emergency Hospital, Glasgow, were summoned to take part in the rescue work and treatment of the casualties from the badly bombed yard of Yarrow and Company. For their heroic efforts that night, numerous rescuers from the hospital were recommended for recognition. Nurse Joan Anderson rescued and tended the injured and was given the BEM, while nurses Morag MacMartin and May Stanley were given King's Commendations for Bravery.

Another courageous woman was Joanna Stavridi, the daughter of a London banker of Greek descent. She was trapped in Greece by the 1940 Italian invasion, where, with her Red Cross training, she began nursing in the front lines. After the Germans invaded to retrieve the Italian defeat, she was evacuated to Crete where she eventually remained, the only British nurse and Matron of a tented hospital of 700 seriously wounded soldiers. During the airborne invasion of the island by the Germans in late May 1941, she tended the enormous numbers of casualties from both sides, finally having them transferred to the island's caves for safety. When the British were forced to withdraw with the less injured casualties, she refused to abandon the worst cases and was captured along with them, whereupon the Germans transferred her to a hospital in mainland Greece. For the exceptional dedication and courage of this Florence Nightingale of Crete, she received no British awards, but Greece gave her the Hellenic Red Cross.

Smaller private societies have also always recognised nurses' heroism. From these stories of bravery, it is not surprising that many nurses have gained the coveted Royal Red Cross (RRC), very highly valued because it acknowledged their skills as nurses. A very special few were given the Florence Nightingale Medal, a rare award and a great honour for its recipients. Its history dates back to 1907, when the Hungarian Red Cross wished to pay tribute to the 'Lady with the Lamp' – Florence Nightingale – who, leading a group of nurses, had worked tirelessly with the wounded soldiers in the hospital at Scutari during the Crimean War, and afterwards had reorganised the nursing profession and facilities. After a survey of national societies, it was decided to have a medal in honour of her life and work but, because the First World War intervened, the first medals were not announced until 1920, which fortuitously was the centenary of her birth; no medals were announced during the Second World War either. Originally it was intended to reward nurses who gave distinguished wartime service, but this was extended to peacetime, too, and from 1991 the award could be given to men in the profession as well as women, and even posthumously.

Florence Nightingale Medal (obverse). (*British Red Cross Museum & Archives*)

Centralised by the Red Cross Society in Geneva, any member countries can nominate their best nurses, once every two years, and these are carefully sifted through so that one country rarely has more than one medalist of the year, and sometimes none. From 1920 up to the end of the century over 1,000 have been awarded.

The medal is roughly oval ending in a point at each end, and shows Florence Nightingale with her lamp. Around its edge are inscribed the Latin words '*Pro Vera Misericordia et Cara Humanite Perennis Decor Universalis*' – 'For True Compassion and Loving Kindness to Humanity, This is an Everlasting Worldwide Honour.' The medal is fastened to the ribbon above by a round brooch encircled by laurel leaves and centred with a large red cross on white.

CHAPTER NINE

Women of the Police, Fire and Prison Services

Although the police wear a uniform very familiar on the streets and in the media, they are still ordinary men and women, who have taken on their work to help and protect the public and their possessions. Over the years their tasks have become more varied, difficult and dangerous, as crime has also evolved and increased. The police can be asked for directions, comment on the weather or deal with suspect bombs. Among the peaceful aspects of their jobs are giving talks in schools; escorting processions, demonstrations, pop concerts or carnivals; searching for lost children or adults; keeping an eye on communities in their workplaces such as hospitals; and attending court cases – but even these occupations have the potential for trouble. Sometimes one group of people have to be protected from another; a not easy peacekeeping role where there are threats, intimidation, disputes, violence, malicious phone calls or letters. In investigating thefts and burglaries they not only have to find facts, but are often required to comfort frightened people. Another duty is attending accidents, frequently on the road and after some of which they have the sad task of reporting serious injury or death to unsuspecting families and helping them through the first stages of shock. They search for drugs, weapons, stolen goods or men who have committed offences. Kidnap, rape and murder are the most serious of the crimes they have to handle, luckily not so prevalent as the media portray. Unfortunately, crime today can be more sophisticated, with personal radios, computers and electronic gadgets. Violence also has become more common.

Those willing to undertake these tasks, and many others, sometimes risk their lives on our behalf. Gradually the role of policing has come to include women. Female talents can be complimentary to those of men and many cases involving women are dealt with by them. Normally the job is far from glamorous, largely mundane, with a proliferation of paperwork, but occasionally it can be very dangerous. And like her male colleague, a policewoman can measure up to that, too.

One kind of work where being a woman member of a police force can be useful is that of acting as a decoy to catch a suspect, in situations where no ordinary member of the public could be asked to take such a risk. An example of this took place in a long, dark lane in Croydon, Surrey, in April 1955. On this twisting path between high walls and trees, much used by everybody as a short cut, a number of violent night-time attacks on women had been reported, and the police suspected them to have been made by the same man.

After duty one night, Woman Police Constable (WPC) Kathleen Parrott was using this lane as a short cut to her home. Thinking of other things, she was not aware of being followed, until a man caught up with her and put a stranglehold on her throat from behind. As she began to scream he tightened his grip, but she managed to swivel around and clawed and beat at her assailant until, driven to her knees, she nearly lost consciousness. In her struggle, before she blacked out, she managed to drag down the mask covering the lower part of his features, and for a split second saw his face. At this point her cries had brought other people to her aid and her attacker ran off. Badly shaken and hurt, she spent a long time in hospital before returning to duty, with a burning determination to catch this man for the sake of other women.

One evening about six weeks later, Woman Police Sergeant (WP Sgt) Ethel Bush was patrolling the path with another policewoman in uniform when she caught sight of a man hiding in the bushes. WPC Parrott, in plain clothes and followed by two policemen, later took the same path to see if he was her former assailant, but he had gone. Even so, the police stationed several of their men around the path at intervals and the woman police sergeant, also in plain clothes, returned as a decoy, hoping to draw him out, the man having appeared long enough for WPC Parrott to identify him. Ethel Bush continued slowly on her way along the path, unable to turn around lest she alerted the man, and so could not tell when suddenly he appeared from behind and dealt her a terrific blow with a branch. Despite her injury she managed to grapple and delay him, her cries alerting the policeman nearest to her. Then things happened in quick succession. The policeman sent his dog over the glass-topped wall where he was hiding and then clambered over it himself, gashing his arm seriously and by bad luck landing on the poor dog. While they were disentangling themselves, the assailant punched the policewoman in the face and made his getaway. WP Sgt Bush was admitted to hospital with a serious head wound.

But the attack had not been in vain. The description of the man was confirmed and made it possible for the police to arrest him the same night. The two policewomen, both nearing forty, were awarded the George Medal and their bravery enabled countless women to walk the path at night in safety.

In 1964, 24-year-old WPC Margaret Cleland was called out on a cold March day in London to try to talk a young father out of committing suicide. He was sitting on the edge of a roof of a tall building, his young baby son in his arms. As the policewoman scrambled onto the roof, the man threatened to jump, so she remained perched precariously on its edge, some distance away. From here she initiated a conversation, finding that he had been living in Cambridge, was very lonely and had told the media that he was going to kill himself there on that day. As it was so bitterly cold the little boy started crying, which gave the policewoman the chance to suggest that the child needed more clothes. Picking up his little coat nearby, she moved forward very gently and wrapped it about the infant's shoulders; at the same time she took hold of the baby with one hand and grasped the father with the other. This action could easily have killed them all if he had then jumped, but fortunately he did not and two policemen nearby leapt forward and overpowered him. WPC Cleland and the policemen escorted the man and his son downstairs and out of the building into the full glare of the media. For her compassionate and selfless action she was awarded the George Medal.

King's Police and Fire Service Medal (reverse). (*R.J. Scarlett*)

The King's Police and Fire Service Medal was established by King Edward VII in 1909 to reward people in either service for 'heroic acts of exceptional courage and skill' or 'instances of conspicuous devotion to duty'. With the heads of different monarchs on the front, it went through some minor changes until 1954, when separate medals were issued for the police and fire brigade and it was decided that the gallantry medal would only be given where the individual had given his life for his action. In 1969, permission was given for recipients to use the letters KPFSM or QPM after their name.

The medal is round and silver, with the monarch's head (uncrowned in earlier years) on the obverse side, with an attractive design on the other. It shows a watchman standing in a draped robe, a large sword, point down, lying against his bent right arm and his right hand on an upright shield inscribed in the upper part with the words 'To Guard My People'. At his feet is a flashing lantern and the background is a fortified city. It is also inscribed with the words 'For Courage' or 'For Distinguished Police Service'. The ribbon is dark blue with a silver stripe on the edges and in the middle. When it marks gallantry, there is a thin red line down each silver stripe. After 1954, the fire brigade had a red ribbon with yellow stripes, gallantry being indicated by a thin blue line on the yellow stripe. The word 'Fire' replaces the word 'Police' in the medal and the recipients can put the letters QFSM after their name.

Only one woman has ever been awarded the King's Police and Fire Service Medal. Tooting Bec Common is an area crossed by a road and much used by the public. Shortly after the Second World War, a series of brutal attacks on women walking alone there in the evenings occurred, when their handbags were snatched. Newspapers labelled the robber the Tooting Prowler. Police officers in plain clothes had been stationed at various points along the common but to no avail and the robberies continued. Thus, only by using a woman as a decoy could the man be caught and Detective Sergeant (Det Sgt) Alberta (Bertie) Watts volunteered.

Carrying a large handbag and dressed as a woman returning from work, she had been out in January 1947 for several nights in thick snow but nothing had happened. At about 6 p.m. one night she noticed a man standing at the corner of the road opposite, watching her. Tightening her grip on her handbag, she continued on her pre-arranged way. Shortly, she heard someone following her, but the man overtook her – obviously not the attacker – but still uncertain the undercover policewoman turned round and started walking back the way she had come. She had hardly gone far before she again heard footsteps behind her and then silence. Steeling herself not to look back, she was suddenly driven to the ground as the man jumped on her back; the snow had deadened his approach. She struggled and tried to hold on to him, but he kicked and punched her, finally wrenching her handbag from her grasp, before running away. Picking herself up and shouting for help, she ran after him, but then she saw that he had been caught by her colleagues who, with great difficulty, arrested him. Det Sgt Watts suffered a black eye, bruising and shock, and was away from duty for nearly a fortnight, but her courage had caught the violent prowler.

Queen's Gallantry Medal (reverse). (*R.J. Scarlett*)

Because of the risks they run in ordinary daily work, which can unexpectedly turn dangerous and which they face with a mixture of common sense, skill and courage, a number of police-women have been given the Queen's Gallantry Medal. It was set up in 1974, primarily for civilians displaying exemplary acts of bravery, which can be awarded posthumously. Round and silver, it has the Queen's crowned head on one side, while on the other are the words 'The Queen's Gallantry Medal', above which is a crown with a spray of laurel leaves on either side. The ribbon is dark blue with a thin rose-pink stripe on a wider pearl-grey central stripe.

Nowhere is bravery more often needed than in the troubled area of Northern Ireland, where police have to not only combat ordinary crimes but also carry out the thankless task of trying to protect the people of the two warring communities, a situation that often results in these courageous officers becoming the target of hatred from both sides. Many lives have been lost, and several women belonging to the Royal Ulster Constabulary have won this medal. One example will have to stand for them all.

In the city of Londonderry, WPC Glynis Breen was walking on patrol duty with a male colleague in May 1982. They were both twenty-one years old. A red van pulled up beside them and, thinking that the driver was needing directions, WPC Breen went to the driver's window. As she did so, a side door in the van opened and she found herself looking into the eyes of a hooded figure holding a rifle. She turned to shout a warning to her

Woman Police Constable
Christine Barclay, Queen's
Commendation. (*Police
Sergeant C. Flynn*)

companion, but as she did so she was felled by bullets in her back and leg. The policeman was also caught in the deadly hail of fire and they both lay on the pavement in a pool of blood. The van drove off, a crowd collected and shortly afterwards they were taken by ambulance to hospital. WPC Breen eventually recovered, but her fellow police officer died.

Another award for courage, not given lightly, is the Queen's Commendation for Brave Conduct. Almost every year a woman police officer has been nominated for it, sometimes more than one. Here are a few examples of the many kinds of courageous acts for which the award can be given.

On school crossing duty in Liverpool in 1970, WPC Nora Taylor yanked a boy to safety from the path of a skidding lorry as it careered down the road towards him. WPC Jacqueline Parish was sent to save a man being threatened with a carving knife by his wife in an alley in Guildford in 1974. Attempting to remove the knife, she was battered around the head by the woman's handbag before being rescued by other policemen. In 1977, WPC

Dianne Bartram and another Lancashire police officer were menaced by a man with a nail bomb, who jumped on their car bonnet. The policewoman wrestled the bomb out of his hands and then helped to overpower him; she fainted when she found it was a live device. WPC Michelle Holt, acting as decoy, was followed by car and on foot by a violent man preying on women in Bristol in 1979. She was attacked and nearly throttled before the man was captured. WPC Kim Catterall and her colleague helped chase four brutal robbers in their Panda car outside Liverpool in 1980. After being attacked with a hammer, she helped to capture one of the offenders, but her colleague was nearly killed. In 1981 in Fife, WPC Christine Barclay aided the senior nursing officer in saving the sleeping residents of a nurses' home in a fire that, because of their actions, claimed only one life. WPC Helen Evans of the Metropolitan Police, in 1981, climbed the scaffolding of a building to talk a young woman out of committing suicide. They were both rescued by the London Fire Brigade. Finally, in Liverpool in 1992, WPCs Leslie Harrison and Ruth Polehill, with two policemen, managed to overpower a violent man wielding a knife and screwdriver. WPC Harrison was nearly stabbed to death.

WPCs Dianne Bartram and Kim Catterall, in addition to their commendations, also received the William Garnett Cup for Bravery. Donated by Alderman William Garnett in memory of his father, it originated from 1930 and was given annually to the Lancashire police officer considered to have performed the most gallant deed of the year. Another recipient was WPC Thompson, who, in 1981 on Blackpool pleasure beach, was attacked and kicked practically unconscious by a mob of youths when she arrested a young girl who had stolen a handbag. Despite this, she hung on to the thief until rescued by colleagues.

A similar award was created by Alderman Goodwin in 1972 for the outstanding policewoman of the year in Durham. In 1985 it was given to WPC Denise White. She and three policemen went to arrest a knife-brandishing husband, with four children inside a house. They had been summoned by his estranged wife. By talking quietly and reasonably to him, the policewoman at length calmed him and he gave himself up.

The Society for the Protection of Life from Fire made three awards to policewomen from the Thames Valley and Tayside police forces, and the Liverpool Shipwreck and Humane Society gave a bronze medal to WPC Denise Morgan for courageously having jumped down onto a narrow ledge – overhanging a 30-foot drop onto concrete below – to rescue a woman from a suicide attempt at Liverpool pier in 1978.

The Royal Humane Society, an international body, awarded their bronze medal to WPC Wendy Heard of the Northumbrian police force. Its highest award – the international and rare Stanhope gold medal – was given in 1992 to another policewoman. A Georgian hotel in London was being refurbished and, to protect the occupants from rain or debris while the work was undertaken, a corrugated iron roof was being erected over the building, fastened to a scaffolding frame. By sheer bad luck, while doing this 25 feet above the hotel, a workman stepped on a sheet of metal that had not been properly attached, and fell 50 feet onto the sloping roof, down which he slid to the flat roof of a fourth-floor dormer window. He was in this precarious position – with the prospect of a further fall, as well as the danger of unstable scaffolding – at the time when WPC Lesley Moore was called to help. She was acting as crew in an ambulance during the 1989 Ambulance Workers' Strike. Seeing the situation, and because of her knowledge of first aid, she volunteered to help, while the policeman with her went to summon further assistance.

Climbing out of the dormer window of a fifth-floor flat, she inched down to the man. As the windows were not in line with one another, she had to cross an awkward gap with a very rickety railing at the bottom, which could have given way. One of the scaffolders held her hand while she swung herself over the gap, enabling her to jump down to the top of the dormer window where the injured man lay. There, restricted by space, in a temperature of 12°C (54°F) and in a high wind, she managed to turn the man over and apply resuscitation. When she had restored his breathing, WPC Moore removed her tunic to make a pillow for his head and put her pullover on him to keep him warm. Then she stayed with him for support for over an hour, until the fire brigade, with specialised equipment, laid planking and ladders to bring him down. Last came the 25-year-old policewoman, mother of three young children, shaking with cold and delayed shock. Sadly the rescued man died later in hospital.

Many men and women of the police have died in performing their duty, but rarely have their names been recorded, nor have they any awards. A plaque was put up to commemorate Yvonne Fletcher, the policewoman shot from inside the building while guarding the Iraqi Embassy in April 1984. The gunman, under diplomatic immunity, escaped punishment. Libya has now accepted full responsibility for her murder and has offered to pay compensation to Yvonne Fletcher's family.

A tragic incident on Blackpool promenade involved six police officers, one of them a policewoman. Who would have thought that trying to rescue a small dog, whose ball had bounced into the sea, would have taken the lives of his master, two police officers and one policewoman? It was a very heavy, dangerous sea that day in January 1983 and, despite the great bravery shown by everyone, the toll was grievous.

The Binney Memorial Medal is given to any member of the general public who helps the Metropolitan Police keep law and order. It commemorates Ralph D. Binney, who died in 1944 while trying to prevent smash-and-grab thieves escaping in London, and so helped the police to capture them. Up to 1996, forty-nine medals have been given, five to women. One of these was Marjorie Condie, who was at work as practice manager in a busy Pinner Medical Centre in 1991. A man came in one day and asked to see a particular doctor, and when he found him absent became agitated and produced a gun. He drove Mrs Condie and two other receptionists into a corner of the room

Binney Medal: a: obverse; b: reverse. (*Worshipful Company of Goldsmiths*)

Marjorie Condie, Binney
Medal. (*Mrs M. Condie*)

out of sight, his aim being to gain publicity in the media over the recent death of his wife. Just then an elderly patient came in and when Mrs Condie was allowed to escort him out, when she whispered to him to call the police. When the telephone rang she was allowed to answer it and again surreptitiously managed to say what was happening. Holding a knife at her throat, the gunman then told her to go upstairs and get the keys to lock the centre, which she did, once again grasping the opportunity to ring the police. When the police arrived, the man once more held a knife to her throat, but after negotiations he released the two receptionists and agreed to let Mrs Condie go in exchange for a police officer, whom he then made Mrs Condie tie up and handcuff. However, shortly afterwards the man gave himself up. Mrs Condie had displayed the utmost calm and consideration for others throughout her frightening ordeal, and received her Binney Medal for helping the police.

Because most of the work of the fire brigade is particularly hazardous – requiring not only skill but great personal strength – the service has not recruited many women, except in a clerical capacity, but there are changes even here.

The earliest examples of bravery in this field appear during the First World War, among those women who received the Medal of the Order of the British Empire in June 1918. Six fire girls are named who were employed in a London munitions filling factory, as well as acting as transport workers. An explosion in their factory resulted in a fire in a corner of the cartridge finishing shed, which quickly spread, setting the whole building aflame. The eighty workers were speedily evacuated, and the fire

Typical munitions factory and trolley, 1915. (*Fleur de Lis Heritage Centre, Faversham*)

girls were quickly on the scene. Despite bullets flying in all directions and the fire moving towards the other buildings, the girls took their hoses right up to the trolley rails beside the sheds and by their concentrated efforts prevented the fire from spreading further. After the London Fire Brigade arrived, they kept their hoses playing on the flames at one end of the building, while the firemen worked on the other. Their efforts helped to save the munitions factory from destruction. Of the firewomen, five were single girls – Minnie Balkham, Elsie Barnes, Gladys Chapman, Rose Saville and Kate Shepherd – and one was married – Mrs K. Marchant. All were under twenty-two years of age. In January 1919, Mrs A. Armitage, a police firewoman at another factory, also received this award.

The Second World War brought about a change in the attitude of regular fire service men. Women were not only employed as clerks, but also telephonists, watch and control room staff, mobile canteen helpers and drivers. Auxiliary fire service women already existed in 1938, but as manpower became stretched to its very limits and the war developed, so did their roles. In London, particularly during the Blitz, they became valuable and necessary. The red fire engines with their bells clanging and firemen hanging on, raced along the cratered, rubble-strewn streets to extinguish fires or smouldering ashes of the many bombed buildings. It was not always appreciated, however, that although they used water on fires, the equipment was powered by that most flammable of liquids, petrol, and on a busy night they would need refuelling.

This was what Auxiliary Firewoman Gillian Tanner volunteered to do during a very bad raid on London docks in September 1940. Her task was to deliver 150 gallons of petrol in cans – each weighing about 17 lb – from her 30-cwt lorry to the quayside. At each fire engine pump – and there were six of them – she had to top up the tanks with a steady hand, knowing that one careless move such as splashing the petrol outside the filler, or catching sparks from any nearby bombs, could set everything on fire, including herself. She continued with her work, despite the bombing around her, until her cans were empty, when she reloaded them and drove back to her depot. Afterwards, even she wondered how she had got away with it. For her courage and coolness in so dangerous an enterprise she received the George Medal.

A BEM went to two firewomen telephonists who stayed at their posts until the lines went dead, while their exchange was on fire. Afterwards, they ran to the nearest working telephone box, one acting as messenger between the fire officer and her friend, while the other phoned through the reports to the control centre, thus keeping the information flowing. In the badly bombed and shelled city of Portsmouth, auxiliary firewomen acting as telephonists also stayed at their posts during bad raids and won the BEM for their efforts. Firewoman Barbara Crosland's BEM was awarded for her work in the control room of the city of Coventry during a frantically busy night when there was heavy bombing.

The dangers of the last few months of 1940 in London alone resulted in 14 firemen killed and over 250 firemen and women seriously injured, and by the end of the war over 327 firemen and women had died, with over 3,000 injured. Such was the toll in just one city. In the country as a whole, auxiliary firewomen were credited with 1 George Medal, 17 BEMs and 40 Commendations for Bravery.

The prison service has long employed female wardens and other workers for its women's prisons, but there seem to be no records of outstanding acts of courage on their part.

However, the general public owes much – sometimes life itself – to the work and protection of these three services, especially the more visible police and fire services. As can be seen, women, though of more recent involvement, have willingly taken their part and shown equal courage.

CHAPTER TEN

Civilian Gallantry MBEs, BEMs and Commendations for Bravery

Among the MBEs and BEMs of the war years, it is difficult to distinguish the awards for gallantry from those given for meritorious service. The latter in itself is valuable but not in the same category as courage.

In the civilian population, beset with restrictions, rationing, evacuees, bombed-out homes, and scares of enemy landings, there were certainly examples of quiet heroism, and the death of a family member in the Services or in enemy raids had to be accepted with sad resignation. Some younger women not absorbed by the Forces, factories or essential civilian services like nursing or the WVS might have gone into the Women's Land Army or the Women's Timber Corps – a healthy but back-breaking revelation for many and necessary work to help overcome the shortages caused during the submarine war, by producing food for beleaguered Britain. Older women with young children, elderly or sick men, and the few younger men still remaining in restricted occupations not only worked in their homes or offices but often took up some form of spare-time war work. Women's participation ranged from Home Guard Auxiliaries, Fire Watching, the Royal Observer Corps, and the Women's Legion to housewives in the Women's Institutes and Townswomen's Guilds, who made do and mended, knitted and jammed, and turned their hands to numerous other smaller tasks. Few did not find something to do to help the war effort.

The MBE is an order of chivalry, and its holder a member of the fifth class of the Most Excellent Order of the British Empire. Instituted in 1917 by King George V during the First World War, it was intended as a reward for any man or woman giving important service to the British Empire of a non-combatant kind, and was thus really for civilians. However, in 1918 a military division was added, mainly to cover nurses and the women's Services. Therefore it could be given not only for devotion to duty but also for courage under hazardous circumstances. In 1957, Queen Elizabeth commanded that MBEs for gallantry should carry silver crossed oak leaves on the ribbon and 1974 saw the gallantry MBE replaced by the Queen's Gallantry Medal. The MBE for distinguished service still remains. The

Member of the Order of the British Empire MBE (obverse).
(*R.J. Scarlett*)

Gallantry Emblem on ribbon of MBE and BEM from 1957.
(*R.J. Scarlett*)

badge is in the form of a cross, each arm ending in three points. Made of silver it is surmounted by the imperial crown. The centre has the motto 'For God and the Empire' in an outside ring, surrounding what used to be a seated Britannia with trident and shield, but in 1937 was changed to the heads in profile of King George V and Queen Mary. The ribbon also altered the same year from purple with a central narrow red stripe for military recipients, to rose-pink edged with pearl-grey, and an extra pearl-grey stripe in the middle for the military; women wore the ribbon as a bow.

One of the earliest MBEs for courage went to Elizabeth Selby in 1920, for her actions after the great explosion at Faversham Explosives Loading Company in 1916. She accompanied her doctor husband after the first small blast was followed by a second huge one. Everything was in chaos. Victims were hastily dug out of the debris before the fire could get to them, even though one or two of the rescuers were on fire at times themselves. There were also continuous explosions of loaded mines in the building.

At the time Mrs Selby was in charge of a small VAD hospital at Sittingbourne and, though unqualified, she knew enough medical procedure to be of great help. She immediately set to work, attending to the injured from the first explosion before going to the scene of the second, where she was located when the third explosion took place. Afraid that there might be more casualties, she hastened to that third area, without considering the risks she ran, and remained there for over two hours, until all those hurt had been evacuated. She was the only woman assisting on the scenes; four months later she was given the silver life-saving medal of the Order of St John. Her MBE took longer to be awarded.

In the Second World War, air raids and the bombing of cities and towns provided many instances of bravery. Aileen Costigan was an ARP warden in Coventry during the November 1940 attack, and among her responsibilities were the people in their individual Morrison or Anderson shelters, as well as the large communal ones. She was on duty at the time and, in her tin helmet and ARP armband, she helped to dig out the many people buried in their demolished shelters and homes. With indifference to her own safety, as bombs continued to fall, she gave first aid to victims and frequently ran to her own home to get hot water for dressings and tea. Since the first aid post and rest centre in her district had been destroyed, she raced through the streets time and time again to attend to people's needs.

In the same raid Mrs Pearl Hyde also set an excellent example. Already a councillor, and a forceful but likeable character who got things done, she was then chief of the WVS in the city. In the thick of the action during the bombing, she shepherded people to shelters and ministered to their needs. She said later, 'You know you feel such a fool standing there in a crater, in pitch darkness at night, holding out mugs of tea and seeing men bring out the bodies, until you learn there's someone in the bombed house who's alive. Then its worth while.' One man, working on a bombed public house, had been handling a very messy body. When she offered him some tea, he hid his hands and asked her to just hold the cup to his lips. 'That tea's jolly good! Just washed the blood and dust out of my mouth,' he commented, then went back with renewed energy to his grisly task. In the following days, disregarding the danger of falling masonry, unexploded bombs and land mines, Mrs Hyde organised the huge task of food distribution.

Pearl Hyde MBE. (*Coventry Evening Telegraph*)

When it became Glasgow's turn to be targeted and Clydeside took a heavy toll, ambulance attendant Mary Haldane distinguished herself by accompanying her vehicle through the fires and the bombs in order to pick up patients in the streets or, in the terrible explosions in the works and factories, sometimes helping to rescue them. Applying first aid she then saw them safely to the emergency hospitals. Her efforts saved many lives and she received the MBE.

Miss Hornby served with the WVS in Wales and Bristol, where she became an expert in firefighting and Civil Defence, and was a regular member of an ARP team. In May 1941, however, she acted as second in command of the Westminster firefighting team in a big air raid on London. When some incendiary bombs landed on her building she helped to put them out. Nearby, a fire erupted inside a chemist's shop. Because of fallen masonry, the only entrance was through a shattered plate-glass window, whose jagged edges were like huge teeth. Miss Hornby volunteered to brave the glass, and holding firmly to her stirrup pump, was thrown bodily head first into the shop by her team so that she could start fighting the blaze with water from the back of the premises. It was a very risky thing to do but fortunately it worked.

A few years later came four rather unusual MBEs to British citizens abroad. The Navy, Army and Air Force Institute, known by the Armed Services as the NAAFI, was set up before the Second World War, and thereafter provided very necessary facilities of food and leisure for tired servicemen and women. By 1943, over 85 per cent of its staff were women. They trained with the ATS and went overseas as members of the ATS or Expeditionary Forces Institute (EFI). Wherever the Services went, at home and abroad, the NAAFI could be found serving cups of tea, pints of beer, sandwiches, otherwise unobtainable toilet necessities, smiles and sympathy, often in the most primitive, difficult and dangerous situations. For hard work under such conditions, Miss Joy was given her MBE.

The second was received by Miss Nicholls. Like two other compatriots who won BEMs for similar actions, she was sent to Greece after the British and Communist-led resistance fighters in 1944 had liberated it from the Italian and German forces. Once peace returned, the Communists and Nationalists fell out, struggling for power, and there was a bitter civil war. In the capital Athens, Miss Nicholls was the organiser of a NAAFI Leave Club and inevitably came under fire as she carried out her duties, many of which involved bringing in supplies from outlying areas. Her award was for bravery under fire.

Other organisations were doing similar work at home and overseas. The Young Women's Christian Association (YWCA) was one. Innez Hargreaves-Heap volunteered to open and run a rest centre and holiday club for Army nurses in North Africa and Italy, in a villa near Algiers and, when Italy surrendered, she was transferred to Bari to open the first Holiday and Women's Club in that country for the nurses and women's Services. Once this was operating she was sent to do the same in Florence. Such centres

Miss M. Joy MBE. (*Mrs B. Anderson*)

were very necessary to take the strain off personnel often too tired to realise it and liable to make costly mistakes. Occupying powers dispatched to liberate a country sometimes faced misunderstandings and outright hostility. For Mrs Hargreaves-Heap it was very hard and difficult work, and she had never been so tired in her life. Nevertheless, with wonderful support from Army and Air Force, it was very rewarding.

Different again, and in the line of actual fire, were the efforts of Nona Baker. She was living a wealthy and cosseted life in Malaya with her brother, eighteen years her senior, who owned one of the country's largest tin mines. In 1941, the Japanese landed on the peninsula. Her brother ordered the mine to be flooded and, with his Malayan foreman, the brother and sister fled to the jungle to escape being imprisoned. They remained in hiding for two years, constantly on the move to avoid Japanese patrols, but at the same time encouraging the workmen of the mine to keep up opposition to the Japanese. When food supplies ceased, they decided to join a Chinese-led Communist guerrilla group in the hills, although Nona's brother was bitterly anti-Communist. Conditions were harsh and squalid and their health, already weakened, deteriorated further as they made exhausting, frequent moves. For the sake of their single female member, the otherwise all-male group were embarrassed about the state of their camp and eventually Nona was sent deeper into the jungle to another guerrilla camp, where conditions were slightly better. At one point, both brother and sister in succession tried to retrieve a cache of arms near the mine, but both failed; the long trek weakened them even more.

In 1944, the Japanese made a major attack on the guerrilla hide-outs. The camps were hurriedly evacuated, with floods of refugees causing complications. Weak and ill, Nona stayed behind to tend her now very sick brother until he died. Fortunately she was given shelter by a Chinese family (at risk to themselves) until she recovered her own health, when she again moved on with the guerrillas.

In 1945 an SOE group from India parachuted in, and Nona was encouraged to edit an anti-Japanese newspaper. This went well until, afraid of being held hostage because she knew of the Communist plans to take over Malaya after the war, she was removed by the SOE group, but saw the surrender of the Japanese in Malaya before leaving. She had lived through five years of nightmare times and had done her best to oppose the Japanese.

Several other foreign nationals also received the MBE for helping in escape lines in Europe, and risking their own and their families' lives to help downed pilots, escapees from prison camps and those condemned by proscription. They were very brave people and many died for their work.

One such was Mrs Hollingdale, who kept a safe house of the twilight underground movement in occupied France. She was the wife of an Englishman and intensely patriotic. By her efforts, it was calculated that she had helped over 210 British soldiers and airmen to escape – one of them was Douglas Bader. Finally she and her husband were arrested and tortured, and only she survived the war.

There are a few later MBEs for gallantry. One went to Mrs Casteldine for her actions when a Trident aircraft crashed at Staines in the 1970s. An MBE for a different kind of courage went to Rebecca Stephens, who became the first British woman to climb Everest in 1993, and then followed it with numerous firsts, climbing the highest mountain in each of the seven continents, including Antarctica, and then sailing to the South Magnetic Pole. She considers that 'the satisfaction in reaching the top [of the mountain] was in direct proportion to the amount of sweat and effort I'd put in'.

In 1922, two medals replaced the former Medal of the Order of the British Empire, neither being orders of chivalry. They were the medals of the Most Excellent Order of the British Empire, the first for meritorious service, the other for gallantry. The second became known as the Empire Gallantry Medal (EGM). In 1937, it was decreed that the ribbon of the EGM should carry a silver laurel branch (see p. 25). When the George Medal was created in 1940, the EGM became redundant because it covered similar ground. The medal for meritorious service still continued, however, but in

Rebecca Stephens MBE. (*Fox Artists Management Ltd*)

1941 its name was changed to the British Empire Medal (BEM), with military and civil divisions. It still included some brave recipients, so in 1957 crossed silver oak leaves were added to the ribbon to indicate this. With the introduction of the Queen's Gallantry Medal (QGM), the BEM for gallantry disappeared. In 1993, the BEM was replaced by the MBE.

The badge of the BEM was silver and circular. It retained the figure of Britannia seated, holding behind her a shield and by her side a trident, all beneath a blazing sun. Under her feet were the words 'For Meritorious Service' and around its edge 'For God and the Empire'. The reverse side carried the monarch's cipher, surrounded by a circle of royal lions couchant, and in 1937 at the base were added the words 'Instituted by King George V'. The ribbon, like that of the MBE, changed in 1937 from the former purple, with a central red stripe for the military, to a new rose-pink edged with pearl-grey, with a central pearl-grey stripe for the military; women wore it as a bow.

Despite carrying the words 'For Meritorious Service', there were a number of gallantry BEMs awarded during the war years. The following give some flavour of the actions for which they were given.

British Empire Medal BEM (obverse) with crossed oak leaves for gallantry (male Civil version) after 1957. (*Sqn Ldr R. Stewart*)

In June 1940, only weeks after the evacuation of Dunkirk, the new Prime Minister, Winston Churchill, announced, 'What General Weygand called "The Battle of France" is over. I expect that the Battle of Britain is about to begin.' And begin it did, in the skies above south-east England, while Hitler prepared his plans for Operation Sealion. Everyone was warned of the danger and told to prepare for invasion, possibly in the shape of parachutists, landing and, in disguise, infiltrating communities. Goodness knows how many innocent nuns were arrested. Rumours and suspicions were rife.

In quiet Hornsea, Yorkshire, Evelyn Cardwell was alone in her farmhouse kitchen listening to the gloomy BBC news on the wireless, when she saw from the window one of her labourers running to the house. 'Parachutists are landing on our fields,' he shouted. As the telephone was not working she called back, 'Send for the police', and the man went off to summon them. On opening the door she saw to her horror a parachutist coming towards her, more than six foot tall. Although she would have preferred to run or hide, she knew her duty. Gathering the shreds of her courage, she stepped out and commanded forcefully, 'Put up your hands!' Perhaps a little surprised at this vehemence from a woman of small stature, the parachutist was nevertheless only glad to be alive, having just baled out of his burning aircraft, shot down by a Spitfire. So once he understood, he complied and meekly handed over his pistol. Evelyn beckoned him to follow her, and marched him down to the police station. In recognition of her courage, she was awarded the BEM, the first given to any woman, Service or civilian.

Scarcely a month later Peggy Prince, an ambulance driver and WVS member at New Romney on the coast of Kent, was called out to try to rescue the crew of a Whitley Bomber, which had been badly damaged in a raid on Germany and had ditched near the coast. The plane had sunk in three minutes, but luckily two of the crew had already been rescued by motor boat. Knowing that there might be other crew members surviving, Miss Prince, accompanied by a soldier, set out in a small canoe to make a search. As they could not see anyone, they returned to the shore, where the soldier left. Still not satisfied, Miss Prince decided to go out and look again. As she passed a buoy she caught sight of a small round object bobbing beside it. Turning, she found a man clinging to the float in the last stages of exhaustion. Somehow, she managed to haul him into her boat and paddle it back. He was the wireless operator of the Whitley, and undoubtedly owed his life to the determination of this young woman with her small canoe.

Many BEMs were awarded for gallant acts during air raids. Joan Westerby was an ambulance driver in the thick of the terrible bombing of Coventry on 14/15 November 1940. Scorning to take shelter, she made no less than eleven separate journeys from the emergency medical centre to different parts of the city to pick up casualties. She remained on driving duty throughout the horrific twenty-four hours, only stopping for rest when others insisted on it, and then resuming shortly afterwards.

In Bristol, Mrs Woodburn-Bamberger was in charge of a mobile WVS canteen, in which she served and drove herself. Knowing that firefighters and rescue crews – as well as the injured, dug from the rubble of their bombed-out homes – were in need of sustenance and hot drinks to fortify them, she voluntarily drove her canteen to some of the worst incidents during and after the appalling May 1941 raids, and often lent a hand in the rescue work.

In Hampshire, Audrey Phillimore was lowered into the cellar of a wrecked house, through a small opening. There she gave first-aid treatment to a trapped and severely injured woman. She knelt by the moaning woman in the dark, hearing the bombs nearby and feeling the walls tremble, knowing they were both in danger but remaining there until they were both released.

In Cheshire, when the first aid post where she was working was severely damaged by a bomb, Gertrude Hawkes saw to the orderly removal of casualties she had been treating to another part of the building and arranged transport to hospital for those needing more treatment. Afterwards she organised the removal and salvage of any useful equipment from the debris.

During another raid, in Hampshire, a bomb landed so close to a party of first-aiders that some were killed. Miss Walker, who happened to be further away, was knocked flat and slightly hurt, but was soon on her feet and taking stock of the situation. She began to try to extricate those still alive, joined shortly by two police officers who, although badly shaken by the blast, dug out the living and brought them to her for attention outside the building. A gas main suddenly burst into flames and there was a risk that the fire might spread, but doggedly the policemen continued their rescue work and Miss Walker her treatment of those injured. By their prompt actions several lives were saved, and their aid continued until the last casualties had been taken to hospital. They were then treated themselves.

The raids on the Liverpool docks in Merseyside often spread over the surrounding area. Mrs Illidge, a WVS member in Bootle, made it her task to cheer and support frightened people whose houses were demolished by the bombing, and often stayed with those who were trapped while the rescue teams fought to get them out. On one occasion, being a particularly small woman at 4 foot 10 inches, she was asked by the rescue teams if she would be willing to crawl into the cavity they had made between the collapsed roof beams of a house, to help the occupants inside, thankfully unhurt. The ruins were in a dangerous state but Mrs Illidge agreed without hesitation, and soon lifted out one survivor, a crying baby, followed by three other people. She emerged last, without injury.

Another kind woman of the WVS was dishing out tea during an air raid. Her mobile canteen was loaded with supplies of food and drink for the beleaguered dockers in Liverpool. Suddenly a bomb landed nearby blasting her and her canteen into the air, to land in the chilly waters of the harbour. Fortunately it was a comparatively soft landing, nor was she seriously injured, but she could not swim. She had already gone down twice before being rescued, pulled out by her hair. Her indignation, however, was vented on her inoffensive canteen. 'There I was bobbin' about in the icy cold water, with me own equipment biffin' me in the face.' This was her only complaint!

The BEM also went in 1942 to two women in a farm on the south coast. As the nearest point to the continent, this area suffered constant attacks, the fields being scarred with filled-in shell holes. Together with the farmer, who was given the George Medal, the two women – Kathleen Mitchell, his wife, and Grace Harrison, a tractor driver of the Women's Land Army – carried on farming under gunfire and air raids, right through the Battle of Britain and afterwards. During intense air raids, the farm was attacked and work on the land had to be temporarily stopped, but in spite of the difficulties and dangers, there was no change in the routine of milking and tending the stock. When cutting corn they often had to take cover under tractor or binder when German aircraft were machine-gunning, and one time the burning fabric of a deflated observation balloon fell over the tractor. By their sustained efforts, bravery and devotion to duty, they remained at the farm and not only saved their own crops, but also those of other evacuated farms nearby.

Out in Greece, Lauretta James and Georgina Beveridge could, in 1944, congratulate themselves on reaching a land of warm sun, friendly people and no war, when they arrived with the Liberation Army. It must have seemed like paradise after the war-torn, grimy and dangerous days of North Africa, Sicily and Italy, where these volunteer leaders of the Young Men's Christian Association (YMCA) had provided rest centres, leisure facilities and canteens for weary servicemen, very near the front lines. However, as soon as the fighting against the German and Italian occupiers had ceased, civil war broke out between the Greek factions. At first the British troops held themselves aloof, but inevitably they became involved, shot at from both sides, and all British women were ordered to go to a specific hotel where they could be guarded by British military police. During the hostilities, the centre of operations was to be at a barracks outside Athens,

Lauretta James and Georgina
Beveridge BEM, in Greece.
(*Mrs G. Merrick*)

once intended for a transit camp, where the YMCA had been. The two
women, knowing how much more the Services now needed their help and
facilities, decided to disobey the order to rendezvous at the hotel and went
instead to the camp. The commandant there was horrified to find himself
responsible for two females, but it was too late to send them back. They kept
the canteen open every day, with the help of some of the Army Catering
Corps, who had been on a course and were now trapped there.

By 1945 things had quietened somewhat and the women were taken
under armed guard to have coffee in the city of Athens and to be presented
with BEMs, 'for courage and devotion to duty under fire'. Later they were
able to open their YMCA in Athens itself.

One postwar award should be mentioned, though it called for a different
kind of courage. Helen Sharman was driving home from work in the science
department of the Mars Manufacturers one day, when she heard on her car
radio, 'Astronaut wanted. No experience necessary'. She rose to the

Helen Sharman OBE.
(*Mr P. Dodds*)

challenge and, along with 13,000 other applicants, started on the long process of selection, through an exhaustive series of physical and psychological tests, until she was one of the two chosen for cosmonaut training in Russia.

Project Juno was to be an Anglo-Soviet space mission, in which Helen was to be the first Briton and the only woman to take part. Eighteen gruelling months later, now speaking fluent Russian, with her sense of humour intact and eager for the experience, she was one of four launched into space in May 1991. She spent eight days on the Mir space station, orbiting the earth and doing commercially useful science experiments. The wonder of space and the hypnotic view of our endlessly beautiful planet would always be with her, but alongside was the sheer courage of a woman daring against the odds to face the discomfort, the work and the danger of being a cosmonaut. For her achievements she was made an Officer of the Order of the British Empire (OBE).

There is also a King's/Queen's Commendation for Bravery or Brave Conduct. The badge is a decorative one mainly intended for civilians and first appeared in about 1943. Starting as a small plastic oval with a pin on the back, it only lasted a few years. Gold in colour and with a red background it was edged with laurels; bisecting it vertically was an upward pointing sword ending with a crown, across the centre of which was a panel carrying the words 'For Brave Conduct'. There was also a duplicate issued with it, to avoid moving it from one item of clothing to another. This unusual badge was unfortunately shortly replaced by a small, silver, brooch-type, laurel leaf spray. In the Services the emblem is a single, small, bronze, oak leaf twig.

King's Commendation for Brave Conduct 1943, Civil (obverse). (*R.J. Scarlett*)

Many commendations were given during the war years, too many to detail, but a few stand out. One was that given to Sarah Ferguson, a civilian stewardess on the ship *Dunbar Castle*, which was sunk by a German submarine. She helped in the evacuation and rescue of passengers.

The next two examples are a little out of the ordinary, because the award was not collected until fifty years later – at the VE-Day commemoration in their village. Both women, great friends, were too busy at the time it was announced to collect their badges, and later forgot about them.

In July 1941 Eva Dickerson and Cicely Bates, both in the Women's Land Army, were working in a field when a Mosquito crashed as it was taking off on a training flight from RAF Great Massingham. One engine had failed and the pilot, trying to circle in order to land near the village, caught a wing on some telegraph wires and the aircraft burst into flames. The two women ran across to help the injured navigator pull the

King's Commendation for Brave Conduct, Service (shown on ribbon of War Defence Medal). (*Sqn Ldr R. Stewart*)

unconscious pilot out of the cockpit. Knowing the aircraft could explode any minute, they somehow managed to carry him behind a hedge into a ditch before everything went up in a roar. Leaving the injured man and her friend, Miss Dickerson ran to the farmhouse to summon help and then assisted in the removal of the two men. Afterwards they both returned to their work as normal. Later, after treatment in hospital, the two men returned to give them engraved bracelets, in gratitude for what they had done.

Much more recently the Queen's Commendation was announced for three of the teachers at Dunblane. Here, in March 1996, a man with a gun

Eva Dickerson, Commendation. (*Sister Laurence-Mary*)

Cecily Bates, Commendation. (*Sister Laurence-Mary*)

had brought terror and death to St Luke's Primary School. A class of five- and six-year-olds were having a physical education session in the school hall. Suddenly a deranged man brandishing a gun burst in and started shooting at the children at random. As the little ones ran in all directions screaming, the teachers tried to shield them; 45-year-old Mary Blake, a special needs teacher, and fifty-year-old Eileen Harrild, their physical education teacher, pulled several of the children nearest to them into a cupboard and kept them quiet, while the man stalked the hall outside finishing off other victims. Gwen Taylor, the class teacher, was not so fortunate. As the children ran to her, she tried to shelter them with her body, but she was hit by six bullets and died with her charges. In the murderous carnage, sixteen infants died and their teacher. Finally the gunman turned the gun on himself. The quiet little village of Dunblane is likely to take a long time to recover from the pointless massacre of its innocents.

Three further commendations should be mentioned but they are different, marking valuable service in the air. The award is an oval silver badge. Two went to women flying in the Air Transport Auxiliary (ATA), during the Second World War. They were 1/Off Cholmondley and Flt Off May. The third was given to Susan Gibbins in 1992. She was a stewardess on a British Airways aircraft flying from Birmingham to Malaga in June 1990. Half an hour after the flight had begun, the windscreen in front of the captain blew out and he was partially sucked out of the aircraft. Crew members rushed forward to hang on to him and regain control of the plane. Mrs Gibbins had to calm and reassure the eighty-one terrified passengers, who had full view of the accident as the door to the cockpit had blown in at the same time. The plane was not fitted with oxygen masks but Mrs Gibbins carefully explained the safety procedures to them and prepared them coolly and confidently for an emergency landing, her composed demeanour preventing panic. The plane touched down safely and no one was injured, much of which circumstance could be attributed to the personality and bravery of the stewardess.

As these examples have shown, even on a lesser level the ordinary public, when confronted by many kinds of danger, can react with common sense and courage.

CHAPTER ELEVEN

Two Civilian Societies – Lloyd's and the Royal Humane Society

Apart from the awards given by a monarch or the government, there are many smaller often charitable societies who recognise, and in many cases try to reimburse as well as reward, actions of bravery where they occur among the ordinary civil population. The awards, like the societies, are many and various, very often dealing with the single theme for which they first came into being. Few would be known to the public at large, and yet their recipients frequently exhibit stories of courage as great as any that have gone before. The following record some of the most noteworthy.

Lloyd's

Lloyd's of London is an international marine insurance body which has, over the years, not only concerned itself in the loss of ships, but also awarded medals for the saving of life from shipwreck. Its first silver medal was handed to the captain of the New York sailing vessel *The Glasgow* in 1839.

There have been four types of medal: one in silver and bronze for meritorious service; one, still in use, of gold, silver and bronze for saving life at sea; one in gold and silver mainly for its chairmen for services to Lloyd's; and the fourth, perhaps the best known, in silver called the Lloyd's War Medal for Bravery at Sea.

The first medal for 'Meritorious Service' to go to a woman came at the end of the last century, when there were still many sailing ships, albeit of iron, plying the seas in long-distance runs. One particular voyage by the *TF Oakes* was to prove unusually long – to such an extent that all the crew had died or were incapable and only the second mate and the captain's wife Mrs Reed had enough strength to bring her to her destination of New York (see Chapter Fifteen).

The second award to a woman for meritorious service went to Miss Ethel Langton. She was the daughter of a lighthouse keeper at St Helen's Fort, off the Isle of Wight. It was March 1926 and her parents had rowed over to the mainland for coal and food. Very rough weather from the Saturday to the

Tuesday prevented their return, and their fifteen-year-old daughter was left at the lighthouse to live on half a loaf of bread and to keep the lighthouse lamp going in a gale. When relieved she was cheerful and had kept the light in perfect order. Her medal was bronze.

The third of these medals – in silver – to a woman went to US astronaut Anna Fisher (see Chapter Fifteen).

Sailing has always been somewhat risky for cargoes, crews and passengers. In 1911, the Princess Royal and others had a narrow escape when their ship, the *Delhi*, was wrecked and they were swept overboard. They were fortunately rescued but there appear to be no awards for their rescuers.

Two medals from around the same time were given for saving life at sea. In November 1908, shortly after leaving Malta, the SS *Sardinia* caught fire, and this spread so rapidly that its master purposely ran the ship aground on some rocks. Most of its passengers were Moorish pilgrims on their way to Mecca, but because of the language problems, when told to abandon ship they refused. It was Kate Gilmour, a stewardess, who finally broke through the language barrier and persuaded the mothers and their children to leave, amid heart-rending scenes. It was only after they were safely away that she allowed herself to be put on a rescue boat. Nearly 100 perished, including 13 members of the crew.

Lloyd's War Medal for Bravery at Sea. (*R.J. Scarlett*)

Three years later a bronze medal for saving life at sea was given to a Frenchwoman, Madame Matelot, the wife of the lighthouse keeper of the Kerdonis Light at Belle-Isle-en-Mer. As could happen in these lonely, exposed places, her husband died suddenly. Before she could be relieved, she and her children kept the light burning by turning it manually all night, since they did not understand the mechanism. Their efforts undoubtedly saved several passing ships from disaster.

The Lloyd's War Medal for Bravery at Sea was established in December 1940, to be given mainly to members of the Merchant Navy and the fishing fleet, which were taking such heavy losses in the German submarine and bombing war, and on whom Britain was dependent for her essential supplies of food and armaments; 530 of these special medals were awarded, and many more would have qualified had they not died with their ships. Of the surviving number of awards five went to women, whose heroism was recognised not only by Lloyd's, but also by other national awards.

The front of the Lloyd's medal shows a seated man, symbolising courage and endurance, leaning on his right elbow. His hand holds a wreath. The fingers of his outstretched left arm curl protectively over a three-funnelled ship on the distant sea. Around the edge are the words 'Awarded by Lloyd's'. On the back is a trident surrounded by a circle of oak leaves and acorns. Across the centre is a ribbon bearing the single word 'Bravery'. The medal ribbon is blue, edged with silver, with a broad silver stripe down the centre.

There have never been many women in engineering, and rarer still are those who have been ship's engineers. Victoria Drummond was one of these, at a time when she was almost unique. A god-daughter of Queen Victoria, she was the first woman to qualify as a marine engineer in the Merchant Navy, and there was no doubt about her engineering ability. When asked about her 'feel' for engines she said, 'Oh, I just talk nicely to them. You can coax or lead engines . . . you must never drive them.' She needed all her skills in August 1940, when she was second engineer on the Panamanian registered SS *Bonita*.

The ship was 400 miles from land when a German four-engined bomber swooped down for the kill. At once the ship's alarm sounded. Miss

2nd Ship's Engineer Victoria Drummond MBE. (*Imperial War Museum*)

Drummond immediately went below and took charge in the engine room. When the first bomb landed, she was thrown heavily against the levers, nearly stunning her. She ordered the other engineers to open the fuel injectors and herself increased the main throttle bit by bit, before ordering the engine room and stokehold staff to get out. She gave them a chance at life but stayed down herself. In ten minutes she had 'talked' to the engines to such good purpose that their lumbering speed of nine knots had risen to twelve and a half, which gave the captain a chance to turn the clumsy vessel quickly and thus avoid further falling bombs, sometimes by inches and seconds. This was the only defence for an unarmed ship.

The bombing, however, had damaged the pipes, electric wires and tubes, and split a joint in the main engine stop valve, so that scalding steam hissed over Victoria's head. Anyone less skilled would have caused it to burst under the extra pressure, but she nursed it through each explosion, easing down when she judged that the bombs were about to fall, holding onto a stanchion as they burst, and then opening up the steam again. The platform on which she stood was littered with bullets and glass, which rained down from the skylight above her as the German plane machine-gunned the ship, but still it sailed on. She stood with one hand stretched above her head, holding down the throttle control as if trying to urge another pound of steam through the straining pipes, a long black streak of fuel oil trickling down her face. Three times the ship swung to avoid the bombs, and finally after 35 minutes the plane flew away, out of bombs and ammunition. When Miss Drummond was able to ease the speed, the ship was in a bad way and leaking water, but it was still afloat, due to the skill and disregard of danger of her second engineer and her captain. In 1941, in addition to the Lloyd's War Medal for Bravery at Sea, Victoria Drummond was given the MBE at Buckingham Palace.

The second of these Lloyd's medals went to Elizabeth Plumb in November 1940. She was a stewardess for the first-class passengers on the MV *Rangitane*, sailing from Auckland to Britain via the Panama Canal. The ship was attacked by three German vessels, who poured shells into her so that she stood no chance of escaping. Once the captain gave the order to abandon ship, it was then the job of the crew to see the passengers safely onto the lifeboats. Several of the crew were noted for acting very bravely in rescuing trapped passengers, Mrs Plumb being among them, except that she had also been badly wounded by shell splinters. Ignoring her own pain, and calmly and quietly exuding an air of great confidence, she escorted her share of passengers into the boats, and showed great concern and kindness for their well-being before she too climbed into one, leaving the sinking ship behind.

It was not long before they were picked up by the enemy vessels, whose German doctors immediately gave treatment to those who had been injured, attended by Miss Plumb, who did all that she could to help. It was only after they had all been settled that she nearly collapsed, and the doctors became aware that the quiet, comforting stewardess was herself badly wounded. For her courage and self-sacrifice she was also given the BEM for gallantry.

Only a few months later, in March 1941, the SS *Britannia*, sailing from Britain to South Africa and India, was sunk 720 miles from Freetown by another German vessel, the *Thor*. Despite creating a smokescreen to escape, the one-gun *Britannia* was outgunned by the *Thor* with three, and her entire gun emplacement and crew were destroyed in the first attack, leaving her helpless. She tried to outdistance her attacker but her pursuer was faster. She transmitted two radio messages before her aerial was brought down, and shell after shell landed on her, creating havoc. Finally, with the ship sinking, the captain signalled the German vessel that he was abandoning ship, but the captain of the *Thor* did not stop his attack, even when he saw the crew and passengers taking to the lifeboats. He only ceased when the ship went down. He then left the boats drifting in the middle of the Atlantic, without picking up the survivors.

Dr Adeline Miller had been ship's doctor and surgeon aboard the *Britannia*. In the sickbay, she tended to the wounded and dying, even when she knew the ship was sinking. Her task continued as she transferred the injured aboard the lifeboats and joined them there. Her care and devotion through the most frightening of situations undoubtedly saved many lives. Two of the lifeboats with the doctor were later picked up by a Spanish ship; the third – after twenty-three days, during which occupants died off one after another – ultimately made land on its own with only twenty-three survivors. Of nearly 500 people aboard the *Britannia*, over half died or were killed and more would probably have perished but for Dr Miller's attention. With the Lloyd's medal, she also received the MBE.

Three months later, in June 1941, the SS *St Patrick* was slipping along the Channel when she was intercepted by a German plane whose bombs scored a direct hit, setting the ship on fire and eventually sinking her. Before the ship went down the wireless operator managed to send a message giving their position, and received a reply. Now it was the task of any surviving crew to get the passengers onto those lifeboats which were left.

Elizabeth Owen was stewardess of the poorer passengers. Making her way by touch to the lower decks where the women's berths were positioned – the lights had failed when the bomb struck – she told those she met to hurry up on deck. At length she reached a door which had jammed closed, behind which she could hear the cries of several women. Knowing they would die in the sinking ship if they were not quickly released, her first attempts to open the door failed, and it was only after she had applied all her strength that she finally forced it open and released five people. Taking the first woman by the arm, Elizabeth told the others to hold on to one another and follow her. Feeling her way in the darkness, she eventually got them up on deck, only to find that there were only five lifebelts left. With no thought of herself, she gave up her own and placed all the women in a lifeboat. About to take place on the boat she suddenly recalled another girl who should have been with them, and who would probably still be on the lower deck. In spite of the protests of the passengers and crew, she determined to try to rescue her too.

Again she made the dark, dangerous journey down to the lower deck, calling as she went. By good luck she located the girl, nearly terrified out of her wits, and brought her up on deck, only to find that the last lifeboats – and all the lifebelts – had gone. Not only that, but the ship was already low in the water and splitting in two. With no time to waste, or they might be sucked down by the undertow when the ship sank, she jumped overboard, holding firmly to the girl, and then swam as far as possible from the vessel. Treading water for two hours, Miss Owen and the girl kept afloat, and during this ordeal she also lent her support to a nurse in the water nearby, while she heartened them and those around with the thought that they would soon be rescued. As indeed they were, by two ships, but Miss Owen and her two passengers were the last to be picked up.

There was, however, a heavy death toll – only sixty people survived – and there would have been more fatalities but for Miss Owen's courageous actions. In recognition of this she received not only the Lloyd's medal but also the George Medal, for saving so many lives.

The *Avila Star* left Buenos Aires early in July 1942, bound for Britain, with nearly 200 passengers on board, many of them volunteers to join the British Services. About 300 miles from the Azores, a German submarine torpedoed the ship. Six lifeboats were launched and by torchlight the crew filled them with passengers, but one boat upended during the launch and another capsized when a second torpedo struck the ship. All its passengers fell into the sea, but about twelve managed to scramble back into the waterlogged boat. Among them were four badly injured men and Maria Ferguson. She was eighteen and wanted to join the WRNS when she reached Britain. Having swallowed a fair bit of oil, she felt dizzy and ill. Nevertheless she did her best to nurse the sick men and keep up their morale in their lifeboat, now almost continuously awash. When the morning revealed their situation, she swam over to two of the other boats and had the injured men transferred. The chief officer ordered the boats to keep together and in convoy they sailed towards the coast of Portugal, the nearest land. Water was rationed and the people in the boats allocated in more even numbers. At this point, Miss Ferguson moved to another boat to be with a friend. This was bad luck, since the boat became separated from the others and it was nearly three weeks before they were found.

To Maria Ferguson, these must have been the worst days of her life, as she watched her companions slowly dying from exposure, wounds, delirium, sickness, starvation and lack of water. Tides and winds blew them off course, storms drenched them and in daylight a merciless sun beat down on them. They all had to bale out the sea water constantly to keep afloat. During this ordeal, Miss Ferguson tended the sick, cheered the depressed, and by her inspiring example and fortitude tried to maintain their hopes and spirits.

Twenty days later they sighted a ship and sent up flares. After previous disappointments they were not too hopeful, but this time the ship sighted them and picked the survivors up. It was a Portuguese destroyer, the *Pedro*

Nunes. On board they were given the best of medical attention, but despite this three more passengers died before they reached harbour. Out of a lifeboat of thirty-nine souls, twenty-five had survived, and all praised the courage and magnificent example of this young girl. After reaching Britain she spent six months in convalescence, before following her original intention and joining the WRNS – despite her experience of the sea. Later she received the BEM as well as the Lloyd's medal, being the fifth and last of the five brave women to receive it.

The Royal Humane Society

Its awards started in 1774 for those drowning at sea. The royal title came from King George III in 1787. Gradually it expanded its scope to that of rewarding any bravery in the saving of human life.

The medal – in gold, silver and bronze – shows a cherub blowing on a torch, representing the symbol of life. Around the edge are the Latin words '*Lateat Scintillula Forsan*', meaning 'Peradventure, a little spark may yet lie hid'. Underneath the cherub are the words, '*Soc Lond in Resuscitat Intermortuorum Instit MDCCLXXIV*', which stands for the 'Society Established in London for the Recovery of Persons in a State of Suspended Animation 1774'. There are two kinds of reverse to the medals. One is for the successful saving of life by the rescuer. Around the outside edge of this is '*Hoc Pretium Cive Servato Tulit*', meaning 'He has obtained this reward for saving the life of a citizen'. Inside the inscription is an oak wreath encircling the words '*Vit Ob Serv D.D. Soc. Reg Hum*' which stands for 'The Royal Humane Society Presented this Gift for Saving Life'. There is a different kind of reverse for the rescuer whose efforts were unsuccessful. Inside the oak wreath are simply the words '*Vit Peric. Expos. D.D. Soc. Reg Hum.*' meaning 'The Royal Humane Society Presented this Gift . . . His Life Having Been Exposed to

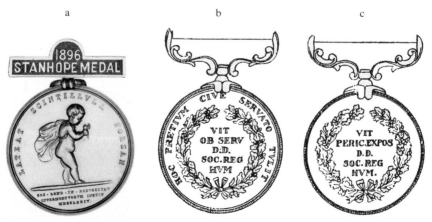

Medal of the Royal Humane Society: a: obverse of both types; b: reverse for a surviving rescuer; c: reverse for a rescuer who died in the attempt. (a: *R.J. Scarlett*; b and c: *Royal Humane Society*)

Danger.' Any acquainted with Latin will have realised that many of the words are abbreviated from their fuller form to squeeze more onto the coin. This gave no trouble to people of the eighteenth century, as Latin was the normal usage for more formal documents and memorials.

Grace Darling and her father were two famous recipients of the Royal Humane Society Gold Medal. In September 1838, in a terrible tempest, the luxury steamship SS *Forfarshire* was wrecked on the rocks near the Longstone Lighthouse in the Farne Islands. Believing that the mainland lifeboat would not be able to be launched in such a storm, 23-year-old Grace and her father rowed their small boat a mile through the heaving seas from their lighthouse, and by a combination of daring, strength and skill managed to take off five survivors. The father then returned with two survivors to rescue the remaining four. Sadly, just four years later, Grace died of tuberculosis.

In 1873, the Stanhope Gold Medal was introduced, in memory of Captain Stanhope of the Royal Navy, who several times risked his life to save others. This medal was to be given to the person showing the greatest gallantry during the year. In 1962, similar humane societies in Canada, New Zealand, Australasia and New South Wales, as well as the Liverpool Shipwreck and Humane Society in Britain, could nominate their best candidates for the Stanhope Gold Medal.

The Stanhope is of gold, its ribbon blue with two narrow yellow stripes inside its black edges. The Society's silver medal ribbon in blue has a yellow stripe in the middle and white edges, while the bronze has a plain blue ribbon.

In Britain, records only show eight women who have been awarded the two higher medals, and of those only three have had the Stanhope Gold. The standard set is very high.

The warm climate and the blue-green seas of Cornwall can often tempt holidaymakers out into waters that frequently turn treacherous. Iris Ryle twice won a medal for rescuing foolhardy swimmers in Constantine Bay. In 1937, assisted by a friend, she swam across the current and the incoming tide, taking a buoy with her, to a husband and wife who had been surf bathing. Three others had also got into difficulties while trying to rescue them. Swimming against the rising current, Iris reached the rock from which she had started, and found that two men had hung onto her line. Her aunt then arrived with her personal lifebelt with a line attached, and the two women set off to rescue the others. The line was too short, but helpers swam out and fastened on an extension. Meanwhile Iris reached the two others, while her friend, also exhausted, hung on. Watchers now helped her by hauling in the line as she made for the shore. Her aunt had turned back as she could not get through the breakers. The rescue of all the persons involved took an hour and Iris Ryle received a Silver Medal for her courage.

Her second rescue was in July 1957. She was now thirty-seven and by marriage had become Princess Wittgenstein. A man out of his depth developed cramp and shouted for help. Two men jumped in and held him up, but were unable to make headway against the current and were being swept out to sea. At this a third man swam out after them but, tiring before he reached them, was himself in danger of drowning. It was at this point that the princess ran into the sea, calling for a lifebelt. Before she had gone far she realised that the rope attached to it was too short, but nevertheless made her way to the four men, three of whom caught onto the short rope streaming behind her. The fourth man managed to swim inshore to grasp a second rope which, having been joined to that on the lifebelt of the princess, enabled them to be hauled safely ashore. This rescue won her a Bronze Medal, but it was a unique achievement to have twice run great risks, to save nine lives.

Grenada, one of the Windward Isles in the West Indies – then a British territory – in October 1945 had a huge cloudburst, causing the rapid rise of a river. When the river burst its banks, the flood swept away twelve houses and drowned twelve people. Petronella Ferguson, in the last stages of pregnancy, was inside one of the houses being carried seaward by the flood, together with her husband and son, who were both drowned. In the terrifying darkness, she heard a cry for help nearby. Abandoning the house, she entered the racing water and managed to reach a young girl of thirteen, clinging to a log and unable to swim. Mrs Ferguson tried to push the log towards what she thought to be the shore, but which a flash of lightning revealed to be the open sea. She fought to turn them around, and after two hours of swimming at last reached land, now close to collapse. Her bravery, especially considering her condition, was rewarded by the Stanhope Gold Medal.

An annual excursion for transport drivers at Cushendall Bay in Northern Ireland nearly ended in tragedy for four of its members in August 1947. They were out in a small boat when one, fancying a swim, dived in and accidentally capsized the boat, containing three non-swimmers. Margaret Ditty, in a caravan on the shore, heard their cries and swam out, followed by two others. Between them they brought in one of the non-swimmers. She then returned with another girl, only to find that a second boat, which had gone to the rescue, had itself overturned with one of the occupants trapped beneath it, his foot jammed in the bottom boards. Finding an unconscious man floating face downwards, the two women supported him until another boat arrived and pulled him on board. Mrs Ditty then dived under the upturned boat and, managing to release the man's foot, helped him to swim to the rescue boat. The first two rescuers, meanwhile, had swum out with an air dinghy to support the remaining two non-swimmers, and all were then rowed or towed ashore by the rescue boat. For her efforts in deep water against a strong ebb tide, Margaret Ditty received a Silver Medal and the other three rescuers a Bronze.

There was a longer interval before the next medal – a Silver – in 1980. The incident for which it was awarded took place on the M2 motorway at Bradgar, Kent. Owing to roadworks, contraflow traffic was in operation. A lorry fully loaded with coal shale had crashed into an overhead bridge pillar, in which it had become partly embedded. Two cars had then piled into it, killing both drivers. The lorry driver was alive, but trapped in his cab and screaming with pain and panic. Elizabeth Bishop, a first year student nurse, was an early arrival on the scene. Without considering her own safety, she climbed into the crushed lorry cab, which was a mess of oil, blood and shale. Here she did her best to give first aid and reassure the injured man with support, encouragement and sympathy. When the rescue crews arrived, sections of the lorry had to be pulled apart to extricate the driver, resulting in dangerous falls of shale and parts, but Elizabeth accepted the risks and remained with the man for over two hours until he was freed. Even afterwards, though mentally and physically exhausted, she wanted to stay with him, until finally persuaded to leave. He subsequently lost both legs, but her intervention undoubtedly saved his life.

Under very different circumstances another woman won a Silver Medal. In December 1984, two British nurses were on holiday visiting the pre-Inca Temples of the Sun and Moon at Moche, Peru. As they were bargaining with a small boy selling pottery, they were suddenly surrounded by bandits. The men attacked the boy, who wriggled free, and then grabbed the nurses, demanding money. The women refused and someone fired a shot, seeming to kill one of the nurses, at which the assailants ran off. Sarah Belshaw, at twenty-two the younger of the two, saw that the bullet had entered her friend's neck on the right and was now lodged on the left side. She was bleeding, choking and turning blue. Miss Belshaw immediately began mouth-to-mouth resuscitation and looked round desperately for help. But there was no one in this isolated area. She was also afraid that the bandits might still be near and strike again. For over an hour she protected her friend, making her comfortable and giving her resuscitation, in between dashing out from the rocks to look for assistance.

Eventually Sarah caught the attention of a villager who was passing with his horse and cart, and they moved her friend onto it, who still needed resuscitation on the long journey across the desert. At a village they transferred to a minibus, which took them first to a hospital in Trujillo, then on to Lima and finally by air to Miami, where her friend went into a deep coma. The friend was finally taken to hospital in Britain. Miss Belshaw, whose bravery and devotion were of quite an exceptional order, returned to her work.

Another Silver Medal came as a result of a bad road accident at Penmorfa, North Wales, in November 1982, in wet weather and heavy fog. Margaret Pritchard, aged nineteen, was a taxi driver following a lorry up a hill, the two vehicles with their lights on because of the conditions. They had both pulled out to pass a parked car when there was a loud crash, and the lorry spun round, its rear end over the opposite hedge and its front towards the taxi. At that very moment, a large articulated petrol tanker appeared out of the fog, coming downhill towards them. Trying to squeeze between the tanker and the lorry to avoid being caught between the two, Miss Pritchard's taxi hit the back corner of the tanker as she passed it. Leaving her vehicle at the side of the road, she returned to see the lorry on fire. Running to the driver, she asked for a fire extinguisher, but he was stunned, trapped by the legs and screaming with pain.

A motorist arriving found a small fire extinguisher, which she used to put out the fire. As there was a strong smell of petrol coming from the now stationary tanker, the motorist managed to find a larger fire extinguisher and stayed with the tanker, in case a further fire broke out. Meanwhile, with great presence of mind, Miss Pritchard found and turned off the master switch in the tanker, which had a full load of 6,000 gallons of petrol and had already leaked about 500 gallons over the road. Returning, she removed the battery from the lorry.

A further car arrived and the driver joined Miss Pritchard as they turned their attention to the tanker driver. He was unconscious, bleeding from head wounds and gurgling, so they sat him up and opened his mouth, clearing it of blood and wiping more away from his head and generally making him as comfortable as possible. Shortly afterwards the police, ambulances and rescue crews arrived and the tanker driver was taken to hospital. The lorry driver, however, was trapped, and since they could not use cutting equipment, for fear of fire, the vehicle had to be broken into manually. It took a long time, but at length he was extricated and taken to hospital.

The next award, recommended by the Liverpool Shipwreck and Humane Society, went on to win the coveted Stanhope Gold Medal. The incident took place in Shadsworth, Blackburn, at the beginning of December 1989. Elaine Walsh and her husband, with her six-year-old son and babe in arms, were returning home when they saw flames inside the front window of a neighbour's house. Leaving his wife and children, Mr Walsh ran off to call the fire brigade. Mrs Walsh, however, thought she could hear moans from inside the house and, knowing that an old man lived there, she suspected him to be trapped inside. Giving her son the baby to look after, and telling him to keep away from the garden, she ran to the neighbour's house. Pushing open the door, she was met by a cloud of thick black smoke, but she still heard moaning. Feeling her way to the living room door, she pushed it open. Terrific heat and a dense wall of smoke almost drove her back, and she saw flames licking up two walls of the room. Guided by her neighbour's moans, she fought her way to his side, finding him on his knees by the settee to which he had crawled but could go no further. His hair was scorched, his trousers had melted onto his legs, and he was choking in the smoke and barely conscious. Despite the dead weight of this heavy man, Mrs Walsh caught hold of him and dragged him out to the hall and then into the garden. It had taken only two minutes at most.

Mr Walsh now returned and, as the old man started coming around in the fresh air, he muttered about his 22-year-old son being still in the house. Mr Walsh ran to the front door to search, but the fire had taken hold and he was driven back by the intense heat and smoke. When the fire brigade arrived they managed to rescue the son from a verandah at the back of the house and both men were taken to hospital. The son was soon released, but his father had to remain there for extensive skin grafts.

The 1991 Stanhope Gold Medal was given to WPC Lesley Moore of the Metropolitan Police, whose account of rescuing a workman in London who had fallen from scaffolding at a hotel, was told in Chapter Nine.

The above stories only concern the highest awards of the Royal Humane Society in Britain, but there were many others, with lesser medals, testimonials, commendations and in memoria, as all rescues, whether successful or not, put rescuers in great danger.

Such awards from Lloyd's or the Royal Humane Society only serve to show that in an emergency many people will try to help, even at their own cost, and these resources of courage are inside most of us, unrecognised until tested.

CHAPTER TWELVE

Other Civilian Societies' Awards and Some Forgotten Women

The Liverpool Shipwreck and Humane Society

a

Liverpool Shipwreck and Humane Society: a: reverse of all the medals; (opposite) b: Marine Medal (obverse); c: Fire Medal (obverse); d: General Medal (obverse). (*Liverpool Shipwreck and Humane Society*)

The Liverpool Shipwreck and Humane Society has existed since June 1839. The awards for saving human life are mainly reserved for the Merseyside area and the majority are for rescues from drowning or fire. Although most awards are won by men, a number have been given to women. The degree of danger faced by the rescuer and the bravery shown are the factors that determine the level of any award. These range from a Gold Medal (to date, none have been given to women), a Silver and a Bronze Medal, with a parchment, certificate and commendation at the lower levels, and there are three groups for the awards: marine, fire and general.

As has already been seen, this Society can also recommend its higher awards for consideration by the national and international Royal Humane Society in respect of the Stanhope Gold Medal, and its 1989 award to Mrs Elaine Walsh went on to gain the Stanhope.

The reverses of the Liverpool Shipwreck and Humane Society's three medals are the same. A coin shape showing a cormorant with beak upraised holding a laurel twig, and wings ready for flight, was inspired by the Liverpool city arms. It is encircled by an oak wreath and around this are the words 'Liverpool Shipwreck and Human Society 1839'.

The main side of the marine medal (see overleaf) shows a sailor kneeling on a fragment of a wreck rescuing a drowning infant from its mother. Above are the words 'Lord Save Us. We Perish'. The ribbon is a plain dark blue.

The obverse of the fire medal shows a fireman in the act of rescuing children from the staircase of a burning house. Below are the words 'For Bravery in Saving Life'. This ribbon is plain, the orange-red of fire.

The front of the coin-shaped general medal shows a Maltese cross, in the centre of which is a medallion of a crown surrounded by a laurel wreath. Outside, around the edge, are the words 'For Bravery in Saving Human Life, 1894'. The ribbon is composed of three red and two white stripes.

Some flavour of the awards given by the Society to women over the years can be judged from the following examples.

The SS *Arabic* was torpedoed without warning by a German submarine in August 1915. Dorothy Kelk, who was a passenger on the steamer, found a seat in a lifeboat that was about to be lowered from the sinking ship. A stewardess was one of the people to be left behind, since there was not enough room for all but, because she could not swim, Miss Kelk bravely gave up her place to the woman. Then, since the ship was going down rapidly, she dived into the water and swam away. Fortunately, she was shortly picked up by another boat. For her action in being willing to risk her own life for another, she was awarded the Silver Marine Medal.

The sea at Blackpool claims victims every year. For this reason in the summer, beach patrol officers are always on hand. Tracey Jones, aged twenty, was one. At the beginning of June 1991, a sixteen-year-old girl got into difficulties while swimming. The sea was rough and a strong gale-force wind was rising. Miss Jones reached the girl near the stanchions of the South Pier, and while making her rescue ran the danger of being thrown against the pillars by the strong sea. Despite this risk she single-handedly managed to bring the girl to safety, for which she was awarded the Bronze Marine Medal.

Silver Medals for rescues from fire have also been given to a number of women over the

b

c

d

century. One was a little out of the ordinary. Elizabeth Kelly was a frail, elderly widow of sixty, just returned from three months in hospital and still very weak. On a night in February 1948 she heard her neighbour screaming loudly, and realised that something was seriously wrong. Still in her nightdress she hurried onto the landing outside her flat. There she saw her neighbour, a woman of eighty-seven, enveloped in flames. Mrs Kelly threw her down onto the floor and tried to beat out the flames with her bare hands, risking setting her own clothes on fire and burning her hands and feet. When others arrived, the flames were all but out, and both women were taken to hospital. Sadly her neighbour was too shocked and burned to survive, but after another long stay in hospital, Mrs Kelly recovered.

Actions of great bravery that cannot be classified under fire or marine rescues come under the general heading. Olivia McNeil, an airwoman who rescued a child who had fallen between the electrified rails at Birkenhead Central Railway Station in 1942, received a Silver Medal. A Bronze was given for the rescue by WPC Denise Morgan of a woman making a suicide bid from Liverpool Pier Head in 1978. These illustrate the types of danger that can suddenly confront anyone. Mary Davidson, in April 1930, was quietly walking along a street in Liverpool when a large lorry came careering towards her without a driver at the wheel. Two children were playing, oblivious to the danger, in the runaway's path. Without considering her risk – only that of the children – she ran forward and caught hold of one child, throwing her aside. She leapt in to save the other, but unfortunately the lorry caught and ran over her so that she died from her injuries. Her husband received the Silver In Memoriam Medal on her behalf.

The Society for the Protection of Life from Fire

Society for the Protection of Life from Fire: a: obverse; b: reverse. (*Society for the Protection of Life from Fire*)

Fire was probably the cause of the gradual development of early man in his primeval forest environment, but it has never been satisfactorily controlled in its life-giving/life-threatening power. Mankind is fascinated by it, uses it and fears it, all at the same time.

While the Liverpool Shipwreck and Humane Society recognises its lethal potential among other dangers to rescuers in its own area, the sole interest of the Society for the Protection of Life from Fire, though only a small body, is to acknowledge, encourage and reward people saving others in small conflagrations throughout the British Isles.

The Silver Medal of the Society has changed slightly over the years. It is coin-shaped, showing on the reverse a man in the heroic mould, carrying a girl, her long hair flowing over his shoulder. On the right by his feet is a smouldering pile of the remains of a brick wall and a roof covered by flames. Around the edge are the words 'Actions are Ours. Results are God's'. The front of the medal shows the name, date and action of the recipient below a crown encircled by a laurel wreath. Around the perimeter are the words 'Royal Society for the Preservation of Life from Fire' and the date of the foundation of the Society, '1845'. The ribbon is bright orange-red.

The Society's records are full of small sums of money, certificates and medals given to rescuers, and they make interesting reading. Details of a few rescues are given below.

Annie Pearson was a mantle saleswoman of a large store in Huddersfield. At about 10 o'clock at night in November 1896, a serious fire broke out in the store. It was caused by one of the apprentices who, in drawing down the blinds in one of the big downstairs show windows, accidentally moved a group of lighted gas burners too close to a quantity of muslin hanging there. Soon the place became a blazing inferno which spread rapidly. Miss Pearson, covering up goods before leaving for the night and hearing noise downstairs, ran down into the street and was concerned to see that most of the male and female assistants were still in various departments upstairs, evidently unaware of the fire below. She dashed bravely into the burning building and fought her way upstairs through the gathering smoke and fire. Warning everyone she saw on the first floor, she continued up to the other floors, possibly sacrificing her own escape. Her actions resulted in the safe exit of all save the chief millinery saleswoman, whom she could not reach. Miss Pearson was the last to leave the burning building alive. For her bravery she received a Silver Medal.

In Sligo during May 1916, two men and two women – Mary and Ursie Downs – working with their father, a grocer, helped to save a mother and her two teenage children from her burning home. That same year fire engineer May Milner and a superintendent in Brighton each received Silver Medals for saving a man and his household from a fire, caused by a fallen lamp.

In 1926, Betty Rattey, a schoolgirl from Thornton Heath, saved her young brother and sister – aged four and six – from a fire caused by a lighted candle falling on clothes. She was given a silver watch – much prized in those days. And in 1935 Nurse Emmeline Buckingham of Exmouth, together with a fireman, rescued her two baby charges from a fire; she too was presented with a silver watch.

Lorraine Duncan of Dundee received a Silver Medal in 1985 for her efforts to save a family from a fierce house fire. One night she was awakened by an explosion in a nearby house. From her window she could see flames pouring from the place so, throwing on a dressing gown, she ran into the back garden of the house. There she met the wife, who said her husband, son and grandchild were still inside. Without hesitating, Mrs Duncan ran into the smoke-filled hall and up the stairs. The four-year-old grandchild was crying in one room, so she opened the door, seized him and took him out into the fresh air. She then attempted to go upstairs again, but was driven back by the heat and dense smoke. But she did not give up: there were still two adults in the house. Running to the front she saw the husband at an upstairs bedroom window, calling for help. Hunting round, she found a ladder with an extension and, placing it against the wall, found it long enough to reach the man, who was able to scramble down it to safety. By now the house was alight from top to bottom, and there was no sign of the son. When the fire brigade arrived, she could do no more. Sadly the son died in the fire, but Mrs Duncan had saved two people.

The Royal Life-saving Society

Mountbatten Medal of Royal Life-saving Society (obverse). (*RLSS*)

Water is another of the essentials for life, but it can also bring about its destruction, particularly at sea. Nevertheless, once a fire has taken hold and spread, technical equipment and expert help are the only ways of dealing with it, whereas people do have it in their own power to save themselves and others from drowning in water by learning to swim, and many have gone a step further in learning the skills of life-saving and resuscitation techniques.

The Royal Life-saving Society began as the Swimmers' Life-saving Society in 1891, to try to prevent some of the 2,000 or so annual drownings in Britain. It changed to its present name in 1904. During this period many countries all over the world were becoming aware of the need of such societies, and there are now many self-governing branches of this Society in the Commonwealth. St John Ambulance Brigade is also a great supporter of its work. Cups, diplomas and medals are issued for several degrees of expertise. In 1951, Earl Mountbatten of Burma, Grand President of the British Society, introduced a Silver Medal named after him, to be awarded each year for a rescue judged to be the bravest of the year, by any member from Britain and the Commonwealth.

The front of the medal shows the arms of the Mountbatten family. On the back is wording running in a circle around the edge. The outer circle reads 'The Mountbatten Medal, The Earl Mountbatten of Burma'. The top half of the inner circle reads 'The Royal Life-saving Society'. Preceded above by the words 'Presented by', the bottom part of the inner circle reads 'The President RLSS.' This Silver Medal is large, presented in a case and has no ribbon.

The first medal in 1951 went to a Canadian man. The second in 1952 went to Sally Jupp of Enfield, Britain, a schoolgirl of fifteen. As she stood on top of a cliff one day, she saw that an older woman had gone to help a small child swimming out of her depth and, before reaching the child, had herself got into serious difficulty, due to the strong current. Sally immediately raced down the cliff path and, throwing aside her shoes and blouse, dived into the sea. She reached the woman only to find she was unconscious, but managed to drag her ashore and applied artificial respiration. While doing so, she called for blankets to keep the woman warm and sent someone for an ambulance. Sally accompanied her to the hospital where the woman in due course recovered.

The next year another woman won the medal. Sybil Higgins of Culleenamore, Ireland, heard someone shouting that two children were

Sally Jupp, Mountbatten Medal. (*Royal Life-saving Society*)

Sybil Higgins, Mountbatten Medal. (*Royal Life-saving Society*)

drowning. They had evidently taken a derelict boat that had floated out to sea and, when they had tried to turn, it had capsized, throwing them into the water some 300 yards from the shore. The five-year-old girl sank beneath the waves; the boy was waving frantically near the upturned boat. Mrs Higgins clambered down the bank, undressing as she went, and swam towards them, noticing that a fully clothed man was also swimming slowly out to the boy, but was reaching the point of exhaustion. She shouted to him to grab the boat, but when she reached it found that the boy, who could not swim, was holding onto the now unconscious man. She grasped him as he lost his grip and placed the child – lashing out at her in terror – onto her chest. Holding the man by his collar she pulled both of them with her as she swam on her back to the shore. By this time both man and boy had been in the water for about half an hour.

About 50 yards from the shore two other people went to help them, one in a rowing boat, by which he towed them back. Artificial respiration was then carried out, but when a doctor arrived he pronounced the man dead. The boy was taken to Sligo Hospital and, after treatment, recovered. The little girl was drowned.

In 1962, Hilary Westerman of Leeds rescued a woman from a park lake, formerly a quarry, where bathing had been forbidden. The woman was unconscious, floating face downwards in the water, her face blue. Miss Westerman, despite being frightened, brought the woman to the bank, where a man helped to pull them out, and she then applied artificial respiration until relieved by the park keeper.

In 1970, Patricia Pope of Wakefield made another rescue, followed by Pauline MacLean of Hamilton, Scotland, in 1977. This rescue took place in Guernsey, one of the Channel Islands, where her elderly mother and father had taken out a dinghy, which was being swept out to sea. As her husband was a non-swimmer, the wife slipped into the water to try to push the dinghy back towards the shore, but she suffered an asthmatic attack. Unable to get her back into the dinghy, Pauline's father tried to catch the attention of those ashore. A few people tried to swim out but had to return, as there was now a strong current and high waves. But luckily the couple's daughter had seen their plight and swam about a mile through heavy-going seas to reach the dinghy. When she reached her, her mother was unconscious, so Pauline supported her until a surf-sailor managed to get her onto his craft and took her ashore. Pauline then swam back through the waves pulling the dinghy containing her father. Her courage and skill had thus saved both her parents.

A Richmond schoolgirl of fifteen was awarded the 1985 Mountbatten Medal. She was Holly Phillips who, with a friend, was taking part in a regatta at Swanage Bay, Dorset. Just off a stone quay, the 10-foot dinghy they were in capsized, and her friend tried to swim after it. He became exhausted after a short distance, since there was a very strong outgoing tide and he was wearing overalls and heavy boots. Seeing his difficulties, Holly swam to his assistance and found him by now semi-conscious and struggling feebly to grasp the mooring line of the boat. She tried without success to remove his heavy boots, and instead towed him back to shore, reassuring him as she went. Halfway there he lost consciousness, but fortunately did not stop breathing. A boat arrived, but it proved impossible to lift the boy's heavy and inert body aboard, so Holly continued to drag him through the water, checking at regular intervals that he was breathing. At the beach two men helped her until the ambulance arrived and two days later her friend made a full recovery.

Special Service Cross

The British Red Cross Society instituted a Special Service Cross in June 1917, mainly as an award to those from abroad who had given special help to the Society in Britain. In 1919, this was widened to include British members and those holding the Military and Albert Medals. In 1941, it was decided to give it only to members who showed 'Special acts of distinction or gallantry'.

Numbers of these awards were given over the years, mainly to civilian housewives who were part-time members of the BRCS. These encompassed the Second World War, when many members of the BRCS were also honoured with national awards.

Special Service Cross (obverse). (*British Red Cross Society Museum and Archives*)

The list of Special Service Cross awards is a long one; a small selection gives some idea of the variety of actions that they covered. In 1941, Mrs Bird of the Bedford branch of the BRCS received it for saving the life of a fellow member who was drowning. High tides and particularly heavy rainfall caused widespread flooding in 1953. At different times and places three members of the Norfolk branch rescued people from the floods and gave first-aid treatment. They were Miss Barclay, Miss Bloomfield and Miss Knights. Also in 1953, Mrs Hazeldean of the Sussex branch won her award for averting injury to a number of schoolchildren. In 1960, Mrs Brittain of Montgomeryshire made a courageous attempt to save the lives of two men who had been electrocuted and, in 1967, the Special Service Cross went to Mrs Hughes of Somerset for rescuing a rider from a fallen horse, at great personal risk. Miss Audrey Morrell of the County of London branch assisted a lady trapped beneath an underground train in 1971 and a rescue by Mrs Anne James of Sussex took place in Majorca in 1973, when she gave artificial respiration to an unconscious man, after a swimming pool accident. From the Northern Ireland branch, Mrs Campbell and Miss Steele assisted during an accident at a motor racing event in 1979 and, in 1988, Mrs Linda Wooten helped to save the life of a victim of a shooting accident, rendering first aid during and after the episode. The plane crash on the Scottish village of Lockerbie killed many people in 1988. Miss Eva Cox helped motorists trapped in a petrol station set on fire as a result of it.

The Carnegie Hero Fund Trust

Carnegie Medal (obverse). (*Carnegie Hero Fund Commission*)

Andrew Carnegie established the Fund in 1904. He was born in Scotland, emigrated with his family to the United States of America, worked his way up to becoming owner of a steel company, and retired as a multimillionaire. The award that he established was at first intended to cover America and Canada, but in 1919 it was extended to Great Britain. Not only did it recognise with a medal brave actions in saving life at the risk of the rescuer's own life, 'to an extraordinary degree' – even if the life was lost in the attempt – but it also aimed to compensate the rescuer and, if injured or dead, the livelihood of the family. It is, therefore, chiefly a civilian award, for men or women. The Deed of Trust opens with the ringing words 'Gentlemen: We live in a Heroic Age'.

The front of the medal shows a large embossed profile of Andrew Carnegie. Around the top edge run the words 'Carnegie Hero Fund' and around the bottom edge 'Established April 15th 1904'. On the back, behind the large panel upon which are inscribed the rescuer's name and deed, are in low relief the map outlines of the United States and Canada, and in higher relief the seals of the United States below, with Canada and Newfoundland above. Around the inscription panel itself are sprigs of ivy for friendship, oak for strength and thistle for persistency above, with sprigs of laurel for glory underneath. The edge of the medal carries the words of St John's Gospel, 'Greater love hath no man than this, that a man lay down his life for his friends.' Once gold, all medals since 1980 are made of bronze.

Among the beneficiaries of the Carnegie Hero Fund Trust awards have been numerous women. The heroic rescues they attempted cover many aspects, such as drowning, fire, traffic accidents, animals, electrocution, deranged people and others. The following accounts illustrate a few.

Sarah Aldridge, a housekeeper in Aberdeen, was seriously injured in 1939 when attempting to rescue two small boys trapped by a fall of steel girders. Rosemary Woolhouse of the ATS in Elgin in 1940 rescued a child from drowning in the River Lossie. Florence Grant of Blyth, Northumberland, lost her life in 1942 while preventing injury to a child who had fallen from the back of a lorry. Margaret Henderson of North Yell, Shetland, died in 1944 after rescuing two of her children and attempting to rescue three others and her father-in-law, after her house caught fire. Jean Froud, aged fifteen and a draper's clerk in Alveston, lost her life in 1944 attempting to save two companions from drowning in the River Avon. Elizabeth Addison of London and Edith Sedgebeer of Looe, Cornwall – both members of the Women's Land Army employed at Breage, Cornwall – in 1946 rescued a German prisoner of war, who was being gored by a bull.

In 1949, Jean Weir, a schoolteacher of Bangor, County Down, with another, rescued a woman from drowning in the sea at Ballyhornan, but lost her own life. Olive Harding, a clerk from Crewe, was injured in 1951 while assisting a woman – since deceased – whose clothing caught fire in a laboratory. In 1952, a young boy was rescued from drowning, following an accident at Kilrea, by his 44-year-old aunt Lavinia Derry, his 69-year-old grandmother Rosetta Derry, and twelve-year-old Ellen McCausland. Lavinia Derry drowned. Also in that year, Ellen Potts, an office cleaner of Finsbury, London, was injured while attempting to prevent further hurt to a child who had been attacked by a bull terrier.

Annie Key and her daughter Beryl, a shop assistant, both of Skegness, lost their lives in 1955 while attempting to rescue the youngest member of their family, a boy aged seven, after an accident on ice, and Shirley Howard of Cardiff, although heavily pregnant, rescued a little boy from drowning in the West Dock, Cardiff, in 1958. Staff Nurse Eileen Robinson of Epsom, Surrey, was seriously injured in 1972 when she tried to help another nurse being violently assaulted by a mental patient at an Epsom hospital, while in 1984 Stella McKenna, an accounts clerk in London, was injured when she tried to prevent a colleague from being stabbed by a deranged man. In 1991, Elizabeth Wynn, a nurse of Lea, Preston, was seriously injured while helping others rescue three people trapped in a crashed car on a motorway near Walsall and, in 1994, Monica Richardson of Leeds suffered severe traumatic stress after intervening successfully in a stabbing incident at a neighbour's house.

The Royal National Lifeboat Institution and the Coastguards

Organisations such as these have remained solidly in the male domain. Women have only been accepted into them relatively recently, and it takes time for them to settle in. Awards such as the Board of Trade Silver and Bronze Medals have been exclusively awarded to men. However, one interesting award of a Silver Medal to a woman by the RNLI dates from the last century. Helen Blyth was daughter of the head lighthouse keeper at Point of Ayre, Isle of Man. Her father was away ill at the time, when on a morning of March 1888 the schooner *Burns and Bessie*, taking coals from Glasgow to Duddon Pier, was caught into a severe gale. Three miles from the lighthouse a tremendous sea struck her, throwing the vessel on her beam ends and washing away her deck house and lifeboat. Half an hour later the schooner stuck on a gravel ledge and the wind was so strong that no line could be thrown aboard to the crew.

Helen, together with the assistant lighthouse keeper and his wife, stood in neck-high water – in imminent danger of being washed off their feet – extending the line to the sailors, on which the lives of all virtually depended, the shore end of the line being held by Helen. As the crew jumped off the schooner into the raging sea, they made for the line and were pulled in. The gale blew sleet into the faces of the rescuers with blinding force. When finally the captain jumped, he was so benumbed with cold that he could not pass the running bowline around his body and was knocked unconscious by a falling spar. He would have died had not Helen dashed into the breakers and, throwing her own clothes line about his neck, dragged him ashore insensible and half strangled, even though she was nearly lost several times owing to the force of the backwash. The rescued men were nursed at the lighthouse by the two women and all recovered.

Some Forgotten Women

It is a sad fact that many women who have died from their brave actions have not been recorded, and some can be named but have received no award, though they displayed no less courage. The British nurse Edith Cavell was one. She helped to shelter over 200 escaping soldiers at her Red Cross hospital in German-occupied Belgium during the First World War. She was eventually arrested, court-marshalled and shot by the Germans in October 1915. Another early agent of the First World War was British employed and Oxford educated intelligence gatherer Louise de Brettignies. Trapped in Lille during the German invasion, she brought back much valuable information when she escaped to Britain. She returned in 1915 to establish the 'Alice' (Dubois) network. Arrested in 1916, she died in a Brussels prison. Nan Hurst, a volunteer FANY ambulance driver badly injured in the battle of Verdun, still continued her work of ferrying injured soldiers to hospital, for which she received a French Croix de Guerre, but no British award, and in the Second World War, Leading Wren Chadwick and Wren Kneebone, manning a naval motor launch on their own, helped in the rescue of six sailors from a bombed ship. They were given silver compacts at the Savoy Hotel by the ship owners for their bravery. Another Wren, Mary Woodhouse, rescued a drowning sailor in the dark at Plymouth, but her actions went unrecognised.

Nurse Edith Cavell. (*Mrs B. Anderson*)

Outstanding acts of courage and devotion were shown by nurses and doctors in the First and Second World Wars. In 1940, a nursing sister on the SS *Oronsay*, which was picking up survivors after the evacuation of Norway and St Nazaire, worked flat out for 72 hours tending rows of wounded soldiers laid out on the decks, and two sisters, Dorothy Field and Molly Evershed, died with their casualties when the *Amsterdam* struck a mine. In all, nine hospital ships were sunk with their patients and staffs during this war.

Four ATS girls helped to put out the fire on a crashed Wellington bomber. They were Privates Jackie Birrell, Eva James and Joyce Middleton, and Lance Cpl Joan Myall. Pte Johnson burned herself badly while dragging a survivor from an aircraft crash, and Pte Morris ferried men and equipment to and fro at a blazing ammunition dump. These are only a few of many brave unrewarded actions.

On the other side of the world, Sister Mary Brand of the QAIMNS continued treating patients among the evacuees from Singapore until her ship went down and, though she was rescued, she died of her wounds. Ursula Bower, dubbed 'Queen of the Nagas' – a fierce head-hunting tribe on the Burma–India border – was an early anthropologist, who during the war organised the tribes to guard the mountain passes and help escaping Allied prisoners. Her men were so feared by the Japanese that the latter never dared enter her area.

Madelaine Barclay ferried SOE agents between France and Britain in her small boat, but was lost at sea during one of these secret journeys. And Madame Marie Smith, married to an Englishman, hid isolated British soldiers and was part of an escape network. She sent useful intelligence to Britain and was always completely unsuspected by the Germans.

In the ATA Amy Johnson was probably drowned when her aircraft was lost in thick cloud. The captain of HMS *Hazelmere* drowned in attempting to save a woman, possibly Miss Johnson, parachuting into the Thames estuary off Herne Bay.

Other women opened their homes to the sick or evacuated families with no recompense. Such women as Marjorie Keens housed over 100 families of SOE or French fighters for short periods during the later stages of the war.

All these received no medals, but we are the richer for their lives and efforts. Other unsung heroines still continue their work at home and abroad, prompted only by their love of humanity and their courage.

CHAPTER THIRTEEN

American Women of the First World War

Medal of Honor Army 1862–96 (obverse). (*Sotheby's*)

The United States of America has been Britain's friend and ally over the course of the twentieth century and through two exhausting world wars, and the interests of the two countries have been largely the same. Indeed there have been many migrations of people in both directions. Courage, however, is no respecter of race or language and is common to all. America has its own medals to reward the brave and there are some women among the recipients.

The Congressional Medal of Honor is a rare badge of distinction. It was established by the navy in 1861 and the army in 1862 as the supreme award for bravery in action involving actual battle with the enemy. Normally it is given in person by the President of the United States and can be awarded posthumously.

The early Army Medal was a five-pointed bronze star with a central round piece. This showed a draped classical female figure with a Roman fasces in her left hand and a shield in her right, driving off Discord, represented as a half-running, crouching male figure brandishing snakes in both hands. The whole was surrounded by a circle of thirty-four stars. Above the medal were crossed cannons standing on a pile of cannon balls on which rested an American eagle with its wings spread wide. On the reverse were the words 'The Congress to . . .' followed by the recipient's name and action. The ribbon of the early Army Medal was blue with red and white stripes, and it was worn as a brooch fronted by a shield of the United States with a cornucopia on either side. The medal and ribbon have gone through several changes. The navy version is also slightly different.

This early form of Army Medal was handed to the unconventional Dr Mary Walker, an army surgeon, for medical services provided on the battlefield during the American Civil War in the nineteenth century. She was the first and only woman to receive it in that or the twentieth century – perhaps this was the reason that it was withdrawn from her in 1916, but reinstated in 1977, long after the good doctor had ceased to care about its vagaries.

After America entered the First World War in April 1917, the Army Nurse Corps, officially established as a branch of the Army Medical Services in 1901, mustered 403 nurses to go on active duty, their numbers being shortly swelled by 2,822 volunteer members from the American Red Cross, who served in hospitals at home and abroad. Army nurses could be found in field and convalescent hospitals, ambulance trains, ships and camps. By November 1918, 21,480 nurses had enlisted and over 10,000 had served overseas. Inevitably some were wounded and there were deaths too, especially in conditions of war in France and Belgium, and also at the end of the war and for some time afterwards, when the influenza pandemic carried off both patients and nurses. About 102 lost their lives while serving with the

Dr Mary Walker, Medal of Honor. (*WIMSA*)

American Expeditionary Force in Europe, Asia, South America and the Philippines, including 6 civilian dietitians serving with the army; 134 army nurses died in the United States.

All war is appalling, but this war was more terrible than any that had gone before. Ships could be sunk by an invisible enemy. Hospitals and quiet places far from the battlefield could be destroyed by bombs from the air. New weapons could bring death and destruction to those trusting in trenches or huts for shelter. They could be run over by motor vehicles, and men could be deafened, maimed or killed from a distance. Gas could choke or blind them. The injured from the front were sad cases, their illnesses increased by dirt, disease and squalor. In conditions like these, any who could offer succour or save lives shone even brighter.

Eva Parmalees and Beatrice MacDonald were two American Army nurses who received Britain's prestigious Military Medal (see Chapter One) for bravery under fire in their military hospitals near the battlefields – an award given to British nurses in similar conditions.

Distinguished Service Cross, Army (obverse). (*M. Salm*)

It fell to three army nurses and a Red Cross nurse serving with them, to be given the highest American honour ever won by the Corps – the Distinguished Service Cross. It was created in 1918 for the army to reward any act of extraordinary heroism against the enemy. Standing next to the Medal of Honor in importance, it can be awarded to any individual, whatever the rank. At the beginning of 1918, about 100 more-elaborate versions of the Distinguished Service Cross were issued to France, but since then the crosses have taken a simpler form. The cross is bronze, with an American spread eagle standing on a laurel wreath. Beneath the eagle is a scroll, attached to three arms of the cross, on which are the words 'For Valor'. On the back is the name of the recipient, surrounded by a laurel wreath. The ribbon is blue, edged with thick red stripes, with a thin white stripe along the inner side of the two red ones. This was the award given to Helen McClelland, Beatrice MacDonald and Isabel Stanbaugh of the Army Nursing Corps, and Jane Jeffrey of the American Red Cross.

The navy had its own Nurse Corps established in 1908. During the First World War, about 1,476 women served at home and abroad, around 327 in Europe in field hospitals, hospital transport groups and Army Nursing Corps units. Lena Higbee, who became Superintendent of the Navy Nurse Corps, was one of them. She worked in medical and surgical wards and theatres, and was the first nurse to be given the Navy Distinguished Service Cross. She received it for meritorious service in showing unusual and conspicuous devotion to work of unusual responsibility. Her efforts produced a most loyal and efficient group of nurses in a very short space of time.

Distinguished Service Cross, Navy (obverse). (*M. Salm*)

The Navy Distinguished Service Cross is equal to that of the army, and was instituted by the navy in 1919. At that time it ranked third in the navy to the Medal of Honor and the Distinguished Service Medal. In 1942, it was changed to stand above the Distinguished Service Medal when it was given for extraordinary heroism or distinguished service in combat action against the enemy.

The medal is a cross in dark bronze, the ends slightly wider and rounded. In the centre in a coin shape is a caravel, a rigged sailing ship on waves. Joining the four arms of the cross is a laurel wreath. The reverse carries crossed anchors with the letters USN (United States Navy). The ribbon is navy blue with a white stripe down the centre.

As might be expected, there were deaths also among the navy nurses; about thirty-six are recorded, three of them, unnamed, from the influenza epidemic. They had evidently continued their work until they dropped, but so outstanding were their contributions that all three were granted a posthumous Navy Distinguished Service Cross.

Other nurses who tended the casualties of war included a small group of African-American nurses, who joined the Army Nursing Corps for a short time but, to their regret, not until the war was over, so they won no awards. Nevertheless, this was breaking new ground, although they lived in segregated quarters and their patients were mainly German prisoners of war and African-American soldiers. Their success provided an example of professional equality for all qualified nurses.

However, a group not accepted by the War Department was that of women doctors. Notwithstanding this, they raised their own funds and went to France under their own organisation as the American Women's Hospitals

Black army nurses, 1919. (*WIMSA*)

in Europe. They wore their own uniform and about 350 of them created their own hospitals and clinics for soldiers and civilians overseas, during and after the war. But they also won no awards.

In fact the list of high-level awards for the First World War is a short one, and mainly dominated by nurses. Many from the army appear in the lists of the Distinguished Service Medal and these date mainly from the occupation of Germany.

Chief Nurse Julia Stimson, formerly a chief of the Red Cross nursing service in France, became a director of the nursing service to the American Expeditionary Force after the war, and finally Superintendent of the Army Nursing Corps until her retirement in 1937. 1st Lieutenant (1/Lt) Carrie Howard served as an army nurse until 1935, becoming Chief Nurse. She was one of the original members of the Army Nurse Corps. These are but two in a long list of nurses who received the Distinguished Service Medal, and around twenty of these also received the British Royal Red Cross award (see Chapter Six) for their devoted efforts.

Distinguished Service Medal
(obverse). (*R.J. Scarlett*)

The Distinguished Service Medal had been established by the army in 1918, at the same time as the Distinguished Service Cross. It was to reward exceptionally meritorious service against the enemy or to the government in a duty of great responsibility.

It is of bronze in a circular coin shape, carrying the American eagle, wings spread, its claws each holding a laurel wreath. Above the eagle are the American stars and the whole design is cut out within the rim, on which are the words 'For Distinguished Service MCMXVIII' (Roman numbers for 1918) on a blue enamel background. On the other side of the medal is a scroll upon a trophy of flags and weapons. The ribbon is white with a broad red stripe at each edge and a thin blue line against the red.

The medal could also be given to civilians who had helped in the war effort. Three women were much associated with the work of the American Red Cross (ARC): Maude Cleveland, Jane Delano and Mary Andress. During the war there were about 8 million volunteers across America who produced clothes, surgical dressings and extras for the troops. Many worked in Red Cross canteens at home and in France for the Forces, and civilians in war-torn areas were also helped by them.

Jane Delano had been a nurse in civil life and in 1909 became Superintendent of the Army Nursing Corps. Even then she was involved in supervising the American Red Cross Nursing Service, to such an extent that in 1912 she resigned from the army to devote herself full-time to this service, building it up as a reserve for the army and eventually becoming its head in 1917. At that time she also helped to recruit army, navy and public health nurses – at least 20,000 entered under her supervision – as well as the Red Cross workers overseas. She worked indefatigably for their welfare, making frequent inspections and visits to boost morale. In 1918, she received the rare Red Cross Gold Medal for Conspicuous Valor. At the beginning of 1919, her inspection tour of overseas military hospitals was cut short when she fell ill at Savenay in France. She wrote in one of her letters home, 'I do not suppose I should complain, after the men put up with so much more!' Three months later she was dead. Her country awarded her the Distinguished Service Medal and she was buried at Arlington National Cemetery.

Another outstanding civilian to receive the Distinguished Service Medal was Mrs James Cushman. She was chairman of the Young Women's Christian Association (YWCA) and worked closely with its counterpart, the Young Men's Christian Association (YMCA). The two combined to provide canteens, rest camps, leisure and recreational facilities for the men at home and overseas. More than fifty of their number served under fire, and many were commended for bravery; thirteen received the French Croix de Guerre.

Commander Evangeline Booth, daughter of the founder of the Salvation Army, also organised a corps of men and women – the latter fondly known by men at the front as 'doughnut girls' – to provide canteens outside home camps and railway terminals, where men arrived hungry and tired. Canteens and other much-needed facilities were also provided for front-line troops. Their mission was 'soup, soap and salvation' and about 109 women served abroad. They often worked so close to the battlefield that they were shelled, gassed, bombed and wounded, 'serving humbly and with distinction'. After the war they made it their task to identify the graves of American servicemen for bereaved families. None of the corps members received awards, but Commander Booth, their inspiration, accepted the Distinguished Service Medal on behalf of the self-sacrifice and loving labour of her fellow salvationists.

Many American women volunteered for the Forces in 1917 'to free a man to fight'. They were enlisting in the US Naval Reserve as yeomen as early as March 1917, though were not permitted to serve overseas. Their tasks were mainly clerical, with a few minor specific occupations. It was popular, however, and nearly 12,000 served their country. Some died later in the influenza pandemic of 1918. The Marine Corps Reserve recruited 305 women to work mainly as clerks and telephone operators; the army, however, employed just 233 women, and those only as civilians. They were a highly trained, bilingual group recruited for the Army Signals Corps as telephone operators, most to be sent to France to help communications between the French and American armies. For their pleasant manners, tact and success in difficult circumstances, they were sometimes called 'Hello Girls'. They greatly helped in the negotiations at Versailles, when the peace

Yeomen Genevieve and Lucille Baker.
(*US Coast Guard*)

terms were eventually signed by America, Britain, France and their enemy, Germany.

Women also enlisted in the Coast Guard but they, too, were limited in what they were asked to do, and were confined to stations in the US. The twins, Genevieve and Lucille Baker, are believed to be the first women yeomen of the Coast Guard.

Apart from nurses, no women in any of the services appear to have gained any awards for courage, but this was mainly because they were seldom put directly in harm's way.

CHAPTER FOURTEEN

American Servicewomen of the Second World War and Beyond

The Second World War was vastly different from the First World War. It had become more technical, demanding and complicated. The war was also waged on many fronts all over the globe. Somewhere in the region of 400,000 American women joined the Armed Forces and their nursing services, many times more than those in the First World War. Statistics are notoriously unreliable but a general picture emerges, including the fact that most of the women were volunteers and young.

Among the highest awards for bravery given in the Second World War, excluding those who worked for the Secret Services, is the Silver Star. It was instituted in 1932 for all the Armed Services, to reward actions of gallantry against, and in direct contact with, an enemy. Though it is given for facing less danger that expected of the Medal of Honor and the Distinguished Service Cross, it nevertheless requires a very high standard of heroism.

Silver Star (obverse).
(*R.J. Scarlett*)

Despite its name, it is a bronze, five-pointed star, gilded. In the centre, within a laurel wreath, is a small raised silver star standing against bronze rays. At the back are the words 'For Gallantry in Action'. The ribbon is more varied; its base is dark blue and in the centre is a wide red stripe with two broad white stripes alongside. Near the edge is a thin white stripe.

The army started recruiting women in 1941, their eventual name being the Women's Army Corps (WAC). About 150,000 women served in it, and 18,000 or so travelled overseas. Around 40,000 of the WAC worked with the US Army Air Force, since during the war the Air Force was part of the US Army. It did not become a separate arm with its own Women's Air Force (WAF) members until 1948.

Major Karen Mast SS.
(*Dr K. Mast*)

Major (Maj) Karen Mast was the only woman aviation cadet in the United States Army Air Corps. After long training on all kinds of American, Australian and British aircraft, the 22-year-old eventually chose an Australian wooden Mosquito Mark XVI, modified to her own specifications, to take her on highly dangerous photographic and confidential reconnaissance missions over Japanese-held territory, from which she, and men like her, rarely expected to return alive. Out of her section of 99, 96 never returned. So far, although suffering bullet wounds in various parts of her anatomy, she had returned successfully with her vital information and photographs. Her last mission is told in her own words, in this much-shortened but graphic account.

An Australian Air Marshal was ready to go with me to get some photographs of a Japanese target in the central mountains of New Guinea.

We took off about 0325 in excellent weather with an empty cabin, except for the extra gas tank and the big American Fairchild camera that the Marshal would use once we were over the target. We had no problems on the way out. The moon was full but we could only see the tops of the clouds. I did not think that Japanese anti-aircraft fire would come very close. Our idea was to quietly slip in to the target before they knew we were there.

The sun came up as we were ready to close in at a power-on rate of speed close to 500 mph. No need anymore to be quiet. Both engines were under full power and we headed straight down. We went from 30,000 to almost 10,000 ft before I started to pull out. The fire was heavy but no shots came close. The Marshal was ready to take pictures in the very short time over the target – 14–20 seconds. I levelled off at close to 2,000 ft and the Marshal took picture after picture as fast as he could. He was back in his seat in a flash. 'Let's get out of here, Major,' he shouted. I was heading up again with the engines straining. We were going up at a dizzying rate. The Marshal was about 15 years my senior and I knew we were climbing too fast for his body to stand it long. I was wondering if I could slacken off a little but I kept searching in my rear view mirror for the Japanese Zeros.

I levelled off a little and suddenly there they were. Six Zeros coming right at us from behind, between us and the sun. I hauled the nose of my big plane up again. I did not know exactly the ceiling of the Tony's. They were too new. I was sure, however, that I could climb out ahead of them and far outrun them, as they would be soon out of fuel. I was wondering if I should make headway, more speed or climb more steeply. I could not do both at the same time, so I levelled off at 31,000 ft and let the Mosquito pick up its tremendous speed. But those pilots would do all they could, even unto death. Suddenly two of them dropped back. 'Out of gas', I thought. I had enough to make it back, but not at this speed. I would soon have to throttle back to cruising speed or we might go down into the dense jungle of the foothills of the mountain range. Another Tony went down. Only two were left that I could see. One was missing and I thought he might be somewhere below ready to pounce. The two I could see kept on after us for a while. I wondered who would come out the winner. Then one wobbled his wings and down he dived. Then I could only see the two Zeros that were left. They were coming up again.

Without enough fuel to get back, they were probably going to ram me if they could. This was an emergency, so I just pushed the throttles wide open. I saw that the two Japanese were falling back again. My air speed was trembling at 465 mph. I hoped the engines would hang together and not blow up, and the wing would not be wrenched off . . . I saw one Tony tip over into a nasty spin. The last enemy plane was now behind and below me, so I pulled at the control wheel again to see if I could get a little more altitude. Up we started, slowly, so slowly to 32,700 ft. This was it. The Tony was below me out of sight, but I was sure he could not get past 31,000 ft and when last seen he was rocking so badly that I knew we were both at our highest altitude, and even a slight slowing would flip either of us into a spin, which I knew would be fatal. We must level off and get back down to thicker air. The Tony had disappeared.

At that moment something sliced through my right wing, just behind the right gas tank. Immediately there was a tremendous explosion and the whole side of the cabin shook and splintered. Glass was flying everywhere. The big aircraft wrenched and seemed to buck. I could hear and feel glued joints separating. I shoved the nose down just as the right wing began to settle into a fatal turn. As we went down under full power the sinking wing stopped falling off and I was able to bring the craft back under sensible control.

I looked around for the Marshal, so that we could both bail out. But he was gone from his seat. He was on the floor behind my seat unconscious, with blood running out of both sleeves and the bottom of his leather flying jacket. I pulled back more and let the plane come down another few thousand feet. I had a brief glimpse of the last Tony's wings going over and over in the terrible inside loop and spin. Down he went out of sight.

I decided my plane was going to fly, though it vibrated badly and shook and jangled. Now I had to help the Marshal if I could. I breathed a prayer and reached out to flip the switch of the auto-pilot. At first it did not seem to take hold, but at last I felt it take over. Being able to see better without my goggles in the bitter wind streaming through cracked and broken windows, I went behind the seats to see what I could do. The cold air would freeze us if we did not quickly get down, but I was over enemy territory and mountains, and I knew they were looking for us. I found the Marshal was badly cut across his upper back, very deeply. His seat had not helped to defuse the harm of whatever had sliced across his body. He seemed to have one artery cut and was bleeding badly in spurts. He would die if I did nothing. I thought to get a tourniquet between his heart and shoulder, so I exposed the artery and tied some bandages around it, tying up the other end. It stopped most of the blood down to an ooze. As he was now coming to his senses, I gave him a shot of morphine, tucked his cut and torn coat around him and opened his parachute's nylon cloth over him to keep him snug from the cruel wind streaking in the broken side window. After checking his oxygen, there was nothing more I could do.

I got back to my frosty seat and switched off the auto-pilot. If we got back in time we might not freeze to death. Anyone with sense would go out the escape hatch and take far better chances with a parachute, but I could not do that and leave a badly wounded man behind. I therefore started to trim the plane as best I could. Some trim leads were blasted away, but some worked and I managed to get the ship under reasonably good balance control. I gave a quick look round and began to get the big plane lower, because we were using oxygen faster than normal and I didn't think I could fly with such cold pinching me close to passing out. Also the mercury pressure on the right engine was below standard. I prayed it would keep running long enough for us to set down in our territory.

No Japanese planes were around as far as I could see, as I put the nose into a gentle down angle. I did not know if the Mosquito would fly on one engine, as badly damaged as it was. Behind me I did notice that the whole right flap had gone, but the plane continued to fly in a remarkable fashion. I had to keep up as much speed as I could to get the Marshal back, and I could only hope whatever fuel we had left would get us back to our field. I had been slowing down, and at 310 mph I decided we could make it back, if nothing else happened against us. I limped along in that fashion for some 80 minutes. We were over the mountains now and going along the southern coast towards the little Aussie air field. We might just make it! Breaking radio silence I got a message through with a good loud signal coming back, warning we were coming in with dangerous damage, and I figured the wheels would not come down. The Air Marshal too was very badly hurt and might even now be dead. When we landed I knew they would be ready with everything – fire truck, ambulance, doctors and a small plane to take the Marshal to the nearest hospital.

My speed was down to around 120 when I came over the outer markers. They said my wheels were down and looked all right, but my right wing had a big hole in it. No time to go around for a good once over, so I aimed right for the central strip and with a lot of rumbling, clanking and hisses we were down and it appeared we were safe. At 80 mph we careened down the landing strip and round onto a fast track to the waiting ambulance. I pulled up and let the plane slow to a stop. The men tore open the door, grabbed the Marshal and whisked him out. I saw a doctor on the run, take out his stethoscope and try to get a heartbeat. They shoved him into an ambulance and tore off to the Dispensary. I was just sitting in the left seat trying to calm down, when the men grabbed me too, because blood was trickling out from under all my flying clothes. I noticed three other men latch on to the big Fairchild camera, stick it into a jeep with armed men and wheel away. Later I found the camera gave the Generals all the information they needed and it was almost worth it. I was picked up bodily and crammed into another ambulance. As we roared away, I could see the ground crew and a lot of pilots and gunners looking at the wreck I had brought back.

My wounds were serious, so I spent time in hospital and was ordered off active missions. As to the Air Marshal, in time he was patched up, and the Australian Government gave him a large sheep ranch with all the animals, tools and help. I guess he became a rich farmer. Later I was awarded my 4th Purple Heart for wounds in combat, and President Harry S. Truman gave me my Silver Star – the third highest decoration the military gives for Heroism in Action.

Four army nurses also gained the Silver Star, just after the Anzio landings by the Allies in Italy. During the fierce fighting on the beachheads and afterwards, their hospitals were nestled in with the combat units. In February 1944, 2nd Lieutenants (2/Lt) Elaine Roe and Rita Rourke were working in the 33rd Field Hospital, when it was heavily shelled. Using flashlights when power lines were cut, they calmly helped to evacuate forty-two patients, heedless of their own danger. At the same time, a tented operating room fell prey to 30 minutes of prolonged shelling. Despite the disruption, doctors and nurses continued at all three operating tables by flashlight, greatly assisted by the efficiency of their supervisor, Mary Roberts. Six nurses were killed during the attack and many military personnel wounded. Among the dead was Lt Ellen Ainsworth, whose outstanding courage caused her to be awarded a posthumous Silver Star; 2/Lt Majorie Truax, a WAC, also gained the Silver Star there.

Many other awards were presented to nurses. In 1940, there were 1,000 Army Nursing Sisters; by 1945, there were more than 62,000 scattered over all the theatres of war, as well as in hospitals at home in America. The navy had about 14,000 nurses, those abroad mainly serving in hospital ships. Ensign Jan Kenleigh was the first naval nurse to fly into Iwo Jima to evacuate casualties and the first at Okinawa. The Army and Navy Nursing Corps were the trailblazers of American women in the war – first in action, first in uniform and first in citations. They suffered deaths in action and eighty-seven became prisoners of war with the Japanese, and one with the Germans. They were also present in most modern conflicts including during 1991 in the Persian Gulf.

The Distinguished Flying Cross, introduced in 1926, is for men and women in any branch of the Armed Forces who have distinguished themselves 'by heroism or extraordinary achievement, while participating in aerial flight'. The award, unusually, was backdated to 1917. The medal is a bronze cross with a four-bladed propeller superimposed on it. Behind the cross is a small square, marked with deep rays, running out from the centre. The reverse is plain except for the person's name and date. The ribbon is blue, with a thin red stripe edged with white down the centre, with a slightly wider white stripe near the border.

Distinguished Flying Cross (obverse). (*M. Salm*)

In 1932, Amelia Earhart-Putnam was one of the first to receive this medal, though she was not in the Services. She was a civilian pilot – an American aviation pioneer – who was the first woman to fly across the Atlantic.

Late in the Second World War, some army nurses became flying nurses, and two of these also won the Distinguished Flying Cross. To be a flying nurse was a hazardous occupation. Often casualties were picked up under fire or with battles almost raging around them. Air ambulances might be vulnerable to enemy aircraft or be shelled from the ground, and they could also crash. Lt Adela Lutz flew more than 150 missions to evacuate the wounded from forward areas. On her last flight she was severely injured and died. 1/Lt Kathleen Dial was in a plane that crash-landed on a beach at Fisherman's Island, New Guinea. Though hurt, she directed the removal of eighteen mentally disturbed patients before collapsing.

For bravery not necessarily in the face of the enemy, the Services created their own branch medals. First came the Soldier's Medal for the army, followed by the Navy and Marine Corps Medal, then the Coast Guard Medal in 1949. As the Air Force was formed later, together with its own nursing service, their Airman's Medal did not appear until 1960. As far as can be ascertained, no women appear in the lists for the last two medals.

Soldier's Medal (obverse). (*M. Salm*)

The Soldier's Medal was instituted in 1926 'for heroism not involving actual combat with the enemy'. This meant that women non-combatants were eligible. The action, however, must involve danger and the risk of the loss of life.

It is an octagonal bronze medal showing the American eagle standing on a bundle of fasces, representing the law. His raised wings have stars on both sides – six to the left with a small laurel crown at the top, and seven to the right. The reverse shows an American shield and the letters 'US'. Above are branches of oak and laurel. Underneath is a blank plaque for the name of the recipient, below the words 'For Valor'. Around the edge is inscribed 'Soldier's Medal'. The ribbon is blue with a wide central stripe lined with seven thin white stripes.

Ten women of the WAC gained this medal in the Second World War. A few are mentioned here. In Algeria in 1943, Private (Pte) Margaret Mahoney (overleaf) saved a soldier attending to the stoves in the WAC kitchen when his clothing caught fire from spilled gasoline. Both were badly burned in the rescue attempt, but survived. Pte Mary Ford (overleaf) tried several times to rescue a drowning soldier in May 1944 at Camp McCoy, Wisconsin. She finally brought him ashore, but he was dead. Among other medallists were Corporals (Cpl) Mary Lynne and Helen Bragdon, and Technician Vivian Withner in October 1944. They worked together to control a fire caused by an oil stove explosion in a women's barracks in New Guinea.

WACs were not the only group to receive the Soldier's Medal. Army nurses were close behind. In fact, 2/Lt Edith Greenwood was the first of any military women to gain this award. In April 1943 at Yuma, Arizona, she helped to rescue fifteen patients from a burning ward in her hospital. And 2/Lt Christine Dahl in Michigan aided in saving the lives of the pilot and crew of a crashed aircraft.

There were others. By far the largest numbers of awards of all kinds went to the Army Nurse Corps during the war. They included presidential

Private Margaret Mahoney SM. (*WAC Museum*)

Private Mary Ford SM. (*WAC Museum*)

citations for nurses who waded ashore to France after D-Day, or served on the Bataan Peninsula and in the battle for the Philippines. Nor did the close of the Second World War see the end of conflicts where American forces and nurses were needed. In Vietnam, for instance, Colonel (Col) Marion Tiernay saved the injured members of a crashed plane and received the Soldier's Medal. And in May 1968, Maj Mary Carr volunteered to help in the operation on a patient at Long Binh who had an explosive device embedded in his skull, and 1/Lt Diane Lindsay, also in Vietnam, successfully intervened when a deranged soldier threatened to blow everyone up with a live grenade. They, too, received Soldier's Medals.

The navy took women into its reserve in 1942 and around 100,000 joined. As they were 'Women Accepted for Volunteer Emergency Service', they became known as WAVES. They did many types of work but were not allowed abroad. In spite of this a few gained the Navy and Marine Corps Medal, notably Ensign Deborah Burnett in 1975, Jessica Brown in 1986 and SA Deborah McBeth in 1995. There are no further details.

The Navy and Marine Corps Medal, instituted in 1942, is awarded for heroism not involving actual combat with the enemy, and is roughly equivalent to the army's Soldier's Medal. It is bronze and octagonal. On the obverse is an American eagle with raised wings holding on to an anchor, lying sideways. From the rope around it hangs a globe showing the American continent. Below is the single word 'Heroism'. The reverse is plain except for the name of the recipient. Its designer died in the Pacific in action during the war. The ribbon has three equal sized stripes of navy blue, gold and reddish-purple.

The Marine Corps Women's Reserve was formed in 1943 and enlisted about 23,000 women. Though employed on many types of work, they could only serve in the United States. In spite of these limitations, several members distinguished themselves by gaining this medal. Two recipients were Gunnery Sergeant (Sgt) Dorothy Kearns and 1/Lt Vanda Brame. The first, in her apartment house in San Francisco in 1961, tried to save a woman from being stabbed to death by her deranged husband. The second award winner, in November 1970 in Iowa, foiled the theft of money from a blind man's shop, and with others chased and caught the thief.

Navy and Marine Corps Medal (obverse). (*M. Salm*)

The Air Medal was established in 1942 and is for personnel from any of the Armed Forces, who have done something heroic or of meritorious achievement beyond the call of duty while on a plane. During the war it could also be given for flying on five long combat missions and was backdated to 1939. It is a sixteen-pointed bronze star. On a very large central globe is an American eagle flying downwards, while clutching in each claw a thunderbolt. The name of the person is on the reverse. The ribbon is dark blue with two broad orange stripes near the edge on either side.

Air Medal (obverse). (*M. Salm*)

This medal was given in very large numbers, mainly to Air Evacuation Nurses. 2/Lt Elsie Lott was the first woman to receive it. She made a record-breaking experimental flight from India, taking nearly a week, to bring five desperately sick soldiers to the USA for special care. And Sgt Henrietta Williams was the first WAC to enter China. She made more than 100 training flights operating the Loran system.

In 1942, the Women's Auxiliary Ferrying Squadron was formed to provide pilots to ferry military planes across the United States. At the same time, a larger organisation called the Women's Flying Training Command came into being to train women pilots to transport larger aircraft. In 1943, the two organisations joined to form the Women's Airforce Service Pilots (WASPS). Though still civilians, they wore uniform, came under army orders and were not allowed overseas.

Barbara Erickson was a WASP, who managed an extraordinary feat for any ferry pilot. She flew 8,000 miles in five days, delivering four aircraft of

Lieutenant Colleen Cain. (*US Coast Guard*)

different types from and to various destinations. For this unusual accomplishment she gained the Air Medal.

Another Service that must be mentioned, though awards were few, is the Coast Guard Women's Reserve (SPARS), formed in 1942. There were about 10,000 of them, working mainly on land. At two shore-based stations, their most important task was the operation of Loran, a secret long-range radio-signal aid to navigation of US military ships and planes.

The Women's Reserve virtually vanished after the war, but came to life again in the 1970s when its women became part of the regular and reserve Coast Guard, thus able to serve at sea or in the air. Three of its women received Air Medals. In 1985, Ginger Barnes gained hers for two sea rescues. In 1989, Kelly Mogk managed a difficult air-sea rescue, and in 1990 Lt Laura Guth made a helicopter rescue of six fishermen from their sinking vessel in the icy Alaskan seas. Colleen Cain was their first helicopter pilot, but she was killed in 1982 when, as a co-pilot, she crashed answering a distress call.

A Second World War navy nurse, Lt Ann Bernatitus, was the first person to wear the bright colours of the Legion of Merit. She was the only navy nurse to escape being a prisoner of war with the Japanese in the Philippines.

Though the Legion of Merit is not a medal for courage, it is interesting just the same, since it is probably the most decorative of American medals. There are four classes. It stemmed from George Washington's 1783 Badge of Military Merit, and in its early years ranked above the Silver Star but below the Distinguished Service Medal. Re-established in 1942, it came to reward numerous types of service to the state. In shape it is a five-rayed cross, each arm enamelled white with red edges and tipped with a gold ball. The arms rest on an enamelled green wreath, the space between bearing two crossed war arrows. A ring of gold surrounds a dark blue centre set with thirteen white stars. The ribbon is light purple with a white edge.

There were many Legions of Merit given during the Second World War, mostly to army women and nurses. A few went to army women after the war and one to air force nurse Clifton Bovee, who saved many lives in a plane crash in Korea.

But in general the postwar years are lean ones in regard to any awards to women, as few servicewomen were left in the services after demobilisation, except for nurses. The need for recruiting more was not recognised until America found itself increasingly embroiled in other, smaller conflicts. The 1950–3 Korean War had about 540 army and air force nurses serving; one died in a plane crash. The 1965–75 Vietnam War had about 7,500 women, the majority of them nurses; fourteen died on duty. In the 1970s–80s most Services assimilated women into the male forces, and in 1983 Operation

Legion of Merit (obverse). (*M. Salm*)

Urgent Fury in Grenada had 170 women in its numbers. Operation Just Cause in Panama in 1989 had 770 women serving, and one woman army captain led her soldiers against Panamanian defence forces. Three female army pilots caught in enemy fire gained Air Medals. The 1990–1 Operation Desert Storm in the Persian Gulf had 40,000 women among its forces; two were, for a few days, prisoners of war with the Iraqis. In 1991 servicewomen were deployed in Honduras, and in 1993 servicewomen were sent with the United Nations Forces to Bosnia and Somalia. Servicewomen joined the United Nations Forces in Rwanda in 1994, and in the 1994 Operation Uphold Democracy in Haiti, navy women served on combat ships, as they also did in the Middle East. And in the closing months of the twentieth century, they are involved with the North Atlantic Treaty Organisation (NATO) and the United Nations (UN) in parts of the former Yugoslavia.

The above indicates the growing role played by servicewomen in the restless post-Second World War years. It also goes to prove, to the curiosity – not to say incredulity – of many male servicemen, that women really are fully capable of taking an equal share in the increasingly technical work of their Service.

CHAPTER FIFTEEN

America – Mainly Civilian Awards

Purple Heart (obverse).
(*M. Salm*)

Civilians as well as Service personnel could qualify for the Badge of Military Merit, now called the Purple Heart. Established by General George Washington in 1782 and revived in 1932 – but backdated to 1917 – it is given to anyone suffering wounds or death in times of war in the service of their country. It is lowest in the order of precedence among personal awards, but is considered one of the most attractive. The name Purple Heart gives a good idea of its appearance. The medal is heart-shaped with a bust of George Washington in its centre, outlined against a purple enamel background. The words 'For Military Merit' are on the back. The ribbon is also purple, edged with white.

In the conflicts where American women were to be found, numbers were wounded and gained this award. For instance, in the Second World War, nineteen women of the US Army Corps were injured during the bombing of London in 1944–5 while posted to England. Because their work outside America often took them to dangerous areas, many Service nurses were wounded or killed by enemy action, their numbers swelled by the American Red Cross volunteers. Even before the United States entered the war, six went down with their torpedoed ship in June 1941. They were the staff of a Harvard University hospital being sent to Britain. Other female Red Cross workers were injured or died abroad. Esther Richards, a medical social worker, was wounded at Salerno during the Italian invasion and in 1944 was killed in the receiving tent at the Anzio beachhead. Others died when their planes crashed and many more were hurt, though the toll for male Red Cross workers was higher. The organisation also sent mobile clubs and canteens to help the Armed Services, wherever there was a need.

The American Red Cross also has its own medal system to reward or recognise its personnel. Its Gold Medal, the highest award, was given to Jane Delano, a First World War recipient mentioned in Chapter Thirteen. The Silver Medal usually went to foreign nationals. The Bronze Medal, 'for Highly Meritorious Service', was given to the families of its workers or nurses who died at home or abroad during the Second World War. There are in addition various badges and certificates of commendation.

In 1920, the International Committee of the Red Cross at Geneva began issuing the Florence Nightingale Medal (see Chapter Eight) to some in member countries who had given exceptional service in connection with nursing. Instituted in 1912, it was held up by the First World War; its first list, in 1920, therefore, was rather longer than usual. Thereafter the medal has been given very sparingly, every two years, usually to no more than one nurse in a country, and sometimes none. America, being a large country, rarely fails to have a suitable nominee, but nearly all are civilian nurses. Of all the honours to a graduate nurse, this is the most coveted.

Civilian women in America have been performing Coast Guard duties longer than there have been official Coast Guards, and the first female employees, in a roundabout way, were lighthouse keepers. Frequently the cause of this was because the men appointed by the Lighthouse Board for this task occasionally died suddenly, leaving a wife or daughter to take their post, who were then allowed to carry on, since their work was satisfactory. Consequently these women were sometimes involved in rescues at sea and were given life-saving medals for their bravery.

The most famous one comes from the last century, but her story is so unusual and shows such high courage that it should be included here.

Ida Lewis makes a rescue.

Idwalley (better known as Ida) Lewis, was the daughter of the Keeper of the Lime Rock Lighthouse, Newport, a Civil War veteran. Four months after taking the post he suffered a stroke, so that from the age of sixteen, Ida had the care of her father, her family and the lighthouse, but was not officially appointed until her father's death in 1872. She developed outstanding boat-handling skills, rowing her siblings to school on the mainland, and made many sea rescues from the age of fifteen, being credited with saving between eighteen and twenty-four lives during her thirty-nine years of official tenure. In 1869, she was given a Gold Medal for life-saving and later, other awards, so that she became almost a public figure.

Another daughter of a lighthouse keeper at Grand Point au Sable, Michigan, received a Silver Life-saving Medal, proving that Ida Lewis was no isolated case. Technological advances eventually phased out women lighthouse keepers at the end of the 1940s, ironically at almost the same time as the US Treasury started issuing its own official life-saving medal in 1949. The picture on one side of this medal is based on that of Lloyd's of London for saving life at sea.

Lloyd's, being an international marine insurance body, awarded one of its medals 'for Meritorious Service' (see Chapter Eleven) to Mrs Reed, the wife of the captain of the US vessel the *TF Oakes* at the end of the nineteenth century, an iron-built sailing vessel, dependent on wind and tide, that plied to and from New York and Hong Kong. In a good run that should have taken about a month, but its return voyage, starting in 1896, took eight months, through the worst of weathers, unable to touch land in between. Most of the crew had died or been incapacitated, including the captain, and even his first mate and wife were barely able to keep on their feet by the time the ship was taken on tow and entered New York harbour with Mrs Reed at the wheel in 1897. At the end of the twentieth century, a Lloyd's medal for Meritorious Service went in 1994 to the American Air Force Major Anna Fisher and her four fellow astronauts for successfully completing their mission to retrieve two rogue satellites from their space shuttle *Discovery*.

In September 1944, a vicious tropical hurricane swept the east coast of America causing 440 deaths, most from wrecks at sea. Winds reached 135 mph. RM3c Irene Ayriss of the US Coast Guard was on duty that afternoon with another girl, in a flimsy radio shack beside the raging ocean. Despite the danger she continued her work, realising that crewmen on the ships at sea were depending on them. When all communications were lost, they were unwillingly removed through waist-high swirling water. She received a commendation for this, and another a year later for her courage and initiative in a severe electrical storm, when her aerial was struck by lightning.

The civilian Florence Finch lived in Manilla when the Japanese occupied it in 1942. Her husband had been killed, and with no income she took a job with a liquid fuel distributing firm run by the Japanese, who had no idea of her American background, only being impressed by her clerical abilities. Soon she was writing out vouchers for fuel for members of the Philippine underground and causing critical items to be shipped away. She also tried to help American prisoners of war with supplies. In 1944, she was arrested, tortured and imprisoned. When released by American troops in February 1945, she weighed a mere 80 lb. Returning to her relatives in New York, she eventually joined the US Coast Guard and, in 1947, was awarded the Medal of Freedom – America's highest civilian honour.

The tragedy of a mine disaster in Pittsburgh in 1904, in which 178 people died, including some rescuers, prompted multimillionaire Andrew Carnegie to set up the Carnegie Hero Fund Trust, to recognise and compensate the bravery of ordinary men and women who tried to save life at the risk and sometimes sacrifice of their own. (The Carnegie Medal is described in Chapter Twelve.) Many women, as well as men, have been recipients of the medal and the fund. A few are given below.

In 1915, Shirley Starkey, a student lodger in Huntingdon, West Virginia, gathered from the noise downstairs that a madman was loose in the house. Running down, she was in time to deflect his aim as he drew a gun to shoot the landlord, only to have the gun turned on herself. The bullet passed through her heart, lodging in her back. Despite this she had enough strength left to throw the man down, and hold him until others took the gun. But while they were attending to her, he drew another gun and fired more shots, fortunately not hitting anyone, and then shot himself dead. Miss Starkey eventually recovered.

In 1934, Effie Haugh, a 58-year-old housewife in St Petersburg, Florida, saved a three-year-old child, who had been electrocuted by a high tension wire on the sidewalk and was still holding it. She tried twice to release its grip, once by jerking its elbow, receiving a huge shock that knocked her off her feet, and the second time by successfully pulling at the child's dress. Both recovered after some weeks in hospital.

In 1946, Grace Bingham, a 44-year-old housewife in Himyar, Kentucky, saved an eleven-month-old baby from burning to death. He had been left unattended in his two-room frame house. In the bedroom, the smoke was so thick and the heat so intense that Mrs Bingham was nearly driven back. Feeling her way to the crib, she found it was empty. Backing to the door she heard the child cough, and guided by the sound alone, groped her way back to the bed. As she did so a burning beam fell nearby and by its light she saw the infant. Catching him up, she put out his smouldering hair and tucking the baby inside the front of her coat ran for the door. Five minutes later the house collapsed. The baby and Mrs Bingham soon recovered.

In Columbia, South Carolina, in 1973, Naomi Clinton was driving her boss – who had heart trouble – home when she saw that a tractor and a lorry, loaded with oil drums, had collided causing a huge fire. One of the drivers had been thrown a few feet away and, though conscious and calling for help, was in danger of burning to death. Because of the intensity of fire and fear of explosions, no one in the watching crowd dared to help him. Alone, Mrs Clinton crawled forward and tried to pull the man away, though spattered with oil and hot rubber from an exploding tyre. At a safer distance she flung herself on top of the him, smothering the flames on his clothes.

When police and ambulance arrived, she had fainted. Miraculously the man recovered.

At Pampano Beach, Florida, in 1992, pilot Kimberly Schuttler, with a friend, stopped a car careering down a busy street with the driver slumped unconscious inside. Sprinting after it, she managed to reach through the car window and wrench the wheel out of the way of oncoming traffic, and then prevent it hitting a glass bus shelter. Her friend managed to reach in and pull the emergency brake. Only Miss Schuttler had minor injuries.

In 1993, in Lawrence, Kansas, seventeen-year-old LaTonya Farmer awoke to a fire in the bedroom of her apartment building where she was sleeping with her three young nieces. She started lowering the youngest girls to the ground, but before she could complete her task she was overcome with smoke and fumes and fell unconscious beneath the window, where her body was later found. The nieces survived.

Also in 1993, Kathleen Pilkerton, a part-time receptionist at a nursing home in Crozet, Virginia, saw one of the elderly residents taking a short cut across a railway line to the home from a shopping trip. The woman suddenly fell and could not get up again. Mrs Pilkerton ran out to help her, but when she heard the horn of a train rounding a bend in the track ran forward, extending her arms in an effort to stop the train. It was too late, however, and it struck both women and killed them.

Raemonda Freeman, Carnegie Medal.
(*Carnegie*)

In 1994, Fawn Walenski of Venice, California, went to the rescue of her partner who was being robbed at gunpoint outside the front door of their apartment block. Told by her partner to go back in, she instead picked up a heavy flowerpot and threw it hard at the intruder, who fired his gun at her, the bullet glancing off her shoulder. Then the assailant ran off with a very sore head.

Laura Shrake, in Matoon, Illinois, rescued the owner of a bull from its attack in 1995. She climbed an electrified fence and struck the bull on the nose with a length of rubber tubing, allowing the badly gored owner to crawl away to safety.

In 1996, Raemonda Freeman received her medal for saving a young man's life in Pittsburgh, Pennsylvania. She had gone to the park with her four daughters to decorate a neighbourhood baseball field for the opening game. Suddenly the pitch was invaded by a gang of youths, shooting at a rival gang already there. People fled, but Mrs Freeman returned when she saw one youth, wounded in both legs, trying to crawl off the pitch. She ran back and shielded him with her own body, advising him to play dead. After a while the shooting stopped and the gang fled, leaving two of their rivals dead, but the one protected by Mrs Freeman, and the brave woman herself, miraculously survived.

Of these many heroines, rewarded by these different societies, it is noticeable that there are representatives from both ends of the age scale – very young and quite old. It is also welcome to see how many people will rise to an unexpected danger, and have the courage to risk their lives for the sake of others.

CHAPTER SIXTEEN

Women of America's OSS

In 1942, shortly after Pearl Harbor had been attacked by the Japanese, General (Gen) Donavan was appointed by the President, Franklin Roosevelt, to set up in the United States an organisation – complementary to the British Special Operations Executive (SOE) – which was to be known as the Office of Strategic Services (OSS). The US OSS combined the work of sabotage and intelligence, using propaganda methods when appropriate. Over 21,642 people worked for it, mainly at its Washington headquarters, and over 4,000 were women. Its agents worked against the enemy in Europe, Asia, the Middle and Far East and Africa. Other countries, of course, had their own secret services.

Though OSS and SOE had the common aim to defeat their enemies, they did not always work harmoniously together, suspicion of the other's motives and interests in the East being the main stumbling block. Moreover, in most spheres of war, the resistance group they were there to help were themselves eager to wipe out their own rivals, preliminary to controlling their countries after the war. Fortunately, most of the US and UK agents worked together on the ground better than others did at the top, being inspired to deeds of enormous courage by simple loyalty and love of their countries. Many OSS agents gained high awards but others quite as brave did not. The majority of those working in an enemy country were men, but some were women.

These came from high and low levels of society – such as daughters of a vice-president and a supreme court judge, debutantes, pilots, clerks and shopgirls. Among their covers were titled names, journalists, prostitutes and nuns. Most were charming, good linguists, clever actresses, persuasive liars, intelligent, adventurous and skilled in many things. Two, who worked in German-occupied France, were rewarded with the rare Distinguished Service Cross.

Lt Jeannette Guyot, as a member of the Corps Auxiliaire Féminin (CAF), part of the French Army but on loan to OSS, was parachuted in during February 1944. As a courier, she had to travel around the country contacting fellow members and finding landing fields for supplies, often carrying compromising equipment. With many narrow escapes she undertook her work with marvellous sang-froid and was never captured.

Virginia Hall is probably one of the best known agents. Actually trained by SOE, she was sent to France twice, once for SOE and once for OSS. Born in America, she studied in Europe and failed to get into the American Foreign Diplomatic Corps except as a humble clerk. In Turkey a septic wound caused her leg to be amputated. She was fitted with an artificial leg she christened 'Cuthbert', and walked with hardly a limp. She was a striking figure – very tall and thin, with soft reddish-brown hair. She possessed a gift for languages. Through all disasters she was rock-steady, with a quick mind, a nose for danger and an unquenchable spirit. Virginia started her work for SOE in Vichy,

Virginia Hall DSC. (*Special Forces Club*)

France, in August 1941. Then moving to Lyons, she lived quite openly under her own name as the foreign correspondent of the *New York Post* (which got few reports from her as she was always busy at 'other things'). She became a regular visitor to the American Consulate and cultivated relationships with socially important people – probably why the Lyons police turned a blind eye to her activities. One agent said of her at the time, 'If you sit in her kitchen long enough, you will see most people passing through with one sort of trouble or another, which she promptly deals with.' She was, in effect, the spider in the midst of a gradually growing web of other networks as well as her own.

This fruitful period ended in November 1942 when Vichy-controlled France was occupied by the Germans, who intensified their search for SOE organisers. Virginia escaped over the Pyrenees just ahead of the Gestapo. Before leaving she signalled London, saying that she hoped Cuthbert would not be troublesome. Forgetting this was her name for her artificial leg, London replied 'If Cuthbert troublesome, eliminate him.' She was held in Spain for some time, but returned to Britain in November 1943 and received an MBE (see Chapter Ten).

Realising the handicap of not being her own wireless operator, Virginia had someone teach her the skill privately, and requested a transfer to the OSS. In March 1944, a British torpedo boat landed her with her wireless set and a male agent in France, with a roving commission to establish a new French resistance group and encourage sabotage between Clermont-Ferrand and Nevers. It was to be the first entirely OSS circuit in France and it became very successful. Living in a one-roomed cottage with only very basic facilities, she tended the cows and helped her farmer hosts in between arranging dropping areas and supplies for her growing Maquis group. The Germans failed to track down either her or her wireless.

After the D-Day landings in the north in June 1944, Virginia was moved in July to the Haute Loire, where she found the mountainous terrain and the people very difficult. Eventually in August, a three-man Jedburgh team landed and with her help they set about arming and training the resistance groups, now grown to three battalions and busy assisting the Allied advance. On her return to London in September, she was asked to organise a new operation planned for April 1945 in Austria, but it was overtaken by events. In September 1945, she resigned from OSS, but was awarded the Distinguished Service Cross for heroism, which, however, she would not accept in public.

Several agents were awarded the Silver Star for their work with the OSS in France. Nancy Wake from Australia received one, but her story is told in Chapter Twenty. Raymonde Granger was another recipient. She was actually a member of the French CAF, as was Evelyn Clopet but, as she had died, her award was posthumous. Magdalena Leones came from the US Army. She worked in the Philippines between February and September 1944, and received her Silver Star for gallantry at Luzon.

Some OSS agents, however, only received the Bronze Star medal although their activity was most certainly in contact with the enemy, sometimes face to face, and the dangers run were as great as those of soldiers even though the combat was mainly of brain rather than brawn.

The Bronze Star medal was established in 1944, but backdated to 1941. It was for any in the Armed Services who had distinguished themselves by heroic or meritorious achievement in military action against a US enemy. Aerial combat or flight was excluded. The medal is of bronze in the shape of a five-pointed star, with a small raised bronze star in the middle and five short rays to each corner. The words 'Heroic or Meritorious Achievement' are on the reverse, making a circle around the name of the recipient in the centre. The ribbon is a light red with a central dark-blue stripe edged with white, and a thin white stripe on either edge.

Bronze Star Medal (obverse). (*M. Salm*)

Because America has a multicultural population, it had a wide choice of individuals to award it to and OSS was a semi-civilian organisation, making the choice larger still. The following are a few of the OSS women agents who received this medal, though far below their deserts.

Madeleine Arcelin, a French civilian, worked as the chief cipher clerk to an inter-Allied mission in the Savoie Departement of France. She was captured by the Gestapo four months later, but did not divulge her knowledge under intense and cruel interrogation. Eventually, learning nothing from her, the Germans sent her to a concentration camp, where she survived under appalling conditions until it was overrun by the Allies. She also received the Medal of Freedom.

Paulette Marteliere was another civilian. She acted as assistant organiser and courier to a resistance circuit in the Loir-et-Cher region of France carrying money and messages daily across the river, almost under fire from the enemy. She also received the Medal of Freedom.

Anne Reybaud, also a civilian, worked in coordination with the Allied armies and particularly with the US Army in their advance into France. She planned many operations and very often exposed herself to great danger from the enemy. On one mission, she was chiefly responsible for capturing an advanced enemy command position, of great benefit to the Allies, who thus obtained men and information vital to them.

Annie Thinesse, as a French civilian, worked on both sides of the line between the American and German Forces. In the Epinal sector, the American Forces were badly in need of information on the presence and disposal of the Germany Army units. The weather was too stormy for any aerial reconnaissance pictures, so it was owing to the daring and self-sacrifice of Miss Thinesse that they received the necessary information. She infiltrated into an area full of German soldiers, in the teeth of fire from both sides, to investigate personally the exact position, layout and strength of the defences of the Moselle Bridge – a vital crossing point for the Allies. Without the information she successfully brought back, many lives would have been lost.

Another girl received her Bronze Star through an unfortunate accident. Gertrude Legendre, a graduate from Virginia, was a civilian just posted into Paris after being in charge of the Washington, and then London, Cable Desk, handling highly sensitive, secret information. On leave and looking for adventure, with a friend, she managed to beg a lift to Wallendorf, at a time when the battle lines were still fluid. But she got more than she had bargained for. The area was still in German hands! Under a hail of bullets she was captured, and in WAC uniform, which regulations had insisted she must wear! Then through intense interrogation as a spy, and imprisonment for six months, she held to her story that she was just a little Embassy clerk. Eventually, through the assistance of a friendly American-educated German, she made a hair-raising escape to an OSS Headquarters in Switzerland and safety.

Not all operations took place in France itself, or directly in the face of the enemy. In summer 1943, SOE set up offices in India and Ceylon. Nominally it was under the South East Asia Command (SEAC) of Lord Mountbatten, a British Commander, to act as part of the war against Japan. SEAC was often jokingly transliterated by those in it as the 'Supreme Example of Allied Confusion'. And maybe it was! It certainly allowed OSS access to information on Indian Nationalist elements, with which it was in sympathy, as well as to operate its own missions into Burma, Malaya, Siam and China.

Here and elsewhere much valuable spadework was done by women who patiently collected and collated minute pieces of information and then gave their advice based on their judgement of the material. It prepared the way very often for important military decisions and saved many lives. These 'back-room girls' were as important a part of a modern army as those who fought in it, and some of these, too, received the Bronze Star.

Captain (Capt) Jeanne Letellier was in the US Army and involved in the establishment of the Women's Army Corps (WAC) on the mainland of Australia and in the forward areas of New Guinea. Her suggestions and solutions to difficult problems contributed to the success of their activities in the south-west Pacific area.

Cpl Barbara Lauwers of the WAC worked with the Psychological Warfare Section of OSS in Italy. When she heard that a number of unwilling Czech soldiers, lukewarm in their loyalties at best, had been conscripted into the German Army on the Italian front, it was her idea to use certain propaganda methods to encourage them to defect. She prepared two leaflets, one in Czech and one in Slovak, to be infiltrated into their lines by German prisoners of war working for OSS. The messages played on their loyalties and advised them to leave a losing side. These were to be accompanied with surrender passes. She also wrote five speeches in their language from 'fellow Czechs', suggesting that they join the Czech Army of Liberation fighting with the Allies in Italy. These were broadcast by the BBC to Czech garrisons. Her efforts were amply rewarded, resulting in the surrender of about 600 Czech soldiers, who changed sides and fought with their own people against the Germans – a valuable addition to the Allies.

A similar ploy was used on Japanese soldiers in Burma, through forged 'official' messages and 'doctored' letters in the soldiers' personal mail. These were examples of 'Black Propaganda' at its best. To this end the popular singer Marlene Dietrich also willingly lent her help to the British and American Secret Services by recording specially 'slanted' songs to be used in German radio propaganda broadcasts to Europe and particularly to homesick German soldiers. Among the best known was 'Lili Marlene', which became a favourite of soldiers from both sides. The singer's reward was a Medal of Freedom.

Staff Sgt Jean Matthew's work was much more mundane. She was a translator and administrator in an army unit, whose task was to control the flow of important censored information to worldwide agencies. Shortages of staff, however, placed an increasing burden on the section, where it was Sgt Matthew's suggestions that helped streamline the workload, even when left with the whole responsibility of the section while in transit to Italy. By ill luck, the three Officers in Charge were all away at the same time leaving the whole section on the Staff Sergeant's shoulders – something never allowed. Nevertheless, she coped somehow, so that the flow of information from her section continued smoothly, and her records were accurate and complete. For such an exceptional achievement she gained the Bronze Star.

Maria Gulovich played a more active and dangerous role. Born and brought up in Czechoslovakia and at this time a teacher, she joined a local uprising assisted by the Russians against the German occupiers. After their defeat, she passed from the Russians to a British and American OSS mission. She became their interpreter and guide through a gruelling, three-month, winter, mountain trek through enemy lines, where only a few survived to reach Russian-occupied Hungary. Here they were the subject of Russian suspicions and Maria was fiercely interrogated but kept their secrets, of which she was then fully aware. Just in time with her survivors, they avoided being sent back to Russia, and were rescued by the British and American authorities. In American uniform she later visited her family, but married and settled in America, her loyalty being rewarded with the Bronze Star.

Two nurses, not connected with the OSS, also received this medal. 1/Lt Cordelia Cook was tending her badly wounded soldier patients in 1943 when her field hospital in Italy was badly bombed. In 1944, she was wounded in another encounter. Whatever her injuries, she continued her work in the wards unruffled and calm, giving confidence to her patients and helping in their recovery. Nurse Helen Grant from Scotland was another to receive this medal for her services to the many American sick during her three-years' internment in a Japanese prison camp.

A further mention should be made of an American woman who, untrained, turned herself into a dangerous spy in revenge for the cruel death of her soldier husband in a Japanese-run Philippine prisoner of war camp. She was Claire Phillips, known to guerrillas and American Army Intelligence as 'High Pockets'. She became the owner and chief artiste of a Manila night club, much frequented by high-ranking Japanese officers, from whom she and her girls drew valuable information. Her activities were eventually discovered and she was tortured and imprisoned. On her liberation and return to America she was given a Citation for Valor.

Back at home, one undecorated and unusual agent, Minneapolis-born Amy Thorpe Pack, worked for both British and American Intelligence under the code name 'Cynthia'. An incredibly beautiful and audacious woman, a true 'femme fatale', she used her wiles on various Foreign Embassy officials in Washington, both before and during the Second World War. Thus she secured valuable information, and particularly on the Vichy French and Italian naval codes, almost sufficient to justify the description of her as 'the spy who changed the course of the war'.

Another society beauty, who in 1942 flew to Helsinki and just failed to persuade a leader in Finland to break away and declare war on Germany, was Therese Bonney. She nevertheless brought back useful military information about Finland.

Many other women, both in and out of the Services, and from various countries, worked with and for OSS. They took messages through enemy lines, encrypted and decrypted signals, collected information, analysed reports, rescued or hid escapers and parachutists, forged documents, mapped and worked out enemy targets, planned supplies for operations, channelled speedily important documents, interrogated prisoners, recruited agents, and trained others. They worked everywhere around the globe. From the mixed nationalities were found interpreters and those who had exact knowledge of areas where they had once lived, vital to those in the field. They were involved in every activity.

Some women died in concentration camps or silently under torture. Many went unknown and unrewarded, others were decorated with many foreign awards. To some fell the Legion of Merit, the Purple Heart, Medals of Freedom, Certificates of Merit or Emblems of Meritorious Civilian Service; to others, nothing. The receiving of awards, particularly in a secret service, was always something of a lottery, but those who gave their energies and abilities to help others and shorten the war, whether rewarded or not, know their own worth, and so do their fellows.

CHAPTER SEVENTEEN

Canadian Services and Police

During most of the twentieth century and the two great wars, in which so many countries were involved, Canada has also shared for a long period in the same honours system at Britain, and so have its women.

The highest award (the Albert Medal; see Chapter Three) for a Canadian woman came in the middle of the First World War, and it was to an eleven-year-old girl, having nothing to do with the war at all. She was Doreen Ashburham, who gained her award in 1916. She and a friend – an eight-year-old boy – had left their homes at Cowichan Lake, Vancouver Island, to catch their ponies, which were grazing some distance away. About half a mile from home they were attacked by a large cougar, which was crouching and ready to pounce, at a corner of their path. They were almost upon the animal before they saw it, and had no time to escape. It first attacked the girl, knocking her face down on the ground and standing upon her back. Instead of running away, the little boy attacked the animal with his fists and riding bridle, driving the cougar off the girl, though at the cost of turning it on himself. Doreen, getting to her feet, came to his rescue, fighting with her clenched hands and her own bridle, and even putting her arm into the cougar's mouth to prevent it biting the boy. By her assault, she succeeded in getting it off the boy, but the creature stood on its hind feet and started to maul her face. At that moment a sudden sound disturbed it, making it turn away and run under the shelter of a nearby log, where it was later killed. The two children, though both badly injured, were able to make their way home.

It was remarkable that two such young children, when attacked by such a fearsome beast and with no real weapons, stayed to help each other instead of seeking their own safety. Both were awarded the Albert Medal, the boy being the youngest ever recipient. Over half a century later, the Albert Medal being then discontinued, Doreen was allowed to convert her medal to the George Cross. She was thus the only Canadian woman of the twentieth century to hold this medal.

In the turmoil of the Second World War, the newly created George Medal (see Chapter Four) was established largely to reward acts of bravery – to a lesser degree than those achieved for the George Cross – by members of the civil population. In 1942, two Canadian women were given this medal. One went to Frances Walsh, a schoolmistress at Big Springs School, near Calgary. She was teaching in a classroom in November 1941, when a training aircraft crashed in the school yard and burst into flames. The airman pupil, though on fire himself, was trying to pull the pilot from the blazing plane when Mrs Walsh ran out. Though risking the danger of fire, she dashed into the burning wreckage and dragged the pupil out. Rolling him onto the ground to extinguish the flames, she saved the airman's life but could not rescue the pilot, who was already dead. With the help of her pupils, the airman was carried into her schoolhouse nearby, where she applied first aid and sent for medical assistance. She was badly burned around the face herself, but made no mention of this until the medical men had dealt with the trainee, when she then allowed them to treat her.

Marion Patterson was brought up in Canada, but came to Scotland in the war. As a member of the ARP, she was on fire-watching duty on the night in August 1941 when the city of Aberdeen was badly bombed in a German air raid. A bomb demolished a tenement building near her, causing a fire to break out. Wielding a stirrup pump, she immediately set to work dousing the fire, which would have proved highly destructive without her prompt attention. Soon afterwards, she heard that a man was alive and trapped in the debris. Ignoring the danger to herself, and with bombs still dropping around, she volunteered – as the smallest person there – to burrow down under the wreckage for 15 feet to see if a way could be cleared through the rubble to the victim. Having reached him, Marion found that he was trapped by a heavy beam across his legs. She then tried to burrow down to free his feet, dust and ash falling around her at every move and threatening to engulf both of them in a living tomb. However, she succeeded, and the rescuers were finally able to draw him up gently, followed by Miss Patterson. She had been in acute danger during the rescue, as evinced by the complete collapse of the building only minutes after she had emerged. After the war she returned to Canada.

A third George Medal was given in Ottawa in 1959, after the war, to Edith Collins, a retired Canadian nurse. In May 1958, she was a widow living with her four children on the island of Viti Levu, Fiji. One night, hearing a noise in her maid's bedroom, she went to investigate and saw to her horror the maid being attacked by a man with an axe. Forgetting the danger to herself, and in a desperate attempt to save her maid, Mrs Collins rushed to try and disarm him, but in her struggle she was twice knocked down and injured. One of her children, hearing the commotion, appeared at the door, and Mrs Collins was again injured as she tried to push the child out of the door to safety. The man then escaped, but was later arrested and turned out to be the maid's husband. The two women were taken to hospital. Mrs Collins recovered but the maid died; a sad result for such a gallant effort.

Canadian nurses were already working with the army in 1885, and became officially part of the Canadian Army Medical Corps (CAMC) in 1901. At the outbreak of the First World War in 1914, they had only 5 nurses in the Corps, but this rapidly grew to 3,141, out of which 2,504 went overseas. They were not without casualties and 46 died on duty. St John

Nurse Edith Collins receives her GM from
Queen Elizabeth II. (*Canadian Forces
Photographic Unit*)

Ambulance Brigade and the Red Cross also contributed their nursing
volunteers and the Queen Alexandra's Imperial Military Nursing Service
(QAIMNS) was added to them. They all saw service in both wars. During
the First World War, in the eastern Mediterranean, France and Belgium,
Canadian nurses tended mostly their own soldiers, in conventional hospitals
well behind the battle lines, or in casualty clearing stations near railways,
which transferred the wounded brought in by field ambulances to the
stationary hospitals. The casualty clearing stations saw nurses – with white
veils flying, white aprons, and sleeves rolled up – preparing wounded men
for surgery or applying dressings, even though they were bone weary and air
raids were continuing above their heads.

Late on a May evening in 1918, two of the hospitals near Etaples were
heavily bombed in an air raid lasting two hours. This was made worse when
at least one enemy aircraft flew low and, aided by the bright moonlight and
the light from the burning huts, machine-gunned those engaged in rescue
work. Patients and staff suffered indiscriminately. For their bravery during
this terrible time, two nurses distinguished themselves and were the first
Canadian nurses to receive the Military Medal (see Chapter One) in the war.

Nursing Sister Beatrice McNair carried out her duties without pause,
throughout the hours of bombing, as if nothing untoward was happening. She
showed the greatest of solicitude for the patients in her hutted wards, never
leaving them untended whatever ensued and wholly unmindful of her
personal safety. Nursing Sister Helen Hanson assisted in the operating hut
while the air raid went on; her courage and coolness helped in a marked
degree to keep the essential operations going. She was ready to carry out any
duty and worked devotedly during the whole bombardment without flinching.

Before May was out Etaples, with its railway bridge and military trains, was the target of further air raids. The last wrecked the St John Ambulance Brigade Hospital and badly damaged the General Stationary Hospital which, being well behind the lines, should have been safe. Bombs hit three of the femur wards, killing one patient and wounding several others. Matron Edith Campbell, whose own office was wrecked, reported that this raid was harder to bear than the others and threw a greater strain on everyone.

For their great courage the Matron and three of her nurses were awarded the Military Medal. Nursing Sister Leonora Harrington remained on duty all night, being largely responsible for upholding the discipline and efficiency in her wards, while Nursing Sister Janet Williamson was in charge of a ward very damaged by bombs. Despite personal danger, she displayed exceptional coolness and calmed any panic, effectively ensuring her patients' evacuation, and reassuring them as they were moved. Nursing Sister Lottie Urquart remained steadfast when four bombs dropped on her ward. Regardless of the risks, she attended to the survivors' injuries, and helped clear up the destruction left by the bombs – a heartbreaking task. She gave an inspiring example of bravery and devotion to duty. Matron Edith Campbell herself was everywhere she was needed. Ignoring the danger, she attended to the sisters who were wounded, and by her own assured manner gave confidence to those working through the night. After this raid these hospitals were considered too vulnerable and they were closed down. The patients were evacuated and the nurses sent to other hospitals in France and Britain.

The Canadian hospital at Doullens, a brick building of several floors, became the casualty clearing centre during the enemy spring offensive in 1918. Many of its patients were victims of mustard gas. At the end of May the hospital was attacked, despite its isolated rural location, far from a railway or factory, and its roof being clearly marked with a cross. In the midnight attack, a good part of the hospital was demolished, causing many serious casualties and deaths among staff and patients alike.

A falling beam injured Nursing Sister Eleanor Thompson who, after rescue, extinguished fires from overturned oil heaters before they could get hold. She was joined in this work by Nursing Sister Meta Hodge, and together they helped the

Nurse Meta Hodge MM. (*Royal Artillery Institute*)

orderlies remove helpless patients from the wards above, sometimes having to slide down the debris where the main staircase had been. For their heroic efforts in evacuating patients both sisters received the Military Medal.

These eight nurses were all members of the CAMC, but another Canadian who worked with them was a member of the QAIMNS and received the Military Medal. She was Acting Sister Marie Lutwick. During a bombing raid on a casualty clearing station in France, she was talking to the Matron and another sister. When the bomb dropped, the sister was killed, the Matron severely wounded, and Sister Lutwick was blown off her feet. Picking herself up, she saw to the comfort of the Matron, and then crossed the bomb-swept open ground between the huts to find help. Having done this, she returned to her duties and carried on for many hours, in a state of near collapse and shock.

When the First World War ended, the sheer hard work and courage of all the Canadian nurses were recognised by the award of the Royal Red Cross (RRC; see Chapter Six) to 64 of their number, and 253 became Associate members (ARRC). They had all established a very fine precedent for the many thousands of nurses who were to follow them from all three Services in the Second World War, and the many smaller conflicts that inevitably occurred in the postwar years.

Mention should be made of another RRC, awarded in 1945 to Flying Officer (Flg Off) Myrtle Armstrong, a nurse in the Royal Canadian Air Force. She was on a posting in Canada responsible for the organisation of a reception and crash ward, as well as the emergency routine dealing with personnel involved in plane crashes. On one occasion during a blizzard, she went alone into bush country to give medical attention to civilians, who were without such help at the time. She was the perfect nurse for emergencies, dealing with them calmly and efficiently, whatever the conditions.

Of the Military Medals of the First World War, two must be noted, given not to nurses but to drivers of First Aid Nursing Yeomanry (FANY) ambulances. Evelyn Gordon-Brown was a Canadian who had joined the FANY in Britain. Sara Bonnel had joined the

Driver Sara Bonnel MM. (*Royal Artillery Institute*)

Canadian Army Service in 1917, driving an ambulance in London. At the end of the year, she transferred to the FANY and both women were sent to France. Often in the thick of battle they had to pick up any injured soldiers they could find, or were instructed to collect, and ferry them in their ambulances to the nearest first aid post or casualty clearing station.

On a night in May 1918, they were both summoned to help at an ammunition dump at Arque, which had been set on fire by enemy bombs and whose only available ambulance had been destroyed in the blast. There were many wounded to evacuate, and there was constant danger of more explosions and fire in the dump spreading. Despite the risks, five FANYs turned up with three ambulances, two driven by Evelyn and Sara, and they succeeded in removing all of the wounded. Their conduct throughout the long, painful and hazardous transfer process to the ambulance was exemplary. This was certainly gallantry and conspicuous devotion to duty under fire, as their citations record.

Returning to Canada, two women in Canadian factories, working for the war effort, won the Medal of the Order of the British Empire (see Chapter Two), designed mainly to recognise the courage of civilian populations when engaged in war work. Accidents frequently happened in factories making dangerous explosives and Jessie Hadd and Clare Sauve in 1919 were awarded with the medal for their courage in saving others and dealing with a fire resulting from an explosion in their factories. Jessie suffered extensive burns as a consequence.

In the Second World War, there was much exchange of ideas and personnel between the Women's Canadian Forces and Britain. Three WREN officers were sent from Britain to Canada to assist in organising and recruiting the Women's Canadian Naval Service (WRCNS) in 1942. The Service grew to over 5,000 women, many going to work in the United States and Britain. In Canada, some worked on board ships and some with the Fleet Air Arm. Today they are integrated with the Royal Canadian Navy. The Royal Canadian Air Force, Women's Division (RCAF/WD) began in 1941, but in 1942 was refounded after a slow start, when four WAAF officers travelled from Britain to exchange ideas. Like the navy women, as well as being employed at home its members were also posted to America and Britain. Today it is integrated with its male Service. The Canadian Women's Army Corps (CWAC) started as an auxiliary corps in 1941 but changed to full status in 1942, their officer ranks and badges being the same as the army.

The nursing service of army and air force were the first to be mobilised in 1940, with those of the navy in 1941. Nurses travelled wherever they were needed in the world. Some were trapped in Hong Kong and imprisoned by the Japanese. About 3,656 nurses served with the army, 343 with the navy and 481 with the air force. The first mobile nurses' force, known as the Canadian Active Service Force (CASF), was also created.

When South Africa agreed to take the wounded from the Middle East in 1941, it requested the Canadian government's permission to recruit 300 Canadian nurses to work with its own South African Military Nursing

Service (SAMNS) on a year's contract. The first contingent of eighty nurses left at the end of that year, being followed in the next year by others. By 1943 most had returned to Canada, but a few married and remained, while in 1947 there were still five Canadian nurses serving in South Africa.

Immediately after the war the nursing services were run down, but were very soon regenerated when the need to nurse returned veterans was realised, and this increase was maintained during the Cold War. In 1959, the medical services of three Armed Forces were integrated, followed in 1966 by the Armed Services themselves.

Although many awards of the MBE and BEM came to women in the Canadian Services during the Second World War and afterwards, few were for gallantry, mainly because women were not knowingly exposed to danger, except perhaps nurses in an emergency.

In 1942, Margaret Brooke was a nursing sister in the Royal Canadian Navy, employed as a dietitian and posted to Newfoundland. Late in the year she was aboard the Newfoundland ferry SS *Caribou*, when an accident caused it to sink. All aboard took to the icy seas. In the water, Sister Brooke tried to save another nursing sister, her friend, showing great courage in the attempt. But though she risked her own life in doing so, her friend finally drowned. Sister Brooke became a Member of the Order of the British Empire (MBE; see Chapter Ten) for her efforts.

In 1944, a small contingent of Canadian St John Ambulance Brigade left for Britain. It was part of a vast joint war organisation of St John and Red Cross members, 641 of whom drove ambulances or assisted in hospitals overseas, many serving at their own expense. At least one party was torpedoed, but survived. With them was driver Constance Hutcheon, who had been requested for a mobile surgical unit of the Westminster Medical Services, to be employed on Civil Defence. Air raids on London had decreased, though people nightly sought safety in shelters at home or in the deep underground tube stations. June and September 1944 marked a change in the raids, when the much more feared unmanned V1 flying bombs and the V2 rockets started to fall indiscriminately. During one of these raids, Driver Hutcheon showed outstanding bravery when assisting in the rescue of injured people from the wreckage of a bombed-out building that was about to collapse at any time. Afterwards she helped at the medical aid post, which the Canadian members of St John had set up in the Leicester Square underground station. For her dedication and work that night, she received the MBE for gallantry.

In December 1944, the Canadian Army Corps was engaged in a particularly fierce battle near Russi in Italy. Lieutenant (Lt) Margaret McCann was the nursing sister attached to an advanced surgical centre nearby when a large shell crashed through the ward, where she was at that minute dressing the stump of a newly amputated limb for a patient. Although the shell narrowly missed her, the draught from it blowing her headdress about, she let nothing disturb her and calmly completed the dressing. She afterwards coolly directed the removal of her patients to another ward. In

Lieutenant Bamford-Fletcher. (*WTS (FANY)*)

1945, she received an MBE for gallantry under fire.

The unusual award of an MBE was earned by Lt Joan Bamford-Fletcher, who had joined the FANY as a driver. After the war she was set the dangerous task of transporting 2,000 women and children 500 miles across the jungle to the nearest port. They had been held as Japanese prisoners of war at a camp in Padang, on the Indonesian island of Sumatra. The Japanese were still on the island, the Indonesians were nervous and none too friendly, and the Allied troops had orders not to interfere, so as not to spark off an international incident. Clearly it was not going to be an easy assignment. Lt Bamford-Fletcher contacted the Japanese Army headquarters still based there and they gave her fifteen vehicles, later increased to twenty-five. She started with forty armed Japanese guards accompanying her and her charges, and ended with seventy, in trucks mounted with machine-guns. She was the only non-Japanese in charge and it shook the soldiers to find a woman in command. Her only link was her Japanese interpreter.

With so many people to transport, she had to divide the numbers up and take them to the coast in about twenty convoys. The roads were bad, they had 5,000 foot mountains and a ferry to cross, and her vehicles broke down regularly – and once she had to deal with 500 hostile Indonesians. At one point there was an accident between two vehicles when her head was cut open, bleeding profusely, and she needed stitches, but she was on the road two hours later, thereby winning the respect of her Japanese escorts, who said they would never marry a European woman – they were too tough! Within thirty days the evacuation was completed and Lt Bamford-Fletcher was presented with a sword by the Japanese captain of the motor company, for her courtesy to his men and as a token of his respect and esteem.

Much later, in September 1967, Captain (Capt) Joan Cashin, a nursing sister with the Royal Canadian Army Corps, found herself near the scene of a Czechoslovakian airliner crash at Gander, Newfoundland. It was the middle of a warm afternoon and she was off duty, lightly clad in sandals and summer clothes. She was one of the first to arrive. On her way she intercepted some of the survivors, stumbling in a daze around the boggy ground. She gave these assistance and instructions for their dispatch to hospital. Questioning some of them in German, she was able to determine the position of the crash. Reaching the smouldering and burning wreckage, Capt Cashin spent five hours from afternoon to night, answering cries for help, searching for the injured and giving aid to the survivors, the fires in the fuselage illuminating the darkness. When she was sure that the last people alive had been found, she went back to her hospital to help with further treatment. Under the most difficult and chaotic conditions she had worked fearlessly and tirelessly, displaying bravery, initiative and resourcefulness, without thought for herself. Her actions certainly saved many lives. In the crash, thirty-three had been killed out of a total of sixty on board the plane. For her heroic efforts she received an MBE for gallantry.

The CWAC gained quite a few British Empire Medals (BEM; see Chapter Ten) for brave actions. Lance Corporal (L/Cpl) Mollie Entwistle was ill in bed with a fever in February 1942, when a fire broke out in her temporary lodgings in Ottawa. Ignoring her illness, she collected together those under her command and led them to a safe place, returning afterwards to help other occupants of the building, until the arrival of the fire brigade. She did this with no thought of the risks to herself.

In September 1943, Private (Pte) Ellen Kerridge was driving an ambulance, carrying three stretcher cases, to Winnipeg. On the journey she ran into a blizzard and had to drive with her window open and her head outside to see the way. Frequently she had to get out into the deep snow to

Captain Joan Cashin.
(*Canadian Forces Photographic Unit*)

search for the road ahead. She turned off her own heater to save the gasoline in heating for her patients. When she ran out of fuel she sent for the Royal Canadian Mounted Police (RCMP) to refill the vehicle. Finally she telephoned her headquarters for help and her ambulance was towed to Winnipeg behind a snow plough. Her actions undoubtedly saved her patients' lives.

Pte Mary Quinlan was involved in a very serious train accident in July 1943, in which six members of the Forces were injured, four seriously. Although hurt herself, Pte Quinlan took charge, giving first aid where she could, and then hobbled a mile to the nearest telephone to summon aid and give detailed information on the accident.

Another BEM went to Aircraftwoman (ACW) Anderson, a member of the Royal Canadian Air Force, Women's Division. Her award was dated June 1944.

L/Cpls Isabelle Sheppard and Patricia Marriott were both involved in a major fire in the garage where their vehicles were parked, at their headquarters in Ottawa in August 1944. After L/Cpl Marriott raised the alarm, she joined L/Cpl Sheppard in leading those drivers they could summon to drive as many of the vehicles as they could rescue from the compound beside the burning building. One vehicle catching fire was dealt with by L/Cpl Marriott. Both women carried on until ordered away from the collapsing building. L/Cpl Sheppard was slightly injured, but they had saved several vehicles from the fire.

Petty Officer (Petty Off) Robertson of the Women's Canadian Naval Service served and lived in London throughout the period of air raids and flying bomb attacks. In work of a highly confidential nature, she never let the disruptions distract her, even when bombs dropped close by. She received the BEM. Joining her, with Commendations, were Lt Diana Spencer and Petty Off Dorothy Hill, both of whom showed courage and leadership while working in vulnerable areas. There were other Commendations to members of the Canadian women's Services who employed over 33,000 women in the Second World War.

In common with other countries, the police forces, like the fire services, have not long employed women in their ranks. The RCMP have only taken women since 1974 and the Professional Fire Service Association even more recently. The highest award won by a woman is the Ontario Medal for police bravery.

In May 1990, a hired boat was reported drifting empty in the sea, half a mile from Strawberry Island in the Mara township. The next day, when a police launch and helicopter were again searching the area, the boat was spotted along the shore of Thorah Island, and a man was seen nearby, fully clothed and walking slowly away from the shore into deeper water. Removing belt and boots, Provincial Constable Suzanne Chaddock, aboard the helicopter, jumped into the water to attempt to save him. It was a risky undertaking, as not only was there some distance from the helicopter to the water – which was exceedingly cold – but she also did not know if the man might be uncooperative, or even attack or harm her. But the man quietly

allowed her to lead him to the shore, being dazed, incoherent and unable to walk without help. The helicopter pilot landed on the island and assisted Suzanne in getting the man to a point on the shore where the launch could pick him up. In hospital it appeared that he could not remember anything after renting the boat.

Monique Bray, a civilian, also won this award for saving the life of a friend from drowning in the icy waters of Lake Agnew, near Espanola, in May 1993. Her friend, with her boyfriend and another, had been enjoying a trip in a paddle boat, which capsized after taking in water. The third person managed to swim to the shore but the boyfriend drowned, leaving her friend struggling in the icy water. Miss Bray, hearing people screaming, saw the girl bobbing about in the water. Knowing her friend was a poor swimmer, and as a terrified crowd watched, she plunged into the freezing water without further thought, swam the 200 metres out to her friend, who was now numb with cold and could no longer move, and brought her safely back to shore. For her life-saving feat, she was also awarded a Carnegie Medal.

A number of other women constables and civilian women have gained commendations for their actions in recent years, among them Mrs Pauline Williams, who in 1978 rescued and gave artificial respiration to a man drowning in a park lake in St John's, Newfoundland. In 1980, Constable Mildred Norry attempted to free victims from a submerged car at Kenaka Creek, near Maple Ridge, British Columbia, and in 1981 at Toronto airport, Special Constable Brenda Lensh very skilfully used artificial resuscitation and cardiac massage on a car accident victim. Constable Delaney-Smith at Ship Cove, Newfoundland, together with a colleague, managed to arrest an armed, drunk, and mentally unstable man in 1988. That same year, civilian nurses Carol McNally and Barbara Clinton, at their hospital on Prince Edward Island, defused a potentially dangerous situation, pacifying a woman with a gun, which probably saved lives. The following year, Constable Shelly Goodwin attempted the rescue of a drowning man in the icy waters of the Assembly Wharf at Nanaimo, British Columbia. In 1990, Constable Bridgit Harris rescued and resuscitated a victim from Cameron's Lake, Antigonish County. Constable Christine Heikkila, with a male colleague, arrested an unstable, knife-wielding suspect at Botwood, Newfoundland, in 1992 and, in 1993, Constable Slobodian arrested a bank robber after a police chase in Mississauga, even though off duty and with her children at the time. In 1994, Constable Kimberly Ashford, with male colleagues, freed a trapped motorist from a blazing car in North Vancouver. The next year, Constable Rorison rescued two passengers from a burning car at Prince George, British Columbia and, in 1995, Constable Tracy Ross forcibly prevented a drunk and depressed woman, intent on suicide, from drowning herself at Tulameen River, Princeton, British Columbia.

From the range and variety of cases, it is clear that Canadian women have played, and are continuing to play, a very useful part in the police and Armed Services, and have shown courage and presence of mind in many untoward emergencies.

CHAPTER EIGHTEEN

The Canadian Honours System

Cross of Valour (obverse). (*Rideau Hall, Canada*)

The Canadian Honours System was created in 1967, and has grown since. Provision was made in the Canadian system for two kinds of award, that of honours for meritorious activities and that of decorations for bravery, a clear line being drawn between the two.

The Cross of Valour was established in 1972 for Canadian citizens, and it is awarded to those – inside or outside Canada – who perform an act of most conspicuous courage in circumstances of extreme peril in the interests of Canada. It can be awarded posthumously. Recipients may place the letters CV after their names.

The medal is a gold cross enamelled in red and edged in gold. A gold laurel wreath surrounds the central maple leaf. The reverse carries the royal cipher and crown in the upper arm of the cross. Along the two horizontal arms are the words 'Valour – Vaillance'. The ribbon is plain red, and for women, worn as a bow, with the tails behind the cross.

This award is very rare and the most highly regarded. Only three women have received the Cross, one was awarded posthumously, and the action for the first came just before the Cross was established.

In November 1971, an airliner was on its way to Alberta. Mary Dohey was a stewardess aboard the flight when a man with a black hood over his head, armed with a shotgun and two bundles of dynamite, threatened to take the lives of the crew and all the passengers on board. Although continually threatened with a gun, Miss Dohey spoke gently to the man to try to pacify him, and succeeded in discouraging him from using the weapons, which would have taken many innocent lives. When the aircraft was diverted, landing at Great Falls, Montana, she was able to persuade him to allow all the passengers and part of the crew, including herself, to leave the plane. At the last minute, however, she remained behind because of her concern for the remaining crew members. She felt that as she had gained some rapport with the man, they might have a better chance of survival if she continued her efforts; but it was a very brave act, as she had no idea if she would come out of the ordeal alive. During the terrifying eight hours of the hijack, her influence diverted the man from violence and, thanks to her selfless act of staying behind, finally brought the torment to an end without the crew being harmed, when under her persuasion, the gunman gave himself up. Hers was the first Cross to be given to a man or woman.

The second Cross to be awarded to a woman was from an event that took place in the Valnicola Hotel in Meritt, British Columbia, in September 1974. A fire broke out on the ground floor of the frame structure building, and spread rapidly. Jean Swedberg was the switchboard operator at the hotel and, instead of escaping herself, she left her post to race through the heat and smoke, alerting the guests in the dining room before running up the stairs to the second storey. By this time smoke had filled the corridor causing the guests to panic. Though fully aware of the conflagration around her, she went from room to room, banging at the doors, ensuring that everyone had been warned. It was only when she reached the last few rooms that the fire shot up the stairwell, completely sealing off her means of escape. Within minutes the hotel was a raging inferno, making it impossible for her to get out. She died in the fire, having saved many lives by her actions, at the cost of her own.

The third brave rescue took place in September 1980. It was early afternoon and Anna Lang was driving her car, with two passengers, over the Hammon River Bridge in New Brunswick. Suddenly a fuel tanker hit her vehicle and rammed it through the bridge's protective rails into the river below. The out of control tanker also plunged into the water and then exploded, spilling its oil and starting a fire which made the whole surface of the river a mass of leaping flames. Despite suffering concussion, and in terror of the rapidly spreading fire and the threat of further explosions, Mrs Lang managed to swim ashore. There she removed her heavy clothing and returned to the submerged car through a wall of flames. With great difficulty, and underwater, she forced open the doors and dragged out a mother and her four-year-old son, and swam with them out of the flames, towards the shore. Two young men, seeing what was happening, jumped in to help and between them everybody landed safely on the river bank. Mrs Lang suffered extensive burns during the rescue, having shown selfless courage of the highest degree.

The Star of Courage is the second of the special bravery awards created by Canada in 1972 and ranks second to the Cross of Valour. It is given to Canadian citizens who, inside or outside Canada, perform an act of

Star of Courage (obverse). (*Rideau Hall, Canada*)

conspicuous courage in circumstances of great peril. It may also be presented to non-Canadian citizens if their actions have been in the interests of Canada. Awarded to both men and women, it can also be conferred posthumously, and recipients can have the letters SC placed after their names. The medal is a silver star of four points with a silver maple leaf at each of the four angles. In the centre is a gold maple leaf, surrounded by a gold laurel wreath. The reverse carries a small royal cipher and crown, below which is the single word 'Courage'. The ribbon is red with a blue stripe near each edge. Women wear it as a bow with the tails behind the Star.

As the degree of courage needed for the award of the Star is slightly less than the Cross of Valour it has been bestowed upon more people, including women; even so, fatalities have occurred in their earning. The following are a few representative incidents.

In the year before the medal was established, there had been an armed robbery in Ste-Thérèse, Quebec. In his attempt to flee from the scene, the robber had been stopped by two policemen, one of whom he had shot. He had then run into a family home, grabbing hold of the twelve-year-old daughter and putting a pistol to her head, threatening to shoot. The police soon surrounded the house and tried in vain to reason with him but, keeping the girl hostage, he refused to give himself up. In trying to negotiate with him, the police agreed to his demand to talk to certain people, among whom was Evelyne Letêcheur, a Montreal newspaper columnist. After speaking to him on the phone, she went to the house and talked to him through the open window. A few minutes later she entered the house. This was taking a grave risk, as having already shot one person, he might easily shoot her too. Fortunately this did not happen and she – and other people with her – went into lengthy negotiations, in which Mrs Letêcheur offered herself as hostage if the man would release the schoolgirl. Finally she succeeded in persuading him to lay down his gun and surrender. The siege thus ended without further loss of life, owing to the heroic action of Mrs Letêcheur, risking her own life to save the girl.

In January 1972, Ula Boudreau of Bathurst, New Brunswick, a mother of six children, smelled burning in her home. Immediately she rushed up to the second-floor bedrooms to awaken her sleeping children. She brought three down the stairs and out to safety, before returning to fetch the other three.

The fire had now spread to the stairs, preventing further escape that way, so she helped one child out through a second-storey bedroom window and another onto the roof of the verandah below, where both were helped to safety by the crowd that had gathered. Exhausted and distraught, Mrs Boudreau finally succeeded in dropping her last child from another window, safe into the arms of those below, before there was a huge explosion and the whole house became a mass of flames, engulfing her in them. She had died as a mother, sacrificing her life to save successfully all six children of her family.

There was an unusual occurrence near Princeton, British Columbia, in July 1975. Margaret Pitkethly, aged sixty-five, was out with her daughter, collecting geological specimens in an old quarry. Mrs Pitkethly, tapping rocks with her hammer and working alongside her daughter, looked up and saw a huge boulder that had become dislodged from a rocky outcrop hurtling towards them. In the split second that this was happening, she also saw her daughter – becoming aware of it – rooted to the spot with fear. All that she had time to do was to push her daughter out of the way. The boulder bounced off the family van before falling onto Mrs Pitkethly, crushing her. Her injuries were such that she died on her way to hospital. Thus a quiet family day, indulging in their hobby, ended in unexpected tragedy.

In March 1976, the ice on the Kissinger Lake at Nitinat Camp, British Columbia, was in a treacherous condition. Tempted by what seemed solid ice, three young children ventured out to a swimming float, about 50 feet from the shore. There the ice gave way and the three plunged into the freezing water beneath. Alerted by their cries, Gail Flynn gingerly crossed the ice to the float – a dangerous thing to do, considering what had happened – and lifted a boy onto the float. She seized a little girl, who was by now lying unconscious in the water and, anchoring herself on the float, gave her artificial respiration, which soon brought her round. Lastly she searched for the third child, a three-year-old girl, and finally made her out drifting under the ice about 15 feet away. Mrs Flynn jumped into the chilling water and swam towards her, breaking the ice with her arms as she went. With half the distance covered, she dived under its frosty surface, and after a few more strokes caught hold of the child's hand. She managed to find her way back, brought them to the surface and again applied artificial respiration, which happily proved successful. Had it not been for Gail's courage and skill all three children would most certainly have drowned.

Violence suddenly erupted in the well-ordered life of schoolteacher Gloria Duncan in May 1984. She was quietly driving home from school on British Columbia's Pinchi Reserve, with two of her pupils beside her in the truck, when she saw two people fighting in a ditch beside the road. Stopping, she saw a man stabbing frenziedly at his wife with a hunting knife, so that she was covered in blood. At great risk to herself, Miss Duncan attempted several times to take the knife away from the man, but he – being a big man with a history of violent behaviour – merely pushed her out of his way. She tried again, this time grabbing both of his arms and managing to topple him over backwards, but he merely scrambled to his feet and continued stabbing at his wife. Miss Duncan then reached for his knife hand, at the same time pulling his other arm back, and was at last able to push him off his wife, who was now lying prone on the ground. Kneeling hard on the man, she told the wife to run away, while she talked to him and tried to calm him down. This seemed at last to work and, releasing her grip, she allowed him to get up and walk away. Running back to her truck, she drove it to where the wife was crawling down the road, too badly injured to get to her feet. She sent her two pupils to summon aid and, with the help of witnesses, lifted the wife into her truck and drove her to meet the ambulance. Gloria Duncan had taken a great risk in tackling a violent man, who could have turned his attack on her, but by her courage she saved the life of his wife.

In July 1991, Lorrane Leech was at Six Mile Reach Reserve, British Columbia, with a small group of children, whom she looked after while their parents were working. Having walked to a nearby fishing ground, they were all sitting in a small circle talking, when suddenly out of a bush sprang a black cougar who pounced on one of the small boys. Without a thought for herself Ms Leech grabbed the animal by the scruff of its neck and forced it to release the boy. The cougar then turned on her, rising on its hind legs, while she wrestled with its front paws. Using all her strength, and yelling for her dog, she managed to push the animal away from the children. Her dog came racing up, and at this the cougar turned and leapt up a tree, where the furious barking of the dog kept it imprisoned. Lorrane then gathered up the wailing, injured boy and the other hysterical children and ran back to the shelter of her house, only a short distance away. But for her courage and presence of mind, the boy would have been mauled to death.

An incident in April 1992, at Minaki, Ontario, shows that even a seven-year-old girl can be a heroine. She was Jocelyn McDonald and was playing with her five-year-old friend when a man approached them. When he told them to remove some of their clothing, she warned her friend not to listen to him. Annoyed by her attitude, the man grabbed her friend, put his hand over her mouth to stifle her cries, and dragged her with him towards his nearby house. Jocelyn pursued him, tugging at her friend, trying to free her, and picking up a big stone hit the man hard with it. The unexpected blow made him momentarily lose his grip, but he soon caught the crying child again and disappeared with her into his house. Jocelyn did not give up. Sneaking inside a minute later, Jocelyn searched for her friend. She found her alone in the bedroom and together they fled the house. Later the man was arrested as a child molester, and Jocelyn was praised for her sense, determination and courage on behalf of a friend.

The last award in the pyramid of recognition for courage is the Medal of Bravery. Established in 1972 for Canadian citizens at home and abroad who have performed an act of bravery in hazardous circumstances, it may also be given to non-Canadians if their action has been in the interests of Canada.

Posthumous awards are allowed. Recipients may put the letters BM after their names. The medal is coin-shaped in silver, with a large silver maple leaf in the middle of a gold laurel wreath encircling it. On the back in the centre is the royal cipher and crown, surrounded by the words 'Bravery' on the left and 'Bravoure' on the right. The ribbon is red, with three light blue stripes, one in the centre and the others towards the two sides. Women wear it as a bow with the tails behind the medal.

There are many incidents for which women have received this award, and again a few examples must stand for the many. In July 1967, a five-year-old boy on

Medal of Bravery (obverse). (*Rideau Hall, Canada*)

holiday with his parents fell into the Pitt River near Hany, British Columbia. His father, unfortunately a non-swimmer, was searching frantically for some kind of pole to reach out to the boy with, when Ruth McWilliams was passing in her car, going to her swimming class. Seeing the commotion on the bank, she stopped and, hearing what had happened, dived into the river. The boy had disappeared beneath the surface, so she swam some 25 feet underwater, but could not see anything because of the murkiness of the river. The attempt almost seemed doomed to failure, when she accidentally bumped into him and brought him to the surface. He was, however, sticky with mud and weeds and he slid from her grasp. Undeterred, three more dives enabled her to locate him again, and she got him onto a float, downstream of the bridge. He was blue and not breathing, and she began resuscitation – without apparent success – but in about quarter of an hour he regained consciousness. As a result of her rescue, in addition to the Medal of Bravery, this seventeen-year-old student also received the Award of Valour from the Girl Guides Association of Canada.

In February 1978, Gail Bunn, a purser on an aircraft which crashed in a blizzard in Cranbrook, British Columbia, seemed one of only two survivors in the tail of the plane. As they climbed out, they heard a child cry for help, and at risk to themselves in the unstable wreckage, returned and rescued her.

In July 1978, Francine Desbiens swam 1½ kilometres in bad weather, to get help for an adult and three children who, collecting shells, had been stranded by the tide on a small island in the St Lawrence River, near Sainte-Anne-de-Pontneuf.

In August 1979, Jane Fleming saved her two-year-old nephew during a tornado at Woodstock, Ontario. They found shelter in a porch where, protected by her body, he remained uninjured. She, however, had multiple arm injuries and had a leg amputated.

In September 1981, Louise Eliott, employed at the Coronation Nursing Home, managed to save a 92-year-old resident from being struck by a train, as he stood in a bewildered state on the railway track. She pulled him away just in time.

Heather Stewart rescued a co-worker from the grip of a jaguar at the Alberta Wildlife Park in April 1992. She struck the animal with a sledgehammer until it went limp, and then dragged the man into her truck and safety. However, in January 1993, Merla Schoenfield was not so lucky. She lost her life while attempting to rescue her husband after their tourist bus, crashing into a power pole, exploded while they were both inside.

In 1994, in Scarborough, Ontario, Tara and Tammy Benn, fourteen-year-old twins, rescued a man from a teenage gang attack and, with others, drove them off. That same year, in July, Anne Berberi and four men helped to rescue and give first aid to some seriously injured victims of a dynamite explosion near Lake Stuart, Quebec. Though in danger of a second explosion, they remained until medical help arrived.

These are only a small selection of the actions of Canadian citizens, who were willing to risk their own lives to help their fellows. This chapter also displays the handsome new medals with which Canada recognises them.

CHAPTER NINETEEN

Some Canadian Societies

Canada also became the beneficiary of the Hero Fund Trust set up in 1904 by Andrew Carnegie, a steel multimillionaire in America, who wished to reward people who tried to save the lives of others at the greatest risks to their own. Each recipient was to be given a gold medal, and if injured or killed, they and their family were to be given financial assistance. (The medal is described in Chapter Twelve.) Here are some of the stories of a few of its recipients.

In March 1912, twelve-year-old Florence Murray saved a six-year-old boy from drowning in the Avon River. He fell into water 5 feet deep from an edge of ice and went under several times. Florence, who could not swim, jumped in and held him up with one hand while dog-paddling with the other towards safety, her clothing keeping her afloat. Other children formed a human chain to drag them to the river bank.

In August 1933, Mary Boulanger tried to save a ten-year-old boy from a fire in the Great Desert, Ontario. He had been trying to fill a cigarette lighter from a can of gasoline in the garage when his sleeve became saturated. It caught fire when he flicked the lighter. He dropped it, and the leg of the overalls of his younger brother was set alight. Mrs Boulanger, a near neighbour, ran outside and extinguished the flames on the younger boy with a woollen blanket, before doing the same to the older boy. Unfortunately, her clothing too caught fire and although she saved the ten-year-old boy, she was enveloped in flames herself, rising above her head. Arriving on the scene, her husband tore her clothing from her but it was too late; she died five days later from burns and shock.

Mary McSween saved a three-year-old boy from drowning in the Mira River at Marion Bridge, Nova Scotia, in April 1948. He had fallen from an ice shelf, 30 feet from the bank. Mrs McSween, in an advanced stage of pregnancy, saw him floating in the water and ran down the hillside to the ice edge, where she knelt and tried to reach the now unconscious child. Being unable to catch him, she slid into the icy water fully clothed, grasped the boy and pulled him to the edge. Another woman, who had followed her, lifted the boy onto the ice with the aid of Mrs McSween, and then helped her out, though the ice was slippery. They revived the child on the bank and, despite Mrs McSween being chilled and suffering shock, she and her unborn child were unharmed.

In March 1962, three young boys were playing together in a sparsely wooded area in Hinton, Alberta. Suddenly a young cougar attacked the six-year-old, knocking him to the ground and biting at his neck. The other two boys ran to the nearest house, occupied by Elsie McEvoy. Although subject to dizzy spells, since she was just recovering from a recent operation and not yet very strong – as well as being of only slight build – she nevertheless ran to the boy and, picking up a 5-foot branch, struck the animal on the head repeatedly. She was badly winded by her run, but continued striking the animal – which growled menacingly at her – until the branch broke, leaving only a small piece in her hand. Still unable to remove the cougar from the boy's body, she finally took hold of the scruff of its neck and jerked it sharply upwards, at the same time striking its nose with her bit of branch. The creature fell to one side, stunned, and Elsie quickly scooped up the child and started to run back to her house with him in her arms. But it was too much for her and she fell to her knees. Wearily looking backwards, she saw the animal had risen on its forepaws, and this gave her the strength to resume her flight with the child. Nearly home, she met with neighbours armed with rifles. The boy was taken from her and driven to the hospital, while she escorted others to where the animal had crawled. Its skull had been fractured by her blows, and it was shot. The child had nearly 150 sutures to his face and neck and narrowly escaped death from severe loss of blood, but luckily he recovered. By her incredible bravery, Mrs McEvoy, despite her weak condition, had saved his life.

By 1995, the number of medals awarded by the Carnegie Hero Fund for Canada and the United States over the intervening ninety-one years was 7,970, and among these 1,621 people had lost their lives in trying to save someone else. In examining the names, it is surprising – but encouraging – to find so many teenagers among the rescuers, but chilling to find that a large proportion of the incidents were caused by fires or drowning, followed in more recent years by assaults and vehicle accidents.

A society established to address one of these too frequent occurrences and to help prevent them is the Royal Life-saving Society (RLSS). Water is not a natural environment for mankind but, as watersports are becoming increasingly popular, there is a need for as many people as possible to be trained from a very young age, not only in the knowledge of how to swim, but also how to rescue and resuscitate those in difficulties. A growing number of professionals are also there to teach and practise those skills, as lifeguards.

Most countries have seen the need for elements of water safety and many visiting dignitaries and sportsmen have spread the message. Lord Desborough was one such and, in 1911, on a visit to Canada, he was partly responsible for forming the Royal Life-saving Branch in British Columbia, but the earliest branch was formed in Ontario in 1908. Canada, in common with four other countries, including Great Britain, eventually became a self-governing branch of the RLSS in 1955, which is coordinated by the Commonwealth Council. International certificates, medals and awards are given for proficiency in the skills, the highest being the Mountbatten Medal (see Chapter Twelve) for saving life from drowning. Only one person, chosen from all the branches in one year, can receive the medal, and the first went to a Canadian man in 1951.

The only Canadian woman to receive the medal, so far, is Lynda Dann of Alberta. On a Sunday afternoon in July 1964, a twelve-year-old boy and a ten-year-old girl wading in Racehorse Creek, Alberta, suddenly slipped into deep water. The boy's father, a non-swimmer, went to their aid and was able to push the boy towards a bystander, who pulled him to safety, but the father and the girl disappeared below the water. At this point, fifteen-year-old Lynda Dann appeared, removed her shoes, and swam out into the deep pool. Following the directions of bystanders, she dived and found the girl floating unconscious a foot or so below the surface. After towing her about 10 yards to the shore, Miss Dann handed her over to a man who successfully applied artificial respiration. She then returned to search for the girl's father. This was made more difficult because of a strong current and the risk of being swept into a nearby whirlpool, formed by the junction of two rivers. After searching around for about 45 minutes in water cold enough to induce cramp, she recovered the body of the father from a depth of only 8 feet of water, where he had drowned. Out of the thirty or so

Lynda Dann, Mountbatten Medal. (*Royal Life-saving Society*)

people present at the time, she appears to have been the only one capable of going to the rescue of the girl and the father in deep water.

The Royal Humane Society has an even longer history. It was formed to award medals and testimonials for bravery and skill in saving human life. Canada has its own society, the Royal Canadian Humane Society, which awards Gold, Silver and Bronze Medals and testimonials. In 1962, the British Society decided to invite all kindred Commonwealth Societies to nominate their best cases for the pre-eminent award of the Stanhope Gold Medal (see Chapter Eleven) for the most meritorious case of gallantry during the year.

In July 1959, at Kooteney River, Six Mile, British Columbia, four children, aged eleven to fourteen, were paddling in shallow water at a sand point on the river's north shore. A little boy, stepping out too far where the bank dropped away and the river was running very fast, got into difficulties. One of his companions, eleven-year-old Edith Bouey, waded out to try and save him, but also got into difficulties. Another companion, Neil Bouey, aged fourteen, seeing his sister in trouble, plunged in and attempted to help both his sister and the first boy. However, Neil was not very strong and had stomach ulcers and he, too, soon found himself in difficulties. The fourth boy plunged in to help Neil and got hold of him, but Neil struggled so hard that he had to be released or he would have pulled the fourth boy under, who returned empty-handed to the shore. He was the only survivor. Two of the other children were still calling for help but, there being no one near to assist them, all three children were drowned. Neil and Edith Bouey, for their doomed rescue attempts, were awarded jointly the twenty-second Gold Medal of the Society, but these were posthumous.

Shortly afterwards, in August 1959, there was another drowning incident. This happened on Lake Ontario, near Hamilton. Mrs George Turnbull had rescued two children from the lake a few days earlier. On this day she was at her home when a boy yelled to her from the beach that one of his friends was in trouble about 150 feet out in the stormy, overcast lake. Without hesitation, Mrs Turnbull ran to the foam-lashed shore and plunged in, fully clothed. She swam out to the twelve-year-old boy, who was by now breathless and on the verge of sinking. She lifted him onto her back and held him above the surface of the waves, until he had recovered enough breath and strength to carry on himself. He then struck out for the shore, but when he arrived, he found that Mrs Turnbull had not been able to follow him. Having used up all her resources of strength in saving the boy, she had slipped under and drowned. Her medal was given posthumously.

The next two awards were for rescues on land. In March 1985, Mary Sommerville, an ambulance attendant at the Toronto Metro, was called to a propane gas explosion at a Toronto downtown building site. The resulting fire had severely burned a worker on a catwalk 15 feet above ground. Without thinking of the danger, Miss Sommerville climbed up a ladder next to the blazing building and found that the man had third-degree burns to all of his body except his feet. His clothes were nothing but charred rags and, although still conscious and trying to walk, he was in no state to be able to climb down himself. She wrapped some sheets around him and stayed with him, doing what she could to help and comfort. Two more explosions from nearby propane gas canisters erupted, threatening to topple the construction crane holding them. Nevertheless, she remained with the man until they were rescued. For her bravery she was awarded a Bronze Medal.

In April of the same year, Brenda Elkins, a former restaurant manager, was passing along a street in Toronto when she saw a motorcycle go flying through the air and a flash of flame coming from it. Without any type of first-aid training, she treated the victim using her common sense. She applied artificial respiration and cardiopulmonary resuscitation when she realised that his heart was failing. Although she had never attempted the techniques before, the motorcyclist responded and remained semi-conscious. Then becoming aware that his leg was bleeding badly, she devised a primitive tourniquet to stop it, and it worked. Finally she saw that he was having trouble breathing, and examination proved that the strap of his helmet was cutting into his neck. She shouted for a knife to cut the strap, and miraculously one appeared from a bystander, so that she was able to release it. Undoubtedly she saved the man's life. One useful point she made after the award ceremony was that, in an emergency, people shouldn't stand around. There is always something they can do to help.

These are only a few instances of the awards by the Royal Canadian Humane Society, whose aim is to reward the bravery of ordinary people when faced by unexpected and often dangerous accidents in their midst.

Awards of the Florence Nightingale Medal – pictured in Chapter Eight – began in 1920. To show the rarity of this exceptional medal, Canada's first recipient was not until Margaret Macdonald in 1927 and, interestingly, it was for her work with the Canadian Expeditionary Forces in the First World War. None were awarded in the Second World War and they have not been very frequent since.

One outstanding woman who received the Florence Nightingale Medal in 1981, also received Canada's own Jean Mance Award in 1980. The latter had been set up in 1971 by the Canadian Nurses Association to be conferred biennially to honour those who made an outstanding contribution to Canadian nursing. The award was named after the first lay nurse in Canada, a nun (the reason we use the name sister today) who founded Montreal's Hotel Dieu Hospital in the seventeenth century which was dedicated to the care of the sick and especially wounded soldiers. Helen Mussallem (overleaf) was cited for both awards as Canada's most distinguished nurse of her time and generation, who had a powerful influence on Canadian health policies and was an outstanding educator of nurses. She had been a dynamic force for the advancement of health care at home and abroad, a prolific author, and an international consultant as an 'Ambassador for Nursing'.

She started as a staff nurse at Vancouver General Hospital, served in the Second World War in the Royal Canadian Army Medical Corps and

Dr Helen Mussallem FNM
and Jean Mance Award.
(*Studio Von Dulong*)

followed this with several degrees, the last being a doctorate at New York's
Columbia University. She had been director of the Schools of Nursing, a
member of the Canadian Nurses Association, sat on Royal Commissions
and become adviser to the World Health Organisation, among various
activities. She was also a lecturer, speaker and chairman to many other
bodies. Her appointments had been legion, and yet within this busy life she
found time to write over forty publications, being considered one of the
most prolific, influential and scholarly authors in the field of health.

She was, of course, one of the many illustrious names which illuminate
the records of the Florence Nightingale Medallists in Canada and the Jean
Mance Awards.

CHAPTER TWENTY

Australian Women of Two World Wars

It was a fine, dry night in July 1917 in France. All was still except for the distant growl of guns. No. 2 Australian Casualty Clearing Station was a little way behind the trenches of the front lines. The people in the makeshift hospital tents, huts and abandoned buildings of Trois Arbres, near Armentières, had settled down for the night. Most of the patients were asleep – the sleep of exhaustion or the drug-relieved daze of amputations. Dim lights glowed in the wards, where behind the serried rows of white beds the sisters kept their nightly vigil. Tomorrow the ambulance trains would return along the railway track nearby and take the sick to larger long-stay hospitals, further away from the front lines, where their wounds or sickness would be fully treated – casualty clearing stations could only deal with emergency conditions and prepare the men for transfer. Despite their position so near the fighting, nurses and patients felt safe, guarded by huge white crosses painted on roofs and ambulances, clearly seen.

Sister Clare Deacon was off duty, sleeping in the nurses' tent. Sister Alice Ross-King was outside, walking along the pathway of duckboards between the huts, behind her male orderly. Sister Cawood and recently arrived Staff Nurse Derren were in the wards. Suddenly, without warning, bombs came showering from the sky. Deafening explosions were followed by huge fires, which swept through the flimsy structure of the hospital, with its sleeping patients helpless for the most part to save themselves.

Sister Deacon's first thoughts, on being rudely awoken, were for her patients, and she ran out towards her shattered ward. The first bomb exploded only a short distance ahead of Sister Ross-King, and when she picked herself up, deafened and stunned, it was to find her orderly dead. She stumbled forward to a scene of horror. Everything was a shambles: protecting walls were alight; men were scattered like wax dolls, half-hidden by fallen roofs and timbers; blood, limbs, bodies were tossed everywhere as from a great wind.

Head Sister Alice Ross-King MM.
(*Royal Artillery Institute*)

The shadows were soon garishly lit by advancing flames, the snow of ash flakes and red sparks setting new fires on men and shelters.

Frantically, with no considerations for their own safety, the nurses began pulling out any live patients they could find in the burning, shattered wards. Those men who could, moved themselves, or were moved by others. All around, the hungry flames leapt and reached out for more victims. Sister Ross-King calmly organised the evacuation of some wards in the path of the flames, amid the crash of timbers and the crackling of fire, mixed with the shouts and cries for help. The sisters frequently risked their lives to rescue patients trapped in burning tents. They were seen running into the smouldering ruins to remove men to safety.

When the fires at last died out, the sisters' promptness, coolness, and courage had saved many lives, and calmed the panic that might well have caused worse casualties. For their bravery in the field on this night of carnage, these four nurses were given the Military Medal (see Chapter One) – the first Australian women to receive this medal in the First World War.

At the outbreak of this war, Australia – already equipped with its own male Service – had sent troops from its coasts to defend its 'Back Door' in the Pacific and New Guinea, and to support Great Britain and the empire. This era also saw the formation of the famous Anzacs, a joint Australian and New Zealand Army Corps, a nickname proudly retained to this day. Wherever the Australian forces went, the nursing sisters were generally not far behind. Some Australian nurses worked with the Queen Alexandra's Imperial Military Nursing Service (QAIMNS), the Red Cross and the Australian Voluntary Hospitals, but by far the greater number served with the Australian Army Nursing Service (AANS). This had already a long and distinguished history, dating from its foundation in 1888, when its members were mobilised in 1914. Nearly 350 AANS saw service in Serbia and over 2,000 were sent to France. By the war's end, 2,692 AANS had been involved.

The newly instituted Military Medal awarded to these first four nurses had been specifically created for civilians or those who were not officers – a status for which the nurses were qualified since they were not commissioned, though treated as officers and allowed to wear their ranks. The medal was to reward a continuous display of bravery or individual acts of gallantry, which could be found even in hospitals in safe areas. Three more sisters soon joined the first four in winning this medal. In the late summer of 1917, No. 3 Australian Casualty Clearing Station was subjected to a particularly violent air raid. With bombs dropping all round, everyone who could was ordered to take cover in safer places than the tented wards. With sublime indifference to the falling bombs, the instructions were ignored by Sisters Alicia Kelly and Rachel Pratt, who were both on duty at the time. Both stayed with their patients in their tents, continuing with their work.

Recently promoted to a sister, quiet, unflappable 31-year-old Sister Kelly during the worst of the raid had told her patients in her wards, 'Put your enamel wash basins over your heads.' She explained quite seriously that, like their steel helmets, this would protect them from shrapnel and the bombs. Of course, she knew very well that this was not so, but she felt that this small subterfuge would give them a greater feeling of security, and prevent the panic which might damage their recovery. One man objected, 'But some of us have no wash basins, Sister.' 'Never mind', advised the ingenious sister, 'your chamber pot will do.' It created quite a picture – rows of wounded soldiers obediently sitting in their beds, solemnly crowned with handbasins and chamber pots, in the confidence that Sister knew best. But it worked! At the end of the raid Sister Kelly was still in the hospital tents, holding patients' hands and soothing them. No one had been harmed and her stratagem had been successful! With Sister Rachel Pratt, the quiet courage and example of them both had put their patients' well-being and safety above their own, and their presence instilled in their men enough confidence to bring them safely through the trauma of bombardment. For their great bravery under fire, they were both given the Military Medal.

Staff Nurse Pearl Corkhill, in August 1918, was on temporary detachment to No. 38 Casualty Clearing Station when it fell prey to two heavy air raids. On night duty she, too, displayed great courage and presence of mind, bringing the total to seven Australian sisters who were awarded the Military Medal in the First World War.

Nursing in all three Services was very much in evidence in the Second World War, though two of them, starting from scratch, were small – 60 naval nurses and 616 air force nurses, compared with 3,477 army nurses (RAANS). An Australian Army Women's Medical Service (AAMWS) was formed to provide non-nursing staff to the Australian Army Medical Corps. There were also a few women doctors in the army and air force. No more Military Medals were awarded – perhaps the novelty of nurses in the front line had worn off – but they were not left behind either in courage or other awards.

Sisters Margaret Anderson and Veronica Torney were among a group of nurses leaving Singapore in February 1942, in advance of the Japanese invasion. They were in the cargo ship *The Empire Star*, which had been pressed into emergency service. It normally had accommodation for only 16 passengers, but this time it carried 2,154 men, women, children and nurses stowed away in its holds, which usually carried frozen meats. Waves of Japanese bombers attacked the ship shortly after leaving Singapore. One was brought down by the ship's own guns but in the fearsome four-hour attack, three direct hits were scored. The nurses had their hands full dealing with the badly injured and dying, many from the crew. Sisters Anderson and Torney, with others, came up from the hold to tend to the injured, and when the cabins where they were nursing them filled with fumes, they took them on deck, believing that the attack was over. It was not. The aircraft had not finished. They made another run, swooping low and machine-gunning the decks. But even this did not deter the sisters. Rather than taking shelter, they covered their patients with their own bodies to protect them and remained on deck attending to their needs. In these actions, Sisters Anderson and

Torney particularly distinguished themselves by their bravery under fire and later. Staff Nurse Anderson received the newly established George Medal (see Chapter Four) and Staff Nurse Torney became a Member of the Order of the British Empire (MBE). The ship they were on survived and, after a stop for emergency repairs, limped safely back to Australia.

Ships were prime, easy targets at this time, but Australian nurses usually travelled this way to their duties abroad – on open seas, hunted by enemy submarines, planes and ships. Nurses were involved in another attack, this time off the Queensland coast, not far from home. It was particularly tragic as the ship was a specially equipped and staffed hospital ship, the *Centaur*, which was torpedoed in the dawn of May 1943 with a heavy loss of life.

Lieutenant (Lt) Ellen Savage (sisters were officially given commissioned rank by now) was one of the medical staff on board, sleeping on a deck where the doctors and nurses were quartered. In the early morning she was practically thrown out of her bunk by two terrific explosions when the ship was torpedoed, setting fire to the vessel. Still in her pyjamas, and tying on her lifebelt, she ran out on deck to find they were sinking so fast that there was no time for her to seek a lifeboat, only immediately jump into the sea. The next minute the ship went down and she was pulled into the deadly whirlpool of suction. It was like being held by a vice, but she finally reached the surface with multiple fractures of ribs, nose and palate, perforated ear drums and many bruises. The ship had gone and there seemed very few people swimming around. Ellen made for a piece of flotsam, where she was joined by an orderly, and later an already overfilled liferaft took them aboard, where her nursing task began.

During that day they tied up with other rafts bearing survivors, and they were patrolled by hungry sharks, who frequently shook the rafts. In the following night, one of the two badly burned men died. At sea, they were marooned for 36 hours. During that time, Lt Savage, despite her own pain, displayed courage of the highest degree. Her fortitude, care for the injured, calmness in the face of odds and her amazing morale upheld all who were with her. They sighted four ships and several planes, and had one frightening encounter with a submarine which surfaced nearby during the night while they were adrift. Eventually a Royal Australian Air Force plane spotted them and they were rescued by an American destroyer. From the *Centaur*, carrying nearly 340 souls, only 64 survived, Lt Savage being the only nurse. For her bravery on the liferaft, she was given the George Medal, only the second Australian nurse to receive it.

The story of another nurse to suffer a horrific ordeal on land and sea is probably well known. Staff Nurse Vivian Bullwinkel was one of a party of 65 Australian nurses in a mixed cargo of about 300, mainly women and children, whose ship the *Vyner Brooke* followed *The Empire Star* out of Singapore on the fateful day in February 1942. They hoped to reach safety in Java, but this was not to be. Though the ship hid among islands during the day, only steaming into the open sea at night, it was discovered by Japanese aircraft two days later and sunk off the coast of Sumatra. Except

Sister Vivian Bullwinkel
MBE. (*Red Cross, West Australia*)

for the severely wounded, most people managed to leave the ship. Their fates were various. Those who finally survived ended up in Japanese captivity.

Sister Bullwinkel was among a group that made it ashore onto Banka Island. The nurses tended the wounded but, being unable to find food and knowing that the Japanese had occupied the island, they all decided to surrender. When the Japanese did arrive, despite the nurses' Red Cross armbands and the Geneva Convention on treating captives humanely, the women were divided from the men and then had to watch the men being marched away. When the Japanese soldiers returned alone, the women watched in stunned silence as they cleaned their blood-stained bayonets. From that moment the women knew they were doomed, but they accepted their fate without panic. Then the soldiers signalled for them to march into the sea and, when they were waist deep, the Japanese machine-guns opened on them. Sister Bullwinkel, towards the end of the line, collapsed into the water, feigning death as a bullet passed through her left side. Later, having drifted unconscious to the shore, she crawled into the surrounding jungle. She was the only woman to survive the massacre.

After two days, sleeping for long intervals and stumbling along in a daze, thirst drove her back to the beach, where she discovered another badly injured British soldier, whom she nursed for ten days. At length, exhausted and starving, they decided to give themselves up, saying merely that they had been shipwrecked, Sister Bullwinkel hiding her wound with a water bottle. They were taken to the coolie gaol in Muntok, and she was eventually sent to various camps on Banka Island and Sumatra. By surrendering to the Japanese, Sister Bullwinkel was united with 31 other Australian nurses who had survived from the *Vyner Brooke,* and with about 300 other women of British, Dutch, Australian and Eurasian nationalities. They lived under terrible conditions: little sanitation, insufficient food and water and hardly any medical supplies. They had to cultivate their own vegetable plots, do hard manual labour for their captors, be subjected to the most degrading treatment, and take part in the frequent Tenko countings – to which their Japanese captors were prone – and all in the blazing sun. Not surprisingly the women suffered from malnutrition, malaria, typhus and other tropical diseases, so that they rapidly lost weight. For the three and a half years of captivity, the nurses in their makeshift hospitals tried to do their best for their fellow internees, but there was little they could achieve without proper medicines or equipment, and had to watch helplessly as most patients died under their hands. More nurses died during this time and out of those who had left Singapore, only twenty-four survived the war.

Release came in September 1945. The camp was so isolated that it had taken two men three weeks to find them. They were finally escorted back to Singapore to recuperate before setting sail back to Australia. In spite of their privations, all the surviving nurses recovered, and for her sterling efforts before and after her capture Sister Bullwinkel became an MBE (see Chapter Ten).

Women in the Armed Forces were never armed and were always non-combatant. They served long and loyally in the Second World War doing much difficult and essential work but they won few gallantry medals – not because they were incapable of such courage but because most were debarred from serving overseas, and, if they went, they were carefully kept out of danger. The exceptions were those posted to Britain who endured the bombing, endemic to those days, and some who, to avoid the limitations in their own country, enrolled in the British Services.

The Australian Women's Army Service (AWAS) began in 1942 and was disbanded in 1945. A total of 20,000 women served in it but no high awards were credited to them for gallantry.

The Women's Royal Australian Naval Service (WRANS) was formed in 1941 and disbanded at the end of the war. They totalled about 3,000 in shore jobs, but they could apply for overseas work.

The Women's Australian Auxiliary Air Force (WAAAF), patterned on the British WAAF, started in 1941 and reached a strength in 1944 of 16,500 personnel; some were posted to Britain. Again disbanded after the war, the women received no gallantry awards.

All three women's Services were re-formed in 1951 during the Korean War and small numbers afterwards remained on a permanent basis. In the

1980s, most were amalgamated with their parent Services. Some naval women saw active service in the Persian Gulf in 1991 with the medical teams and on board supply ships.

During the Second World War, there was an unusual woman who was very much involved in the war in the Pacific. She was fifty-year-old Ruby Boye, who was with her husband on Vanikoro in the Solomon Islands when the war with the Japanese in the Pacific began. She was given the chance to leave in 1942, for fear of capture, but she and her husband elected to stay. They had realised the importance to the Allies of the Coast Watcher

Ruby Boye BEM Coastwatcher. (*Navy News, Australia*)

Organisation, to which they both belonged. The teleradio station, of which Mrs Boye was the operator, was the only link with the Santa Cruz group and served also as an emergency relay station in communicating reports from coast watching stations in the Solomons to Vila, the American Navy base in the New Hebrides. In addition to transmitting and relaying her coast watching reports in code, Mrs Boye also daily furnished useful meteorological data obtained from her own readings. Such details were of great value to the Americans in the battles fought in the Coral Sea and the Solomon Island area.

The Japanese knew she was nearby and their aircraft flew low over Vanikoro several times. For safety, it was decided to move the tall radio mast and equipment across the river from their home. Unfortunately, the suspension bridge across the water had been destroyed in a cyclone but, undaunted, Mrs Boye crossed the crocodile-infested river by punt four times daily, often in torrential tropical downpours, and then ploughed through ankle-deep mud to her station to transmit the messages. In 1943, it was considered that Mrs Boye should be in uniform, in case of capture as a spy by the Japanese. Her new uniform, as an honorary 3rd Officer in the WRANS, was dropped to her by parachute.

By 1944 – with the effort and strain of the work telling on her – Mrs Boye became ill and was taken off the island. Her place was taken by four US naval men. Her unpaid, courageous work, which greatly helped the Allied forces, was repaid by the award of a BEM (see Chapter Ten) and many lesser awards from Australia and America. She also became a life member of the WRANS Association.

Not to be forgotten in this war must be women's participation on the Australian Home Front, through voluntary work, on behalf of over 8,000 funds, Australia-wide, half of which were affiliated to the Australian Red Cross Society (aside from their VADs) and the Australian Comforts Fund. In

1943, the Red Cross alone had over 315,000 members. Women also put their names down on the Women's Voluntary National Register (WVNR) and in 1941–2, until pre-empted by the Directorate of Manpower, it recruited women for the Services. Their civilian voluntary efforts were certainly not to be ignored.

Also during the Second World War, the British, Americans and French – to mention only those with whom the Commonwealth was most closely associated, since there were many others on both sides – operated secret services, to encourage resistance groups and sabotage against the enemy and to receive information. This was especially important in France, which was intended as the base for the big Allied D-Day entry into Europe, to drive out the invading Germans. Britain employed the Secret Intelligence Service (SIS) and the Special Operations Executive (SOE). Women from all countries of the Commonwealth and Britain, with the right qualities and abilities, were engaged in these, and some saw active service in the field, working with the underground resistance in occupied countries.

Nancy Wake was one of the women whom the war rendered exceptional, and she was one of its unusual heroines. Her parents, both New Zealanders and therefore by definition British, left New Zealand in 1914 when she was two, and she was brought up in Sydney, Australia. Youthful wanderlust took her to America, Britain and France, where in November 1939 she married a Frenchman, Henry Fiocca. She thus became officially French, which, despite her husband's death late in the war, she still technically was when she was awarded the George Medal in July 1945 by the British government. Australian nationality was created in 1949, at the time she took up Australian politics. Later in Britain she married an Englishman, both finally returning to Sydney, which she always considered home. Her true nationality is therefore somewhat confused.

Ensign Nancy Wake GM. (*Special Forces Club*)

Nancy helped to oppose the Nazi occupation of France twice, returning after her first venture as a First Aid Nursing Yeomanry (FANY) trained officer of SOE. Had it not been for the war she might have continued the life of a very rich, sophisticated lady, dedicated only to her husband – an almost millionaire steel industrialist in Marseille – and the pleasures of wealth. She threw herself into everything wholeheartedly, with the inexhaustible energy of abundant health and an insatiable lust for life. She was a mass of contradictions. She always saw the funny side of even the most serious of situations and yet could weep for days heartbrokenly over a minor tragedy. She could speak the faultless French of the cultured classes and in a minute drop into the argot of the street. She considered many men close and dear friends, but remained virtuously loyal to her husband. She could live in the most destitute, squalid conditions and yet insisted on wearing a luxurious nightdress to sleep at night. Nancy adapted quickly to any new situation and could coldly calculate and minimise the risks for others, yet on a personal level showed a complete disregard for her own safety – she almost seemed invulnerable, and faced danger without turning a hair. She was decisive, tough and a brilliant organiser, and yet would run any risk to help a friend. She was a nurse who would faint at the sight of blood and could not face a corpse, yet she willingly caused the deaths of many Germans, and once barehandedly actually killed one herself – though the memory haunted her. She could drink any man under the table and be the life and soul of many a raucous party, but sometimes she needed time and space on her own in quiet. She led a huge, unruly bunch of hard-bitten Maquisards by sheer force of character and example, who became devoted to her, and yet she still retained all her femininity and foibles, which she could on occasion use to gain her own, perfectly legitimate, ends. She was a practical realist with the foresight and creative imagination of a dreamer.

Nancy Wake began her war career as the erratic driver of a converted ambulance. Later, in October 1940 at Marseille, she came by accident into contact with various British officers, on parole from a nearby fortress. Supplying them with necessities led her into other activities, so that gradually she was drawn into a resistance network. She began to lead a double life as the 'White Mouse' sought after by the Gestapo, though there was nothing mouse-like about her. Work extended to helping men on escape routes out of France, often accompanying them herself. Once she was arrested, imprisoned, tortured and interrogated for four days, but her ready wit and tongue confused her questioners and her friends extricated her by a trick. Then, fearful of losing her, London arranged for her to use one of its escape routes over the Pyrenees to Spain and thence Gibraltar and Britain; even then, there were several close shaves on the way.

In Britain, burning with the desire to help France and to see her husband again, Nancy offered her services to the Free French, who were suspicious of her, and then the F Service of SOE under her unmarried name of Wake. On the explosives course, she shared a room with Violette Szabo and once, for a joke, dispersed a trenchful of fellow trainees and her instructor with a live grenade. After an unremarkable career in training, in February 1944 she parachuted into France near Montluçon with a male agent. She was to become Madame Andrée and help the Maquis of the Auvergne as a saboteur. By ill luck both her organiser and wireless operator, who were to be landed by Lysander at the same time but over 100 miles away, were quickly captured by the Gestapo. Thus the two free agents were deprived of the means of contact with the main Maquis groups.

This serious setback did not defeat Nancy. By devious means, she not only sent away her unsuitable fellow agent but managed to meet the unsavoury and stubborn chief of the area and, when a new wireless operator eventually arrived, she began arranging arms drops to a much more reliable group leader. Finally, after the chief's defeat by the Germans – she had always been horrified by French carelessness of security – Nancy found herself virtually the head of around 7,000 men, who became her devoted followers when they found she could summon the supplies they needed, take care of their security, and was willing to accompany them on their guerrilla raids against the enemy.

After D-Day, the enraged Germans amassed 22,000 men to try to destroy her Maquis, now dispersed over a wide plateau. Nancy's foresight minimised their casualties and allowed them to slip away undefeated, to further harass the German convoys sent to relieve their hard-pressed Normandy troops. Nevertheless, the resulting loss by her wireless operator of both codes and wireless caused Nancy to undertake alone, a dangerous, gruelling, 500 kilometre cycle ride to retrieve them. She succeeded in less than 72 hours.

Many times while with the Maquis, Nancy attended the parachute drops, which she always vetted and planned. Sometimes, in later months, they produced more SOE agents, as well as uniformed Americans, to help instruct the Maquis on the newer type of weapons available. In August 1944 came the long-awaited Allied landings in the south of France, and the skirmishes of Nancy's Maquis with the Germans increased. But this was nearly the end, as the enemy was fast withdrawing and Nancy could openly wear her uniform. Shortly, she was able to set up her headquarters at a grand château near Montluçon, and it was here that she took the salute of a march past of 10,000 Maquisards to celebrate her twenty-seventh birthday. After the fall of Vichy, the triumphant celebrations were ruined for Nancy when she heard of the dreadful death of her husband, who had been tortured to discover her whereabouts. His money, too, was gone, and so she found herself penniless.

September 1944 marked the end of Nancy's work for the Maquis. Later she found herself heaped with honours, not only the George Medal – surely too little for her actions – but also American and many French awards, for her courage, tenacity and leadership.

After the Second World War with its trauma and dangers, there were fewer opportunities for gallantry awards such as the George Medal, but one more fell to a twenty-year-old Australian teacher, May Gibbs, in October 1972, in the state of Victoria.

Lunch was over in the little junior school in Faraday, and the children were about to begin their lessons again. They were all from the scattered farming families in the remote district near Castlemaine. Suddenly the door burst open and two armed men rushed in. There was panic and the little children clustered around their teacher for shelter. Leaving a ransom note for one million dollars, the men took them all out into the back of their van. Then they drove off with the teacher and the children to a concealed hiding place in a thick forest, where they parked.

It became dark and with it came great cold, for which the children had no suitable clothing. Miss Gibbs pretended to the children that this was all a game. She told them stories and sang to them to keep up their spirits and prevent them growing too frightened. Throughout the long night she saw to their needs as best she could, but the children were cold, tired and hungry, the freezing temperatures sharpening their appetites and discomforts, only offset by their teacher's leadership and seeming confidence. She, however, was frightened for herself and even more on behalf of the children, being unsure of their captors' intentions, only aware of their pitiless cruelty, and knowing that they were sleeping in the front of the van, merely a short distance away from their huddled, miserable captives.

Just before dawn the two men left, hopeful of picking up the ransom. Realising they had gone, Miss Gibb took this heaven-sent opportunity to try to engineer their escape. Prolonged banging on the back door proved unsuccessful but, knowing how much damage children can cause, she encouraged them all to kick hard at it – giving them much needed exercise if nothing else. To their good fortune their combined efforts loosened it enough to enable them to squeeze out.

Then, at a run, she and the children endeavoured to put as much distance as possible between them and the van, struggling through dense bushland, until they found a road. She had no idea where they were, but a road must lead to some area of population, she felt, so they followed it, although every time they heard a car they had to take cover in case it was the returning kidnappers. This greatly slowed them down. Also the youngest children quickly tired, so that they had to stop to rest frequently.

At long last, on the following morning they were found and taken to safety, the children's well-being and morale largely due to Miss Gibbs' courage and example.

There seems to be only one other of the British higher awards for courage during the postwar years. This is the BEM given to Leading Aircraftwoman (LACW) Kathleen Pearson of the Women's Royal Australian Air Force for her actions in June 1954. She was a young, diminutive, round-faced brunette, based at No. 1 Stores Depot, Tottenham.

Two girls were talking in the recreation room of their station, warming themselves before the open fire, when the clothing of one of the girls caught fire, and she drew away screaming. LACW Pearson, the other person in the room, attempted to smother the flames, but the panic-stricken girl broke free and tried to run away. LACW Pearson did not give up, but ran after her. After a short struggle she managed to throw her to the ground and rolled her in the carpet, being the only thing near at hand. To her relief the flames were extinguished, and LACW Pearson ran for more assistance. She herself had received second-degree burns during her courageous attempt to help the girl, as well as having run the risk of her own clothing catching fire. There is no doubt that her presence of mind and prompt and gallant actions were responsible for saving her friend's life. Despite their burns, both girls eventually recovered.

Courage, it proves, is just as prevalent in peacetime as in war.

CHAPTER TWENTY-ONE

Australia's Own Bravery Awards

Star of Courage (obverse).
(*Government House, Australia*)

At about the time when Canada was considering its own awards system, so was Australia, with the result that the Australian awards for bravery appeared in February 1975. They were in four grades, depending on the degree of courage displayed by the individual, and were mainly intended for the civilian population. Starting from the highest, they were the Cross of Valour, the Star of Courage (pictured), the Bravery Medal and a Commendation for Brave Conduct. There was also a Group Citation for Bravery.

The medals are given to Australian citizens, but can reward non-Australians who are acting in the interests of Australia, or even actions outside the country, if they are done in Australia's interests, and can include Service personnel if their action is not in the face of the enemy. They can also be awarded posthumously.

The Cross of Valour is for those who act with the most conspicuous courage in circumstances of extreme peril. Recipients may use the letters CV after their names. The medal is a cross of gold, with rays at the four angles, ending in a central shield on which are the arms of Australia; above is a small star. From the top of the cross is attached a crown, above which is a bar bearing the words 'For Valour'. The ribbon is dark red with a broad light red stripe down the middle. The reds represent venous and arterial blood. It is such a rare medal that it appears no woman has yet received this high decoration in the twentieth century.

A quite different situation occurs in the case of the second award. Up to 1995, ten of these beautiful medals have been given to women, the largest number in the 1980s. The Star of Courage is for those who have acted with conspicuous courage in circumstances of great peril. Recipients may use the letters SC after their names. The medal is a silver, seven-pointed star, the surface cut with many facets of overlapping points. In the centre is the coat of arms of Australia surmounted by a small star. At the tip of the central point of the medal is a crown attached to a bar carrying the words 'For Courage'. The ribbon is light red with a broad central dark red stripe.

Late in an afternoon of 1981, Peta-Lynn Mann, a twelve-year-old schoolgirl, was with a close family friend travelling upriver in a small air boat in Palm Springs, Northern Territory, to see wildlife. They both jumped out when the boat grounded in shallow water, and as the man with her tried to free it, his pistol fell into the river, so he waded in to get it back. Suddenly Peta-Lynn heard him cry out and saw that a 13-foot crocodile had caught his arm in its jaws, snapping it with a loud crack. Instinctively, Peta-Lynn turned to flee to the boat for safety but then, oblivious to her own danger, turned to help him instead. Catching at his other arm, she tried to pull him away as hard as she could. A grim tug-of-war ensued. After a few minutes the crocodile let go, so that Peta-Lynn was able to haul her companion towards the bank. Unfortunately, this was only a momentary respite, as the crocodile once more attacked. Catching the fleeing man by the buttock, the creature spun him round in the water, but Peta-Lynn hung on. With an awful tearing his flesh came away, again releasing him, allowing Peta-Lynn to drag the badly mutilated and bleeding victim to the bank and stumble with him to his van. Without experience in driving, she somehow managed to start the vehicle and drove as well as she could away from the river and the crocodile. It must have been a terrifying drive, with a moaning man beside her, slippery

The Queen presents Peta-Lynn Mann SC with her medal (centre, in white blouse). (*Royal Humane Society, Australasia*)

with blood, and schoolgirl Peta-Lynn shaking with shock and effort and half frightened out of her wits. Reaching their camp, she dressed his wounds as best she could, and radioed for help. She then took the wounded man back in the van and drove for about an hour, to shorten the journey before the rescuers could meet them and take him to hospital.

Because of her great heroism in the battle with the crocodile and afterwards, the man's life had been saved several times over. In addition to being one of the youngest recipients of the Star of Courage, Peta-Lynn Mann was also given the Royal Humane Society's Clarke Gold Medal and the Rupert Wilks Cup and Silver Medal.

Another unusual, medal-winning incident took place in February 1983, when Lorraine McLeod, a nurse in the Argyle Diamond Mines at Kununurra, Western Australia, was accompanying an injured man on a helicopter to Camp Nicholas. He was strapped to a stretcher on the helicopter's skid, below the machine. Five minutes after take-off, the helicopter's tail rotor was fouled by a pillow slipping from the patient's head and flying into it. With its balance lost, the helicopter went into a spin and crashed, bursting into flames. The nurse and pilot, both seriously injured, managed to struggle free, but the patient was still strapped within the wreckage amid the fire, the flames from which were leaping 10 to 12 feet high. In spite of her spinal injury, the fire, and the risk that the helicopter might explode at any minute when the fire reached the fuel tank, Nurse McLeod struggled to her patient, undid his retaining straps and freed him from his position under the port side fuel tank, which had already caught fire. Dragging him after her, she had only managed to get about 9 feet away when it exploded. By her actions Nurse McLeod showed the greatest of courage and devotion to a patient in her care.

The next occurrence that brought its heroine the Silver Star took place at Taronga Park Zoo, New South Wales, in December 1988. Employee Christine Mueller went to join a colleague who was taking photographs of the tigers. She was outside the cage when she saw one of the tigers seize her friend from behind. Running into the cage, despite the danger, she seized her friend's legs and tried to pull her head and neck away from the tiger's jaws, but the animal was too strong. After a struggle, she felt her friend slip out of her grasp and watched the creature pull her further away from the exit. Miss Mueller made several more attempts to rescue her friend, repeatedly running back into the cage and trying to drive off the tiger, but to no avail. The tiger refused to let go. Finally hearing the screams, a keeper arrived to help and between them they manoeuvred the tiger and its mate into an adjoining enclosure, and got it to release her friend. The woman was immediately taken to hospital where, despite the desperate and courageous efforts of Miss Mueller in circumstances of terrifying danger, she later died of her dreadful injuries.

In February 1989, Lillian Marshall was driving from Maryborough to Biggenden, Queensland, when her car collided with another at the approach to a bridge. Badly shaken by the accident, she found herself unable to stand but, hearing a noise from the other car, realised that the driver was still inside and probably slipping into unconsciousness. She also saw flames coming from its engine, so she crawled over and tried to open the car doors, but they were stuck. Returning to her own car for tools, she came back and, propping herself up against the side, smashed the rear window, which enabled her to open the door at the rear. She then crawled inside to try to drag the driver out.

The car was filling with smoke and she found that the driver was trapped in the front seat and she was unable to release him. Not giving up, she edged further into the vehicle and this time, with strength she did not know she possessed, she managed to drag him over the top of the seat into the back of the car. The whole vehicle was now in flames. She had just swung the driver's feet outside the door when another motorist stopped and came to help her. Between them they got the unconscious man out of the burning car. In her rescue attempt, Miss Marshall received burns to her thigh, arm and hand, but she had saved the other motorist's life. She also received the Star of Courage.

In June 1989, Sharon O'Leary was at home in her apartment building at Wynnum West, Queensland, when she heard a neighbour screaming for help. Running to the flat next door, she found a woman lying on the floor, bleeding from wounds on her arms. A man, armed with a knife, was standing over her. Without thinking of her own danger, or that she might be the next victim of his attack, Mrs O'Leary struggled with the man and, directing the knife away from the woman's head, succeeded in pulling the woman halfway out of the flat. With a mighty push, she sent the attacker off-balance and took the opportunity to help the woman to her feet and down to the car park. After this she returned to the grassed area in front of the flats, where the woman's daughter was playing, and, taking hold of the child, ran towards the mother. Hearing the report of a gun behind her, she momentarily let the child go and then, picking her up, continued to run. Hearing a second shot, she felt the child go limp in her arms and at the same time felt a burning sensation in her right arm, so she knew that she had been wounded. She stumbled and fell to the ground, the child slipping from her arms. Then she blundered to her feet again. To her horror, as she ran she saw her own son playing outside the flats and she shouted to him to run away quickly; luckily he heeded her. Afterwards, she managed to summon the police before collapsing.

Another neighbour, Barbara Clark, had seen Mrs O'Leary falling to the ground with the child and then running away. Without thought for herself but to save the child, Ms Clark hurried to pick her up and carry her to safety, but received a shot in the lower back, causing extensive internal injuries. Both woman and child lay on the pathway in full view of the gunman, until the arrival of the police.

Mrs O'Leary and Ms Clark had done their best to rescue the mother and child, taking risks and receiving injuries in doing so, and showing great courage. They both received the Silver Star.

In March 1992, the Star was awarded for a different kind of rescue. Rachelle McNiven was standing near the baths at North Narrabeen Beach, New South Wales, when she saw a boy being swept out to sea by a strong current in very stormy conditions, towards a line of frothing breakers. Even though she knew how dangerous the situation was, she felt that she had to do what she could to help. Running to some nearby rocks, she dived in and swam out to the boy. There followed 40 frightening minutes, as she supported, encouraged and comforted the boy while she tried to bring him back through huge waves and violent breakers. Although they were carried nearly 300 metres off shore, and suffered both physically and psychologically, Rachelle remained with the boy, and by her courage sustained them both in battling with the stormy seas, until others were able to take over and bring them both to safety on the beach.

Bravery Medal (obverse).
(*Government House, Australia*)

The third award is the Bravery Medal. It is for those who have displayed acts of courage in hazardous circumstances. Recipients may put the letters BM after their names. The medal is coin-shaped and cast in bronze. In the centre is the coat of arms of Australia, surmounted by a small star. They both lie on a background of graduated mimosa blossoms set inside a 24-pointed star, the tips of which touch the rim of the medal, the edge being smooth. Resting on the medal is a crown, above which is a bar carrying the words 'For Bravery'. The ribbon has alternating dark red and light red stripes.

Many more women have been awarded this medal than the Silver Star. Among them are the following. In the evening of an April day in 1988, a light aircraft crashed in bushland near Boambee Beach, New South Wales. On board was Pamela Davidson, who saw another passenger kick open a window, climb out and run off. She followed suit, but then bravely turned back to try to aid the other passengers. One man responded to her calls and she helped him out. Suddenly she heard a hissing followed by an explosion. Flames shot along the ground, catching Ms Davidson who was thrown forward. Scrambling away from the flames she rolled on the ground to extinguish her burning clothes. The police arrived and she was taken to hospital to be treated for 65 per cent burns, which she would not have received had she not returned to save a fellow passenger.

Taroona High School was on an excursion to the Esperance Adventure Camp in Tasmania, during July 1990. After spending three hours exploring Mystery Creek Cave, two teachers and some students were returning to its entrance. They had to cross a creek of rushing water, which in their absence had risen to knee-high, so for safety's sake it was decided to form a human chain. Frances O'Neill was the second person to cross, when the girl behind her lost her footing and was swept away in the strong current. Frances plunged back into the creek and, catching her friend, managed to keep her head above water, but got into difficulties in doing so and called for help. Joanne Cuthbert, a teacher and joint leader of the caving group, rushed to the students, but the current was now so strong that it carried all three down the creek and out of sight, where they subsequently drowned. The Bravery Medal was thus awarded posthumously to Frances O'Neill and Joanne Cuthbert for their brave but unsuccessful rescue attempts.

Another incident took place in Strathfield Plaza shopping complex at Greenacre, New South Wales, in August 1991. Carol Dickinson, her daughter and a friend were chatting in a coffee lounge at the Plaza when a male customer began shooting at people indiscriminately. The friend immediately went to disarm him and, to help by creating a diversion, Mrs Dickinson, without regard for her own safety, leapt onto a nearby table. Shielding her daughter with her own body, she pushed her to safety, but was shot by the gunman as she did so. The gunman was disarmed, but Mrs Dickinson died from her public-spirited and sacrificial act.

In November 1991 at Sunnybank, Queensland, sixteen-year-old Angela Burke saw a young boy being attacked with a broken beer bottle by a gang of youths. While her male friend turned on the youths, she moved without hesitation to help the boy, giving first aid for his serious wounds, and comfort and protection until the ambulance arrived.

In May 1995, Gwenda Hunt, through her very brave actions, saved the life of an eight-year-old boy who was being attacked by a bull terrier, in South Yarra, Victoria. Ms Hunt was looking after a group of young children at the time. With her bare hands she tried to pull the dog off the child, who was being bitten at the back of the neck and the head. The animal then turned on Ms Hunt who, in the process of protecting the boy with her body, was severely mauled on her hand and leg. Before it could be stopped, the dog again attacked the boy, this time biting him in the stomach. Finally, someone managed to haul the creature off. Both Ms Hunt and the boy required surgery and extended treatment in hospital. Ms Hunt showed considerably bravery in tackling the dog single-handedly, and probably saved the boy's life.

Naomi Lennox protected a doorman under attack at a Perth nightclub in Western Australia in February 1996. He was being attacked by twenty-five bikers armed with baseball bats and iron bars. After trying unsuccessfully to find a telephone to call the police, she saw that the doorman was being viciously beaten, with blood spurting from his head. Disregarding her own safety and fearing that the man might be killed, she stepped between him and the attackers, and pleaded with them to stop. She was struck on the arm and a baseball bat was thrust under her chin, but she still stood her ground and remained until the men broke off and left. Then she assisted the injured man into a ladies toilet and hid him in a cubicle until the ambulance arrived.

By intervening and standing firm in the face of a very threatening situation, she showed great courage, and afterwards ingenuity in hiding the man.

Commendation for Brave Conduct. (*Government House, Australia*)

Numerous women have gained Commendations for Brave Conduct, the fourth among the bravery decorations. It is for anyone who performs an act of bravery considered worthy of recognition. The award takes the form of a gold frond of mimosa, with a few blossoms below the leaves. It is set diagonally on the lower part of a light red ribbon.

There are many examples of women going to the aid of those in danger of drowning, and nearly as many, including women police officers, who have risked their lives to save others from fires, usually in the home. There are also instances of rescues from car accidents and even robbers tackled and captured, but most worrying is the prevalence of attacks on women, either with fists, knives or guns, where other women, at great personal risk, intervene. An optimistic note is struck, however, by the number of young children who try to help. A few unusual cases are of interest.

In December 1989, six-year-old Erin Eva, at Largs Bay, Southern Australia, managed to drag her grandmother free when she fell on a railway line with a train approaching and, in March 1991, near Green Point, New South Wales, Senior Woman Constable Kay Piggott helped with others to rescue an injured firefighter from a rapidly advancing bush fire. At Dunalley, Tasmania, in November 1992, Gail Lennox attempted to avert the suicide of an emotionally disturbed man, a friend and neighbour, while in June 1993, off Byron Bay, Queensland, diving instructor Sally Neale swam out to a vessel to comfort a distressed woman whose husband had just been attacked by a large shark. In August 1994, at Bayview Heights, Queensland, 74-year-old Patricia Watt rescued her elderly husband who was being mauled by a wild pig and, using a metal-framed chair as a shield, kept it at bay until her husband could get safely inside the house.

As can be seen, bravery is not as uncommon as might be imagined, and can come in many forms.

CHAPTER TWENTY-TWO

Other Australian Awards

Australia does not lack in bodies anxious to encourage and reward bravery by ordinary people from its population. The Royal Humane Society is one such. Australia, being a large continent, has two of these organisations – one for New South Wales and one for Australasia.

Inspired by the loss of the pilot schooner *Rip*, and the heroism there displayed, the Victoria Humane Society was founded in September 1874. It became the Royal Humane Society of Australasia in 1882 and four years later incorporated Fiji. Recognising bravery was its chief aim, but it also introduced a relief fund for recipients or dependents who might need it. There are currently four classes of award: Gold, Silver and Bronze Medals and a Certificate of Merit. Only the Gold can be given posthumously.

Royal Humane Society Medal, Australasia (obverse). (*Royal Humane Society, Australasia*)

Since its inception, a few other special awards have been introduced. Sir William Clarke instituted the Clarke Silver Medal in 1881 for the single most outstanding case of bravery each year in Australasia. Sometimes none is deemed suitable. In 1952, the Rupert Wilks Trophy was introduced by a widow in memory of her husband, to be given to the most outstanding case of bravery in a year by a child of thirteen or under.

The Stanhope Gold Medal is given to the one person yearly who has displayed the greatest bravery, and its recipient is chosen not only from Australia but from all the kindred Royal Humane Societies of the Commonwealth, including Britain. It is therefore the most internationally important of all the awards, and the greatest honour.

The only woman in Australasia to win the prestigious Stanhope Medal is Beryl Smith. On a morning in November 1992, she was working in her back office on the third floor of the Mercy Hospital in East Melbourne, Victoria, where she was the hospital administrator and business manager. She heard that there was a deranged and armed man rampaging through several floors of the hospital, shooting and swearing at staff and patients, and he was now in her reception area. This matter was part of her responsibilities and, angry at such disruption, she stormed in, demanding to know what was wrong. Confronted by a man with a gun, it was revealed that he had been harassing the hospital for over a year after treatment for a broken wrist, and had developed a schizophrenic's hatred for the staff and one girl in particular. He told Mrs Smith that he had just killed the wrong girl upstairs, and wanted to find and kill the right girl, but if Mrs Smith got in his way, he would kill her too. 'It was then that I realised I'd better drop my plummy administrator voice and use my Aussie voice instead,' she said later. She kept him talking for ten minutes, while deliberately edging away from the desk, under which she could see the receptionist hiding. At this point the man agreed not to kill Mrs Smith, but shot her in the leg before running into the next room. Grabbing a door handle and leaning against the wall for support, she felt that she must still appear to be the dominant party, despite the pain she suffered, and waved away a doctor in hiding nearby who wanted to tend her. She knew that the gunman would be back, as the room he had entered had no other exit. She therefore remained in control of herself in order to protect her fellow workers and others in close proximity.

He did return but, ignoring her, dashed upstairs to the roof, where after some while he was talked into throwing his gun down and surrendering himself to the police. As soon as the emergency was over, Mrs Smith allowed herself to be taken down to surgery. For her courage in confronting the gunman, and protecting others at the risk of her own life, she also received the Clarke Gold Medal and the Australian Bravery Medal.

Clarke Medal (obverse). (*Royal Humane Society, Australasia*)

Four women have won the Clarke Gold Medal, including Reta-Lynn Mann, mentioned in Chapter Twenty-One, and Mrs Smith. The stories of the others are given below.

Ellen Devine was in her home at Wandibindle Station, Queensland, in 1925, when one of her hired hands came to her demanding that she send out one of her girl employees, whom he wanted to shoot, having already shot another of the men on the station. Instead Mrs Devine locked herself, her children and the girl into a room. The man followed and demanded that she let him in, and when she refused he threatened to get an axe and break his way in. While he was away, Mrs Devine decided to take the great risk of talking the man out of his intention. Therefore, locking the door behind her, she went out onto the verandah steps to meet him when he returned with the axe. When he did, she advised, cajoled and pleaded with him until finally she persuaded him to throw away his weapons. She then led him away from the house and engaged him in conversation until help arrived.

In February 1946, Elizabeth Williams of North Ballarat, Victoria, was walking near a railway line when she heard the whistle of the Adelaide Express in the distance. At the same time, to her horror, she saw two children playing on the line, oblivious to the approaching train. Heedless of her own danger, and shouting to the children, she climbed the fence between her and the track and sprinted out onto the line. She pushed the elder child to safety and then ran after the younger one who, laughing, was toddling straight into the path of the oncoming Express. Catching the child in her arms, she had just enough time to clear the track and roll down the embankment alongside before the train thundered by, missing her by inches.

The Clarke Silver Medal also went to four women. The first on record was Doris Simons in 1919. The second was given to eighteen-year-old Clarice Cozens, a clerk in Wangaratta, Victoria, who saved a fourteen-year-old boy in the cart of a bolting horse. Although she lost her footing and was dragged 50 yards, she succeeded in stopping the horse and saved the boy from injury. The third medal went to a fifteen-year-old domestic servant, Lorna Wilhelm. In December 1940, in Holmesdale, Southern Australia, she was in the kitchen with her employer and her baby when the cooker exploded into flames. At great risk to herself, and after several attempts by both women, Miss Wilhelm eventually managed to reach the baby and bring it to safety. The fourth silver medal was given to Joy Newmann of Yeppoon, Queensland, for her actions in December 1985. She was on the beach with a friend and their children, who were paddling happily. Suddenly one child was swept out to sea and she dived in to save it, but had to choose between releasing the terrified child's choking grip or allowing them both to be swept through the waves further out to sea. Eventually two men in a boat rescued them. Mrs Newmann by then was so exhausted, she had already gone under once.

There were numerous Royal Humane Society Silver and Bronze Medals, but some of the children who received the Rupert Wilks Trophy and Silver Medal should be mentioned.

In March 1961, Jane Crothers of Northampton, Western Australia, was playing with friends on a jetty when she saw a man struggling in the sea nearby. Without hesitation, this eleven-year-old girl plunged in and swam him back to shore and safety. Unfortunately, he collapsed a minute later from a heart attack.

Colleen Bachmann, aged seven, in July 1966 was a passenger in a car which somersaulted into a water-filled ditch near Fernvale, Queensland. She managed to scramble out and then, on her

Rupert Wilks Cup (obverse). (*Royal Humane Society, Australasia*)

own, pulled out the five children with her. All except one of the four adults drowned.

Adele Quinn of Swansea, Tasmania, saw that a small boy, swimming in the Swan River on his sister's back, had fallen off, and in his panic was choking her. Twelve-year-old Adele rescued him and then went to the rescue of his bigger, heavier sister, who had sunk to the bottom of the river. She brought her to the surface and with help managed to bring her to the shore, where she recovered.

Peta-Lynn Mann was also one of this select company in 1981.

Royal Humane Society Medal, New South Wales (obverse). *(Royal Humane Society, New South Wales, Australia)*

There is also a long list of those whose rescues cost them their lives. The Royal Humane Society may award a posthumous Gold Medal to the bravest, and an inscribed silver salver with a commemorative certificate to the next of kin, with the rescuer's name recorded in the archives.

The New South Wales Royal Humane Society is separate from that of Australasia, and there are several marked differences. Its inception arose from the loss of the paddle steamer *Yarra* and its crew in July 1877. Then called the Humane Society, it was set up to reward human bravery when saving or endeavouring to save a life, and to give relief to their dependants. In 1968, it changed its name to the Royal Humane Society of New South Wales.

Major awards of this Society are just Silver and Bronze Medals, a Certificate of Merit and Letter of Commendation. There is also the Sir Neville Pixley Book Award to children under fourteen. Gold is reserved for the Stanhope Medal, the most senior and highest of all awards open, since 1962, to all kindred Commonwealth Societies.

The only Stanhope Medal awarded to a woman in New South Wales was given to Dulcie Kalms of Temora, for her actions in November 1980. A car containing four young people ran off the road and, colliding with a heavy steel telegraph pole, burst into flames. Mrs Kalms, sleeping in a nearby house, was awakened by the sound of an explosion. From her bedroom window she saw the vehicle on fire with its headlights still on. Suspecting casualties, she woke her daughter in the next bedroom and gave her instructions to call the police and ambulance. Leaving her, she ran to the scene of the accident, where she saw a girl lying on the grass beside the car, and a young man nearby. Shouting at the young man to get away, she dragged the girl further from the vehicle, before turning her attention to those left in the car. One was a young man in the passenger seat, slumped across another young girl, who seemed to be wedged under the driving wheel. Both were unconscious and perhaps dead. As the door was jammed, she tried those at the rear of the vehicle. They were also immovable, but the window of the offside door was open. Leaning through this, she tried to drag the man from the front seat, towards the opening. This seemed to rouse him, and with her help he managed to climb through the window, but fell to the ground outside due to his injuries. Mrs Kalms tugged him through a fence and induced him to crawl to safety.

The front of the car was now well alight, so again from the window she attempted to pull the injured girl out, but she was wedged under the steering wheel with her seat belt on. As Mrs Kalms struggled to release the girl's seat belt, flames were beginning to lick around the girl's legs. Coming to consciousness, she began to scream and struggle, and as soon as the seat belt was released, Mrs Kalms managed to drag her backwards and through the open window. Meanwhile, the grass around the car had caught fire, so Dulcie Kalms returned to the first girl and pulled her further away from the flames. Shortly afterwards the petrol tank exploded and the whole car was engulfed in a fireball. Mrs Kalms suffered a slight arm burn, and the four young people recovered after two months in hospital, owing their lives entirely to her prompt and heroic actions.

In 1949, an exception was made by the Society, which gave a Gold Medal to Nurse Gwen Smith, who risked her life to help her Matron in August 1949 at the Strathallan Hospital for Crippled Children in Turramurra. A drunken man with a knife was attacking the Matron, and when Nurse Smith unhesitatingly grappled with him with her bare hands, he stabbed fiercely at her face. Worse might have happened had not two visiting Rotarians appeared and felled the man, who was later handed over to the police. Nurse Smith had to have thirteen stitches in her face.

Because the Royal Humane Society's Silver Medal is normally the highest that New South Wales gives, its list of women recipients is quite a long one. Below are the circumstances of a few of the more unusual ones.

In March 1915, eleven-year-old Beatrice Anderson saved a six-year-old – her sister – from drowning in the Murray River, despite a strong current running. In November 1922, eleven-year-old Edna Craigie, together with a thirteen-year-old boy, saved the lives of several children swept by a heavy wave into deep water at Tuggerah Lakes. Thelma Shea and two men rescued a woman surfer in April 1924, who, caught by a strong undertow, was being drawn out to sea at Coff's Harbour beach and, in December 1925, Emma Cantwell rescued from fire in a neighbour's house at Berrigan, four children – ranging from nine months to five years – who had been left alone while their mother was out. In July 1932, Dorothy Barber saved her brother from drowning in Cundibach Creek, while in August 1942, Barbara Mack saved the life of a three-year-old boy who had fallen in the water from Neutral Bay Wharf, despite the danger from the currents and sharks.

In January 1944, eleven-year-old Betty Smith lost her life trying to save a little boy from drowning at Throsby Creek, near Newcastle; he panicked and they both sank, but he survived the ordeal. In March of that year, Private (Pte) Dorothy Williamson of the Australian Women's Army Service was the only person to dive in and rescue a soldier from drowning in the harbour at Manly Wharf, while in December, Emily Hawkins lost her life in trying to save two young schoolgirls in a swimming pool at Northville. Elsie Higgins of Oatley West, in June 1946, rescued a baby from the burning home of a neighbour, who had just left the house and, in January 1949, thirteen-year-old Margaret Pope of Harbord made a gallant attempt to rescue a man carried out in a strong undertow at Freshwater. The rescue was completed by a life-saver.

In April 1951, Fae Channon of Smithfield, Mount Colah, climbed down a disused well in the bush, into which two children had fallen, thereby saving the life of one of the children and, in June 1958, nine-year-old Judith Wangman, at Bonshaw, was alone in the house with her three small sisters and brother, when the house caught fire. She managed to lead her sisters to safety, but her brother could not be rescued.

There are many more Bronze Medals that have been awarded to women but the most interesting cases are the children given the Sir Neville Pixley Book Award, one of which must have gone to the youngest recipient ever. She was Emma Geurts, aged five. In November 1993, at Engadine, her mother was pinned beneath her car in her drive. No one else being near, she sent her little girl to summon aid. The child used the preset button on their telephone and spoke to the police. By careful questioning and with the help of the directory services, they were able to establish the actual address and location of the accident and send the emergency services to rescue the mother. Emma stayed calm during the ordeal, knowing her mother was trapped and injured. She had remained by the phone giving all the help she could, a remarkable achievement for so young a child.

Mention must also be made of two awards specifically for nurses, and though they are not meant to reward gallantry, there is often a great deal of professionalism displayed under the most difficult of circumstances, which almost amounts to heroism.

The first is the Royal Red Cross (RRC; see Chapter Six), a medal instituted by Queen Victoria and proudly held by many Australian nurses in both world wars and afterwards. The first Australian presented with an RRC in 1884 for her nursing in the Zulu War was Mary Armfield, and the second, in 1901, went to Martha Bidmead. This attractive medal is considered an accolade to a recipient's nursing skills, and is held by nurses in all the Commonwealth countries, and even – during the First World War – by a few American nurses.

The second, international, award given by the Red Cross is the Florence Nightingale Medal, mentioned more fully in Chapter Eight. Over the years quite a few Australian nurses have been nominated. Evelyn Conyers, Matron-in-Chief of the Australian Imperial Forces during the First World War, was one of the earliest to receive this medal, when it was introduced in 1920.

Judged on her war years in Gallipoli, Egypt, England and finally France, where her common sense, tact and ability achieved miracles in the most chaotic of circumstances, Matron Grace Wilson in 1925 became Matron-in-

Chief of the Army Nursing Reserve, having held that post for a short time at the end of the war. She received the RRC in 1916 and the Florence Nightingale Medal in 1929.

In 1947, Captain (Capt) Vivian Bullwinkel, then an MBE, received the medal in respect of her Second World War services, as did Major (Maj) Alice Appleford – formerly Alice Ross-King – who, after winning the Military Medal in the First World War, had retired to have a family and then rejoined in the Second World War as Senior Assistant Controller of Victoria, with responsibility for about 2,000 servicewomen. Her organising skills made a great impact on fund-raising and she was fully committed in assisting the Red Cross and Service charities. No one in contact with her could not be impressed by her sense of duty, her sterling character, her humanity, sincerity and kindness.

Rose Huppatz – 'Hup' to her friends – had served with the Royal Australian Army Nursing Service during the Second World War in Egypt and Australia. When demobilised, she returned to the staff of the Royal Adelaide Hospital, where she eventually became Matron, retiring in 1966. She was always an active member of many nursing organisations, chiefly as State President of the Royal Australian Nursing Federation. She also helped

Matron Rosa Huppatz
MBE FNM. (*Mrs C. Harris-Bodfish*)

to found, and eventually became President of, the Council of the College of Australian Nursing. She was additionally involved in the Returned Sisters' League. Her interests were wide and she had an effective way with words. She could be very definite, and quietly set about getting what she thought was right, with lots of tact and a happy approach to the problems. In character she was a warm and genuine person, considerate, courteous, quiet and gentle. In 1966, she received the MBE and in 1963 was awarded the Florence Nightingale Medal for her contribution to Australian nursing.

In 1965, Margaret Edis was the first Western Australian to be awarded the Florence Nightingale Medal, and in 1969 it was conferred on Sister Kathleen Tweedy. A member of the Red Cross, she played a key role in bringing a blood transfusion service to the territory of Papua and New Guinea, being responsible for the recovery of the sick and injured indigenous population. To encourage the enlistment of donors from the people, she learned some of the native languages and regularly visited the villages and members of the village councils. To help her in her job, she

Matron Margaret Edis MBE FNM. (*Red Cross, West Australia*)

wrote a booklet in pidgin explaining her work to the villagers and it is still used extensively in the territory, so that today the blood transfusion service is an organised and smooth running one, thanks to the selfless loyalty and earlier sheer hard work of Sister Tweedy.

The 1995 medal was awarded to Red Cross relief worker Nurse Mary James, mainly for her efforts in the war-torn African countries of Somalia and Rwanda. She packed a lot of experience – much of it very harrowing – into a very short time. Starting with providing support to illegal immigrants, she joined seven other relief workers as a public health nurse in Somalia on a nine-month mission, and then was the only Red Cross representative to join the Special Air Service of the Australian Army at Kigali Hospital in Rwanda, providing emotional support to the soldiers. 'I spent a lot of my time listening,' she said. Faced with some of the horrors seen in that country, this service was essential.

Courage comes in many forms, great and small. Australia can be grateful that so many of its women have risen to meet its challenge.

CHAPTER TWENTY-THREE

New Zealand Civilian and Service Awards

The peace of the little seaside village of Aramoana, a short distance from Dunedin, was shattered one night in November 1990, as terror stalked its houses and woodlands. It was here that New Zealand – a country whose total population is less than half that of London in Britain – acquired its only woman George Medallist (see Chapter Four) of the twentieth century.

Eva Dickson made an unlikely heroine. Aged seventy-two, a widow with two artificial hips and restricted arm movements through surgery, she lived with her son, who did everything for her, including hanging out her washing. Late that day, hearing shots being fired nearby, her son went out with his dog to find out what had happened and, concerned, Mrs Dickson made her own slow, painful way outside to investigate. She saw smoke coming from a neighbour's house, not knowing that a gunman had deliberately started a fire there. She stopped a man walking in the direction of the disturbance but, while they were speaking, the gunman appeared and began firing, so they both fell to the ground, the passer-by severely wounded in the lower back and unable to move. Mrs Dickson dragged him to the side of the road and then crawled to a nearby telephone booth, where she urgently summoned an ambulance and the police – no easy task when she was so crippled. Afterwards she returned to the injured man at the roadside and remained there trying to comfort him. A while later, worried about the delay in medical aid, and not realising that the police had cordoned the area off preventing entry, she struggled back to her home and made further emergency calls. At this point she was advised for her own safety to remain out of sight, and to stay where she was. Later, the injured man was rescued by the police but he died of his wounds.

Meanwhile, Mrs Dickson, in the dark – her only light coming from the burning house – and praying that her son would arrive back safely, continued her tense vigil, crawling from the window to the telephone, giving the police valuable information of the gunman's movements and activities as far as she could see them. Alone in the house and in constant fear of an attack by the gunman – whose shots she could regularly hear – Mrs Dickson bravely carried out her self-appointed task throughout the long, terrifying night.

There were many brave actions during that terrible time, both by members of the public and the police. Thirteen people died in the massacre

Eva Dickson GM. (*Otago Daily Times*)

instigated by the deranged gunman, including Mrs Dickson's son, who had been an early victim. One policeman received a posthumous George Cross. The terror ended the next day, when the gunman himself was shot. The most heartening feature of Mrs Dickson's actions, for which she was awarded the George Medal, is that even the most disabled person can help in an emergency.

A number of nurses were already assisting the army in South Africa well before the First World War, but the New Zealand Army Nursing Service (NZANS) was not really established until 1911, following Lord Kitchener's visit, although no nurses were accepted until 1913. On the outbreak of war they were immediately mobilised and around 600 served from 1914 to 1918.

New Zealand has cause to be proud that one of these nurses achieved the distinction of being awarded the Military Medal (see Chapter One). The daughter of a doctor in Wellington, New Zealand Laura James was early imbued with the idea of a medical career. She trained and became a sister in Wellington Hospital but joined the Queen Alexandra's Imperial Military

Nursing Service (QAIMNS) in November 1910, thereafter nursing in several military hospitals in Britain. She was mobilised as a sister in August 1914, and went with a group of nurses to France, where she continued to serve, usually in casualty clearing stations near the front line, for the greater part of the war. She won distinction early on, receiving a Bronze Star in 1914, was Mentioned in Despatches in 1916 and was given the Royal Red Cross (RRC) in 1917. In July of that year she was awarded the Military Medal 'for Devotion to Duty', while serving as Sister-in-Charge of the operating theatre on a night when the site was being shelled. Continuing her duties with calm assurance, although she knew that she might at any minute be killed, she showed heroism of the highest kind. Nor was this the only instance of her courage, as she had often been under heavy shelling before. Laura James ended the war as Acting Matron of a large hospital for the wounded in Italy, being one of the very few New Zealand sisters to have served there during the war. This tall, slight sister, noted for her efficiency and care of her patients, was always respected and admired by all who knew her.

Sister Laura James MM. (*Royal Artillery Institute*)

Only the sisters of the NZANS were called upon to serve in the First World War, but it was a very different picture in the Second World War. There, all three male Services had their female equivalents in uniform, serving their country.

The Women's War Service Auxiliary (WWSA) was set up when war broke out, to coordinate the efforts of many women's voluntary organisations. It sorted out the enlistments for the Services with the National Service Departments. It also recruited, selected and trained part-time workers for canteens, defence offices and other duties. As a result, in December 1941, a contingent of WWSAs were sent overseas for hospital and clerical work, later to be absorbed by the women's army. This had been formed in 1942 as the New Zealand Army Auxiliary Corps, soon to be known as the Women's Army Auxiliary Corps (WAAC). Their kind of work widened as the war extended, and they eventually served overseas, especially in the Pacific, as the threat to New Zealand from Japan was just as great as that of Germany to Europe.

Women were also accepted for service with the navy from 1942, there having been no call for them until Japan entered the war. They were at first employed as writers, cooks, stewards and wireless operators. Their title finally became the Women's Royal New Zealand Naval Service (WRNZNS). Numbers were always small, but about 5,000 served, mainly in their home country.

The Women's New Zealand Auxiliary Air Force (WNZAAF), known more commonly as the Women's Auxiliary Air Force (WAAF), began in 1941 to relieve manpower shortages. It soon became an integral part of the New Zealand Air Force as its trades and its postings overseas expanded. In 1954, it was renamed the Women's Royal New Zealand Air Force (WRNZAF).

At the end of the war, in common with other Commonwealth countries, the women's Services were disbanded – all except the nurses – to be revived when New Zealand's forces became involved in other conflicts.

An interesting note can be added in regard to the WAAF. In 1951, a New Zealand WAAF was sent to Britain to bring 100 British WAAF back to help the New Zealand force. On the journey one fell ill and returned home. From that time the group became known as 'The Ninety-Nine'. Many became New Zealand residents – mainly by marriage – and others joined them later, so that many former British WAAF are now found in ex-WAAF Associations throughout New Zealand.

As for some of the higher awards and decorations, several army nurses became Officers of the Order of the British Empire (OBE; see Chapter Six). Ida Willis, who served in the First World War and afterwards became Matron-in-Chief from 1934 to 1945, was one, as was Tina Smeeton, who went on active service and heard about her award at that time. A doctor of the New Zealand WAAF, Wing Officer (Wg Off) Main, became an OBE in 1949 and Eva Mackay, a New Zealand Army nurse, had the same honour during the Second World War.

A number of women in the services gained MBEs and BEMs during the Second World War, but it does not appear that any were for gallantry. Some interesting ones, however, deserve mention.

Section Officer (SO) Frances Bryers, of Maori race, joined the WAAF in 1942, where she was widely and affectionately regarded by other servicewomen, while high ranking male officers rated her as an 'absolute gem'. As a Section Officer, she was the person responsible for bringing British WAAF members to New Zealand. She was made a Member of the Order of the British Empire (MBE; see Chapter Ten) in 1960, and was possibly the first servicewoman in the Commonwealth to be granted the Queen's Warrant by Queen Elizabeth II. Matron-in-Chief Nutsey also received the MBE in 1945 for her work in charge of army nursing.

A more unusual case was an MBE for a civilian, and this was certainly for courage. Merle Farlane was a nurse with the New Zealand Methodist Medical Mission in the Solomon Islands of the south-west Pacific, on the island of Vella Lavella. She declined to be evacuated when the Japanese invaded, and lived in the jungle helping wounded and crashed Allied airmen and arranging their onward passage in native canoes, by night, to Allied islands up to 200 miles to the south. Ten months later, the Allied High Command ordered her to leave, when they finally heard of her presence. The Japanese looked for her long and hard, and if they had caught her she would have been interned at the very least, and probably shot. She later held a commission in the New Zealand Army Nursing Reserve and for the rest of the war served as a charge sister at New Zealand Army hospitals and casualty clearing stations. A very brave woman of whom to be proud.

A number of British Empire Medals (BEM; see Chapter Ten) were given to non-commissioned officers. Most were New Zealand WAAFs, for meritorious service. One was to a Wren, Dorothy Pinson, who started work in the canteen section as Chief Wren, moved to an Officers' Mess and remained in the navy until 1949. Her BEM was awarded in 1951. Daphne Donell served as a VAD before joining the women's army, where she was sent abroad to do medical nursing, ending up in Italy. After the war she became a great supporter of the joint council of St John and the Red Cross, becoming eventually treasurer of the Red Cross. She formed a senior citizens' club and was active in many other clubs and the Presbyterian Church. For her work in the community she was given the BEM in 1971.

Not many women have achieved the Queen's Commendation for Brave Conduct. Julienne Horn was thus honoured for her actions during her holiday in Britain in 1974, when she was visiting Hampton Court. Someone called for help from a number of people who were milling around. A man was trapped down a manhole, unconscious from underground fumes. No one seemed to take any notice, perhaps suspecting a hoax. Infuriated by their lack of cooperation, Julienne scrambled down the manhole herself, having to wade through mud up to her knees along a tunnel. At the end, behind a pump, a man was slumped, unconscious and being held up by two others. They needed a third person to pull him from the other side. This Miss Horn did and dragged him towards the manhole, but no one above would help to get him out, so she pulled him up as the two others pushed him from below. He was a big man, slippery with mud, and she was less than nine stone, but somehow she managed to drag him out through the hole. Once outside no one would even give him a coat, despite his being so cold that she thought he would die. So she gave him hers and with her efforts started him breathing again. Meanwhile, the friend she had been with had called an ambulance. One of the bystanders broke the glass summoning the fire brigade – but too late to be of any use. In view of the public apathy, she certainly deserved her Commendation.

In 1978, Jean Donnelly of Masterton went to the assistance of a woman in her town, who was being attacked by her husband. The man, mentally disturbed, wanted to kill her with the iron bar he was wielding. He was waving the weapon indiscriminately about him, injuring Mrs Donnelly, who was trying to protect the woman. Finally, she managed to wrestle the iron bar away from him, and thereby almost certainly saved the woman's life. She received a Commendation for her bravery.

Katherine Burrell's award dates from the two years she was working part-time as a prison nurse. In 1984, she was the last out of her section at the Arohata Youth Institute, when a fire was started in one of the cells by an inmate who was being held in custody on remand for murder. She had set fire to her mattress, which was smouldering and making such black, noxious smoke that it was choking her and threatening the safety of those in the cells around her. When the fire alarm sounded, Mrs Burrell went through the long, slow process of locking and unlocking doors to get to the right corridor, and then the right cell.

Inside, the smoke was very thick. A blanket had been thrown over the mattress to stifle any flames and she could only see a clear space of a few inches at floor level but nothing else. It was so black that she did not even realise that the light was on. She knew the bed was behind the door and groped her way there first, but the inmate was not in it. The sprinklers came on and everything became drenched, including Mrs Burrell. She grabbed the mattress and hurled it out into the corridor, before going back to search for the woman, finally finding her slumped, unconscious, beside the door. She had stopped breathing, though she still had a pulse. So on the floor in the wet, Mrs Burrell carried out mouth-to-mouth resuscitation. The firemen came in afterwards asking about burns, but there were none. The woman was taken off to hospital for the night, and Mrs Burrell was left to settle the other women in their cells and reassure them, before she was able to go home and change her smoke-damaged, wet clothing. Her prompt action had undoubtedly saved the inmate's life.

On a morning in July 1987, Lee Vogel was acting as a parent volunteer supervisor of a school patrol crossing in Christchurch for the Waimairi Primary School. The patrol was in operation, with the signs extended to require the drivers to stop, and four children at that moment were crossing the road. Suddenly Mrs Vogel realised that an approaching car would not be able to stop, and ran out onto the crossing in an attempt either to wave the car down or to pull the children from its path. Despite her efforts the car did not brake and it struck three of the children and Mrs Vogel, badly injuring them. Mrs Vogel had received the worst of the impact, with a crushed vertebra and head and leg injuries. The children suffered a dislocated hip and cuts requiring stitches. But for Mrs Vogel's intervention, the children would have been more seriously injured or perhaps even killed. She well deserved her Queen's Commendation for Brave Conduct.

The last Commendation dates from that terrible day and night at Aramoana in November 1990, and it went to Chiquita Holden, a nine-year-old girl. When the gunman started firing shots, she was visiting friends nearby. She heard shouting and then saw her father go from their house to that of a neighbour, where there seemed to be an argument, followed by some more shots and then silence. Chiquita now feared that her father might have been killed, since an armed man almost immediately ran into the house where she was and started shooting at them. Before her terrified eyes her best friend and her elder sister were killed, and she was badly wounded

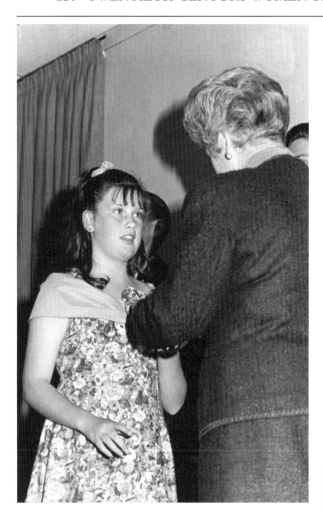

Chiquita Holden (age 9),
Commendation. (*Otago
Daily Times*)

in the stomach and the leg. Her instinctive reaction – rather than to cry or ask questions – was to flee from the house to warn her neighbours and obtain help. As she dashed past two young boys playing nearby she screamed at them, 'Run away. Run away' and, realising she was in earnest, they did so, undoubtedly saving their lives.

At the next house, Chiquita stumbled through her story to incredulous occupants, who calmed her down and then drove her back to her house, which she found on fire. She was again the victim of further gunshots, so that she was quickly whipped away to safety by shattered neighbours. For so young a child, she showed remarkable presence of mind and stamina despite her injuries, and determined courage and public spirit in trying to save others, having seen at least two people, whom she loved, killed in front of her. She was certainly a real heroine.

Hester MacLean RRC FNM. (*Director Nursing Services*)

Lieutenant Colonel Daphne Shaw RRC. (*Director Nursing Services*)

The New Zealand nursing profession has two awards for devotion to duty, and skill in their profession. They are also tied to efficiency and self-sacrifice, which often requires great courage.

The first, established by Queen Victoria in 1883, is the RRC (see Chapter Six) a most coveted decoration. The earliest recipient was a Miss Crisp in 1883, followed by Miss Williamson in 1901. A number were awarded in both world wars but only a few since. Three army nurses who were recipients were Hester MacLean in the First World War, Eva Mackay in the Second World War and Daphne Shaw, who was the last surviving nurse from the Vietnam War and received her medal in 1984. There were, of course, others, and many more who became Associates of the Royal Red Cross (ARRC), described as the Royal Red Cross, Second Class, but no less worthy none the less. It is frequently a stepping stone to the RRC.

The second award – the Florence Nightingale Medal – is truly international. Given by the Red Cross, it is mentioned more fully in Chapter Nine. A steady stream of New Zealand nurses have been considered worthy to receive this award. In 1920, one of the first medals was given to Hester MacLean, mainly in respect of her care of the sick and wounded in the First World War. More recently, Judith Owen received it in 1995. She had acted as a field nurse in some of the most dangerous war zones, the last being Yugoslavia. In 1997, it was awarded to a Southland nurse, Sheryl Thayer,

Nurse Sheryl Thayer FNM. (*Mr J.B. Haigh*)

for her services of almost ten years in many of the areas torn by war. Sadly she was one of the six Red Cross nurses shot dead as they slept in a hospital compound near the Chechen capital of Grozny. It was the first posthumous award given.

Over the past decades New Zealand has gradually introduced some distinctive National Royal Honours. Under consideration is a revised integrated New Zealand system including gallantry and bravery awards, similar to those introduced in Australia and Canada. It was felt that uniformed or not, men and women who served their country, their community and their fellow citizens by performing brave actions at risk or sacrifice of their lives, deserve recognition in their own country.

CHAPTER TWENTY-FOUR

New Zealand Awards from Other Societies

In common with many Commonwealth countries, New Zealand has its Royal Humane Society, founded in 1898. Prior to its formation, awards were given first by the British Society and then by the Australasian Society but at the turn of the century it broke away to develop on its own.

As well as having funds available to help those affected by their rescues, it confers awards for bravery in the service of humanity, ranging from Gold, Silver and Bronze Medals to Certificates of Merit, Letters of Commendation and In Memoriam certificates. In 1898, the Stead Gold Medal was instituted for very conspicuous acts of bravery and this is equivalent to Australasia's Clarke Medal. In 1962 came the Stanhope Gold Medal (see Chapter Eleven), the pre-eminent award shared by Britain and all the Commonwealth Societies for the most heroic rescue carried out by one person, man or woman, during a year. It has not yet been won by a New Zealand woman, though New Zealand's Royal Humane Society has awarded several of its own Gold Medals to women.

The first of their Gold Medals went to Jean Donaldson of Christchurch in October 1906. She was the Matron of the Waltham Orphanage. Just after midnight, she was awakened from sleep by the sounds of breaking glass and crackling wood. At first she thought it was a burglary but, when she got up, she found that the building was in fact full of smoke, with flames already burning around the back staircase, leading to the kitchen. Miss Donaldson awakened the assistant matron and together they set about evacuating the children to safety. There were thirteen children sleeping there and the women's work was made all the more difficult because of the thick, suffocating smoke, which by now was filling each room. The children were taken down the front staircase – which had not been touched yet by the flames – and they had reached the safety of outdoors when it was discovered that one child was missing – there were only twelve present. Miss Donaldson, knowing where the child was probably to be found, immediately re-entered the burning building and, at great risk to herself, ran upstairs to hunt for him in the smoke. She finally located the boy and brought him down to safety.

The second Gold Medal came in 1930. This rescue was felt to be the most outstanding ever accomplished, and was followed by letters of praise, flowers and telegrams from all over New Zealand. On a morning in

February at Muriwai Beach, several members of a group who had gone swimming found themselves in great peril. Out to sea there was a strong undertow, with heavy breakers and treacherous shifting sands. Eighteen-year-old Chloris Munro swam out to the struggling surfers and with difficulty managed to bring one woman safely back to land, not leaving her until she was assured she was in good hands. Then she plunged into the surf once more. The next rescue proved to be much harder, struggling with a heavy man and huge waves crashing down on them. But despite this she eventually brought him within reach of others, who took him the rest of the way to shore. And though she was tired and weakened by the battering of the waves and her supreme efforts so far, Chloris could not leave the last man to drown, so struck out for the third time. However, as she neared the last young man, he disappeared beneath the waves. In those conditions, as the sea was growing rougher, it seemed impossible for her to dive down and find him, but luck was with her. As she swam she saw his arm rise above the water, and then the motion of the waves swept him towards her until he was almost within reach. With a sudden spurt of energy, she ploughed through the water and at last managed to grasp him, although by now he was unconscious. There followed another epic struggle against the surf, but finally she succeeded in bringing him close enough to the shore, now several hundred yards further up the beach, for others to complete the rescue. None the less, it took nearly three hours of artificial respiration before he recovered consciousness, and Chloris was near to exhaustion. This saving of three adults in such difficult conditions took enormous strength, determination and courage on the part of Miss Munro.

An unusual rescue was made by Jessie Ewing, a fifty-year-old woman. In June 1954, she was a passenger on a tram descending a steep hill in Wellington city. Suddenly the motorman collapsed over the controls, and the tram gathered speed as it went downhill. Realising what had happened, Miss Ewing rushed forward and tried to get at the controls, but she was unable to move the man's heavy body. The air brake, which would have helped, was underneath him and out of reach, and the only other thing was the handbrake. Desperately she tried turning its tight, stiff handle, but although it caught, it was too late. The tram crashed at high speed, killing the motorman and one passenger, while the other passengers, including Miss Ewing, were seriously injured. For her brave efforts, she received the Silver Medal of the Royal Humane Society.

A number of other Silver and Bronze Medals went to women. Charlotte Short was given the latter for the rescue of her boss – a big, heavy man – at Omanu Beach near Mount Maunganui in November 1988. With some of her colleagues, she was enjoying a relaxing weekend after a hard working week. Three of them decided to swim in the surf before lunch. Her boss, a non-swimmer who was only walking in his own depth, found it cold and decided to leave the water. Mrs Short, a moderate swimmer, suddenly saw his face change and realised he was in trouble. He had lost his footing in one of the rip-formed holes which abounded on the beach and, being unable to touch bottom, he had panicked. Ignoring the danger to herself, Mrs Short went to grab him, but he pulled her under as well. She struggled with him until he lost consciousness – really quite fortunate, since she was then able to get hold of his arm and drag him back to their depth. Her other colleague, a strong swimmer, had gone far out but, seeing there was trouble, was making his way back as fast as he could. The surf was heavy and he took some time, so it was left to Mrs Short to do what she could. When she finally hauled her boss out of the water and up the beach, he had turned purple and looked dead. Nevertheless, she attempted mouth-to-mouth resuscitation and heart massage, which she vaguely remembered from her schooldays, and, to her relief, after about ten minutes he began to revive. An ambulance arrived, summoned by a nearby householder, and he was taken to hospital where he made a full recovery.

The Mountbatten Medal (see Chapter Twelve) was instituted by the Grand President of the Royal Life-saving Society in 1951, as an annual award for the most gallant rescue or rescue attempt from drowning undertaken throughout all the Societies of Britain and the Commonwealth, of which the Royal Life-saving Society of New Zealand is a member.

The medal has only been awarded once this century to a New Zealand woman – Penny Clayton. The dramatic rescue took place in the sea off a Dunedin beach in January 1988. Penny Clayton, an eighteen-year-old student, was in the clubhouse at Brighton Beach, eating her lunch. It was late in the morning, very hot and with a strong southerly wind whipping up the waves, so that the surf was quite high. There were about 300 people on the beach and nearly 100 in the water. As a member of the St Clair Surf Life-saving Club, Miss Clayton was on duty patrolling the city's beaches and, as she ate, she kept an eye on what was going on. Suddenly, through her binoculars, she spotted a swimmer in trouble. He had been caught in a strong current, decided to turn back and found he couldn't. He tried to get onto a spur of rocks, but they were covered in seaweed, very jagged and slippery, so that every larger seventh wave swept him off, sending him somersaulting under the water four or five times. He was nearly at the point of giving up, despite being a strong swimmer, his blood everywhere from being badly cut by the mussels on the rocks and in danger of drawing sharks.

Penny Clayton, Mountbatten Medal. (*Royal Life-saving Society, New Zealand*)

At this juncture, his wave for help was seen by Miss Clayton, who dashed from the clubhouse, grabbed a rescue tube on the beach and ran through the crowds to the water. Because the sea was so rough and the current so strong, it took her over ten minutes to reach the man. Once there, she had quite a fright to see him looking so ill – in shock and bleeding – but he was at least breathing properly. She reassured him and he jumped into the rescue tube, but a wave hit them and washed them again onto the rocks, cutting both of them. At that stage even Miss Clayton was scared since, when they re-entered the water, the current, the wind and the waves were making it too difficult for her to return with the man to Brighton Beach, and she was nearly defeated. Also, no boat could reach them in the heavy surf, so she had to rely on only what she could do. She decided, therefore, to swim out to sea, to clear the rocks, and then swim around the cliff face to try to make for the next beach, Ocean View. At the same time she was concerned about the blood seeping into the water from their lacerations, as she knew it would attract sharks. There was nothing else for it but to make the attempt, so she set out, risking her own life for his. The man was very heavy to tow, and took a lot of strength to pull, so that Penny was tiring very rapidly. At one stage, she thought they were not going to make it back to the shore. Her arms were getting weak, and she thought she might pass out, but she kept on doggedly – being more afraid for the man's life than her own – and talked to him constantly, telling him they would soon be back on shore and that everything was going to be all right.

About 25 minutes later they reached shallow water and she dragged him wearily up the beach before sitting down to check his wounds. Though covered with cuts, his worst injury was a badly cut toe, which made walking difficult. She therefore had to half-carry him ½ kilometre up the cliff face of the cove, covered with tussocks and rocks, until they came to the road which led to the surf club. There she dressed his injuries, which were later checked, and it was found that no hospitalisation was necessary.

Miss Clayton had been a lifeguard for three years, but this was her first rescue. For her courage, she received not only the Mountbatten Medal but also the Kingsland Memorial Medal. The latter had been instituted by the Royal Life-saving Society of New Zealand in 1957 in memory of a member, Arthur Kingsland, and was given annually to a New Zealand holder of an award by the Royal Life-saving Society or the Surf Life-saving Association, who had made the most courageous rescue from drowning in that year.

She was not the only woman to receive the Kingsland Memorial Medal, as in 1991 it was also awarded to Louise Lewis for a rescue she had made in Auckland Harbour in May of that year. It happened on the Waiheke Island ferry, *Quickcat*, when, in mid-crossing, a passenger saw a man jump overboard from the stern of the ferry into the Motuihe Channel. It was believed that he was a psychiatric patient under escort. Miss Lewis, clad in her uniform trousers and shirt, was swiftly lowered overboard with a lifebuoy in hand, into the very cold, choppy sea, and swam out to the man. He did not want to be helped and dived beneath the surface several times to

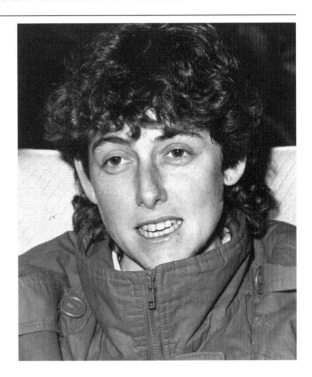

Louise Lewis, Kingsland Memorial Medal. (*New Zealand Herald*)

avoid her, and when she caught up with him he would not make any real attempt to float. She knew if he were left any longer he would certainly drown. She had to pull him by his hair to get him onto the lifebuoy – not easy, as he was a solid man much bigger than she was – and though at this point he did not struggle, he did not cooperate either, so that it was like trying to move a dead weight. Then she headed back to the catamaran ferry, which by then had a cargo cage dangling alongside. With great effort, she pushed the man into the cage, both landing on it together in a heap. They were then winched on board by a crane on the ferry's foredeck. Miss Lewis went to change and the man was taken to the sickbay and later passed over to the police. When Miss Lewis reappeared to continue her duties, she was very embarrassed to find herself given a standing ovation by the passengers, who had watched in fascination during the rescue.

From the sea to the air – and in a much earlier time, unfortunately with no award – mention must be made of a New Zealand woman who was one of the pioneers of the early days of flying. It took very great courage then to go alone into the unknown, entrusting herself to the flimsy planes of those days – especially over the great expanses of oceans, with no ship in sight, no communications, and little chance of rescue if she came down. This is what Jean Batten dared. In her wood and fabric Gipsy Moth, and later a Percival Gull 6, she broke the woman's solo record for the flight from Britain to Australia in 1934 and then made the first direct flight from Britain to New Zealand in 1936. The next year she broke both records simultaneously, out and back to Australia and Britain. She was one of the few women Liverymen of the Guild of Air Pilots and Navigators of the City of London. A woman and a record of which to be proud.

Another courageous islander without official awards was Isabella Scott. She was one of the first nurses to make a special study of birth and babies. Coming from a large and not very rich family, she eventually trained as a children's nurse and in 1910 started her own private hospital in Mataura. She was in her early forties when the First World War broke out and volunteered to nurse her wounded countrymen in Britain during the war. Returning in February 1919 to her hospital in New Zealand, she spent the rest of her career there, bringing about 1,500 babies into the world. Because of her connection with the war, she also became a great supporter of the Returned Servicemen's Association (RSA) and sometimes their committees met in her sitting-room. The society finally gave her their Gold Star for her services to it – she was the first woman to receive the award. Joyce Bennett also received the award in 1993 for her welfare work for the RSA.

The Girl Guides of New Zealand have their own awards for bravery, life-saving and courageous conduct. When so many rescues of all kinds have been made by young girls, it it not surprising to find such courage recognised. They have Silver and Bronze Awards and certificates, as well as a Star of Merit, given to any member who has displayed great bravery under suffering. After a serious operation Sarah Hodder, a Queen's Guide and Leader of Tuatea in Auckland, received this award in 1996 for her inspirational attitude. It also went to Betty Hard in 1992 and Lynne Payne in 1994, and these are only the most recent instances.

Though of small population, the quiet, welcoming islands of New Zealand have had their share of frightening – and uplifting – incidents, and have produced many records of bravery. The sea, their friend and enemy, has created a number of heroines, and the nursing profession in its own gentle way has made a gallant and caring contribution to the whole. Through two world wars and other conflicts, New Zealand women, both in and out of uniform, have always given their assistance, and though not always rewarded, it has not gone unnoticed. May their courage continue in the years ahead: 'Ko ērā e kawe ana i te mahi i runga i te toa, neke atu rānei, i te tawheta, i te nohonga rānei o rātou hei papa mō tā rātou i mahi ai, e tika ana kia tohua' (Those who serve with bravery or distinction, at risk or sacrifice of life, deserve due recognition).

CHAPTER TWENTY-FIVE

South African Awards

South Africa is the home of a large population and many peoples, and has suffered much internal strife and turbulence. As part of the older British Commonwealth, it has also made its contribution of Service personnel to the Commonwealth forces in the two world wars.

Its women have always proved to be excellent nurses. A nursing order of nuns existed in 1850 – three from various orders received the Victorian Royal Red Cross before 1900 – and the first military nurses were in evidence as early as 1877. But it was not until December 1913 that an officially organised Service was proposed, although there were at the time no nurses in it. Fortunately, in August the next year, Elizabeth Creagh was appointed Matron-in-Chief. She was a former member of the Queen Alexandra's Imperial Military Nursing Service (QAIMNS), who had stayed in South Africa after an earlier nursing stint. She had the drive, the experience and the organisational skills to establish firmly the South African Military Nursing Service (SAMNS), a name it retained for many years. There was no lack of volunteers, and its nurses worked in South African hospitals where they tended the injured from the war in German-African territories. Contingents were also sent to hospitals in Britain and France, as well as to casualty evacuation centres there. They also served on the hospital ship the *Ebani*. The service was rapidly disbanded after the First World War, but two military hospitals remained in the country, still staffed by SAMNS sisters. For Elizabeth Creagh's magnificent contribution to South Africa and Britain, in 1920 she was made an Officer of the Order of the British Empire (OBE; see Chapter Six). Her deputy, Miss Nutt, also a former member of the QAIMNS, was another to be granted this honour.

Matron-in-Chief Elizabeth Creagh (later Stanford) OBE, FNM. (*South African Medical Health Service*)

One other sister from this war deserves a mention. Margaret Dewar volunteered to nurse at the front. After working a short time in a London hospital, she embarked for France to nurse the South African soldiers wounded on the Somme. Her hospital was at Abbeyville, the frequent subject of air raids because it lay so near to the front lines. In December 1916, she was sent, via Britain, to a hospital in Salonika, Greece, at a time when the Turks and Bulgarians were approaching the port. Two weeks later, shells started landing on the hospital. Sister Dewar and fellow South African Sister Calhoun began evacuating patients and, during the heavier part of the shelling, Sister Dewar protected one of her patients with her own body. A shell hit the ward, and a piece of shrapnel pierced her chest. Her patient was saved, but Sister Dewar died in her friend's arms. She was, unfortunately, not the only nursing casualty in this war.

During the Second World War, South Africa – very conscious of Italian inroads in Africa – directed much of its war effort to East and North Africa, and only later to the Middle East. Nurses naturally followed the fighting forces, and the SAMNS – their numbers supplemented by VADs from the Red Cross and St John Ambulance Brigade – was revived for this vital work at home and abroad. Their first Matron-in-Chief was Constance Nothard, who had already served with distinction in the First World War, and in the interval, until she was free to take up her post, Elizabeth Creagh – now aged sixty-seven and using her second married name of Stanford – gallantly kept things going before finally retiring in 1941. Constance Nothard remained until the end of the war and became the first President of the South African Nursing Council.

In 1943, around 300 Canadian nurses arrived to make up the South African shortfall of qualified nurses. All nurses served in hospitals both inside and outside South Africa: in hospital ships, in ambulance trains and as casualty evacuation nurses on aircraft. No nurses lost their lives as a direct result of enemy action in this war, but there were a few deaths while travelling on duty.

Demobilisation followed the end of the war, but sufficient numbers of nurses were left to staff the military hospitals remaining, and one aircraft was kept for air ambulance duties. In 1950, a reserve was created, becoming active in 1956, and subsequent internal and external pressures produced variable levels of personnel. In 1972, SAMNS became an integrated part of the greater South African Medical Service (SAMS) whose name it then adopted to the sorrow of former members.

The distinctive honour of the Royal Red Cross (RRC; see Chapter Six) was given to many nurses of the SAMNS during the two world wars. About 26 were presented in the First World War and over 110 RRC (2nd Class), more commonly known as the Associate of the Royal Red Cross (ARRC). These were for demonstrating professional skill and devotion in nursing and were greatly valued by the recipients.

One of these was Mildred Fynn. Trained in South African and London hospitals, she was called on active service in 1915 and sent to France in the following year. By those who knew her, she was described as utterly selfless, compassionate, warm-hearted, serene, and with a great sense of humour – lovely in appearance as well as in disposition. Never asking others to do what she would not herself do, she was highly regarded by all, especially the soldiers she nursed, and never spared herself, particularly for those who were dying. To her they were 'her boys'. She was invested with her RRC at Buckingham Palace in 1919.

Daisy Roberts gained her RRC in the Second World War. Joining in 1941, she saw service in many South African hospitals, and became Senior Matron in Bari, Italy, where she headed a huge complex. She was regularly Mentioned in Despatches for gallant conduct and received her RRC in 1945, the year after Matron-in-Chief Nothard. It would appear that RRCs were scarcer in the Second World War – about thirteen were awarded, with approximately the same number of ARRCs.

The former Matron-in-Chief Elizabeth Creagh was honoured by the rare Florence Nightingale Medal (see Chapter Eight), in its first awards in 1920 – hardly surprising considering her outstanding work and abilities – and after the Second World War, Matron-in-Chief Stoney of the SAMNS was presented with the medal in 1947. Another Matron-in-Chief, Constance Nothard, had to wait until her work on the Nursing Council and other peacetime organisations were recognised before she was given the Florence Nightingale Medal in 1961. Most other recipients came from the world of civil nursing.

Six South African nurses in Italy in 1944.

Southern Cross Medal. (*South Africa National Museum of Military History*)

Military nurses also gained several South African postwar awards for their actions. Eighteen received the Southern Cross Medal, a silver award which had been established in 1975 for men and women of the defence forces of officer status who had displayed the utmost devotion to duty. It shows the Stars of the Southern Cross in a centre medallion, around which are set five groups of three larger rays, among smaller ones. Established at the same time for those of the defence forces not of officer rank but for similar qualities, the Silver Pro Merito Medal appears to have only been given to two Sergeant nurses, and those in 1968. Coin-shaped, it shows a red protea flower – the emblem of South Africa – surrounded with a wreath of protea flowers. The Pro Patria Medal has been given to numerous personnel of all ranks, from 1977 until the present.

At the beginning of the Second World War, the Women's Auxiliary Defence Corps (WADC) was set up to take volunteers for the future Services and, in various measures ending in 1940, the Women's Auxiliary Army Service (WAAS) and the Women's Auxiliary Air Force (WAAF) were given their regulations and organisation. In fact the WAAF had been slightly ahead of the game, because of their connection with women pilots – of whom more later – and became the first uniformed full-time Service, specifically created to work side by side with the South African Air Force, and in 1941 was involved on a large scale with technical training. Over 10,000 women joined. There was also a subsidiary, part-time Women's Voluntary Air Force, whose members lived at home and which was officially recognised in 1941.

Pro Merito Medal. (*South Africa National Museum of Military History*)

The WAAS was also waiting in the wings, with its main object to release men for active service. Their chief tasks were to deal with paperwork and food, but some ambulance drivers and canteen workers were attached to the (male) Union Defence Force, and some staffed military hospitals specifically created for sick servicewomen.

In late 1943, the Women's Auxiliary Naval Service (SWANs) came into being – the youngest of all the South African Services, although forty-seven clerks were already serving on shore with the navy. The SWANs served in clerical, technical and communications roles, as their work was mainly connected with specialised shore-based naval defence systems.

There was also a very small Women's Auxiliary Military Police Corps (WAMPC) founded in 1942 for patrol and investigative work.

All these Services were based in South Africa, but about 600 army and air force women did get postings overseas.

The inspiration of a woman pilot in Johannesburg, Marjorie Egerton-Bird, created the South Africa Women's Aviation Association (SAWAA) in 1938, when the dangers of approaching war could be foreseen. Its object was to familiarise women with flying and all it involved. It was to appeal to both those already flying and those who had not even thought about it. The Association was run by several enthusiastic and experienced women pilots with many flying hours to their credit, some being instructors in their own right. At the outbreak of the war, it was recognised by the government as the South African Voluntary Auxiliary Air Unit, and attached to the South African Air Force to carry out ferrying and training duties in the Communications Squadron. They were contemporaneous with the British Air Transport Auxiliary, which at least one member went over to join.

Women were only employed in the Services for the duration of the war, and with its sudden end with Japan, demobilisation took over, although a contingent of 250 servicemen and women marched in the London Victory Parade in 1946. It was not until further conflicts occurred both inside and outside South Africa that women were again needed in the Services.

Because of their small numbers and the majority of them being kept well away from any fighting – with the exception of nurses – there was little opportunity for servicewomen to gain any awards for gallantry. It appears that most of those made OBEs were senior officers, many of whom had worked extremely hard and had overcome many obstacles to make their Service function. Those made Members of the Order of the British Empire (MBE) and awarded the British Empire Medal (BEM; see Chapter Ten) were mainly army and air force women who had acquitted themselves well in their postings overseas, but there was one SWAN, Chief Petty Officer (CPO) Margaret Forbes, who achieved the BEM for her disciplinary and instructional ability at home.

Awards for courage generally came from the Services, but a medal was given by the Royal Humane Society (see Chapter Eleven) of South Africa in 1945 to Mollie Leith, a Leading SWAN, for an action outside her Service context. She was with another Leading Seaman when they noticed a sailor had capsized his canvas canoe in Saldanha Bay and could not right it again. He was not a very good swimmer, but he struck out for the shore. There was a fairly heavy swell, and the onlookers saw with mounting horror that a large shark was cruising not far off. Nevertheless the serviceman and woman decided to try to help the man. With considerable difficulty they reached a rock some distance from the shore and near to the sailor. Then they swam out and by great good luck were able to rescue the man, by now exhausted, and bring him safely to the beach before the shark took notice. For their bravery and efforts they were both awarded the Bronze Medal of the Society.

Many awards have arisen from South Africa's internal troubles, or those imported through her land borders. Isolated places like farms have been easy targets and, whatever the cause, those living there often have had to fight for their lives and their families.

The South African Police Medal for Combating Terrorism may be awarded to the police, or by the police, to any person who has performed any outstandingly brave action in repelling terrorists. The medal is of bronze with a five-pointed bevelled star upon a laurel wreath. The ribbon is white with two broad red stripes on either side of the central panel and a thin red stripe near both edges.

A schoolgirl aged fifteen was an unusual recipient of this medal. In February 1980, Sonja Dressel was sitting quietly on the open verandah of her parent's farmhouse in Namibia, South-West Africa, in the cool of the morning. Behind her she could vaguely hear the voice of her father, who was trying to phone a friend. Her mother was in the kitchen and her invalid brother in the bathroom. Her father came out to join her, complaining that the telephone was dead and he couldn't get through. Jokingly she replied, 'I expect the line has been cut by terrorists!' To lonely farmsteads these were a continual threat. The next moment her joke became reality when they saw a group of armed men jumping over the fence near the farmhouse. Father and

Police Medal for Combating Terrorism. (*South African Police Service*)

Sonja Dressel (age 15), South African Police Medal. (*South African Police*)

daughter immediately ran indoors, he to the kitchen, she to a bedroom where she knew a semi-automatic rifle and her father's revolver were kept. As Sonja was loading the rifle, she heard shots. She dashed to the verandah and, seeing men running towards the house, she raised her rifle and opened fire. They stopped and scattered. A minute later her mother shouted that there were men behind the house. She crawled back inside and started firing from a back window. By now she knew that her father was dead, and that she was the only one left to protect her family. After a few more shots, the raiders seemed to give up and ran off as suddenly as they had come. By her courage and presence of mind she had saved most of her family.

In 1961, South Africa left the Commonwealth and became a republic, and the former King's/Queen's Medal for Bravery, created especially for them, fell into disuse. It was replaced in 1970 by the Wolraad Woltemade Decoration for Bravery. This was mainly intended for South African civilians or for members of the Forces not eligible for Service honours. Recipients must have saved, or tried to save, the lives of people or their property by an act of conspicuous bravery in the face of extreme danger.

Woltemade Decoration for Bravery.
(*Lt Col P.F. Joubert*)

The medal was made in gold and silver. The story of the picture on the obverse is an interesting one, and the illustration was similar to the medal it replaced. Wolraad Woltemade was an elderly dairyman of German origin, employed by the Dutch East India Company. In June 1773, the ship *The Jonge Thomas*, resting at anchor in Table Bay, parted its cables in a great gale and was driven ashore into the Salt River mouth. Woltemade, seeing this, rode his white horse through the heavy surf eight times and brought fourteen survivors ashore. On his eighth and final hazardous trip, both horse and rider were so exhausted and overladen with panic-stricken sailors that they were overwhelmed by the waves and drowned. His heroic action is commemorated on this medal, showing Woltemade on horseback rescuing a sailor from the waves. Around the edge are the words 'For Bravery' and 'Vir Dapperheid'. The reverse carries the arms of South Africa with the words 'Republic of South Africa – Republiek van Suid-Afrika'. The ribbon is blue with orange edges. This decoration was superseded in 1988 by the Woltemade Cross for Bravery.

Until 1981, no woman had ever received the Wolraad Woltemade Decoration for Bravery, so that Wendy Gibson-Taylor was the first. In January 1981, she was in the family's Glenmore Beach Hotel, breast-feeding her first baby, when a woman rushed up to call for help. A party of schoolgirls with their teacher had gone swimming in the beach below; some

Wendy Gibson-Taylor, Woltemade Decoration. (*Mrs W. Gibson-Taylor*)

had got into difficulties and they were in danger of drowning. Mrs Gibson-Taylor ran to the beach and, hearing that there were at least two children who had been swept out by a current into deeper waters, could see that there was no one else able to help them. She plunged into the water but, after swimming a short distance, realised that the current had already swept the girls too far north towards an old wreck and rocks for her to reach them that way. She returned to the beach and ran instead to a craggy spine, the Portobello Rocks, making her way barefoot over the jagged ridges until she came to a suitable place from which to make her second attempt.

One of the girls had been washed against the rocks and was hanging onto an outcrop with the waves breaking over her. Mrs Gibson-Taylor swam through the narrow gully in between and, though by now tired by her exertions, managed to drag the child, somewhat larger and heavier than herself, away from the rock. Then she ploughed with her through the breaking waves to the gully, and carried the helpless, semi-conscious girl up the main rock ridge. By this time she was much cut by the rocks herself and was bleeding. The inlet where she had climbed from the water was treacherous at the best of times, and this wasn't. On the ridge, she was met by a man who relieved her of the child, taking her back to safety.

Meanwhile, Mrs Gibson-Taylor saw another girl struggling in the water some distance away. Without giving herself time to catch her breath, she again braved the rocks and ran further north, this time carrying a lifeline given to her by the man. Swimming with it through yet another inlet, and then clambering over more rocks, she again dived into the sea, only to find that the line had snagged on the rocks. Attempting to loosen it used up precious energy. At length it came free, and Mrs Gibson-Taylor struck out for the second child, who was in open water. On reaching her, she managed to keep the girl's head above water, but the current had now swept them still further north, and the lifeline she had struggled to keep could not be used to tow them ashore. But the waves became her friends, and carried her and her precious burden back to the rocks and washed them right up. From there she and the girl were helped back to the shore where she started mouth-to-mouth resuscitation, but when she became too tired another person took over. Staggering to her feet, she returned to the hotel to phone the hospital.

Mrs Gibson-Taylor had not been swimming regularly for more than a year, and finally collapsed from exhaustion, cut all over and bleeding. A doctor who later examined her found that, apart from her wounds and bruises, she must at some stage have taken a hard knock on the head. Normally she was too nervous to swim in the sea alone, knowing how treacherous it could be, and only went beyond her depth when with her husband, a former professional life-saver. Her award was given for her bravery in selflessly placing her life in peril in order to save the lives of two drowning children. For her actions that day, she also received the South African Surf Life-saving Association's Bravery Award, and the World Life-saving Organisation's Gold Medal for Bravery.

Recent information on the sinking of the cruise ship *Oceanus*, off the coast of South Africa in the 1990s, came to hand. Here several people attempted the rescue of drowning passengers, performing acts of great heroism. Among these were three women: Lorraine Betts, Geraldine Massyn and Lynn Greig. It also appears that Ms Betts was offered a Woltemade Award for Bravery, but refused it on the grounds that they were all three equally as brave. The Rotary Club of South Africa, however, recognised their courage and awarded each a medal for bravery.

Conclusion

As the millennium draws to a close, we come to the end of a long journey through what has been, for the most part, a violent century. Humankind and the unpredictable elements, as always, have sought to wreak havoc on our everyday lives. Despite the many tragedies, we have found the effects softened by the presence of sacrifice and triumph, compassion and anger, channelled into deeds of heroism, great and small.

Although most were reactions in the heat of the moment – with a few sustained over weeks and sometimes years – they nevertheless display the human spirit at its highest. The sense of adventure and meeting a challenge is present in all of us, as is the distinction between good and evil and the desire to put right what we see is wrong. Courage and kindness on behalf of others, often strangers, are what distinguishes the human race from the rest of creation.

Praise is a poor word to use to honour those about whose heroism we have read in these pages, and the courage displayed will serve as a proud beacon for the years to come. If it exists in one century, it must surely continue into the future. May the dangers be fewer, but may they be met with the same spirit of self-abnegation and courage as before.

We look back with gratitude and forward with hope.

Key to Abbreviations

Women's Services

Great Britain (GB/UK)
ATA   Air Transport Auxiliary (WWII)
ATS   Auxiliary Territorial Service (Army) (WWII)
BRCS   British Red Cross Society
PMRAFNS   Princess Mary's RAF Nursing Service (WWII)
QAIMNS   Queen Alexandra's Imperial Nursing Service (WWI & WWII)
QARANC   Queen Alexandra's Royal Army Nursing Corps (Postwar)
QARNNS   Queen Alexandra's Royal Naval Nursing Service (WWI & WWII)
QMAAC   Queen Mary's Army Auxiliary Corps (WWI)
RAF   Royal Air Force
RAFNS   Royal Air Force Nursing Service (WWI)
RNNS   Royal Naval Nursing Service (WWI)
RAMC   Royal Army Medical Corps
SJAB   St John Ambulance Brigade
TANS }   Territorial Army Nursing Service (WWI)
TFNS }   Territorial Force Nursing Service(WWI & WWII)
WAAC   Women's Auxiliary Army Corps (WWI)
WAAF   Women's Auxiliary Air Force (WWII)
WRAC   Women's Royal Army Corps (Post)
WRAF   Women's Royal Air Force (WWI & Post)
WRNS   Women's Royal Naval Service (WWI & WWII)
FANY }   First Aid Nursing Service   }
WTS   }   Women's Transport Service }

United States of America (US/USA)
ANC   Army Nurse Corps (WWI & WWII)
ARC   American Red Cross
ARCNS   American Red Cross Nursing Service
AWS   American Women's (Voluntary) Services (WWII)
NNC   Navy Nurse Corps (WWI)
SPARS   Women's Reserve of the US Coast Guard (WWII)
USAAF   US Army Air Force (WWII)
USCGR   US Coast Guard Reserve
USN   US Navy (Post)
USNR   US Naval Reserve (Post)
WAAC   Women's Auxiliary Army Corps (WWII)
WAC   Women's Army Corps (WWII)
WAF   Women in the Air Force (Post)
WAFS   Women's Auxiliary Flying Squadron (WWII)
WASPS   Women's Air Force Service Pilots (WWII)
WAVES   Women's Reserve of the US Naval Reserve (WWII)
WMC   Women Medical Specialist Corps (WWII)
WMCR   Women's Marine Corps Reserve (WWI & II)

Australia (A)
AAMWS   Australian Army Medical Women's Services (WWII)
AANS   Australian Army Nursing Service (WWI & II)
AWAS   Australian Women's Army Service (WWII)
(R)AANS   (Royal) Australian Army Nursing Service (WWII)
WAAAF   Women's Australian Auxiliary Air Force (II)

| WRAAF | Women's Royal Australian Air Force (Post) |
| WRANS | Women's Royal Australian Naval Service (II) |

Canada (C)
CAMC	Canadian Army Medical Corps (WWI)
CANS	Canadian Army Nursing Service (pre WWI)
CWAC	Canadian Women's Army Corps (WWII)
RCAFNS	Royal Canadian Air Force Nursing Service
RCAMC	Royal Canadian Army Medical Corps (nurses) (WWII)
RCNNS	Royal Canadian Naval Nursing Service
WIDS	Canadian Air Force Women (WWII)
RCAF/WD	Royal Canadian Air Force Women's Division (WWII)
WRCNS	Women's Royal Canadian Naval Service (WWII)

New Zealand (NZ)
NZAAC(NZ)	New Zealand Army Auxiliary Corps (WWII)
NZANS	New Zealand Army Nursing Service (WWI & II)
WAAC	Women's Auxiliary Army Corps (WWII)
WAAF	Women's Auxiliary Air Force (WWII)
WRNZAF	Women's Royal New Zealand Air Force (WWII)
WRNZNS	Women's Royal New Zealand Naval Service (WWII)
WWSA	Women's War Service Auxiliary (WWII)

South Africa (SA)
SAMS	South African Medical Service (Late Post)
SAMNS	South African Military Nursing Service (all Services)
SAWAA	South African Women's Aviation Association (WWII)
SWANS	South African Women's Auxiliary Naval Service (WWII)
WAAF	Women's Auxiliary Air Force (WWII)
WAAS	Women's Auxiliary Army Service (WWII)
WADC	Women's Auxiliary Defence Corps (WWII)
WAMPC	Women's Auxiliary Military Police Corps (WWII)

Service Ranks

Air Cdre	Air Commander	LACW	Leading Aircraftwoman
Capt	Captain	Ldg	Leading
Cdr	Commander	Lt	Lieutenant
Chf	Chief	M	Master
Cmt	Commandant	Maj	Major
CSL	Chief Section Leader	Sect Off/SO	Section Officer
Cpl	Corporal	Sgt	Sergeant
Col	Colonel	SL	Section Leader
Fg Off	Flying Officer	Snr Wtr	Senior Writer
Flt Off	Flight Officer	Sqn Ldr	Squadron Leader
Gp Capt	Group Captain	Sub	Subordinate
L	Lance/Leading	Wg Cdr	Wing Commander

Nursing

A	Acting	Cmt	Commandant
AARC	Associate of the Royal Red Cross	D	Deputy
		FNM	Florence Nightingale Medal
Amb	Ambulance	ic	in charge
As/Asst	Assistant	Jun	Junior
Att	Attendant	L	Lady (not wife of a Lord)
BRCS	British Red Cross Society	Mas	Masseuse
Ch	Charge	MIC	Matron in Chief
Chf	Chief	Pr	Principal

Qmstr	Quartermaster	Spec	Special
Prob	Probation/ary/er	Super	Superintend/ent/ing
R	Reserve	Sur	Surgical
RRC	Royal Red Cross	Th	Theatre
Sen	Senior	VAD	Voluntary Air Detachment
SJAB	St John Ambulance Brigade		

General

A	Acting	OSS	Office of Strategic Services (US)
AA	Anti-Aircraft (Ack Ack)		
A/c	Aircraft	(P)	Posthumous Award (died before receiving it)
Admin	Administrat/or/ion/ive		
ARP	Air Raid Precautions	P	Police
Amb	Ambulance	QE	Queen Elizabeth
Att	Attendant	R/Res	Reserve
As/Asst	Assistant	RUC	Royal Ulster Constabulary
BCRA	Bureau Central de Renseignements et d'Action	SIS	Secret Intelligence Service (UK)
BRCS	British Red Cross Society	SJAB	St John Ambulance Brigade
Br	British		
C	Constable (Police)	SOE	Special Operations Executive (UK)
CAF	Women's Army (French)		
Cdr	Commander	Stdss	Stewardess
Clk	Clerk	Sub	Subordinate
d	died	Super	Superintend/ent/ing
Det	Detective	Tech	Technician
d/o	Daughter of	Tel	Telephon/e/ist
Dr	Doctor	VAD	Voluntary Aid Detachments
Dvr	Driver	W	Women/Wireless/Warden
ENSA	Entertainments National Service Association	WAFS	Women's Auxiliary Fire Service (UK)
FANY/WTS	First Aid Nursing Yeomanry/Women's Transport Service	w/o	Wife of
		WIMSA	Women in Military Service for America, Memorial Foundation Inc.
Hosp	Hospital		
Jun	Junior	WL	Women's Legion
M	Motor	WPC	Woman Police Constable
Mec	Mechanic	W/T	Wireless Telegraphy
Med	Medical	WVS	Women's Voluntary Service
Merch	Merchant	UK/GB	Great Britain
MID	Mentioned in Despatches	US/USA	United States of America
MT	Motor Transport	YMCA	Young Men's Christian Association
NAAFI	Navy Army & Air Force Institute	YWCA	Young Women's Christian Association
Op	Operator		
Off	Officer		

Appendix

Great Britain

GEORGE CROSS (GC)

08–08–69	Harrison Miss Barbara Jane	BAOC		20–08–46	Sansom Odette Marie Céline	Lt FANY/SOE
05–04–49	Inayat-Khan Noor	Asst Sect Off WAAF/ SOE (P)		17–12–46	Szabo Violette Reine Elizabeth	Ensign ATS/FANY/ SOE (P)

ALBERT MEDAL (AM)

28–03–11	Wolsey Hilda Elizabeth	Nurse GC		17–08–20	Emmett Mrs Florence	
31–01–13	Holley Elizabeth	Nurse		20	Hopkins Ethel	Nurse
31–01–19	Batt Alice	Nurse VAD		20–11–35	Allen Florence Alice	Nurse GC
31–01–19	Carlin Gertrude Walters	Sister TFNS		21–07–44	Everitt Mrs Elizabeth Anne	(P)
31–01–19	Fraser Harriett Elizabeth	StaffNurse TFNS GC		01–11–49	Vaughan Miss Margaret	GC
31–01–19	White Gladys	Sister BRCS		14–05–68	Hanson Mrs Nanette	(P)

EDWARD MEDAL (EM)

19–04–10	Hugill Miss Hannah		28–09–25	Peyto Mrs Lilian

EMPIRE GALLANTRY MEDAL (EGM)

06–09–32	Townsend Miss Emma José	GC		01–02–37	Ashraf Begum un-Nisa	GC
02–03–34	Thomas Dorothy Louise	Sister GC		19–07–40	Pearson Joan Daphne Mary	Cpl WAAF GC

THE MOST EXCELLENT ORDER OF THE BRITISH EMPIRE – GALLANTRY AWARDS

Dame (DBE)

Turner Margot	Sister QAIMNS

Commander (CBE)

01–01–98	Atkins Vera	Sqn Ldr SOE		08–06–50	Franklin Olga H	Sister QARNNS

Officers (OBE)

07–03–41	McGreenery Mrs H	Amb Att WVS		23–12–47	Walden I	Temporary Pr Matron/ Sister QAIMNS(R)
07–03–41	Dakins Mrs FD	Amb Dvr WVS			Spedding	Matron QAIMNS
01–12–42	Cawston Muriel E	Asst Supt/Sister QARNNS			Innes	Sister QAIMNS
22–08–44	Stone VK	Sister PMRAFNS		92	Sharman Helen	Woman Astronaut

Members (MBE)

01–01–20	Selby Elizabeth	Asst Matron		44	Joy MM	NAAFI
06–40	Davies Kathleen B	Sister QAIMNS		01–01–45	Nicholls D	WVS NAAFI
20–12–40	Carter Muriel Audrey	Jun Cdr ATS		01–01–45	Hornby MG	WVS
07–02–41	Costigan Aileen	ARP		28–12–45	Huskin LM	Sister QAIMNS(R)
07–12–41	Hyde Pearl M	WVS		29–12–45	Hourigan ET	Sister QAIMNS(R)
17–03–41	Hanbury Felicity	Asst Sect Off WAAF		01–02–46	Sturrock Sybil Anne	WAAF/SIS
21–06–41	Haldane Mary B	Amb. Att		02–46	Turner Margot	Sister QAIMNS
09–07–41	Drummond Victoria Alexandrina	2nd Eng Br Merch Navy		46	Brusselmans Anne Madame	
17–02–42	Miller Dr Adeline Nancy	Ship's Surgeon		46	Baker Nona	Civilian
				46	Marsden Alexandrina	Matron
01–01–42	Franklin Olga H	Supt Sister QARNNS		46	Hargreaves-Heap I	YWCA
11–06–42	Jones Letitia	Sister PMRAFNS		02–12–58	Pillsbury Margaret	YWCA Baghdad
20–10–42	Grace Pamela IN	3rd Off WREN		11–06–66	Beasley Barbara Gordon	QARNNS/VAD
10–10–44	Whittaker Alexandra	2nd Off WREN		50s	Race Ida	QE Overseas Nursing Service
10–11–44	Stainton RE	Sister QAIMNS(R)				
10–11–44	Stringfellow D	Sister QAIMNS(R)		70s	Spencer Marjorie	QE Overseas Nursing Service
10–11–44	Thompson D	Sister QAIMNS(R)				
10–11–44	Thorpe PM	Sister QAIMNS(R)		72	Casteldine	Trident Nurse
29–12–44	McNickolas L	Sister QAIMNS(R)		09–93	Stephens Rebecca	Mountaineer
29–12–44	Roberts E	Sister QAIMNS				

The following have various dates 1944 to 1949. Earliest ones were transferred from the Civil to the Military Sections of the MBE.

Baseden Yvonne	Flt Off WAAF/SOE	Nearne Jacqueline	Lt FANY/SOE
de Baissac Lise	Capt FANY/SOE	O'Sullivan Patricia	Sect Off WAAF/SOE
Butt Sonya	Asst Sect Off WAAF/SOE	Rolfe Lilian	Asst Sect Off WAAF/SOE
Cormeau Yvonne	Flt Off WAAF/SOE	Rudellat Yvonne	Ensign FANY/SOE
Granville Christine	Flt Off WAAF/SOE	Sansom Odette MC	Lt FANY/SOE
Inayat-Khan Noor un Nisa	Asst Sect Off WAAF/SOE	Szabo Violette RE	Ensign ATS/FANY/SOE (P)
Knight Margaret DF	Ensign FANY/SOE		
Hall Virginia	SOE/OSS	Walters	Asst Sect Off
Latour Phyllis	Sect Off WAAF/SOE	Anne-Marie	WAAF/SOE
Nearne Eileen	Lt FANY/SOE	Witherington Pearl	Flt Off WAAF/SOE

George Medal (GM)

Second World War

18–07–41	Anderson V	Nurse		09–10–42	Knee EAM	Asst Nurse
13–06–41	Bateman L	Dr		17–01–41	McGovern C	Asst Matron
08–05–41	Beardshall M	Nursing Orderly		27–06–41	McNairn AJ	Dr
14–02–41	Bick C	ARP Despatches (14yrs)		17–01–41	Marmion P	Staff Nurse
				21–02–41	Newman MSJ	Asst Nurse
27–06–41	Billig H	Dr		23–09–41	Owen EM	Stdss Ship
25–04–41	Boulton ME	Matron		07–02–41	Perkins ME	Nurse
07–07–41	Brown M	Nurse SJAB		13–12–40	Quinn B	ARP SJAB (17 yrs)
07–07–41	Burton JE	Matron		07–02–41	Rattenbury G	WVS
30–09–40	Clarke D	Amb Dvr WVS		15–11–40	Reid VE	Nurse Asylum
13–12–40	Ede R	WVS		24–04–41	Rosser REM	Nurse
08–08–41	Fitzgerald ME	Amb Dvr		03–01–41	Steele M	Tel Sup
09–05–41	Fleming M	Staff Nurse		30–11–41	Stevens EL	Asst Matron Maternity
30–05–41	Frampton VEA	Nurse Maternity		30–09–40	Straw SVC	ARP
06–06–41	Gardner DK	Prob Nurse		31–01–41	Tanner GK	Aux Firewoman
23–01–46	Granville MC	Flt Off WAAF/SOE		14–02–41	Thomas EG	Matron
23–03–45	Greaves SM	Lt Sister QAIMNS(R)		24–01–41	Thomas MF	ARP Nurse
30–09–40	Hepburn BJ	Amb Att WVS		09–05–41	Turner AR	Asst Sen Nurse
07–03–41	Hollyer WP	Tel ARP		31–01–41	White DM	Nurse WVS BRCS
07–07–41	Horne E	Sister				VAD

Post-war

14–06–55	Bush EV	Sgt Policewoman
05–04–66	Chard FJM	Sister
18–08–64	Clelland MS	Policewoman
22–06–54	Holland F	Nurse
14–06–55	Parrott KF	Policewoman
14–06–97	Potts L	Nursery Nurse
02–07–48	Richards ME	L Cpl ATS
25–09–51	Vearncombe Miss M	
14–05–68	Young M	Prob Nurse

KING'S POLICE AND FIRE SERVICE MEDAL (KPFSM)

28–10–47	Watts Alberta May	Det Sgt Policewoman

MILITARY MEDAL (MM)

First World War

01–03–18	Abraham Maud Alice	Sister Civil Hosp Reserve
18–12–17	Alexander Annie	Sister BRCS
01–09–16	Allsop Beatrice Alice	Sister QAIMNS(R)
	Ballance Margaret H	Sister SJAB
	Batten Winifred Eleanor Sarah	Dvr VAD
30–07–18	Bemrose Jane	Sister SJAB
	Becher	Sister QAIMNS
30–07–18	Bianconi M O'Connel	Dvr FANY
	Blair Mavis Agnes	A Sister QAIMNS(R)
04–03–18	Broome Florence	Sister Civil Hosp Reserve
31–07–18	Brampton Winifred A	Nurse BRCS
04–06–18	Brown Mary Agatha	A Sister QAIMNS(R)
21–02–19	Bovey CM	Nurse VAD
17–09–17	Bowles Linda	Sister QAIMNS
04–03–18	Boyd Ann Georgina	Sister QAIMNS
01–03–17	Byrne Ellen	A Sister QAIMNS
30–07–18	Callander Edith Beveridge	Dvr FANY
31–07–18	Campbell Mary Gwyneth	Nurse BRCS
15–11–16	Carruthers K	Sister CCS Midlands
19–10–18	Cartledge Ethel Grace	Forewoman QMAAC
30–07–18	Cavanagh Moyra Cavanagh	Asst Nurse SJABVAD
03–07–18	Chappel P	Dr QMAAC
19–02–17	Chisholm Marie Lambert Chisholm Gooden	Nurse BRCS VAD
	Chittock Mabel A	A Matron SJAB
26–05–17	Colhoun Annie Rebecca	Staff Nurse QAIMNS(R)
30–07–18	Courtis Elsie A	Dvr FANY
30–07–18	Crewdson Dorothea	Nurse BRCS ML VAD
	Cridlan EM	Dvr FANY
08–07–18	Cross	Unit Admin QMAAC
	Cuthbert Galantha M	Sub Sec Ldr BRCS VAD
	Dascombe Beatrice	Staff Nurse QAIMNS(R)
	Davidson Margaret	Dvr FANY
	Davis Mary E	Sister QAIMNS
	Dewhurst Nellie	Dvr FANY
18–12–17	Devenish-Mears Ethel Isabella	A Matron QAIMNS(R)
30–07–18	Dickinson Hilda M	Dvr FANY
30–07–18	Dickson Stella Primrose	Dvr FANY BRCS VAD
26–05–17	Dobbs Daisy Ellen	Staff Nurse TFNS
01–09–16	Easby Norah	OBE Sister QAIMNS(R)
01–03–17	Eckett Elizabeth Jane	Staff Nurse TFNS
	Elmer W	Dvr FANY
30–07–18	Elwes Winifred M	Dvr VAD
	Evans Mabel Louise	Sister QAIMNS
	Fabling Katherine SM	Nurse FANY VAD
30–07–18	Faulder Evelyn B	Sgt FANY
	Faulkner Aileen Maud	Dvr FANY
01–09–16	Feilding Lady Dorothea ME	Munro Motor Amb
11–01–18	Foley Mary Gladys Corrinia	OBE Sister QAIMNS
22–01–19	Forse Lilian Audrey	Nurse VAD
04–06–18	Foster Dorothy Penrose	Sister TFNS
30–07–18	Freshfield Katherine M	Nurse VAD
	Galvin Nellie	A Sister QAIMNS(R)
	Garrett Ethel	Staff Nurse QAIMNS(R)
08–07–18	Gibson Margaret Annabella Campbell	Unit Admin QMAAC
17–09–17	Gilbert Louisa Mary	Staff Nurse QAIMNS
16	Gleeson Helen	Dvr Munro Motor Amb
30–07–18	Gordon-Brown Evelyn	Dvr FANY
03–07–18	Gregory Lily Anne	Nurse VAD
	de Guerin Minnie Maude	A Sister QAIMNS(R)
	Hawkins Winifred	Sister TFNS
26–11–17	Herbert Julia Ashbourne	Sister TFNS
31–07–18	Hounslow Edith	Nurse SJAB VAD
18–12–17	Humphries Elizabeth Mountford	Matron TFNS

01–09–16	Hutchinson Ethel	Staff Nurse QAIMNS(R)
11–01–18	Jennings Mabel	Sister ic TFNS
18–04–18	Johnson Sarah Evelyn	Staff Nurse QAIMNS
29–01–18	Johnston Gertrude	Sect Ldr VAD
29–01–18	King Eileen	Sister QAIMNS
18–12–17	King Gladys Victoria	Nurse VAD
19–11–17	Laughton Dorothy Ann	Sister TFNS
	Lowe Katherine Robertson	Staff Nurse TFNS
	MacLean Christine	Staff Nurse QAIMNS
	Mahoney Kaite	Sister QAIMNS
25–11–18	Marshall Mary Devas	Sgt FANY
	Maude Etherinda	Sister QAIMNS
14–06–18	Maxey Kate	Sister ic TFNS
	McGinnis Molly	Sister SJAB
	McGrath Annie M	Staff Nurse QAIMNS
18–12–17	Mears Ethel Isabella Davenish	Sister QAIMNS
	Mellor Juliet V	Sen Sect Ldr VAD
	MontBatten Winifred ES	Commander BRCS
	Moreau Emilienne	Nurse SJAB & BRCS
	Moseley Rachel Gertrude	Ensign FANY
30–07–18	Munroe Susan Deverell	Staff Nurse QAIMNS(R)
	Naughton Dorothy Anne	Sister TFNS
24–01–17	Nolan Mrs Louisa	Civilian
	O'Connell Mollie	Dvr FANY
	Panton Helen Elizabeth	Staff Nurse TFNS

	Pennell Josephine R	Dvr FANY BRCS VAD
	Peyton-Jones G	Sgt Major FANY
18–12–17	Repton Helena Kate	Matron BRCS
30–07–18	Richardson Mary	Cpl FANY
30–07–18	Robinson Charlotte Lilian Anne	Sister QAIMNS
	Roy CM	Sister ic QAIMNS
25–11–18	Russell G Ellen	Cpl FANY
17–09–17	Spense Cissy	Sister QAIMNS
08–10–18	Stubbs Mary Bushby	Dvr FANY
19–11–17	de T'Serclaes Baroness Elsie Blackhall	Munro Motor Amb
	Thompson Ethel Kate	Nurse QAIMNS
30–07–19	Thompson Muriel	Ensign FANY
18–12–17	Thompson Nella Helen Ann	Sister TFNS
19–02–17	Thurstan Anna Violet	Sister BRCS
30–07–18	Todd Constance Elizabeth	Matron SJAB
30–07–18	Toller Lucie MM	Sister QAIMNS
	Trotter JE	A Sister QAIMNS(R)
01–09–16	Tunley Mabel Mary	Matron QAIMNS
21–02–19	Turner HM	Nurse VAD
	Urquart CMC	Dvr FANY
15–07–19	Valentine Selma Amy	Nurse FANY BRCS
30–07–18	Warner Catherine	Sister SJAB
19–11–18	Watkins Ethel Frances	Sister QAIMNS(R)
18–12–17	Weir Annie McKenzie	Nurse BRCS VAD
19–11–18	Wilkinson Louise	Sister QAIMNS(R)
24–01–17	Williams Mrs Florence Ada	Civilian
	Wood Minnie	Sister ic QAIMNS
01–09–16	Whyte Jean Strachan	Staff Nurse TFNS

Second World War

10–11–41	Hearn Avis AJ	A Cpl WAAF
05–11–40	Henderson Elspeth C	Cpl WAAF
05–11–40	Mortimer Joan E	Sgt WAAF
20–12–40	Robins Josephine MG	Cpl WAAF
05–11–40	Turner Helen E	Sgt WAAF
10–01–41	Youle Joan M	A Sgt WAAF

Post-war

18–09–73	Warke SJ	L/Cpl WRAC

QUEEN'S GALLANTRY MEDAL (QGM)

1978	Haire Anne	Inspector Police RUC
1980	Pearson Alison	Constable RUC
1982	Breen Glynnis	Constable RUC
1995	Graham Lesley	Constable RUC
1995	Martin Heather	Ex-Constable RUC

ORDER OF THE BRITISH EMPIRE

British Empire Medal (BEM) – Gallantry

07–40	Cardwell Evelyn M	WVS
08–40	Prince Peggy	WVS
27–12–40	Marsh Nina	Leading Wren WRNS
03–01–41	King Alice	ARP Warden
18–01–41	Westerby Joan	Amb Dvr BRCS
05–41	Woodburn-Bamberger FC	WVS
27–06–41	Anderson Joan	Nurse
09–41	Illidge LB	WVS
30–09–41	McGeorge Pamela	Wren WRNS
	Crossland Barbara	Firewoman AFS/NFS
	Baker Elizabeth	Nurse BRCS
07–03–41	Farr Mary	Midwife BRCS
	Hawkes Gertrude I	BRCS

07–03–41	Leaver Evelyn	Midwife BRCS	
	Phillimore Audrey		
	PD	BRCS	
09–10–42	Walker Jessie E	Asst Nurse BRCS	
09–10–42	Britt Mary M	Asst Nurse	
09–10–42	Walker Mary AD	Asst Nurse	
24–03–42	Jerome Daisy	Nurse	
22–05–42	Harrison Grace L	Women's Land Army	
22–05–42	Mitchell Kathleen M	Farmer's Wife	
22–05–42	Plumb Elizabeth	Ship Stdss	
01–12–42	Caplan Fay	QARNNS VAD	
01–12–42	Tait Susan P	QARNNS VAD	
01–12–42	Wylie Joan	QARNNS VAD	
11–01–43	Richardson MI	Private ATS AA	
11–03–43	Johnson MM	Private ATS	
16–12–43	Ferguson Maria E	Civ/WRNS	
24–12–43	Ellis Lillian	Cpl WAAF	
	Harris	Petty Off WRNS	

14–03–44	Booth Elizabeth	Wren WRNS
14–03–44	Holden Alice	Cpl WAAF
05–05–44	Golland Grace C	L Cpl ATS AA
10–11–44	Crowhurst V	Private ATS
10–11–44	Harcup HM	L Cpl ATS
01–01–45	Beveridge Georgina	YMCA
01–01–45	Fisher DGB	Sgt ATS
01–01–45	James Lauretta	YMCA
01–01–45	McVey MA	Sgt ATS
03–45	Cosgrove Viola M	Amb Dvr BRCS
03–45	Payne Olive E	Amb Dvr BRCS
13–03–45	McKinlay Kathleen	LACW WAAF
23–03–45	Harradine A	L Cpl ATS
14–06–45	Cross Ivy	LACW WAAF
15–03–46	O'Brien M	Private ATS
01–01–47	Enston N	Private ATS

MEDAL OF THE ORDER OF THE BRITISH EMPIRE
First World War

Medals – Civil Division

24–08–17	Algar J	01–01–18	Burrell M	24–08–17	Ede LM	11–06–18	Hibbard HM
15–01–19	Allison E	11–06–18	Burt EM	1917–18	Edwards MA	01–01–18	Hickey ENE
11–06–18	Allum AE	01–01–18	Busby L	01–01–18	Egan N	06–07–20	Hobday EM
06–07–20	Anderson J	01–01–18	Butler E	11–01–18	Enefer EH	01–01–18	Holdsworth VI
11–06–18	Andrews G	01–01–18	Butler GE	01–01–18	Evans K	11–06–18	Hollamby RE
15–01–19	Ansell EE	11–06–18	Calrow G	11–06–18	Everard ER	01–01–18	Holly A
15–01–19	Armitage A	11–06–18	Carpenter AE	11–06–18	Fakeley EE	01–01–18	Holmes J
11–06–18	Arthur LM	01–01–18	Cass FM	06–07–20	Fenwick A	01–01–18	Holttum Mrs
06–07–20	Ash J	01–01–18	Carlton LM	11–06–18	Ferguson A	15–01–19	Honey JR
01–01–18	Auger EA	15–01–19	Caunce M	01–01–18	Finbow RF	15–01–19	Hooper CK
11–06–18	Austin BM	11–06–18	Chapman G	01–01–18	Fisher J	06–07–20	Hopkins AM
15–01–19	Barber VM	15–01–19	Chester E	01–01–18	Fisher M	11–06–18	Howe IL
11–06–18	Barlow AA	01–01–18	Clarke A	11–06–18	Fletcher E	01–01–18	Hurst D
11–06–18	Barnes E	01–01–18	Clarke ME	01–01–18	Flintoff B	15–01–19	Hunt J
15–01–19	Bartlett FCJ	15–01–19	Clough JW	15–01–19	Gafford E	01–01–18	Hunt M
01–01–18	Beaufort BO	15–01–19	Coleman KE	15–01–19	Gemson FE	11–06–18	Hunter AK
01–01–18	Beaumont FE	01–01–18	Coles G	11–06–18	Gibson M	06–07–20	Hutchinson EE
11–06–18	Beck EA	06–07–20	Connoughton S	15–01–19	Gittings EP	15–01–19	Hutt FG
15–01–19	Bennett JA	11–06–18	Cope L	11–06–18	Gittings P	06–07–20	Isles FM
01–01–18	Bessent MG	06–07–20	Copsey E	01–01–18	Godfrey MAL	15–01–19	Jacobs MH
06–07–20	Bevan EM	11–06–18	Cowell E	24–08–17	Golding V	11–06–18	Jackson A
11–06–18	Beverley LA	01–01–18	Cox MR	01–01–18	Goodenough E	01–01–18	Jackson F
11–06–18	Binns MA	1917–18	Croucher MV	06–07–20	Grant A	11–06–18	Jamison MJ
15–01–19	Birch E	01–01–18	Cunningham S	11–06–18	Grasham LF	06–07–20	Jeffries NE
01–01–18	Bostock LA	11–06–18	Cunnington MP	15–01–19	Gray GL	15–01–19	Johns GMM
15–01–19	Bound J	06–07–20	Curtis EG	15–01–19	Green M	15–01–19	Johnson AN
15–01–19	Bowring F	11–06–18	Cuthbert I	01–01–18	Hanson A	01–01–18	Johnson E
01–01–18	Bramwell M	24–08–17	Daniel N	01–01–18	Harman EL	06–07–20	Johnson Mrs
01–01–18	Brisley A	01–01–18	Dartnell LJ	11–06–18	Harrison RE	11–06–18	Johnstone MD
01–01–18	Brooke E	06–07–20	Davies E	01–01–18	Hartley M	15–01–19	Joyce M
11–06–18	Brown AM	11–06–18	Davies L	06–07–20	Hayes K	15–01–19	Kallend EC
01–01–18	Brown E	01–01–18	Davies VA	11–06–18	Haylock FM	01–01–18	Keenan M
01–01–18	Brown M	15–06–18	Davis HL	11–06–18	Haynes EM	06–07–20	Kent A
24–08–17	Bruce M	06–07–20	Davis M	01–01–18	Head E	01–01–18	Kiaer M
11–08–18	Bullions ADS	15–01–19	Dawkins MR	01–01–18	Healey AA	01–01–18	Kipling RK
01–01–18	Burdett-Coutts	24–08–17	Dixon	06–07–20	Heath AM	11–06–18	Kirk E
	MW	11–06–18	Donovan EA	11–06–18	Henbrey EM	15–01–19	Knight M
		01–01–18	Easter BAF	01–01–18	Herrington GE	11–06–18	Knott R

11–06–18 Lancaster A	01–01–18 Morphet N	01–01–18 Rock M	06–07–20 Thomas F
06–07–20 Lavie GL	11–06–18 Morrisroe C	24–08–17 Rose A	11–06–18 Thompsett MA
01–01–18 Laws AM	01–01–18 Mulholland M	06–07–20 Rushton L	15–01–19 Thompson HCL
01–01–18 Leeds EM	06–07–20 Muskett K	11–06–18 Saville R	01–01–18 Trout E
01–01–18 Lethbridge M	01–01–18 Nelson J	11–06–18 Scamer DE	01–01–18 Venus EE
11–06–18 Lightbody J	11–06–18 Newton O	15–01–19 Shell ML	15–01–19 Verney CD
11–06–18 Lindsay J	01–01–18 Newton V	11–06–18 Shepherd K	24–08–17 Vicars DG
06–07–20 Long EK	15–01–19 Nicholls D	11–06–18 Shepherd M	15–01–19 Vincent EP
01–01–18 Ludlow A	06–07–20 Nicholls EM	15–01–19 Sims F	15–01–19 Vining DO
06–07–20 Martin K	15–01–19 Ougham ET	15–01–19 Sinclair M	15–01–19 Waddell C
15–01–19 MacInnes M	01–01–18 Palmer NEA	01–01–18 Sleeford M	01–01–18 Walker M
11–06–18 Mackern J	15–01–19 Passfield KH	01–01–18 Smith BE	01–01–18 Wallace LB
11–06–18 Marchant K	15–01–19 Payne N	15–01–19 Smith C	15–01–19 Waller MC
11–06–18 Marlow EV	01–01–18 Pearson A	11–06–18 Smith CEF	01–01–18 Ward AJ
01–01–18 Marsh D	01–01–18 Peeters G	01–01–18 Smith FEE	01–01–18 Ward N
15–01–19 Marshall R	01–01–18 Pendreigh M	24–08–17 Smith L	11–06–18 Watkins EW
01–01–18 Mason MJ	15–01–19 Perritt BF	15–01–19 Smith L	01–01–18 Watson FM
06–07–20 Matthews G	11–06–18 Perritt GP	01–01–18 Spash H	15–01–19 Watson JB
01–01–18 Maw EB	01–01–18 Peters AM	15–01–19 Spense L	01–01–18 Watt A
01–01–18 McCann A	11–06–18 Philbrick BS	15–01–19 Spink E	01–01–18 West DK
01–01–18 McIntyre ML	15–01–18 Plummer AE	01–01–18 Stanyon L	15–01–19 Westrope G
15–01–19 McKenzie E	01–01–18 Potter EL	15–01–19 Stead CHA	15–01–19 Wheeler M
01–01–18 Merralls AD	06–07–20 Powell E	01–01–18 Steed E	01–01–18 Whibley DF
11–06–18 Messiter FE	11–06–18 Price A	01–01–18 Steggel FE	11–06–18 White EE
11–06–18 Middleton G	01–01–18 Pullen F	01–01–18 Steward FE	15–01–19 Wilding EA
01–01–18 Mills R	01–01–18 Pullinger EM	11–06–18 Stokes EK	01–01–18 Wilkinson MA
11–06–18 Mitchell F	15–01–19 Randall G	11–06–18 Storey L	24–08–17 Williams M
11–06–18 Mitchell I	15–01–19 Rate A	01–01–18 Storey M	01–01–18 Wood G
1917–18 Mitchell OC	15–01–19 Robinson FAG	11–06–18 Swabridge C	11–06–18 Yates A
01–01–18 Moody M	24–08–17 Robinson L	15–01–19 Taylor E	15–01–19 Young ML

Medals – Military Division

09–05–19 Bell EB	CSL WRNS	09–05–19 Evans MF	CSL WRNS
09–05–19 Carter M	CSL WRNS	09–05–19 French DE	Snr Wtr WRNS
09–05–19 Coleman EF	Snr Wtr WRNS	09–05–19 Hayter R	CSL WRNS
09–05–19 Cummings K	CSL WRNS	09–05–19 Henderson HF	Tel Op WRNS
09–05–19 D'Arcy M	CSL WRNS	09–05–19 Jenner H	Mt Dvr WRNS
09–05–19 Dart GO	CSL WRNS	09–05–19 Maunsell MESE	CSL WRNS
09–05–19 Davies AM	CSL WRNS	09–05–19 Perrett EO	CSL WRNS
09–05–19 Dennis AF	CSL WRNS	09–05–19 Reid AA	Snr Wtr WRNS
09–05–19 Dove AE	MT Dvr WRNS	09–05–19 Smith J	CSL WRNS
09–05–19 Dove D	CSL WRNS	09–05–19 Tidman IG	CSL WRNS
09–05–19 Duckworth M	CSL WRNS	03–06–19 Brisley M	Member WRAF
09–05–19 Duncan K	Snr Wtr WRNS		

KING'S/QUEEN'S COMMENDATIONS FOR BRAVERY/BRAVE CONDUCT

27–12–40 Marriott Irene M	Wren WRNS	21–02–41 Williams Mairie	Amb Dvr ARP
40 Jago-Brown EA	3rd Off WRNS	02–41 Hanford	WVS
Warren Winifred M	Nurse	02–41 Paulson	WVS
Campbell W	Nurse	27–05–41 Coleman AM	WVS Vol
McMartin Morag	Nurse	27–05–41 Taylor ER	ATS Vol
01–01–41 Weaver DG	WVS	16–05–41 Randall Mary	Petty Off WRNS
18–02–41 Gaunt Clarice	Petty Off WRNS	27–06–41 Stanley May	Nurse
21–02–41 Carter Hilda AM	WAFS (Fire)	06–41 Tudball MG	Amb Att WVS
21–02–41 Griffith Hilda J	WAFS	08–41 Restall	WVS ARP
21–02–41 Sargent Jean E	WAFS	16–12–41 Shipton Phyllis L	Sister QARNNS
21–02–41 Young Anita	WAFS	24–03–42 Dick BH	L/Cpl ATS
21–02–41 Hefford Hilda	ARP	05–05–42 Lunnon Winifred	3rd Off WRNS
21–02–41 Lewis Eva	ARP	08–42 Whimster	WVS
21–02–41 Wells Carrie	Amb Off ARP	01–12–42 Turnbull Elizabeth	Petty Off WRNS

03–12–42	Gibbs PJ	Sister QAIMNS		75	Warrilow Eva	Det C Police
42	Ferguson Sarah	L Wren WRNS		77	Bartram Dianne	WPC Police
09–10–42	Cartwright Florence E	Asst Nurse		78	Patterson L	Ex Det C Police
07–09–43	Smith Helen E	L Wren WRNS		79	Holt Michelle	WPC Police
44	Paton Amy A	L Wren WRNS		80	Kearns Janet	WP Sgt Police
44	Moyes Agnes S	Petty Off WRNS		80	Catterall Kim	WPC Police
15–09–44	Abercrombie E	Sister QAIMNS		83	Barclay Christine	WPC Police
07–11–44	Bates Cecily	Women's Land Army		83	Early Helen	Det Sgt Police
07–11–44	Dickerson Eva	Women's Land Army		83	Evans Helen J	WPC Police
14–11–44	Wilson Brenda	L Wren WRNS		84	Edmiston Kareen	Sgt Police
01–12–44	Bacon F	Private ATS		85	Kane Sharon	Ex Det C Police
29–12–44	Evershed M	Sister QAIMNS (P)		85	Bowden Thelma	Det C Police
29–12–44	Field DM	Sister QAIMNS (P)		85	Barkley Lyn	Sgt Police
45	Leigh Vera E	FANY/SOE (P)		85	Brown Faith	WPC Police
45	Bennett PM	Flt Capt ATA		85	Thompson IE	Ex WPC Police
25–09–51	Haseleen Esme M	Secretary		85	McCullough FK	Ex Res C Police
03–10–50	Ferris Ethel K	Sgt Med WAAF		94	Harrison Leslie	WPC Police
22–11–52	Cambell H	Private QARANC		94	Polehill Ruth	WPC Police
54	Jones Audrey M	Lt QARANC		95	McKinney Mary	Res C Police
28–11–58	Edinger Elizabeth	Shorthand Typist		14–06–97	Blake Mary	Teacher
70	Taylor Nora	WPC Police		14–06–97	Harrild Eileen	Teacher
11–74	Milton IR	Stdss VC10		14–06–97	Mayor Gwen	Teacher (P)
74	Parrish Jacqueline	WPC Police				

CIVIL AWARDS

LLOYD'S MEDALS

Medal for Saving Life at Sea

25–11–08	Gilmour Kate	Stdss SS *Sardinia* (Silver)		28–06–11	Madame Matelot	w/o Keeper Kerdonis Lighthouse (Bronze)

Medal for Meritorious Services

18–07–96 to 18–03–97	Mrs Reed	w/o capt of *TF Oakes*; 1st medal to woman
20 to 23–03–26	Langton Ethel	d/o Keeper St Helen's Fort Lighthouse (Bronze)
12 to 14–11–84	Fisher Anna Lee	US Astronaut Space Shuttle *Discovery* (Silver)

Lloyd's War Medal

25–08–40	Drummond Victoria Alexandrina	2nd Eng SS *Bonita*		13–06–41	Owen Elizabeth May	Stdss SS *St Patrick*
26–11–40	Plumb Elizabeth	Stdss 1st Class MV *Rangitane*		05–07–42	Ferguson Maria Elizabeth	Passenger SS *Avila Star*
25–03–41	Miller Adeline Nancy	Dr Ship's Surgeon SS *Britannia*				

ROYAL HUMANE SOCIETY (RHS)

Stanhope Gold Medal

1948	Ferguson Petronella	Housewife		1992	Moore Lesley Allison	WPC
1990	Walsh Elaine	Housewife				

RHS Medal

1838	Darling Grace	d/o Lighthouse Keeper (Gold)		1980	Bishop Elizabeth	Student Nurse (Silver)
1895	Verity Kate	(Bronze)		1983	Pritchard Margaret Eirian	Taxi Dvr (Silver)
1937	Ryle Iris Mary	Hotelier (Silver)		1984	Belshaw Sarah Jane Esther	Nurse (Silver)
1957	Wittgenstein Princess Iris Mary	(Bronze)		1990	Moore Lesley Allison	WPC (Silver)
1947	Ferguson Petronella	Housewife (Silver)				
1947	Ditty Margaret Elizabeth	Housewife (Silver)				

ROYAL LIFE SAVING SOCIETY (RLSS)

Montbatten Medal

1952	Jupp Sally Elwin	1970	Pope D Patricia
1953	Higgins Sybil	1977	McLean Pauline A
1962	Westerman Hilary	1985	Phillips Holly Jacqueline

LIVERPOOL SHIPWRECK AND HUMANE SOCIETY

Marine Medal (Silver)

1915	Kelk Dorothy	1934	Hume Jean
1919	Leach Nancy	1934	Bravey Louise
1924	Meesham Maud	1936	Hogg Doris
1925	Thew Margaret	1938	Byatt Elsie
1925	Linley Berenice	1938	Rose Doris
1925	Linley Mabel	1938	Scott Mary
1926	Dobbie Elsie	1944	Preston Mona
1926	McLellan Dorothy	1948	Wilkinson Norma
1933	Blore Alice		

Marine Medal (Bronze)

37 Bronze including
1991   Jones Tracey

Fire Medal (Silver)

1914	Stenhouse Margaret	1927	Passmore Mabel
1914	Harris Edith	1931	Morris Freda
1915	Evans Edith	1940	Kells Elizabeth
1916	Neill Edith	1948	Kelly Elizabeth
1920	Gilooly Dorothy		

Fire Medal (Bronze)

22 including
1989   Walsh Elaine

General Medal (Silver)

1930	Davidson Mary	1942	McNeill Olivia	WAAF

General Medal (Bronze)

6 including
1978   Morgan Denise   WPC

CARNEGIE HERO FUND TRUST

1908	Wharton Ethel	1912	Ash Maud MA	1913	Jones Grace	1917	Bond Lillie M (P)
1909	Hugues Maggie	1912	Davis Maud	1913	Woodruff Grace (P)	1917	O'Higgins Mary
1909	Nicholls Florence	1912	Davison Annie	1914	Birch Elsie	1918	Caird Margaret
1909	Nicholls Mary	1912	Munro/Grant	1915	Buckthorpe Violet	1918	Campbell Maggie
1909	Weir Mary		Jessie A (P)	1915	Turvey Hilda	1918	Goodacre Louisa
1909	Smith Annie	1912	Munro/Ross Alice	1916	Blakeley Doris A	1918	Tisdall Irene
1910	Davison Margaret A	1912	Greaves Eleanor	1916	McNeill Winifred FJ	1918	Nance Jeniver
1910	Chivers Jane	1912	Kirk Mrs MC	1916	O'Neill Margaret	1918	Oakham Elizabeth
1910	Wright Frances	1912	Lewis Mary A	1916	Wakeman Louisa E	1918	Williamson
1910	Gisborne Fanny	1912	Parker Alice E	1916	Nolan Louisa		Margaret G
1910	Footman Frances	1912	Stephenson Elsa	1916	O'Neil Margaret	1918	Nuttall Kathleen
1911	Wilson Jessie	1912	Davies Annie (P)	1917	Daniels Janet S	1919	Stein Zoe
1911	Jacques Amy M	1912	Holley Elizabeth	1917	Dixon Isabella	1919	Pickett Rose L (P)
1911	Harvey Mary E	1912	Waylor Ada	1917	Bruce Maud	1919	Kerr Elizabeth
1911	Howell Sarah J (P)	1912	Price Doris	1917	Kensington	1921	Allen Muriel
1911	Craigiel Mrs	1913	Howe Mary J		Charlotte	1921	Mitchell Rena

1921 Young Agnes	1932 Illsley Sarah C	1943 Mepham Bertha C (P)
1923 Heatly Mary	1932 Seecking Emma L	1944 Henderson Margaret M (P)
1923 Kinley Margaret M	1932 Riddle Mary (P)	1944 Atkinson Ivy R (P)
1923 Hamer Margaret	1932 Ellard Eithne	1944 Endersby May D (P)
1925 Payto Lilian	1932 Jackson Margaret A	1944 Froud Jean M (P)
1925 Price Margaret J	1932 Jones Kathleen M	1944 Millner Rosemary
1926 G Batstone Gladys (P)	1933 Ashton May (P)	1944 Thomas Lilian
1926 Doyle Susan (P)	1933 Deasy Eileen	1945 McCahill Mary J
1926 Smith Margaret (P)	1933 Ackerley Mary F (P)	1945 Doyle Alice
1926 Edmunds Edith	1934 Bravey Louisa F (P)	1945 Hughes Elsie W
1926 Herman Muriel	1934 Cameron Isa	1945 Tindall Hannah W (P)
1926 Hughes Joyce	1934 Chamberlain Anne (P)	1945 Nathan Florence (P)
1926 Eveson Milicent M (P)	1934 O'Hanlon Mary	1945 Hetherington Edna
1926 Harwood Mabel M	1935 Crampton Ethel (P)	1945 Smith Annie A
1927 McArdle Nora (P)	1935 Hemphill Kathleen A (P)	1946 Addison Mary E
1927 Williams Annie E	1935 Ketteridge Florence	1946 Casey Kathleen
1928 Dow Ingrid YG (2 rescues)	1935 Norwood Mary C	1946 Cooke Phyllis E
1928 Franckeiss Madge	1935 Pope Winifred	1946 Dyke Muriel
1928 Fraser Ella	1935 Thomas Ivy E (P)	1946 Gant Rosina E
1928 Haigh Elsie (P)	1935 Gilson Sarah (P)	1946 Fisher Dorothy M (P)
1928 Lindley Hilda M (P)	1936 Wiseman Elizabeth	1946 Gore Lilian (P)
1928 O'Hagan Elizabeth	1937 Bunker Margaret	1946 Muir Edna M (P)
1928 Trainer Rose E	1937 Gates Sarah (P)	1946 Sedgbeer Edith M
1928 Williams Edith	1937 Parsons Rose	1946 Stead Violet
1928 Hall Olive	1938 Ivermee Nellie A	1946 Burrows Margaret M
1928 Papple Janet C	1938 Springett Barbara	1946 Barton Lilian (P)
1929 Anderson Kathleen C (P)	1939 Aldridge Sarah E	1947 Baldwin Patricia M (P)
1929 Moubray Marianne C	1939 Gath Ellen (P)	1947 Price Gwenora
1929 Noble Mysie	1939 Cartwright Joan A	1947 Wills Ivy
1929 Dewsberry Nancy	1940 Donoghue Mary M (P)	1947 Patmore Dorothy (P)
1929 Higgins Julia	1940 Pedelty Elsie	1947 Shanahan Evelyn (P)
1929 King Alice (P)	1940 Pickles Julia (P)	1947 Austin Margaret
1929 Olsson Harriet J (P)	1940 Thomas Marian E (P)	1947 Hibbs Isobella
1929 Wilson Margaret I (P)	1940 Crisp Alice	1948 Baker Rosina E (P)
1929 Leary Kate	1940 Woolhouse Rosemary	1948 Chaloner Irene
1929 Madigan Florrie	1941 Ford Phyllis M (P)	1948 Habens Lyn V (P)
1929 O'Brien Dorothy (P)	1941 Hope Elsie A (P)	1948 Howard Marjorie (P)
1930 O'C Clarke Marie (P)	1941 Baker Rose E	1948 Pocock Kathleen M
1930 Law Annie (P)	1941 Page Sarah A (P)	1948 Spring Beatrice FJ
1930 Marchant Eva M	1941 Green Mary (P)	1948 Wilson Betty (P)
1930 Ayris Elizabeth (P)	1941 Anderson Annie E (P)	1948 Cox Eva M
1930 Bialostocki Annie	1942 Keery Ruby (P)	1948 Jones Ruby
1931 Chappell Jessie	1942 Grant Florence (P)	1948 Wilkinson Stella
1931 Levy Edith (P)	1942 Cook Effie GS	1949 Lyons Margaret A (P)
1931 Schon Gwendoline J (P)	1942 Barber Doreen (P)	1949 Gardner Eliza
1931 Utton Daisy H	1943 Hills Daphne	
1931 Wilce Marion	1943 Fabian Dulcie E	
1932 Barnett Edna	1943 Knowles Millicent (P)	

1949 Glazier Emily M
1949 Kay Maureen
1949 Weir Jean I (P)
1950 Howse Blanche
1950 Howell Nicola
1950 Deasy Eileen (P)
1950 Reynolds Monica (P)
1951 Stanton Mary
1951 Gregg Shelagh
1951 Vearncombe Marjorie
1951 Harding Olive
1951 Percival Charlotte G
1952 Derry Lavinia (P)
1952 Derry Rosetta
1952 McCausland Ellen M
1952 Fowler Mary P
1952 Potts Ellen
1953 McClarnon Sarah M (P)
1954 Hammond Gladys
1954 Holland Sister Freda
1954 Iredale Barbara C
1954 Iredale Adeline
1955 Key Annie S (P)
1955 Key Beryl (P)
1955 Tanner Hilary
1955 O'Sullivan Myra
1956 Buck Elsie FE
1958 Lewis Beatrice
1958 Howard Shirley A
1958 Leslie Catherine
1958 Green Pamela M (P)
1958 Clydesdale Eileen (P)
1959 Bishop Flora
1959 Maguire Mary M (P)
1959 Casey Margaret (P)
1971 Murgatroyd Annie
1973 Robinson Eileen S
1974 Komunyckyj Josephine (P)
1974 Mitchell Margaret (P)
1975 Pegg Evelyn
1977 Nevard Patricia (P)
1985 McKenna Stella C
1991 Wynn Elizabeth J
1995 Richardson Monica J

SOCIETY FOR THE PROTECTION OF LIFE FROM FIRE

(A short selection of names)

1896	Pearson Annie	(Silver Medal)	1917	Shepherd MJ	
1916	Downs Mary		1926	Rattey Betty	
1916	Downs Ursie		1926	Buckingham Emmeline	
1916	Milner May		1971	Cocks Ettie	
1918	Robson Louisa	(Silver Medal)	1971	Crawley Flora	
1917	Messenger Lily		1985	Duncan Lorraine	

ROYAL NATIONAL LIFEBOAT INSTITUTION

1888	Blyth Helen	d/o Head Lighthouse Keeper	1888	Wallace Mrs	w/o Asst Lighthouse Keeper

SPECIAL SERVICE CROSS BRCS

1941	Bird J	Bedford Branch	1954	Evans D	Staffs
1943	Dawson	Essex	1955	Niblock V	N Ireland
1943	Hughes E	Berks	1957	Gibbings C	Devonshire
1943	Skinner D	Norfolk	1958	Day J	Kent
1944	Dalby J	E Riding Yorks	1959	Costin M	Kent
1944	Thorogood	Beds	1959	Bailey JA	Staffs
1944	Currall	Belfast	1960	Burrell D	Northumberland
1944	Irvine HJ	Middlesex	1960	Brittain R	Montgomeryshire
1945	Wilkins P	Hamps	1965	Braxton C	Wilts
1945	Froud J	Warks	1966	Bidwell I	Kent
1947	Brandrick GM	Staffs	1967	Hughes D	Somerset
1947	Macfarlane SG	Scotland	1971	Morrell A	Co London
1948	Cairns H	Belfast	1971	Lutfoot DE	Essex
1948	Thomas H	Ceylon	1973	Davies EM	Kent
1948	Pinchon M	E Riding Yorks	1974	James A	Sussex
1950	Brown L	Herts	1978	Davis D	Kent
1951	Cooper	London	1979	Campbell I	N Ireland
1953	Barclay H	Norfolk	1979	Steele M	N Ireland
1953	Bloomfield K	Norfolk	1988	Wooten L	Northants
1953	Knights L	Norfolk	1988	Hill S	Dorset
1954	Hazeldean	Sussex	1989	Cox E	Lockerbie
1954	Watson D	Kent			

LOCAL POLICE AWARDS
William Garnett Cup for Bravery (Lancs)

1977	Bartram Dianne	WPC	1980	Catterall Kim	WPC
1980	Wright	WPC	1981	Thompson	WPC

Goodwin Award (Durham)

1985	White Denise	WPC

Binnie Medal (London)

1951	Richards Mrs PH		1973	Burns Mrs J
1955	Myers Mrs W		1993	Condie Mrs M
1957	Moss Mrs EM			

FLORENCE NIGHTINGALE MEDAL (FNM)

1920	Jones Beatrice Isabel	QAIMNS	1923	McCarthy Maud Emma	
1920	Lambert J.	RNNR	1927	Browne Sydney	
1920	Maxey Kate	Sister TFNS	1929	Swift Sarah	
1920	Minchin Lucy	Sister India	1931	Smith Anne Beadsmore	
1920	Smith Gertrude Mary Wilton	Sister QAIMNS	1933	Still Lloyd	
			1935	Becher Ethel Hope	
1920	White Gladys Laura	Sister BRCS	1937	Carter Maynard Linden	

1939	Phillips Agathe Mary		1973	Stromwall Sonia Lenie	
1939	Musson Ellen		1975	Quinn Remone Susan	BRCS
1947	Blair Emily Mathisson		1977	Ash Patricia Margaret	BRCS
1949	Watt Catherine		1977	Fraser Helen Clare	BRCS
1951	Deale Doris		1979	Elvidge Diana Mary	
1953	Bridges Daisy Caroline		1979	Gilbert Eileen	BRCS
1955	Jorden Ellen Priscilla	Sister BRCS	1981	Cookson Helen	BRCS
1957	Cockayne Elizabeth		1983	Morris Susan	
1961	Colquhoun Olive Laura	Sister	1983	Riordan Josephine	Sister
1961	Craven Marjorie Eden	BRCS	1985	Ryding Diane	
1963	Adams Janet Patience	BRCS	1987	Edwards Phyllis Eileen	(P)
1965	Folke Mary Sheelagh McConnel		1987	Kerr Annette	
1967	Hills-Young Elaine	BRCS	1989	Lamb Elizabeth	
1969	Lancaster Eva G	BRCS	1991	Bertschinger Claire	
1971	Jones Gwyneth Ceris	BRCS	1993	Perkins Mary Elizabeth	
1971	Houghton Marjorie	BRCS	1995	Hayward-Karlsson Jennifer Ann	
1973	Cholmeley Helen Joyce				

Australia

UK AWARDS

THE MOST EXCELLENT ORDER OF THE BRITISH EMPIRE – GALLANTRY AWARDS
Members (MBE) – Gallantry

1946	Bullwinkel Vivian	Staff Nurse AANS	1942	Torney Veronica	Staff Nurse AANS

GEORGE MEDAL (GM)

22–09–42	Anderson Margaret	Staff Nurse AANS	17–07–45	Wake Nancy	Ensign FANY/SOE
25–08–44	Savage Ellen	Lt AANS	23–01–73	Gibbs Mary Elizabeth	Teacher

MILITARY MEDAL (MM)
First World War

28–09–17	Cawood DG	Sister AANS	16–10–17	Kelly Alicia Mary	Sister AANS
28–09–17	Deacon Clare	Sister AANS	16–10–17	Pratt Rachel	Sister AANS
28–09–17	Derren Mary Jane	Staff Nurse AANS	23–08–18	Corkhill Pearl Elizabeth	Staff Nurse AANS
28–09–17	Ross-King Alice	Head Sister AANS			

ORDER OF THE BRITISH EMPIRE
British Empire Medal (BEM) – Gallantry

1944	Boye Ruby	Coastwatcher/ Hon 3rd Off WRANS	21–01–55	Pearson KW	LACW WAAAF

AUSTRALIAN AWARDS

STAR OF COURAGE (SC)

01–05–79	Allen Elizabeth Florence	17–09–90	Mueller Christin
29–04–80	Quazim Esme	21–10–91	Clark Barbara Ann
23–08–81	Mann Peta-Lynn	21–10–91	O'Leary Sharon Elaine
14–05–86	McLeod Lorraine Kaye	29–03–93	McNiven Rachelle
17–09–90	Marshall Lillian Beryl	02–03–94	Chillemi Tiani Michelle

BRAVERY MEDAL (BM)

01–05–79	Martin Ann Louise	29–04–80	Partington Katherine Bridgette
29–04–80	Coulton Merril Elizabeth	12–11–86	Long Jennifer Anne

21–10–87   McLune Catherine Sally
16–03–88   Kemp Tracey Lee
21–12–88   Eathorne Carolyn Joy
21–12–88   Lowther Sharon Marie
21–12–88   Newmann Joy Annette
21–12–88   Peterson Julie Ann
09–08–89   Grice Leonie Gaye
20–04–90   Yabsley Cheryl Linda   (P)
17–09–90   Ascrizzi Connie   (P)
17–09–90   Davis Megan
17–09–90   Dowling Grace Philomena   (P)
17–09–90   Purcell Caroline
16–03–91   Chee Catherine Ann
16–03–91   Davidson Pamela Jane
16–03–91   Dyer Elizabeth Anne
16–03–91   Jackson Sandra

21–10–91   Cuthbert Joanne Louise   (P)
21–10–91   O'Neill Frances Jane   (P)
04–05–92   Pang-Quee Lena Mary
04–05–92   Walters Debra Anne
29–03–93   Burke Angela Leigh (16 yrs)
29–03–93   Dickinson Carol   (P)
29–03–93   Hensler Priscilla Anne
29–03–93   Mattiske Janelle Anne
29–03–93   Robinson Joy Rosalie
02–02–94   Buckley Gail
02–03–94   Petricevic Robyne Lynne
02–03–94   Smith Beryl Ellen
25–03–96   Brown Jane Edith
07–08–96   Hunt Gwenda Jean
12–03–96   Lennox Naomi Louise

COMMENDATION FOR BRAVE CONDUCT (CBC)

1992	Baird Hannah Marie (13 yrs)	
1984	Bell Sherilee Kate	
1997	Bourke Patricia	P Sgt
1992	Brown Julie Annette	
1991	Campbell Robyn Corrine	
1983	Carver Mary Ann	
1997	Chadwick Natalie Anne	
1989	Chalkley Clare Catherine	
1990	Cleary-Munro Lea	
1989	Collingridge Kathy Jean	
1982	Conniff Suzanne	
1979	Conrad Jennifer May	
1991	Cooper Holly Dwan	
1993	Copley Neesha Irene	
1997	Dal Zotto Marisa	
1981	Dunkley Carole Ann	
1994	Dunstan Emily Rae	
1993	Edwards Marguerite Therese	WPC
1990	Egoroff Jean Doreen	
1988	Ellery Joyce Evelyn	
1990	Eva Erin Lee (6 yrs)	
1985	Fletcher Kathryn Jill	
1992	Foye Beverly Anne	
1996	Gardner Tracey Christine	
1991	Gay Sandra May	
1987	Gerry Catherine Ann	
1990	Gladman Judyth	
1994	Gretch Louise Katherine	
1988	Harper Lynne Elizabeth	
1982	Haskew Sue-Ellen Kaye	
1983	Howard Jade-Leah	
1991	Howe Melissa Anne	
1992	Jury Sandi Louise (7 yrs)	
1978	Kavanaugh Wavenie	
1997	Leigh-Gordon Kerri	
1994	Lennox Myra Gail	
1990	Liddington Sarah Emma (13 yrs)	
1979	Lohmann Rosslyn Kay	
1997	Matti Suzanne Marie	
1995	Milton Joanne Therese	
1990	Moir Diane Jarlath	
1995	Neale Sally Fiona	
1995	Nord Frances Marie	
1993	Parremore Jodie Lee (10 yrs)	
1989	Patterson Allison Margaret	
1991	Pattison Debbie Joan	
1991	Phelan Rebecca Anne (10 yrs)	
1992	Pigott Kay Lorraine	WPC
1979	Pittaway Debrah Anne	
1989	Porch Catherine Jean	
1993	Shaw Ellen Suzzanne	
1989	Shelton Debra Leanne	
1984	Simpson Christine Lynn	
1980	Stanyer Jacqueline Faye	
1995	Tegel Jordana Brenda	
1992	Thomson Sally Ann	
1995	Van Den Bosch Karen Marietta (16 yrs)	
1988	Watkins Sharon Anne	
1995	Watt Patricia Margaret (74 yrs)	
1980	Williams June Marie	
1983	Wright Brianna Kate	
1997	Yoon Sun-Young (Sonya)	

OTHER CIVIL AWARDS

ROYAL HUMANE SOCIETY (RHS)

Stanhope Gold Medal

1981	Kalms Dulcie	Housewife New South Wales	1992	Smith Beryl Ellen	Med Practice Manager Australasia

Clarke Gold Medal (Australasia)

1925	Devine Ellen Mary	Housewife		1981	Mann Peta-Lynn (12 yrs) Schoolgirl	
1946	Williams Elizabeth	Housewife		1992	Smith Beryl Ellen	Med Practice Manager

Clarke Silver Medal (Australasia)

1919	Simons Dovis Isabel		1940	Wilhelm Lorna Hilda (15 yrs) Servant
1930	Cozens-Clerk Clarice		1985	Newmann Dr Joy Annette

Rupert Wilks Trophy & Medal (Australasia)

1962	Crothers Jane Elizabeth (11 yrs)	1977	Quinn Adele Sandra (12 yrs)
1966	Bachmann Coleen Maree (7 yrs)	1981	Mann Peta-Lynn (12 yrs)

RHS Gold Medal (New South Wales)

1949	Smith Gwen	Nurse

RHS Silver Medal (New South Wales)

1915	Anderson Beatrice Evelyn (11 yrs)		1944	Williamson Dorothy Angela	Private AWAS
1922	Craigie Edna M (11 yrs)		1944	Hawkins Emily Alice (P)	
1924	Shea Thelma		1946	Higgins Elsie Mary	
1925	Cantwell Emma May		1949	Pope Margaret (13 yrs)	
1932	Barber Dorothy Jean (13 yrs)		1951	Channon Fae (14 yrs)	
1942	Mack Barbara Ann (15 yrs)		1958	Wangman Judith Ann	
1944	Smith Betty Ellen (11 yrs) (P)		1980	Kalms Dulcie	

Neville Pixley Book Award (New South Wales)

1995	Geurts Emma (5 yrs)	

Posthumous Awards (Australasia)

1926	Richards Mary Kathleen	Clerk		1970	Cowborn Paula Jean (13 yrs)	
1927	Brewer May	Teacher		1972	Pitkin Rhona Fay	
1927	McDonald Kathleen Margaret	Teacher		1976	Haynes Marie Estelle	
1937	Blake Ann Clarice (16 yrs)			1978	Troedel Margaret Andrea	Biochemist
1948	O'Flaherty Clara Amy (15 yrs)	Kitchenmaid		1981	Lange Janine Patricia	
1948	Marchini Lily (13 yrs)			1982	Moore Dorothy Anne	
1952	Dowell Liola Maria (62 yrs)			1984	Livingstone Beverley Eleda	
1954	Comper Judith (15 yrs)			1987	Papaionnou Georgina	Student
1956	Wakefield Irene Ethel DB			1987	Markoska Vesna	
1958	Woodfield Helen			1989	Wood Sheryl Maree	
1958	Russel Cheryl Ann (11 yrs)			1990	Cox Marion Louisa	
1961	Hardy Gloria Dawn			1990	O'Neill Frances Jane (14 yrs)	
1962	Marchant Anne Theresa			1990	Cuthbert Joanne Louise	Teacher

FLORENCE NIGHTINGALE MEDAL

1920	Conyers Evelyn Augusta	1951	Paschke Olive	1963	Huppatz Rose Zelma	1979	Harler Edith Elizabeth
1929	Wilson Grace Margaret	1953	Bowe Ethel Jessie	1965	MacIntosh Lucy Wise	1979	Leak Jenny Elizabeth
1933	Cornwell Edith	1953	Johnson Edith	1965	Edis Margaret Dorothy	1981	Johnson Bridget Agatha
1935	Pidgeon Elsie Clare	1953	MacDonald Sarah Charlotte	1967	Lawson Betty Constance	1983	Edwards Ailsa Betty
1937	Kellett Adelaide Maud	1955	Marshall Lucy Thelma	1969	Doig Edna Dell	1983	Leach Anne
1947	Sage Annie Moriah	1957	Abbott Joan	1969	Ferguson Jean Elsie	1985	Tyler Ella
1947	Bullwinkel Vivian	1959	Daymon Phyllis Mary	1969	Tweedy Kathleen	1987	Ryan Berenice Nonie
1947	Moriarty Barbara	1959	Chomley Patricia Downes	1971	Docker Betty Bristow	1987	Nissen Elizabeth Eleanor
1949	Storey Ruby Evelyn	1961	Maloney Margaret Jean	1971	Fall Constance Amy	1995	Roberts Vera
1949	Appleford Alice Rose	1961	Headberry Jean Evelyn	1977	Deal Patricia G	1995	James Mary
1951	Malcolm Rita			1977	Schultz Bartz		

Canada

UK AWARDS

GEORGE CROSS (GC)

AM 21–12–17   Ashburnham Doreen (11 yrs)   GC 21–10–71

THE MOST EXCELLENT ORDER OF THE BRITISH EMPIRE – GALLANTRY AWARDS
Members (MBE) – Gallantry

01–01–43 Brooke Margaret Martha	Lt WRCNS	10–46 Bamford-Fletcher
44 Hutcheon Constance	Dvr SJAB	Joan	Ensign FANY
07–07–45 McCann Margaret Jane	Lt RCAMC	08–06–68 Cashin Joan A	Capt RCAMC

GEORGE MEDAL (GM)

11–06–42 Walsh Frances	Teacher	02–12–58 Collins Edith Gladys	Ret'd Nurse
04–12–42 Patterson Marion	Fireguard		

MILITARY MEDAL (MM)
First World War

08–07–18 Bonnell Sara	Dvr FANY	01–06–18 Lutwick Marie Dow	A Sister QAIMNS(R)
30–07–18 Brown Evelyn Gordon	Dvr FANY	29–01–19 McNair Beatrice	Sister CAMC
24–09–18 Campbell Edith	Matron CAMC	24–09–18 Thompson Eleanor Jean	Sister CAMC
29–01–19 Hansen Helene Elizabeth	Sister CAMC	24–09–18 Urquart Lottie	Sister CAMC
24–09–18 Herrington Leonara	Sister CAMC	24–09–18 Williamson Janet Mary	Sister CAMC
24–09–18 Hodge Meta	Sister CAMC		

MEDAL OF THE ORDER OF THE BRITISH EMPIRE

15–01–19 Hadd Jessie	Factory worker	06–07–20 Sauve Clare M	Factory worker

ORDER OF THE BRITISH EMPIRE
British Empire Medal (BEM) – Gallantry

09–01–43 Entwhistle Mollie	L/Cpl CWAC	01–01–45 Marriott Patricia Marguerite	L/Cpl CWAC
05–06–43 Kerridge Ellen Millicent	Private CWAC	01–01–45 Sheppard Isabelle	L/Cpl CWAC
01–01–44 Quinlan Mary Lillian	Private CWAC	01–01–46 Robertson Margaret Elizabeth	Petty Off WRCNS
08–06–44 Anderson AM	ACW1 RCAFWD		

COMMENDATION FOR BRAVE CONDUCT (CBC)

15–12–44 Margarete Helen	Nursing Sister RCAFNS	01–01–45 Spencer Diana	Lt WRCNS
01–01–45 Kovalchuk Helen	Private CWAC	01–01–46 Hill Dorothy	A Petty Off WRCNS
01–01–45 Newman Grace Adah	L Cpl CWAC	01–01–46 Owen Vivian Wilson	A Ldg Patrolman WRCNS

CANADIAN AWARDS

CROSS OF VALOUR (CV)

12–11–71 Dohey Mary	Stdss	09–09–80 Lang Anna	Car Dvr
04–09–74 Swedberg Jean	Switchboard Op (P)		

STAR OF COURAGE (SC)

14–02–71 Paterson Irene (16 yrs)	03–05–73 Larose Claire (16 yrs)
14–05–70 Moddejonge Geraldine (14 yrs) (P)	29–07–75 Poulin Louise (15 yrs) (P)
28–01–72 Boudreau Ula (P)	29–07–75 Pitkethly Margaret Lucretia (65 yrs) (P)
12–10–71 Letêcheur Evelyne	19–05–73 Panton Kathryn Louise (P)

16–09–76 Bishop Chris Ann (15 yrs)
04–03–76 Flynn Gail
30–07–76 Swayze Anna Gertrude
20–07–78 MacDonald Sandra Joan   (P)
08–05–78 May Dawn Kathleen
25–01–78 McInnis Deborah Ann
25–01–78 MacLean Deborah Jean
03–05–78 McCann Barbara Ann   (P)
14–03–79 Morrison Jane Ellen
06–12–79 O'Brien Sharon
18–12–80 Hewitt Doreen
07–04–82 Kinch Mary Eleanor Michelle   (P)
28–07–82 Milanovic Kristine Ruth   (P)
25–07–82 Boudreault Brigitte (14 yrs)

09–01–83 Semeniuk Ora Daisy
17–01–84 Newell Margaret Elizabeth   (P)
14–05–84 Duncan Gloria May
03–08–85 Lifely Lilia
13–01–87 Gagnon Gisele
01–08–88 Garcia Maribel   (P)
04–07–89 Nolan Grace Marilyn
04–11–90 Betts Tiffiney (12 yrs)
03–07–91 Leech Lorrane Sybil
23–06–92 Beaucher Suzanne-Marie
25–04–92 McDonald Jocelyn (7 yrs)
14–12–93 Maracle Sheila Ruth
19–02–95 Bjornson Mary Ona

MEDAL OF BRAVERY (MB)

1967	McWilliams Ruth	1982	McCauley Gerda Anna	1988	Annable Karen
1968	Buchanan Theresa (16 yrs)	1982	Young Aileen	1989	Beaton Irene
1971	Potts Donna Claudette	1982	Horner Laura Lee Margaret	1989	Provost Nathalie
1972	Morissette Suzanne	1982	Gulka Olga Nurse	1990	Soucy-Proulx Johanne
1973	Dale-Harris Ann	1983	Balcom Mona Jean	1990	Kushneryk Stacy Alison
1973	Cornish Margaret	1983	Semeniuk Saralyn Marie	1991	Amaral Isattina
1974	Stewart Pamela Anne	1983	Provost Tracey (10 yrs)	1991	Hardy Janice
1976	Boyce Louise (13 yrs)	1983	Sartorelli Francesca	1991	Browning Janice Elaine
1976	Brock Diane Constable	1984	MacInnis Edith Marie (14 yrs)	1992	Stewart Heather Ann
1976	Kennedy Rhona Dawn	1984	Palmer Deborah Ann	1992	Cote Lise
1976	Skinner Judi Ann		(14 yrs)	1992	Rioux Rachel (6 yrs)
1976	Meshake Glenda Mary	1984	Keefe Diane Margaret Dru	1993	Morin Nicole Monique
1977	Gagnon Rita	1984	Marszowsky Donna Jean		(14 yrs)
1977	Burns Paulette Elizabeth	1984	Proulx Dana Firewoman	1993	Warlop Pascale
1978	Bunn Gail Lois	1984	Saunders Maude Firewoman	1993	Roach Mary Beatrice
1978	Desbiens Francine	1984	Volk Lisa Patricia Mary		(13 yrs)
1979	Berry Colleen (13 yrs)		(11 yrs)	1993	Schoenfeld Merla Lorelle
1979	Serbyniuk Colleen Lynn	1984	McHale Susan Elizabeth		Elizabeth (P)
	(11 yrs)	1985	Van Dam Carla	1993	Simpson Terry Ann
1979	Fleming Jane	1985	Truscott Barbara Ann	1993	Benn Catharina Margaretha
1979	Ritchie Judy	1986	Chappaz Michele	1993	Harris Stephanie
1980	Foote Jessie Ann (10 yrs)	1986	Young Lorna	1993	Kramil Kelly
1980	Jones Karen Olive Evelyn	1986	Parrent Alison	1993	Sparkes Rond
	(12 yrs)	1986	Blagen Lori Jean	1994	Duncan Lynn Constable
1980	Byrne Mildred	1986	Patterson Bonnie Kathleen	1994	Ashford Kimberley
1980	Hughes Dorothy	1986	Gibbons Wendy Lee		Anne Constable
1980	Doskas Darlene	1986	Lawson Pamela Ann	1994	Benn Tammy (14 yrs)
1981	Bailey Jean	1986	Brierly Julie	1994	Benn Tara (14 yrs)
1981	Davenport Darla	1986	McLean Charmaine (11 yrs)	1994	Bings Annel
1981	MacDonald Lise	1987	Hargrove Sandra Lee	1994	Berberi Anne
1981	Schwab Kerry	1987	Buhagiar Despina	1994	Matthews Amy Jeannine
1981	Elliott Louise Nurse	1988	Golley Yvonne G		(15 yrs)
1981	May Geneva	1988	Howard Susan Melodie-Joy	1994	Wilkes Jennifer Anne
1981	Stillwell Dorothy	1988	Reimer Rose-Marie		(12 yrs)
1982	Poullett Jacqueline	1988	Viscusi Sherley Belle Nurse	1995	Klingbeil Kerry-Jo Savannah
1982	Halkett Doris		(P)	1995	Newell Patricia Carman

ROYAL CANADIAN MOUNTED POLICE
Ontario Medal for Police Bravery

22–05–90 Chaddock Suzanne E   Provincial Constable   05–93 Bray Monique Kathleen   Civilian

COMMANDING OFFICER'S COMMENDATION

20–07–78 Williams Mrs Pauline
17–12–80 Norry Mildred Ann   Constable
06–03–81 Lensh Brenda   Spec Constable
16–08–88 Delaney-Smith PM   Constable
24–02–88 McNally Carol Ann   Nurse
24–02–88 Clinton Barbara   Nurse
02–01–89 Goodwin Shelley Lee   Constable

03–06–90 Harris Bridgit Ann   Constable
05–01–92 Heikkila Christine E   Constable
25–02–93 Slobidian J Constable
15–12–94 Ashford Kimberley
           Anne   Constable
26–03–95 Rorison DM   Constable
10–05–95 Ross Tracy Lee   Constable

OTHER CIVIL AWARDS

CARNEGIE MEDAL

1909	Rattenbury Bertha
1913	Lewis Doris E (14 yrs)
1915	Armstrong Ethyle J
1915	Murray Florence (12 yrs)
1918	McKinnon Mary A
1919	Ford Ada W
1919	Slack Myra G
1920	Tilston Phyllis A (13 yrs)
1923	Payne Iris VM (15 yrs)
1926	Perry Phyllis K (15 yrs)
1927	Brown Dorothy F (14 yrs)
1928	Brown Mary Evelyn (14 yrs)
1930	Clarke Jane Schubert (11 yrs)
1934	Boulanger Mary A
1934	Ullock Frances H (14 yrs)
1935	Gilmore Marion Lorrain (14 yrs)
1937	Luton Rena M (16 yrs)
1938	Blackadar Kathleen D
1946	McCabe Olwen K
1947	Joyce Alma Romalds (62 yrs)

1949	McSween Mary Pearl
1953	Holman Ethel L
1954	McKenzie Marjorie I (13 yrs)
1959	Horne Norma Belle (15 yrs)
1962	Brennan Kathleen M
1962	Harvey Norene Anne
1962	La Pierre Catherine
1962	McEvoy Elsie H
1965	McCormick Anna A (64 yrs)
1965	Strudwick Carol Anne (14 yrs)
1965	Vidler Mary Lou
1966	Dokken Julie C
1966	Fagan Brenda Beth (16 yrs)
1967	Llewellyn Donna Marie
1972	Moddejonge Geraldine (14 yrs)
1975	Stewart Pamela Anne
1976	Swedberg Jean C
1977	Flynn Gail

1979	MacLean Deborah Jean
1979	McInnis Deborah Ann
1984	Milanovic Kristine Ruth
1985	Palmer Deborah Ann
1985	MacInnis Edith Marie (13 yrs)
1986	Duncan Gloria
1986	Lifely Lilia
1986	Newell Margaret E
1987	Gibbons Wendy L
1989	Buhagiar Despina
1989	Gagnon Gisele
1989	Viscusi Sherley Belle
1990	Beaton Irene J (67 yrs)
1990	Nolan Grace Marilyn
1992	Browning Janice E
1992	Hardy Janice Eileen
1992	Smith Leanne
1993	Beaucher Suzanne-Marie
1993	Posey Brenda
1993	Stewart Heather Ann
1995	Bray Monique Kathleen

ROYAL CANADIAN HUMANE SOCIETY

11–07–59 Bouey Edith (11 yrs) (Gold Medal) (P)
06–08– 9 Turnbull Mrs George (P)

03–85 Sommerville Mary
        Beth   (Bronze Medal)
04–85 Elkins Brenda

ROYAL LIFE SAVING SOCIETY
1964   Dann Lynda R   (Montbatten Medal)

FLORENCE NIGHTINGALE MEDAL

1927	Macdonald Margaret Clotilde
1929	Hartley Anne
1931	Tremaine Vivien Adlard
1935	Gunn Jean Isabel
1939	Browne Jean Elisabeth
1949	Russel Edith Kathleen
1953	Emory Florence HM
1957	McArthur Helen G
1963	Wilson Mona Gordon

1967	Girard Alice M
1971	Pepper Evelyn Agnes
1973	MacAulay MJ
1975	Ouellet Jeannette
1977	Percy Dorothy M
1979	Rossiter Edna Elizabeth
1979	Aitken M George
1981	Mussallem Dr Helen Kathleen
1981	Thorpe Ethel LM

1983	Lowe Elizabeth
1985	Wilson Mary Emily
1987	Lehman Jane Bryant
1987	Grenier Cecile Emelia
1987	Robinson Barbara Ann
1991	Carrier Marie Anna Elisabeth
1995	Roberts Vera

JEANNE-MANCE AWARD

1971	McArthur Dr Helen	1979	Labelle Dr Huguette	1986	Kergin Dr Dorothy
1974	Creelman Dr Lyle	1980	Mussallem Dr Helen	1988	Rovers Dr Maria (P)
1974	Girard Dr Alice		Kathleen	1990	Stinson Dr Shirley
1974	MacLennan EA Electa	1982	Splane Dr Verna H	1992	Glass Dr Helen
1977	Chittick Dr Rae	1984	Emory Dr Florence	1994	Miner Louise
1979	Allen Moyra	1984	Lefebvre Sister Denise	1996	Neylan Margaret

New Zealand

UK AWARDS

THE MOST EXCELLENT ORDER OF THE BRITISH EMPIRE
Members (MBE) – Gallantry

    42   Farlane Merle   Sister NZANS

GEORGE MEDAL (GM)

20–12–91 Dickson Eva Helen (72 yrs)

MILITARY MEDAL (MM)

18–07–17 James Laura Elizabeth Sister QAIMNS

QUEEN'S COMMENDATION FOR BRAVE CONDUCT

11–04–79	Donelly Jean Susan	20–12–91	Vogel Lee Frances
27–08–87	Burrell Katherine	20–12–91	Holden Chiquita Danielle (9 yrs)
	Agnes Prison Nurse	74	Horn Julienne

OTHER CIVIL AWARDS

ROYAL (NEW ZEALAND) HUMANE SOCIETY

1916	Doughty Kate			1969	Armstrong Lois Joy (Silver Medal)
	Phillips	(Silver Medal)		1993	Winslade Evelyn (Silver Medal)
1923	Aburn Daphne May	(Silver Medal)		1906	Donaldson Jean (Gold Medal)
1954	Ewing Jessie	(Silver Medal)		1930	Munro Chloris (Gold Medal)
1965	Ford Judith Ann	(Silver Medal)			Short Charlotte (Bronze Medal)

ROYAL LIFE SAVING SOCIETY (NZ)

08–01–88	Clayton Penny	Montbatten Medal	1991	Lewis Louise	Kingsland Memorial Medal
1989	Clayton Penny	Kingsland Memorial Medal			

GIRL GUIDES ASSOCIATION (NZ)
Star of Merit

1992	Hard Betty	1996	Hodder Sarah
1994	Payne Lynne		

FLORENCE NIGHTINGALE MEDAL

1920	MacLean Hester	1961	Ramsay Doris Ogilvy	1987	Rodger-Cecchi Glenys L
1947	Campbell Irene Flora	1961	Rudd Edith Mary	1991	McMahon Jennifer
1949	Cooke Helen	1963	Gidall Mary Ann	1993	Parker Phillipa
1951	House Edna Jean	1965	Jackson Muriel	1993	Smith Wendy Dymphna
1953	Coleman Isla Noeline	1969	McTamney Moyra Clare	1995	Owen Judith Christine
1957	Wells Catherine Lynette	1975	Simpson Ngaire	1997	Thayer Sheryl (P)
1959	Cameron Flora Jean	1981	Crisp Megan		

South Africa

SOUTH AFRICAN AWARDS

WOLTEMADE DECORATION FOR BRAVERY
1982   Gibson-Taylor Wendy Lorraine

SOUTH AFRICAN POLICE MEDAL
1981   Dressel Cornelia (15 yrs)

PRO MERITO MEDAL

1968	Steenkamp HMH	Sgt SAMNS		1968	Kent E	Sgt SAMNS

SOUTHERN CROSS MEDAL

1965	Maree MM	Col SAMNS	1978	de Bruin GE	Col SAMS
1966	Roode EM	Capt SAMNS	1978	Scheepers B	Cmdt SAMS
1966	Smit LM	Capt SAMNS	1982	Collins HM	Col SAMS
1972	Erasmus AE	Col SAMS	1982	von Maltitz J	Cmdt SAMS
1976	Jager ME	Col SAMS	1985	Jooste EC	Cmdt SAMS
1976	Lowden BG	Maj SAMS	1987	Wanliss MA	Maj SAMS
1976	Steyn A	Capt SAMS	1988	Swanepoel MES	Col SAMS
1977	Vivier DE	Maj SAMS	1988	Burger EMC	Col SAMS
1978	Dique SC	Col SAMS	1992	Rose L	Col SAMS

ROYAL HUMANE SOCIETY (SA)
01–01–45 Leith Mollie   SWANS (Bronze Medal)

SURF LIFE SAVING ASSOCIATION OF SOUTH AFRICA
Gibson-Taylor Wendy Lorraine   Silver Medal & Citation for Heroism

ROTARY MEDAL

1998	Betts Lorraine		1998	Greig Lynn
1998	Massyn Geraldine			

OTHER CIVIL AWARDS

FLORENCE NIGHTINGALE MEDAL

1920	Creagh ER	1955	McLarity J
1947	Harper MM	1961	Nothard CA
1947	Stoney ME	1963	Marwick II
1947	Waugh EJ	1965	Freeman VM
1947	Frewen EJ	1969	Simpson AN
1947	Vandecar RM	1969	Searle C
1949	Pheiffer ME	1971	Radloff DH
1951	Borcherds MG	1977	Venter ME

United States of America

GALLANTRY AWARDS TO WOMEN

CONGRESSIONAL MEDAL OF HONOR
1862   Walker Mary   Dr Army Surgeon

DISTINGUISHED SERVICE CROSS

First World War

McClelland Helen Grace	ANC (R)	Jeffrey Jane	Nurse ARC
MacDonald Beatrice	ANC	Higbee Lena Sutcliffe	NNC
Stambaugh Isabel	ANC (R)	3 unnamed	NNC (P)

Second World War

Guyot Jeannette	Lt OSS	Hall Virginia	OSS

DISTINGUISHED FLYING CROSS

Second World War

02–08–32 Putnam Amelia Earhart	Civilian Pilot	Lutz Adela E	ANC (P)
		Dial Kathleen R	1st Lt ANC

SILVER STAR
Second World War

Roe Elaine Arletta	Lt ANC	Leones Magdalena	Special Agent, US Army
Rourke Rita Virginia	Lt ANC	Granger Raymonde	OSS
Roberts Mary L	Lt ANC	Wake Nancy	Ensign OSS/SOE
Ainsworth Ellen	Lt ANC (P)	Truax Marjorie S	2nd Lt WAC
Clopet Evelyn	OSS (P)	Mast Karen R	Maj USAAF

SOLDIER'S MEDAL

Second World War

Maloney Margaret H	Private WAC	4 unnamed	WAC
Ford Mary Jane	Private WAC	Dahl Christine Catherine	2nd Lt ANC
Lynne Mary T	Cpl WAC	Decker Margaret	2nd Lt ANC
Bragdon Helen C	Cpl WAC	Greenwood Edith	2nd Lt ANC
Withner Vivian C	Tech WAC	Stephenson Orah D	1st Lt ANC
Lavrich Marie	Private WAC		

Post-war

Carr Mary J	Maj ANC	Tierney Marion	Col ANC
Lindsay Diane M	1st Lt ANC		

NAVY AND MARINE CORPS MEDAL
Post-war

Barnwell Barbara O	Staff Sgt Marine Corps	Young Sheryl L	L Cpl Marine Corps
Kearns Dorothy L	Gunnery Sgt Marine Corps	Burnett Deborah A	Ensign USNR
Brame Vanda K	1st Lt Marine Corps	Brown Jessica L	AO3 USN
		McBeth Deborah A	SA USN

MARINE CORPS MEDAL (WITH V FOR COMBAT)

Leaverton Shirley E	Capt Marine Corps	Reinholz Ruth F	Lt Col Marine Corps
Holleran Ruth J	Lt Col Marine Corps		

DISTINGUISHED SERVICE MEDAL

First World War

Delano Jane A	ARC (P)	Cleveland Maud	ARC
Andress Mary Vail	ARC	James Mrs Cushman	YMCA

Booth Evangeline	Cdr Salvation Army	Leonard Grace E	Chf Nurse 1st Lt ANC
Patterson Hannah H	Council of National Defence	Milliken Sayres L	Asst Supt Capt ANC
		Molloy Jane G	Chf Nurse 1st Lt ANC
Shaw Anna Howard	Council of National Defence	Mury Edith A	Asst Supt ANC
		Poston Adele S	Chf Nurse ANC
Lilliam Aubert	Chief Nurse ANC (P)	Rhodes Marie B	Nurse
Banker Grace D	Chf Tel Op Army Signals Corps	Rulon Blanche S	Asst Supt Capt ANC
		Ryan Lilliam J	Chf Nurse 1st Lt ANC
Brennan Cecilia A	Chf Nurse ANC	Sheehan Mary E	Chf Nurse 1st Lt ANC
Brown Katherine	Chf Nurse ANC	Shelton Nena	Chf Nurse 1st Lt ANC
Burns Sophy Mary	Chf Nurse 1st Lt ANC	Sinnott Catherine G	Nurse 2nd Lt ANC
Cameron Reba G	Chf Nurse 1st Lt ANC	Stimson Julia C	Chf Nurse Maj ARCNS
Coughlin Edna M	Nurse ANC		
Flash Alice H	Chf Nurse ANC	Sweet Ethel E	Chf Nurse ANC
Goodrich Annie W	Contract Nurse	Thompson Dora	Supt ANC
Howard Carrie L	Chf Nurse 1st Lt ANC	Vandervort Lynette L	Chf Nurse ANC

Second World War

Blanchfield Florence E	Supt Col ANC	Goman	Col ANC

BRONZE STAR MEDAL
Second World War

Arcelin Madeleine	OSS	Combites Inez E	2nd Lt ANC
Gentis Mary Antonia	OSS	Cook Cordelia E	1st Lt ANC
Grant Helen Gordon	Nurse UK	Craig Rose C	1st Lt ANC
Gulovich Maria	OSS	Dennis Thelma	1st Lt ANC
Lauwers Barbara J	WAC/OSS	Dickson Grova Nelle	2nd Lt ANC
Ledi Arsene	(CAF)/OSS	Dupont Isabelle	2nd Lt ANC
Legendre Gertrude	Civ/WAC/OSS	Huffman Isabelle	2nd Lt ANC
Letellier Jeanne	Capt WAC	Loe Maude/Lonnette	2nd Lt ANC
Marteliere Paulette	OSS	Miernicke Frances A	2nd Lt ANC
Matthew Jean	Staff Sgt WAC	Anna Smith M	2nd Lt ANC
Reybaud Anne Marie	OSS	Spillman Anna H	2nd Lt ANC
Thinesse Annie	OSS	Wood Sue Elva	2nd Lt ANC
Baltzer Katherine C	2nd Lt ANC	Zadylak Anne Stella	1st Lt ANC

COMMENDATIONS FOR HEROISM

Brajkovich Catherine A	WAC	Mutter Carol A	Lt Col WAVES
Ayriss Irene A	Coast Guard	Streeter Ruth C	Col WAVES
Wohl Ruth	Coast Guard	Davis Josephine G	Gunnery Sgt Joint Service

COASTGUARD ACHIEVEMENT MEDAL

1980	Cain Colleen A	Lt USCGR

CITATION FOR VALOR

1945	Philips Clare	Civilian

MEDAL OF FREEDOM

1947	Finch Florence Ebersole	WAVES	
	Arcelin Madeleine	OSS	
		Marteliere Pauline	OSS
		Dietrich Marlene	Civ

ARMED FORCES EXPEDITIONARY MEDAL

Gebers Josephine S   (with Combat Action Ribbon) Staff Sgt WAVES

US BRITISH AWARDS

MILITARY MEDAL (MM)
First World War

MacDonald Beatrice M   ANC   Parmalees Eva Jean   ANC

THE MOST EXCELLENT ORDER OF THE BRITISH EMPIRE – GALLANTRY AWARDS
Members (MBE)
Second World War

Hall Virgina   OSS/SOE

CIVIL AWARDS

RED CROSS
1918   Delano Jane A   (Gold Medal for Conspicuous Valor) ARCNS

LIFESAVING MEDAL
1869   Lewis Idawalley Zorada   (Gold Medal)

LLOYD'S MEDAL FOR MERITORIOUS SERVICE
1887   Mrs Reed w/o capt of *TF Oakes*   1984   Fisher Anna Lee   US Astronaut

FLORENCE NIGHTINGALE MEDAL

1920	Hay Helene Scott	1937	Butler Ida F	1959	Leone Lucile Petry
1920	Johnson Florence Merriam	1939	Mathews Stella	1959	Sleeper Ruth
1920	Russel Martha M	1947	Danielson Ida W Lt Col	1961	McIver Pearl
1920	Meirs Linda K	1947	Lippman Mrs Walter	1961	Hauge Cecilia H
1920	Foerster Alma E	1949	Dines Alta Elizabeth	1963	Magnussen Ann K
1920	Gladwin Mary E	1949	Roberts Mary M	1963	Dorsey Nan L
1923	Noyes Clara D	1951	Blanchfield Florence A	1963	McManus Louise R
1925	Minnigerode Lucy	1951	Nelson Sophie C	1969	Reiter Dean Frances
1927	Fitzgerald Alice	1953	Petersen Annabelle	1981	Freeman Ruth Dr
1929	Stimson Julia C	1955	Bradley Ruby G	1983	Sundberg Alice M
1929	Hall Carrie M	1955	Stewart Isabel Maitland	1985	Angleton Dolores L
1931	Fox Elizabeth Gordon	1957	Porter Elizabeth Kerr	1987	Wilson Ruthelle Duke
1933	Heilman Charlotte Miller	1957	Sheahan Marion W	1993	Adkins Claudia Dr
1935	Vaughan Elsbeth Hosig	1959	Taylor Effie J		

CARNEGIE HEROINE MEDAL

1914	Briggs Phebe	1916	Holliman Flonnie S	1918	Starkey Shirley L
1914	Coburn Lillian M	1916	Prince Eva E	1919	Clarke Lily B (13 yrs)
1914	Guy Margaret F	1916	Suhr Karoline K (14 yrs)	1919	Dekker Kate
1914	Haven Lola E (12 yrs)	1917	Danson Ethel J	1919	Goff Dorothy E (16 yrs)
1914	Hunt Anna L	1917	Dickey Eunice A	1919	Graeber Gladys G
1914	Parker Beryl	1917	Hunter Leonore U	1919	Holstein Frances B
1914	Spanke Frances (14 yrs)	1917	Jenkins Nellie M (14 yrs)	1919	Kisner Margaret
1914	Thomas Sophia E	1917	Ludlum Alberta I	1919	Riter Hazel R
1914	Vanlandingham Ruth	1917	Nelson Helen V (12 yrs)	1919	Sears Mary E (14 yrs)
1915	Bell Grace L	1917	Sexton Edna M (12 yrs)	1919	Smith Mary E (15 yrs)
1915	Branham Lucy G	1917	Shaw Lillian E	1919	Wascoe Elizabeth M
1915	Brunelle Viola M (11 yrs)	1917	Wolfe Chloe A	1920	Brown Marjorie A (14 yrs)
1915	Crummel Hazel D	1918	Brittingham Susan T	1920	Clark Hilda M
1915	McNeely Ruth E	1918	Brown Augusta B	1920	Clougherty V E (15 yrs)
1915	Reed Irene H	1918	Bush Gertrude (16 yrs)	1920	Draheim Cora L (14 yrs)
1915	Ruslander Flora E	1918	Combe Carrie M	1920	Goldsmith Mariana T
1915	Sornberger Irene L	1918	Hughes Mary V		(12 yrs)
1915	Vannah Bessie A (16 yrs)	1918	Morrow Marcella	1920	Heidcamp Mary
1916	Cooper Olive MJ	1918	Nahm Frieda FG	1920	Leach Sarah A
1916	Crouch Bess D (14 yrs)	1918	Riordon Catherine E	1920	Lundeberg Karin S
1916	Crouch Lucille		(12 yrs)	1920	MacKenzie Edith M

1920	Merrill Gertrude M
1920	Smiley Louise B (13 yrs)
1921	Ball Elizabeth M
1921	Beatty Frederika
1921	Bukosy Ella E
1921	Crocker Nannie B
1921	Darrow Laura J (16 yrs)
1921	Dodge Helen F (11 yrs)
1921	Doubleday Eva C
1921	Hague Miriam
1921	Miller Inza M
1921	Reck Marion E (13 yrs)
1921	Young Mary M
1922	Bassett Caroline S (13 yrs)
1922	England Isabelle (14 yrs)
1922	McCullough Donna A (16 yrs)
1922	Smith Josephine C M
1922	Standifer Agnes D (13 yrs)
1923	Buhner Mary A
1923	Ernsberger Kathrine E (10 yrs)
1923	Grimsley Nancy J
1923	Hertlein Hilda E (12 yrs)
1923	Jarrell Lill S
1924	Brennecke Margaret
1924	Bryson Viola I
1924	Crowell Mae T
1924	Geist Helen G
1924	Matthews Jewell M
1924	Oswald Margaret L (12 yrs)
1924	Richardson Kathryn E
1924	Wagener Dorothy D (13 yrs)
1924	Yocom Lora A
1925	Beard Esther R
1925	Dorr Helen M (14 yrs)
1925	Good Edna M (15 yrs)
1925	Justice Ruth L
1925	Lovelace Imogene C (9 yrs)
1925	Mason Helen E
1925	Strickler Josephine E (13 yrs)
1925	Wise Elizabeth S (15 yrs)
1926	Dickey Helen G
1926	Geary Alice R
1926	Nelson Mary B
1926	Wertz Evelyn M (16 yrs)
1927	Bellus Lena E
1927	Corgiat Louise A (15 yrs)
1927	Gallinger Verna M (13 yrs)
1927	Johnson Esther J
1927	Lindsay Ruby H (15 yrs)
1927	McConnell Alverna
1927	McMahon Janice B (12 yrs)
1927	Mizerak Susanna (11 yrs)
1927	Robison Helen C
1927	Sherwood Susan R (11 yrs)
1927	Taylor Betty C
1927	Thompson Mildred V (14 yrs)
1927	Webb Hazel I
1927	Woods Frances C

1928	Allen Beryl C (14 yrs)
1928	Baldwin Blanche I (15 yrs)
1928	Baskin Sadie E
1928	Brynhildsen Svanhild M
1928	Campbell Minnie I
1928	Citron Anna
1928	Corbitt Tawlie I
1928	Fahey Dorothy E
1928	Foley Marguerite C (15 yrs)
1928	Fridgen Catherine M (15 yrs)
1928	Ghear Elizabeth E (12 yrs)
1928	Herlihy Irene F (13 yrs)
1928	Hession Monica F
1928	Ingram Elva M
1928	Irwin Mabel F
1928	Levis Louise F
1928	Olger Mae L
1928	Raynard Maybel I
1928	Talman Helen C (11 yrs)
1929	Beinert Anna E
1929	Gorthy Frances J (16 yrs)
1929	Lankford Mary B (16 yrs)
1929	Martin Agnes I (12 yrs)
1929	Muller Barbara H
1929	Ross Ida M (15 yrs)
1929	Wooddard Edna F (16 yrs)
1930	Disbennett Myrtle
1930	Ferris Myrtle G
1930	Larocque Dora R (15 yrs)
1930	Moore Claribel
1930	Shetka Marian (14 yrs)
1930	Stange Eva J
1931	Brenneman Anetta L
1931	Cavenagh Jane T (14 yrs)
1931	Foster Klemye S
1931	Furlong Catherine W
1931	Hagood Helen
1931	Jenkins Ruth I
1931	Koske Winifred A
1931	Massey Thelma R
1931	McCartan Florence M
1931	Pappalardo Margaret F (13 yrs)
1931	Rogers Jeanette S (12 yrs)
1931	Smith Maxie L
1931	Wilson Maryland W (13 yrs)
1932	Akins Marian V
1932	Allen Glendora E (10 yrs)
1932	Blizzard Emma L
1932	Hoopes Katherine M
1932	Isbell Jane E (13 yrs)
1932	Kitelinger Nellie M (15 yrs)
1932	Rivers Grace E
1932	Sirmons Mary B (15 yrs)
1932	Weber Caroline J (16 yrs)
1932	Wells Grace L (14 yrs)
1932	Williams Margaret F (14 yrs)
1933	Fitch Marguerite A
1933	Huffaker Mary L
1933	Leftwich Evelyn C (15 yrs)

1933	Lyne Gladys M
1933	Ohl Bertha M
1933	Overstreet Evelyn E (10 yrs)
1933	Rollins Fanny L
1933	Scurlock Ethel S
1933	Trice Anna K
1933	Whitehead M Omega (14 yrs)
1934	August Lucy E (8 yrs)
1934	Bennett Matilda (15 yrs)
1934	Cantwell Nora E (15 yrs)
1934	Clark Josephine E
1934	Marinelli Lena (13 yrs)
1934	Papcke Evelyn M
1934	Robinson Marion W
1934	Stearns Grace M
1934	Van Tassell Agnes M (15 yrs)
1935	Brown Marion C
1935	Deel Suzanna A (12 yrs)
1935	Geaney Ellen
1935	Hart Wilma R
1935	Haugh Effie C
1935	Hayter Dessie
1935	Moyer Kathryn G (13 yrs)
1935	Murray Allie M H
1935	Nightingale Mildred E
1935	Patterson Nellie B
1935	Petrie Marian G
1935	Stewart Christine
1936	Barber Violet M
1936	Coldiron Dell (12 yrs)
1936	Prince Margaret L
1936	Reso Margaret M
1937	Baukat Lillie B
1937	Beebe Shirley (14 yrs)
1937	Davenport Velma K (14 yrs)
1937	Garvin Gwendoline I
1937	Hendrick Violet L
1937	Joyce Edna M
1938	Larson Dorothy L
1938	Snyder Margie J (15 yrs)
1938	Sullivan Helen R
1938	Williams Margie C (16 yrs)
1939	Gray Fern
1939	Krause Evelyn StJ
1939	Randolph Elinor I (15 yrs)
1939	Schuck Betty O (16 yrs)
1939	Scott Luella R
1939	Siniawski Sabina
1940	Austill Mary (9 yrs)
1940	Bailey Dorothy J (16 yrs)
1940	Cotta Marjorie E
1940	Fabbri Yolanda G
1940	Fitzgerald Kathryn T
1940	Jones Irene
1940	Mason Elizabeth R
1940	Shields Patricia L (9 yrs)
1940	Sivils Nadine V (16 yrs)
1941	Bacher Jean D
1941	Bedell Norma A (13 yrs)
1941	Cady June E (11 yrs)

1941	Cober Emily J (15 yrs)	1951	Tremblay Virginia	1959	Hayes Marie T
1941	Grill Martha E	1951	Warner Florence	1959	Hilton Mattie M
1941	Harrison Oleta	1951	Woods Mattie Y	1959	Hoffman Estelle
1941	Hecht Helen	1952	Davis Ruth	1959	Kopp Barbara A (14 yrs)
1941	Holloway Wilhelmina	1952	Fairbank Virginia M (16 yrs)	1959	O'Neill Shirley F
1942	Campbell Glenna L	1952	Frye Margaret E (15 yrs)	1959	Pettit Alida E (15 yrs)
1942	Feiring Elizabeth (14 yrs)	1952	Gore Eileen C	1959	Smith Margaret E (15 yrs)
1942	Funk Amelia K	1952	Kroeger Deanna J (13 yrs)	1959	Weaver Ethel S (70 yrs)
1942	Garrelts Hattie F	1952	Mason Jane M	1960	Boehnen Mary E
1942	Moakler Doris M (15 yrs)	1952	Mork Betty M (16 yrs)	1960	Bruno Matilda F
1942	Rush Margaret F (13 yrs)	1952	Mork C Marie (13 yrs)	1960	Friederich Teresa
1943	Hewitt Wilma L	1953	Fishburne Iva B	1960	Matthews Elizabeth M
1943	James Barbara A (10 yrs)	1953	Fisk Doris H	1960	McKinley Flora S (63 yrs)
1943	Johnson Lella D	1953	Johnson Mary H	1960	Sutton Blanche E
1943	Nash Frances K	1953	Kimberley Cora B	1960	Szabo Lois E
1943	Nesson Dorothy C (10 yrs)	1953	Monroe Carolyn G (15 yrs)	1960	Walton Marcia J (14 yrs)
1944	Benson Glorianne (15 yrs)	1953	Whisler Sarah E	1961	Hull Mary L (12 yrs)
1944	Desonia Patricia A (15 yrs)	1954	Benoit Eileen	1961	Hull Sharon L (13 yrs)
1944	Plummer Bertha C	1954	Haar Marilyn B	1961	Iverson Laurel A
1944	Vorwerk Kathleen L (12 yrs)	1954	La Marche Lynne L (14 yrs)	1961	Miller Donna A
1945	Francoeur Lillian C	1954	Ludvigsen Hildur A (15 yrs)	1961	Ridout Mozelle L (16 yrs)
1945	Gregg Ruth P	1954	Murillo Rosalie G (13 yrs)	1961	Wharton Shirley C
1945	Hays Emma W	1954	Parker Nellie J	1961	Wrobel Paula A (12 yrs)
1945	Kaiser Hazel M	1954	Pereira Theresa	1962	Hynes Constance F (16 yrs)
1945	Miller Doris J (16 yrs)	1954	Rodriguez Eleanor R	1962	Johnson Nanette L
1945	Nazzaro Ruth S	1954	Scribner Alice D	1962	MacLeod Helena M
1945	Shepard S Gertrude	1954	Zimmerman Darlene J	1962	Peterson Violet F
1945	Thomas Margaret G L	1954	Zimmerman Genevieve J	1962	Ramirez Isabel N
1945	Webster Dorothy D	1955	Coppock Catherine L	1962	Sullivan Viola
1946	Ball Rita J	1955	Culver Ruth C	1963	Clark Sheila A
1946	Bingham Grace L	1955	Flores Felicidad C	1963	Grytness Lasca J
1946	Dunn Mary A (11 yrs)	1955	Flores Isabel S	1963	Lucca Diana M
1946	Haydon Mary (63 yrs)	1955	Mason Mildred D	1963	Makowsky Rochelle S
1946	Stone Elizabeth C	1955	Parker Lady Helen	1963	Nulsen Linda J (16 yrs)
1946	Ulen Violet H	1955	Paulson Mona F	1963	Schmidt Lindo F (16 yrs)
1946	Vickers Margaret N	1955	Rivet Myrna D (15 yrs)	1963	Shaw Alberta
1946	Westall Sara O	1955	Weaver Helen L	1963	Snover Lyla M
1947	Burkett Barbara J (12 yrs)	1956	Bunn Eleanore B	1964	Aloisio Matilda
1947	Erickson Teresa P	1956	Chaffinch Eleanor M	1964	Banks Bessie E
1947	Hanson Ermel F		(15 yrs)	1964	Eymer Elizabeth L
1947	Hunter Katie B (13 yrs)	1956	Frischknecht Margaret	1964	Gibson Deborah M (15 yrs)
1947	MacLachlan Marion F		(12 yrs)	1964	McGhee Lynn M (10 yrs)
1947	Park Marilyn J	1956	Johnston Virginia	1964	Race Mary A
1947	Rice Margaret E (15 yrs)	1956	Kearney Beryl D (12 yrs)	1964	Railsback Marita M
1948	Schickling Wanda G	1956	Kochs Dorothy	1964	Romer Lene
1948	Skillin Thelma M	1956	Miller Geraldine L	1964	Seigars Dee A (16 yrs)
1949	Davidson Barbara V	1957	Anderson Rose M (16 yrs)	1964	Van Wagner Sandra F
1949	Hiller Merilyn C	1957	Burch Beatrice N	1964	Vozier Marsha S
1949	Krumpotick Jeanette PA	1957	Guthrie Carol A	1964	Wilbrecht Mary K
1949	Sippel Barbara A (10 yrs)	1957	McMurdo Hazel E	1964	Wylie Karen B
1949	Smalling Mary P	1957	Schieb Patricia J (12 yrs)	1965	Bailey Kathleen S
1949	Urban Anna R	1958	Hayden Marion L	1965	Cahill Bridget A
1950	Adams Ruth M	1958	Keil Irma C	1965	Dowdell Mary A (13 yrs)
1950	Boston Nancy M	1958	Koonce Judith E	1965	Gilpin Linda L
1950	Bradshaw Edena B	1958	Lindeman Nellie M (64 yrs)	1965	Kenczka Lois J
1950	Gutman Polly S	1958	Mahlmeister Katherine	1965	Luduc Theresa E
1950	McKee Rosemary	1958	Seabrook Elizabeth (15 yrs)	1965	Martin Katherine S
1950	Sickler June (15 yrs)	1958	Sindelar Ethel L (16 yrs)	1965	McGee Ella V
1950	Toepp Sally T	1959	Boero Sharon L (16 yrs)	1965	Neininger Evelyn M
1950	Yowell Mary C (66 yrs)	1959	Bryan Evelyn S	1965	Sipos Mary B
1951	Housley Mary F	1959	Colquitt Pearl W (65 yrs)	1965	Townsend Mary E
1951	Littlefield Thelma M	1959	Davis Jeanne F	1965	Van Riper Carol A

1965	Vartanian Rogene A	1973	Wallace Carolyn L	1987	Stone Sherry C
1966	Anderson Lois M	1974	Hafer Marion J	1987	Wilson Mary S
1966	Beasley Teresa E (15 yrs)	1974	Mannock Betty R	1988	Bell Donna M
1966	Bruch Barbara J	1975	Hirtz Elizabeth A	1988	Drury Christina (16 yrs)
1966	Burdette Barbara L (14 yrs)	1976	Gibson Cynthia M (14 yrs)	1988	Gries Connie S
1966	Carr Dolores J	1976	O'Dell Sarah L	1988	Pierdolla Sallie R
1966	Crawford Patricia G (13 yrs)	1977	Pittman Norma K	1988	Shatto Elizabeth S (16 yrs)
1966	Guthrie Joyce M	1978	Collins Anitra L	1989	Finkbeiner Katherine
1966	Korgan Florence A	1978	Leonard Margaret E	1989	Kekumo Lavina
1966	Michaud Barbara M (14 yrs)	1978	Reed Dolores B	1989	Magnant Kemrey
1966	Roshone Edna L (14 yrs)	1979	Betts Joanne (14 yrs)	1989	McMahon Mary MK
1966	Swoboda Harriet N	1979	Gregg Nancy A	1989	Porter Lynn LL
1966	Yokots Stefany A	1979	Kline Ethel H (60 yrs)	1989	Shelley Deborah J
1967	Bowden Marian E	1979	Miller Sharon L	1990	Boczek Denise
1967	Buckles Mary L (14 yrs)	1979	Reece Louise	1990	Caylor Karen A
1967	Buckles Tanja L (13 yrs)	1980	Apgar Teresa LM	1990	Duemler Christine VG
1967	Cannon Louise E	1980	Gosnell Mary E	1990	Killen Melody S
1967	Doane Rose E	1980	Mariscal Myrna F	1990	Lamb Betty B (69 yrs)
1967	Hardin Jacquelyn K (16 yrs)	1980	McGowan Janet H (14 yrs)	1990	Mauro June A
1967	Heath Linda M	1980	Motta Barbara E	1991	Hagan Sherry L
1967	Kalinowski Susanne M	1981	Schweitzer Anita C	1991	Hohl Karen
	(12 yrs)	1982	Fluno Donna E	1991	James Hazel (66 yrs)
1967	Mehelich Jean	1982	Gloston Deborah B	1991	Jonas Judith H
1967	Pedee Louise A (12 yrs)	1982	Maw Brenda S	1991	Schellsmidt Kristy M
1967	Power Billie J	1983	Fisher Mary H	1992	Davis Mildred F
1967	Rivers Mary M	1983	Gilginas Janice A	1992	Fenner Stephanie K
1967	Rodriguez Gloria (12 yrs)	1983	Hartsock Carolyn B (14 yrs)	1992	Iben Cheryl A
1967	Sorrells Connie M (16 yrs)	1983	Shulder Helen B	1992	Jordan Adriene L
1967	Vallero Louise P	1983	Wilson Bonita O	1992	Moreno Guadalupe
1968	Martuscelli Anna M (68 yrs)	1984	Atteberry Jill A (13 yrs)	1992	Munson Janice
1968	Mayberry Sylvia J	1984	De Kett Janet LF (12 yrs)	1992	O'Donnell Shirley
1968	Mulcahy Virginia	1984	Machel Tina M (14 yrs)	1992	Riley Ellen A
1968	Roberts June E	1984	Payne Alverna A	1993	Baker Mary B
1969	Donaca Virginia L	1984	Whittington Dorothy B	1993	Barnes Terreatha L (11 yrs)
1969	Feltz Karen F		(63 yrs)	1993	Beyer Jennifer C
1969	Lockhart Annie M (64 yrs)	1985	Finn Raimie (12 yrs)	1993	Brewer Sue L
1969	Patterson Grace L (64 yrs)	1985	McBride Geraldine T	1993	Griffith Lisa M
1969	Speel Judith E		(67 yrs)	1993	Schlachter Karyn B
1970	Adamchick Donna J	1985	Norman Shirley A	1993	Schork Valerie J
1970	Anderson Nancy	1986	Boring Kristine E (11 yrs)	1994	Brooks Deberah C
1970	Barnes Mayme L	1986	Brayboy Mary E	1994	Farmer Latonya S
1970	Corrigan Kathleen A	1986	Flores Bertha	1994	Guerra Janean R (11 yrs)
1970	Sharp Reta R (12 yrs)	1986	Harrison Leatrice (10 yrs)	1994	Jacquette Elvira (69 yrs)
1970	Thompson Martha L	1986	Isbell Maura J	1994	Pilkerton Kathleen M
1970	Waroe Deborah L (13 yrs)	1986	Markor Patricia M	1994	Robbins Rhonda S
1971	Cromartie Hazel M	1986	Moore Lucille (75 yrs)	1994	Schuttler Kimberly J
1971	Hittelman Marilyn M	1986	Quick Pamela S	1994	Terry Denise
1971	Thibodeau Anita M	1986	Shively Rita S	1994	Valdez Lucy J
1971	Ward Marianne I	1987	Babcock Lucille (65 yrs)	1994	Walenski Fawn
1972	Barker Linda D (13 yrs)	1987	Bellamy Joy	1995	Chemsak-Mackie Laurie
1972	Bayerle Shirley E	1987	Brooks Kelli L (13 yrs)	1996	Driggers Rejuvia L
1972	Campredon Wava T (70 yrs)	1987	Coleman Marianne R	1996	Freeman Raemonda O
1972	Fontes Cynthia	1987	Crowley Mary (14 yrs)	1996	Johnson Vivian
1972	Klein Jo-Ann L	1987	Griffith Rose M	1996	Salbeck Shelly
1972	Plumlee Elinor L	1987	Kirk Kim L	1996	Schaeffer Patricia
1972	Schichko Lisa V	1987	Mazzetti Gail	1996	Shrake Lora K
1973	Clinton Naomi T	1987	Morrison Ann M	1996	Whitehead Linda M
1973	Edwards Karen K (13 yrs)	1987	Rossiter Teresa		
1973	Stewart Diana J	1987	Ruhling Constance H		

Bibliography

Abbink, H & C. *The Military Medal and its Canadian Recipients 1916–22*, Alison Pub Co., 1987

Abbott, PE & Tamplin JMA. *British Gallantry Awards*, Nimrod Dix & Co., 1981

Alexander, Barron & Bateman. *South African Orders, Decorations and Medals*, Human and Rousseau, Capetown, 1986

Anderson, B. *We Just Got On With It*, Picton Pub Ltd, 1994

Anderson, K. *Heroes of South Africa*, Purnell and Sons (SA) Pty Ltd

Angus. *Medals and Decorations*, New York, 1975

Ashton, M. *Canadian Medal Rolls – DFM 1939–45*, Lorimer D., Charlton Press, Toronto

Ashton, M. *Canadian Medal Rolls – Distinguished Conduct and Military Medal 1939–45, 50–53*, Lorimer D, Charlton Press, Toronto, 1960

Aynes, E. *From Nightingale to Eagle*, Prentice Hall Inc, New Jersey, 1973

Bannister, C. *7,000 Brave Australians, History of the Royal Humane Society of Australasia 1874–1994*, RHS Australasia, 1996

Bate, CK and Smith, HG. *For Bravery in the Field. Recipients of the Military Medal, Army 1919–91*, Bayonet Pub, 1991

Beauman, KB. *Partners in Blue*, Hutchinson, 1971

Bellafaire, J. *The Women's Army Corps, Commemoration of WWII Service*, US Army Centre of Military History, 1995

Bellafaire, J. *The Army Nurse Corps, Commemoration of WWII Service*, US Army Centre of Military History, 1995

Berry, L (ed.). *Canadian Almanac and Directory 1993*, Canadian Almanac & Directory Pub. Co., Toronto, 1993

Bidwell, S. *Women's Royal Army Corps*, Leo Cooper, 1997

Birdwell, R. *Women in Battledress* Fine Editions Press, New York

Bisset, I. *The George Cross*, 1961

Blackstone, GV. *A History of the British Fire Service*, Routledge Keegan & Paul, 1957

Blatherwick, FJ. *Canadian Orders Decorations and Medals*, Unitrade Press, Toronto, 1985

Blatherwick, J. *Royal Canadian Air Force Honours Decorations and Medals 1920–68*, FJB Pub, 1991

Blatherwick, FJ. *A Thousand Brave Canadians 1954–89*, Unitrade Press, Toronto, 1991

Bleicher, H. *Colonel Henri's Story* (ed. Borchers & Colvin), Kimber, 1954

Boddington, J. *Canadian Lifesaving Medals and Other Awards*, Military Collectors Club of Canada, 1982

Bousquet, B & Douglas, C. *West Indian Women at War*, Lawrence & Wishart, 1991

Bowden, J. *Grey Touched with Scarlet*, Hale, 1957

Braddon, R. *Nancy Wake*, Cassell & Co. Ltd, 1956

Brant, JG & Collins, DF. *First Ten Years, Queen's Gallantry Medal*, Medals Year Book, Whittacker, 1984

Brant, JG. *Queen's Birthday Honours List 1988*, BAC Books, 1988

Brant, JG. *New Year's Honours List 1989*, BAC Books, 1989

Brant, JG. *Honours List, Northern Ireland 1969–88*, BAC Books, 1989

Brant, JG. *Honours & Awards Who's Who 1974–87*, Whittacker, 1988

Brass, R & Thomas, W (gen gds). *Register of Canadian Honours*, Canadian Almanac & Directory, 1991

Brome, V. *The Way Back*, Cassell & Co. Ltd, 1957

Brown, G & Pannall, R. *The Conspicuous Gallantry Medal*, Pacific Pub. Co., Vancouver, 1977

Brown, GA. *Lloyd's War Medals for Bravery at Sea*, W Canada Distributors, 1992

Bryers, F. *The WAAF Book; A Scrapbook of Wartime Memories*, Christchurch, New Zealand, 1982

Buckland, C (ed.). *Medals Year Book*, Leo Cooper, 1996

Burne, J (ed.). *Chronicle of the World*, Longmans, 1989

Campbell, C. *World War II Fact Book 1939–45*, Macdonald, 1985

Calder, A. *The People's War*, J. Cape, 1969

Cambray & Briggs. *Red Cross & St John's War History 1939–47*, SJAB, 1949

Campion, M. *Jupiter's Children*, Liverpool University Press, 1998
Campion, P. *The Honourable Women of the Great War and the Women's Who's Who*, printed Math and
    Sons, Bournemouth, 1919
Carrol, FG (ed.). *Register of the George Cross*, This England Books, 1985
Caroll, JM. *Medal of Honor, History and Recipients*, Amereon Ltd, 1976
Caroll, JM. *Congressional Medal of Honor Library, Names, Deeds, Korea*, Dell Pub. Co. (US), 1987
Caroll, JM. *Congressional Medal of Honor 1939–46, Names, Deeds, WWII*, Dell Pub. Co. (US), 1987
Cheeseman, EC. *Brief Glory (ATA)*, Harborough Pub. Co. Ltd, 1966
Churchill WS. *Second World War*, Cassell and Co. Ltd, 1954 (9 vols)
Clarke, JD. *Gallantry Medals and Awards of the World*, P Stephens Ltd, 1993
Clayton, A. *The Enemy is Listening*, Hutchinson, 1980
Clayton, GJ. *The New Zealand Army History 1840–1990s*, New Zealand Army, 1990
Clifford, ML & JC. *Women Who Kept the Lights; History of Female Lighthouse Keepers*, Cypress
    Communications, Williamsburg, 1993
Collett-Wadge, D. *Women In Uniform*, Sampson Low, 1946
Collier, R. *The City that Would Not Die*, W Collins Sons & Co. Ltd, 1959
Condon, JPB. *The Military Medal Awarded to Women*
Congdon, P. *Behind Hangar Doors*, Sonik Books, 1985
Cookridge, EH. *They Came From the Sky*, Heinemann, 1965
Coulthard-Clark. *Diggers, Makers of Australian Military Tradition*, Melbourne University Press, 1993
Cowper, JM. *The Auxiliary Territorial Service*, War Office, 1949
Cowper, JM. *A Short History of Queen Mary's Army Auxiliary Corps*, WRAC Assoc., 1967
Cox, MD. *British Women at War*, John Murray & The Pilot Press, 1941
Crawford, J. *North from Taranto, New Zealand & the Liberation of Italy 1943–5*, New Zealand Defence
    Force, 1994
Crawford, J. *Atlantic Kiwis, New Zealand & the Battle of the Atlantic*, New Zealand Defence Force, 1993
Crofton, E. *The Women of Royaumont* , Tuckwell Press, 1997
Cruickshank, C. *The Official History of SOE in the Far East*, OUP, 1983
Curnock, G. *Hospitals Under Fire*, Allen & Unwin, 1941
Davies, MD. *Twin Trails, Story of Flynn & Southey Families*, KB Davies, Salisbury, S Africa, 1974
Davies, TJ. *South African Roll of Honour 1914–18*, Roberts Medals, 1991
Davis, KS. *The American Experience of War*, Secker & Warburg, 1947
Demarne, C. *Our Girls, Story of the Nation's Wartime Firewomen*, Pentland Press, 1995
Dickson, HP. *Badge of Britannia*, Pentland Press, 1990
Diver, R (ed.). *Shoulder Sleeve Insignia etc, of US Armed Forces*, Rex Military & Co., New York, 1941
Dobell, D. *Kaitaia and Its People*, Whangarei, New Zealand, 1982
Dorling, HT & Guille, LF. *Ribbons and Medals*, G Philip & Sons, 1963
Dowe, SF. *The Canadian Military Register of Foreign Awards*, FS Dowe Pub., Ottawa, 1979
Drummond, C. *The Remarkable Life of Victoria Drummond, Marine Engineer*, Institute of Marine
    Engineers, 1994
Ebbert, J & Hall, B. *Crossed Currents, Navy Women from WWI to Tailhook*, Brasseys (US), 1993
Edmond, L. *Women in Wartime*, New Zealand, 1986
Eisler, R. *Chalice and the Blade*, Harper & Row, New York, 1988
Escott, BE. *Women in Air Force Blue*, P Stephens, 1989
Escott, BE. *Mission Improbable*, P Stephens, 1991
Escott, BE. *Our Wartime Days*, A Sutton, 1995
Ewing, E. *Women in Uniform*, Batsford, 1975
Farmery, PJ. *Police Gallantry 1909–1978*, Periter & Assoc., 1995
Fevyer, WH. *George Medal*, Spink, 1980
Fitzgerald, HM. *History of the United States Navy Nurse Corps 1934–Present*, ASA, 1968
Fitzgibbon, C. *The Blitz*, Wingate, 1966
Foot, MRD. *SOE in France*, HMSO, 1966
Foot, MRD *Six Faces of Courage*, Eyre Methuen, 1978
Foot, MRD. *SOE 1940–46*, BBC, 1984
Forward, N. *The White Mouse*, Australian Large Print Ltd, Melbourne, 1987
Foster, J. *An UnAmerican Lady*, Sidgwick & Jackson, 1980
Forsyth, DR. *Medals for Gallantry & Distinguished Conduct Awarded to Natal, Cape Colony and Union
    Defence Force Units*, Private, 1991
Forsyth, DR. *Decorations Awarded to Natal, Cape Colony and Defence Force Units 1877–1961*, Private,
    1981
Forsyth, DR & Davies. *King's Commendations Military Recipients, Union Defence Force*, Roberts
    Medals Publications, 1991

Forsyth, DR & Davies. *Gallantry Medals Awarded to Natal, Cape Colony and Union Defence Force Units 1877–61*, Roberts Medals Publications, 1991

Forsyth, DR & Davies. *Orders of Chivalry, Foreign Decorations and Awards to Natal, Cape Colony & Union Defence Force Units 1977–1961*, Roberts Medals Publications, 1991

Frank, MEV. *Army and Navy Nurses Held as Prisoners of War during WWII*, Office of Asst Secretary of Defence (US), 1985

Freeman, RA. *Britain at War*, Arms and Armour, 1990

Gavin, L. *American Women at War*, 1998

Gawler, J. *Lloyd's Medals 1836–1945*, Hart Pub., Toronto, 1989

Gibbon, JM & Matthewson, MS. *Three Centuries of Canadian Nursing*, Cassell & Co. Ltd, New York, 1953

Gleeson, J. *They Feared No Evil. Women Agents of Britain's Secret Armies* Robert Hale, 1976

Glesson, J & Waldron. *Now It Can Be Told*, Paul Elek

Gordon, EL. *British Orders and Awards*, Kay & Ward, revised 1968

Grant, D. *The Thin Blue Line (Glasgow Police)*, J Long, 1973

Graves, C. *Women in Green; Story of the WVS*, Heinemann Ltd, 1948

Greer, RF. *The Girls of the King's Navy*, Sono Nis Press, Victoria, Canada, 1983

Hakins, C. *Women of Glory*, Longacre, 1980

Haldane, E. *The British Nurse in Peace and War*, John Murray, 1923

Hall, MR & Sweet, HF. *Women with the YMCA Record*, International Committee of YMCA, 1948(?)

Halliday, HA. *Honours and Awards to Canadian Army Nursing Personnel 1936–46*, Private, 1996

Hamilton, AD et al. *Hamilton's Coin & Medals Despatch*, ed. RJ Molloch

Harland, K. *Queen Alexandra's Royal Naval Nursing Service*, RN Medical Service, 1988

Harper, B. *Petticoat Pioneers: South Island Women of the Colonial Era – Book 3*, Wellington, New Zealand, 1980

Hare-Scott, K. *For Gallantry, The George Cross*, Peter Garnett Ltd, 1951

Harrison, A. *Grey and Scarlet, Letters from Army Sisters on Active Service*, Hodder & Stoughton, 1944

Hay, I. *One Hundred Years of Army Nursing*, Cassell & Co. Ltd, 1953

Hayward, JB (ed.). *Honours and Awards of the Army, Navy and Air Force 1914–20*, JB Hayward, 1979

Henderson, DV. *Dragons Can Be Defeated – George Medals Progress 1940–83*, Spink and Son Ltd, 1984

Henderson, DV. *Heroic Endeavour – Complete Register of Albert, Edward and Empire Gallantry Medals & How They Were Won*, Hayward & Son, 1988

Henderson, DV. *Fashioned into a Bow*, Pentland Press, 1995

Hess, JF. *WAAC's At Work*, Macmillan & Co., New York

Hieronymussen. *Orders, Medals and Decorations of Britain & Europe*, Blandford Press, 1966

Hocking, P. *Dictionary of Disasters at Sea during the Age of Steam 1829–1962*, 3 vols, Lloyd's Register of Shipping, 1964

Holm, MG. *Women in the Military*, Presidio Press, US, 1982

Howgrave-Graham, HM. *Metropolitan Police At War*, HMSO, 1947

Hilsinger, MP & Schofield, MA. *Visions of War, WWII in Popular Literature & Culture*, Popular Press, Bouting Green University, US, 1992

Hutton, JB. *Women in Espionage*, Macmillan, 1971

Hyde, HM. *Cynthia*, Hamish Hamilton, 1966

Ingram. *Women in the Armed Forces*, Smithsonian University, US, 1992

Irwin, RW. *War Medals and Decorations of Canada*, 1969

Jackson, R. *Heroines of WWII*, A Barker, 1976

Jameson, K & Ashburner, D. *South African WAAF*, Shuter and Shooter, Pietermaritsburg, South Africa, 1946

Jarvis, SD & DR. *Cross of Sacrifice 1914–19*, Roberts Medals Publications, Aldermarston
> vol. 4: 'NCO's, Men & Women of the UK & Commonwealth Royal Navy, Royal Marines, Royal Naval Air Service, RPS and RAF 1914–1921', 1996
> vol. 5: 'Officers, Men & Women of Merchant Navy & Mercantile Fleet Auxiliary', 1989
> vol. 9: 'Female Officers, Nurses, Enlisted Women & Civilians'

Jocelyn, A. *Awards of Honour, Orders, Decorations, Medals and Awards of Great Britain and the Commonwealth from Edward III to Elizabeth II*, Adam and Charles Black, 1956

Johnson, D. *The City Blaze*, William Kimber, 1980

Johnson, RE. *Guardians of the Sea, History of US Coastguard 1915–86*, Annapolis Naval Institute Press, 1987

Johnson. *War Medals*, 1971

Jones, L. *A Quiet Courage*, Bantam Press, 1990

Jones. *America's Medal of Honour Recipients*, Highland Publications, 1980

Kelley, N & W. *Royal Canadian Mounted Police*, Hurtig Pub., Edmonton, 1973

Kendall, CJ & Wingate. 'Gallantry Awards', *Numismatic Circulars* Oct 1955 & Sep 1960, Spink & Son Ltd

Kendall, G & Corbett, D. *New Zealand Military Nursing*, Auckland, 1996

Kenny, C. *Captives*, University of Queensland Press, St Lucia, 1988

Kent de Long. *War Heroes, Stories of Congressional Medal of Honor Recipients*, Greenwood & Praiger Pub., 1993

Kerrigan, EE. *American War Medals & Decorations*, King Press Ltd, 1964

Kiel, S Van W. *Those Wonderful Women and their Flying Machines, Unknown Heroines of WWII*, Four Directors Press, 1990

King, A. *Golden Wings*, Pearson, 1956

King, S. *Jacqueline*, Arms and Armour Press, 1989

Kramer, R. *Flames in the Field, Four SOE in France*, Michael Joseph, 1995

Laffin, J. *Women in Battle*, Abelard-Schuman, 1967

Laver, MPH et al. *Sailor Women, Seawomen, SWANS, a History of the South African Women's Auxiliary Service 1943–49*, SWANS History Publication Fund, Simonstown, 1982

Lenemann, L. *In the Service of Life*, Mercat Press, 1994

Leslie, A. *A Story Half Told (ATS)* Weidenfeld & Nicholson, 1988

Leslie, JH. *An Historical Roll with Portraits of those Women of the British Empire to whom the Military Medal has been Awarded during the Great War 1914–18 (Parts 1–5)*, Sir WC Leng, Sheffield, 1919 & 1920

Lloyd's. *Lloyd's War Medal for Bravery at Sea 1941–47*, Corporation of Lloyd's, 1947

Lock, J. *The British Policewoman: Her Story*, Hale, 1979

Longmate, N. *Air Raid*, Hutchinson, 1957

Lorain, P. *Secret Warfare*, trans D Khan, Orbis, 1984

Lucas, N. *WPC Courage*, Weidenfeld & Nicholson, 1986

Lucas, N. *Heroines in Blue*, Weidenfeld & Nicholson, 1988

Lucas, YM. *WAAF With Wings*, GMS Enterprises, 1992

Lynn, Vera, Cross, R & J de Gex. *Unsung Heroines, Women Who Went to War*, Transaction Pub., 1993

McBride, B. *Quiet Heroines*, Chatto & Windus, 1985

McDermott, P. *For Distinguished Conduct in the Field, Register of DCM 1920*, 2 vols, published for the DCM League by J Hayward, 1994

McDowell, CP. *Military & Naval Decorations of the United States*, Quest Pub. Co., 1985

McIntosh, E. *The Role of Women in Intelligence*, Assoc. of Former Intelligence Officers, McLean, Virginia, 1989

McIntosh, E. *Sisterhood of Spies*, Naval Institute Press, US, 1997

MacKersey, I. *Jean Batten, The Garbo of the Skies*, MacDonald, 1991

Macksey, K. *The German Invasion of England July 1940*, Arms & Armour, 1980

MacPhail, IIM. *The Clydebank Blitz* , Clydebank Town Council, 1974

Macphail, A. *Official History of the Canadian Forces 1914–19*, Medical Services, 1925

Marlow, J (ed.). *Virago Book of Women and the Great War*, Virago Press, 1998

Marshall, A. *Guinness Book of Winners*, Guinness Pub., 1997

Marwick, A. *Home Front*, Thames & Hudson, 1976

Mason, U. *Britannia's Daughters*, Cooper, 1992

Masson, M. *Christine, Search for Christine Granville*, Hamish Hamilton, 1975

Masters, D. *In Peril on the Sea, War Exploits of Allied Seamen*, Cresset Press, 1960

Matthews-Laughton, V. *Blue Tapestry*, Hollis & Carter, 1949

Mayo, JH. *Medals and Decorations of the British Army & Navy*, A Constable & Co., 1987

Mercer, D (ed.). *Chronicle of the Twentieth Century*, Longmans, 1988

Merton, E & Reither, J. *Women Pilots with the American Air Force 1941–44*, MAAH Pub., 1946

Messenger, C. *WWII Chronological Atlas*, Bloomsbury, 1989

Minney, RJ. *Carve Her Name with Pride*, Newnes, 1956

Mitchell, D. *Women on the Warpath*, , J. Cape, 1965

Monick, S. *South African Civil Awards 1910–90*, South African Museum of Military History, Johannesburg, 1990

Morden, BJ. *Woman's Army Corps 1945–78*, Centre of Military History, US Army, 1990

Murphy, EF. *Korean War Heroes*, Presidio Press, US, 1992

Nicholas, E. *Death Be Not Proud*, Cresset, 1958

Nicholson, GWL. *Canadian Nursing Sisters*, Samuel Stevens, 1975

Norman, E. *Women At War, Story of 50 Military Nurses Serving in Vietnam 1960–1965*, University of Pennsylvania, 1990

O'Brien, B. *Aromoana, 22 Hours of Terror,* Penguin Books New Zealand Ltd, 1991

Oliver, B. *The British Red Cross In Action,* Faber & Faber, 1966

O'Shea, PP. *Honours, Styles and Precedences in New Zealand,* Wellington, 1977

O'Shea, PP. *An Unknown Few,* PD Hasselberg, Wellington, New Zealand, 1981

Overton Fuller, J. *Noor-un-Nisa Inayat Khan, Madeleine,* Gollancz, 1952

Overton Fuller, J. *The Starr Affair,* Gollancz, 1954

Overton Fuller, J. *The German Penetration of SOE,* Kimber & Co., 1975

Overton Fuller, J. *Double Agent,* Pan, 1961

Pallas, SM (ed.). *Canadian Recipients of the Canadian Auxiliary Forces Officers' Decorations & the Colonial Auxiliary Forces Long Service Medal 1958–90,* The Graphic Printing, Ottawa

Parkman, MR. *Heroines of Service,* Ayer Pub. Inc., 1977

Pearsall, R. *Lifesaving, the Story of the Lifesaving Society,* David & Charles, 1991

Piggott, J. *Queen Alexandra's Royal Army Nursing Corps,* Leo Cooper, 1975

Pinson, B. *Women of South Taranaki, their Stories,* Hawara, New Zealand, 1993

Popham, H. *FANY 1907–84,* Secker & Warburg, 1984

Power, JR. *Brave Women and their Wartime Decorations,* Vantage Press, US, 1959

Price, A. *Blitz on Britain,* Ian Allen Ltd, 1977

Purves, AA. *Medals, Decorations & Orders of the Great War,* JB Hayward, 1975

Purves, AA. *Medals, Decorations & Orders of WWII,* Hayward & Son, Polstead, 1986

Pushman, M. *We All Wore Blue,* Robson Books, 1989

Pyle, F. *Ack Ack,* Harrap, 1949

Ramsey, WG (ed.). *The Blitz, Then & Now,* 3 vols, After the Battle Pub., 1987

Rattray, J. *Great Days in New Zealand Nursing,* G Harrap & Co. Ltd, 1961

Riddle, DK & Mitchell, DG. *Distinguished Conduct Medal to Canadian Expeditionary Force 1914–20,* Kirby Malton Press, Winnipeg, 1991

Reid, PJ & Witlieb, BL. *The Book of Women's Firsts,* Random House, New York, 1992

Renders, S. *No Place for A Lady,* Portage & Main Press, Canada, 1992

Roberts (ed.). *Honours & Awards for Cyprus Campaign,* Roberts, Titan House, Aldermaston

Roberts (ed.). *Honours & Awards for Kenya Campaign,* Roberts Pub.

Roberts (ed.). *Honours & Awards for Near East (Suez),* Roberts Pub.

Robertson, EM. *WAAF At War,* Mullaya Pub., Australia, 1974

Robinson, V. *Sisters In Arms (Gunners),* Harper Collins, 1996

Robson, LL. *The First AIF, Study of Recruitment 1914–18,* Melbourne, 1970

Ross. *Rebel Rose,* Harper Bros, 1954

Rossiter, ML. *Women In Resistance,* Praeger Pub. Ltd, US

Rowes, AK. *United States Military Medals & Ribbons,* Tokyo, 1971

Sainsbury, JD. *For Gallantry in the Performance of Military Duty,* Samson Books, 1980

Schneider, D & C. *Into the Breach, American Women Overseas in WWI*

Schuon, K & L & Ronald, D. *Service Women and What They Do,* Franklin Watts Inc., 1964

Seedey, C. *American Women and the US Armed Forces,* National Archives Fund Trust Board, 1992

Seedies. *Roll of Naval Honours & Awards 1939–59,* Ripley Registers, UK, 1989

Serclaes, Baroness de T'. *Flanders and Other Fields,* Harrap, 1964

Sharman, H. *Seize the Moment,* Gollancz, 1992

Smith, RH. *OSS,* University Press of California, 1972

Smythe, J. *Will To Live,* A Barker

Smythe, J. *The George Cross,* A Barker, 1968

Somerfield, M & Bellingham, A. *Violetta Thurstan, A Celebration,* Jamieson Library, 1993

Stanistreet, A. *'Gainst All Disaster,* Picton Press, 1986

Stephens, R. *On Top of the World,* 1994

Stevenson, C & Dorling H (ed.). *The WAAF Book,* Hale & Iremonger Press Ltd, Sydney, Australia, 1984

Stone, G (ed.). *Women War Workers,* G Harrap & Co., 1917

Strandberg, JE & Bender, R. *Call of Duty, Military Awards & Decorations of the US,* RT Bender Pub., 1994

Stratford, DO & Collins, HM. *Military Nursing in South Africa 1914–94,* Chief of National Defence Force, 1994

Stremlow, MV. *History of Women Marines 1946–77,* History & Museums Division Headquarters Marine Corps, Washington, 1986

Stremlow, MV. *Free a Marine to Fight, Women Marines in WWII,* WWII Commemorative Series, 1994

Strome-Galloway, Q. *The White Cross in Canada 1883–1983,* St John Ambulance, Ottawa, 1983

Tamplin, JMA. *Various Notes and Articles on the Meritorious Service Medal,* Journal of Orders and Medals Research Society, 1973–75

Tancred, G. *Historical Record of Medals and Honorary Distinction Conferred on British Navy, Army & Air Forces from the Earliest Period,* Spink and Son, 1911

Taprell-Dorling, H. *Ribbons and Medals,* London, 1972

Taylor, A & Doddington, D. *Honoured by the Queen, Recipients of Honours,* Auckland, 1994

Taylor, E. *Women Who went To War,* Robert Hale Ltd, 1988

Taylor, E. *Heroines of WWII,* Robert Hale Ltd, 1991

Taylor, E. *Front Line Nurse,* Robert Hale Ltd, 1997

Taylor, RJ. *Kiwis In The Desert,* New Zealand Defence Force, 1992

Terraine, J. *The Right of the Line, RAF in the European War 1939–45,* Hodder & Stoughton Ltd, 1985

Thomas, RCW. *The War in Korea 1950–53,* Gale & Polden Ltd

Thompson, J. *Imperial War Museum Book of War Behind Enemy Lines,* Sidgwick & Jackson, 1998

Thompson, RJ. *The Coast Guard and the Women's Reserve in WWII,* Coast Guard Historian's Office, US, 1992

Thurstan, V. *Field Hospital and Flying Column,* Putnam & Sons, 1915

Tickell, J. *Odette,* Chapman Hall, 1949

Tickell, J. *Moon Squadron,* A Wingate, 1956

Tilley, JA. *History of Women in the Coast Guard,* Commandants Bulletin, US, 1996

Tilley, JA. *Out of Uniform, Civilians in the Coast Guard,* Commandants Bulletin, US, 1994

Treadwell, ME. *US Army in WWII, Special Studies, The Women's Army Corps,* Washington DC Army Dept, 1954

Tucker, G. *The Naval Service of Canada,* King's Printer, Ottawa, 1962

Uys, I. *South African Military Who's Who 1452–1992,* Uys Pub., 1992

Verity, H. *We Landed by Moonlight,* Ian Allan Ltd, 1978

Walker, A. *Official History of the Medical Services RAN & RAAF, Australian in War 1939–45,* RAMS 1961

Walters, AM. *Moondrop to Gascony,* Macmillan, 1946

Wallington, N. *Firemen At War,* David and Charles, 1982

Wallington, N. *999 Accident and Crash Rescue Work of the Fire Service,* David and Charles, 1987

Wallington, N. *Images of Fire,* David and Charles, 1989

Ward, I. *FANY Invicta,* Hutchinson, 1955

Weatherford, D. *American Women in World War II,* 1990

Webb, AM (ed.). *The Natzweiler Trial,* William Hodge, 1949

Werlich, R. *Orders & Decorations,* Washington

West, N. *Secret War, Story of SOE,* Hodder & Stoughton, 1992

Wicksteed, MR. *A Chronology of the New Zealand Army,* Government Printer, 1988

Wigmore, L & Harding, B. *They Dared Mightily, Australian VC & GC,* Australian War Memorial, Canberra, 1963

Williams, VS. *WASP, Women's Air Force Service Pilots in WWII,* Motorbooks, 1994

Williams, VC. *WAC Women's Army Corps,* Motorbooks, US, 1997

Willoughby, MF. *The US Coastguard in WWII,* Annopolis US Naval Institute, 1957

Wilmot, C. *Struggle for Europe,* Collins, 1952

Wilson, A & McEwen, JHF. *Gallantry, its Public Recognition in Peace & War at Home and Abroad 1887–1938,* OUP, 1939

Wynne, B. *Count Five and Die,* G Mann, 1958

Wynne, B. *No Drums . . . No Trumpets,* A Barker Ltd, 1961

Handbooks and Books (no authors given)

Royal Australian Air Force, a Brief History, AGPS, Dept of Defence, 1981

MTE Journal 1941–5, MTE & DRAF, 1946

AP3234 – 2nd WW 1939–45, Women's Auxiliary Air Force, AHB, 1953

Book of the WAAF, Amalgamated Press, 1942

WAAF In Action, Adam & Charles Black, 1944

The Women's Auxiliary, Johannesberg, Feb 1941

Official Yearbook of Union of South Africa – South Africa & the Great War, 1946

Shoulder Sleeve Insignia etc, Rex Military Co., US, 1941

South African Pamphlet Collections – Box 97 – OBE & MBE

South African Decorations and Medals, Dept of Defence, Union of South Africa

Moments of History, US Coast Guards

Kiwis in the Air War over Europe & North Africa 1939–45, New Zealand

New Zealand Honours List – Wellington
Lloyd's War Medals for Bravery at Sea – Extracts from Lloyd's *Shipping Gazette 1941–46*, Pub.
  Corporation of Lloyd's, London, 1947
Encyclopaedia Britannica
The Times Concise Atlas of the World
Australia in the War 1939–45, 22 vols, Canberra Australian War Memorial:
        Series I, *The Army*, 7 vols, 3 by G Long
        Series II, *The Navy*, 2 vols, GH Gill
        Series III, *The Air*, 4 vols, 2 by J Herrington, 2 by SJ Butlin
        Series IV, *Civil*, 5 vols, 2 by P Hasluck
        Series V, *Medical*, 4 vols, AS Walker

Papers and Leaflets

London Gazette, Supplements 1916 onwards
Government Gazette of South Africa
New Zealand Gazette (extracts)
Canada Gazette Part I
South African Digest, 1981
Liddel Hart Collection, Papers of Lady Mary Denman, Director Women's Land Army 1939–46
General Orders, War Dept (Army), May 1919, South Africa
Prologue, National Archives, Washington DC
Lists of Albert & Edward Medals & Other Awards & Papers – HO45, Home Office
Lists of King's/Queen's Fire Service Awards, Home Office
Lists of Police Honours and Awards 1954–96, Home Office
Reports of Red Cross Awards, 1920–95
Reports:
  Florence Nightingale Awards, 1920–95
  Royal Humane Societies (various dates), Australasia, NSW, New Zealand
  Carnegie Hero Fund Commission (various dates), US, Canada, UK
  American Red Cross, National Awards – Various
  New Zealand's Royal Honours System, Report of the PM's Honours
Honours Advisory Committee, Sept 1995
US Women In the Military, Where they Stand – Hoisels, Gormley and Ford Foundation, 1994

Journals and Magazines

I am indebted to many of the following for printing my requests for information:
Sabretache – Journal of the Military Historical Society of Australia
American Legion Magazine
Athena – Journal By and For Women Veterans (US)
Police Review & Gazette (UK)
The Soldier (UK)
Servamus – South African Police Magazine
WRAF Officers' Gazette (UK)
WAAF Association News (UK)
The Volunteers – Journal of New Zealand's Military Historical Society
The Canadian Legion
Nursing Review (Australia)
Navy News (Australia)
The Register – Newsletter – WIMSA (US)
Canadian Nurse Magazine
Air Force Women Officers Associated News (US)
Women's Transport Service (FANY) Gazette (UK)
The WREN (UK)
ATA Association Newsletter (UK)
Orders & Medals Research Society Handbook (UK)
Touchdown – British Airways Journal
The Job (UK)

The Pennant (UK)
Nursing Standard (UK)
Women's Memorial – Special Calendars 1995 & 96 (US)
Saga Magazine (UK)
WI Newsletters
British Commonwealth & Ex-Service League
National Geographic Magazine – various articles esp. Dec 1944 & '42

Special thanks to:

My local library (the staff of whom must have been horrified at my peculiar requests but patiently searched for them); Bette Anderson (UK); Lynette Beardwood – Captain i/c Linguists & Records WTS/FANY (UK); Mrs Mary Campion (UK); Mrs Elizabeth Cox (UK); Mr Gervase Cowell – Chairman Historical Sub-Committee, Special Forces Club (UK); Mr J Haigh (New Zealand); Mr Hugh A Halliday (Canada); Mrs Frances Horsburgh – ATA (UK); Staff of Dept Printed Books – IWM; Colonel PF Joubert (South Africa); Sister Laurence Mary (UK); Mr John Lloyd – Home Office; Mr John B Long – Commonwealth Secretary General RLSS (UK); Mrs Ursula Mason – WRENS (UK); Major MH McCombe – Curator QARANC Museum (UK); Ms Susan McGann – Curator Royal College of Nursing Archives (UK); Major Constance Moore – Army Nurse Corps Historian (US); Mrs Margaret Oliver (Australia); Mr Arthur Percival – Hon Director Fleur de Lis Heritage Centre (UK); Mrs Nancy & Sue Plummer (Canada); Mr RJ Scarlett (UK); Mr Philip O'Shea – New Zealand Herald of Arms; Lady Joan Price (South Africa); Mr Alan Probert (UK); Mrs Margaret Salm (US); Ms Kathryn Sheldon – Curator WIMSA (US); Dr R Shroder – Social History Collection, University of N Carolina (US); Squadron Leader Peter Singleton – AHB (UK); Mrs Lesley Smurthwaite – National Army Museum (UK); Mr Anthony Staunton (Australia); Captain Decia Stephenson – i/c Records, WTS/FANY (UK); Lady Sibyl Stewart (UK); Squadron Leader Robert Stewart (UK); Ms Lesley Thomas – Curator WRNS Collection Royal Naval Museum (UK); Major General Christopher Tyler – Secretary RHS (UK).

And MANY other correspondents.

General Index

Index of Heroines Named in Text

Page numbers given in **bold** refer to photographs.

Index of Medals

Page numbers given in **bold** refer to photographs. Page numbers given in *italic* refer to descriptions of medals.